The Profession
and Practice
of Consultation

*A Handbook for Consultants,
Trainers of Consultants,
and Consumers of
Consultation Services*

June Gallessich

The Profession
and Practice
of Consultation

Jossey-Bass Publishers

San Francisco · Washington · London · 1983

THE PROFESSION AND PRACTICE OF CONSULTATION
A Handbook for Consultants, Trainers of Consultants,
and Consumers of Consultation Services
        by June Gallessich

Copyright © 1982 by: Jossey-Bass Inc., Publishers
                      433 California Street
                      San Francisco, California 94104
                              &
                      Jossey-Bass Limited
                      28 Banner Street
                      London EC1Y 8QE

Library of Congress Cataloging in Publication Data

Gallessich, June.
        The profession and practice of consultation.

        Bibliography: p. 439
        Includes index.
        1. Social service consultants. I. Title.
HV10.5.G34   1982   361.3'2   82-8948
ISBN 0-87589-527-1   AACR2

Manufactured in the United States of America

The paper in this book meets the guidelines for
permanence and durability of the Committee on
Production Guidelines for Book Longevity of the
Council on Library Resources.

JACKET DESIGN BY WILLI BAUM

FIRST EDITION
        First printing: August 1982
        Second printing: November 1983

Code 8218

*The Jossey-Bass
Social and Behavioral Science Series*

Preface

This book is for the members of an emergent profession, women and men who are now involved in the part-time or full-time practice of consultation and those who will enter this exciting field. Although written especially for human services consultants—social and behavioral scientists, mental health professionals, and management and public administration specialists who consult in public and private human services institutions—the book is concerned with the field as a whole. It examines the social role and purposes of consultation, its body of knowledge and principles, and its development as a new profession. Because of this generic orientation, the book will be of interest to all consultants. It should be a useful resource to professionals who in mid-career consider moving into the practice of consultation and to trainers who, in professional schools, continuing education programs, and in-service programs, educate and supervise beginning consultants. Consumers, the administrators who employ consultants, will find the information in this book helpful in choosing, using, and evaluating consultation services.

The practice of consultation is rapidly growing, spurred by requests from modern work organizations for assistance in using highly specialized and developing technology to meet the changing needs of a turbulent world. Consultants' services provide a crucial interface through which knowledge, technology, and perspectives from specialized disciplines enter organizations and help their staff members solve problems and maintain or increase their productivity. Pressures on these organizations due to their dependence on complex human processes, the increasingly specialized nature of work, and the need to make continual adaptations to the changing environment suggest that demands for consultation will continue and perhaps escalate. The practice of consultation can be expected to grow not only in size and scope but also in its importance to the well-being of society. From time to time, professionals from all fields will find themselves drawn into the consultant role. For many professionals, consulting will be a full-time occupation.

A discrepancy is apparent, however, between social needs and available professional competencies. Consultation concepts and processes are not well understood. Most professional training does not include consultation theory and practice. Many professionals, in fact, assume that experience in a particular field—for example, social work or communications—is adequate preparation for consultation. But helping others with their work is a far more intricate process than working directly on one's own task. Moreover, the organizational milieu is fraught with conflicts that may ensnare consultants and leave them impotent. Lacking specific concepts and principles to guide them, consultants must rely on the practices and principles of their primary professions; these may, at times, fit the new role, but they are often dysfunctional.

A major purpose of this book is to bring together the concepts, principles, and practices now scattered across a number of fields to define and present in one volume the core of knowledge needed for effective practice as a consultant. My assumptions are: (1) consultation is a complex process for which specialized preparation is needed, (2) although consultants' practices vary greatly, they share a common role (technical adviser) and serve a common purpose (helping organizations increase their effectiveness), and (3) consultants, therefore, need a common body of knowledge to equip them to serve in this role.

A second major purpose of this book is to analyze this emerging profession from a sociological perspective. To this end, I examine its roots, current status, and prospects. I identify the developmental tasks that must be accomplished if consultants are to reach their potential for serving society. By stressing the generic aspects of consultation, I hope to heighten the awareness of commonalities among consultants from different fields. Although generally invisible to one another, they share the responsibility for the future of consultation. Through this book, I hope to promote the bonding needed for vigorous development of this new field and to promote standards of excellence.

By taking a broad approach to consultation, I intend this book to serve as a bridge connecting concepts and practices from a number of fields. It reflects a dozen years of experience in a wide range of consulting activities and efforts to find the central differences and similarities of diverse consultation approaches. In my introduction to consultation in 1965, Ira Iscoe taught me the classic tenets and practices of mental health consultation, a model that he had learned in postdoctoral training with Gerald Caplan. Four years later, through training in National Training Laboratories Institute programs, I discovered a different model, organization-focused consultation based on social and psychological theories. At that time, these two bodies of consultation theory and practice were entirely separate. Publications in neither field referenced the other. The contrasts between them created considerable dissonance in my thinking; but I, like many others, began to identify not only their differences but also their commonalities. I began to use both—often in integrated forms—in my practice and teaching. My training and experiences in the fields of group therapy and group processes—and especially the tutelage of Earl Koile and Michael Kahn—brought still other perspectives to my thinking about consultation and made me aware of the importance of group phenomena in both creating and solving problems in the workplace. One

additional major body of knowledge entered into my conceptualization of consultation theory and practice through Robert
Reiff, a seminal thinker in the fields of community psychology
and social policy. Discussions with Reiff were very helpful in
sharpening my conception of the differences between the roles
and responsibilities of the consultant and those of the advocate.

From varied experiences as a practitioner and trainer
came other stimuli that expanded my thinking about consultation. I began to raise and struggle to answer crucial questions regarding consultation practices. From students and colleagues I
learned about consulting approaches taken by different disciplines and about the behavioral model of consultation. From
my own experiences and my supervision of others I learned
about the commonalities and differences in consulting in different types of organizations and about the uses, advantages, and
disadvantages of still another consultation model, program consultation. From my own failures and successes and those of my
students and colleagues, I discovered the typical dilemmas that
consultants face and the infinitely varied ways in which these
arise and can be resolved. I became acutely aware of a common
problem—ambiguity and confusion about the nature, goals, and
boundaries of the consultant role—that often has disastrous consequences. Unless consultants have developed and held on to a
clear set of principles and values, they are likely to succumb to
internal and external pressures to behave in ways that are inappropriate, that may create uneasiness and distrust in their
consultees, and that even, at times, can be destructive.

I have organized this book in four major parts. Part One,
"An Emerging Profession," presents and develops concepts that
I later elaborate. Chapter One explains the book's purposes and
identifies the generic roles, functions, and boundaries of consultation in its various settings. To further illuminate the purposes
and responsibilities of the consultant, I compare this role with
more familiar ones, such as teacher and supervisor. Chapter Two
examines consultation from a sociological perspective. I review
the roots and early stages of consultation and the steps through
which it is now being professionalized. I raise questions about
peer leadership and the profession's future. Human services

agencies are the topic of Chapter Three. The two major goals of this book cannot be fulfilled without an understanding of these institutions, which have shaped and continue to shape the profession of consultation. Moreover, a thorough understanding of the structure, dynamics, and problems of these agencies is an essential element in the consultant's body of knowledge. I apply several conceptual frameworks in examining organizational structure and processes.

Because of professional barriers, consultants are often unaware of the work of consultants from fields other than their own. Part Two, "Models for Practice," delineates the diverse forms, concepts, and methods used by consultants. Chapter Four reviews some of the efforts to classify consultation practices and identifies five primary sources of variability—the consultant's conceptualization of the problem, goals, strategy, role, and values. These dimensions are the basis for discussions in Chapters Five through Ten, in which I describe the conceptual and methodological bases of six major approaches: educational and training, clinical, mental health, behavioral, organizational, and program consultation. These chapters also include illustrations that vividly depict the unique practices of each model.

Regardless of the model they choose, all consultants go through similar processes, beginning with preliminary discussions with agency representatives and ending with termination of the consulting relationship. Part Three, "Common Processes, Principles, and Practices," is concerned with such processes. Chapter Eleven provides basic information for the beginning consultant by answering such questions as how to contact potential client organizations and how to set fees. Chapters Twelve through Fifteen describe the processes involved in each major phase of consultation (entry; relationship building; data gathering, diagnosis, and intervention; and evaluation and termination) and suggest guidelines for effective management of each process.

Part Four, "Developing the Potential of Consultation," returns to the analysis of consultation as an evolving profession. In Chapter Sixteen, I consider the impact of two forces, social change and peer associations, on the profession. I identify a developmental failure—the lack of clarity about the profession's basic principles and values. As a consequence, the profession faces role identity problems, which I review and for which I suggest solutions. Professional associations, in order to express their commitment to serve society, typically evolve ethical codes that contain principles for competent and ethical performance by their members. Codes for consultation are, in general, lacking. Chapter Seventeen proposes an ethical code to guide individual consultants, trainers, and consumers. I hope it will be considered by consultant associations and help move the profession toward a stronger service commitment. The future of a profession is also shaped by its training. Chapter Eighteen reviews two dominant consultation training patterns—a traditional, intraprofessional pattern and an innovative, interprofessional pattern—and their implications. I suggest two training models, one that would provide minimum levels of competencies needed for the practice of consultation as a subspecialty and one for a doctorate in consultation and a career in the new profession of consultation.

It is my hope that this book will help raise the standards of consultation practice and move the profession to higher levels of social consciousness and responsibility.

In addition to the mentors named previously, I owe a great deal to numerous other individuals who helped me develop and organize the concepts in this book. I am indebted to many clients but particularly to Betty Alverson, Allen Becker, Dorothy Blume, Archibald Montgomery, Kathryn Respess, Don Rippy, and Sister Antoinette. Interactions with students were crucial in the evolution of my ideas. I am especially grateful to those who worked with me as teaching assistants—Barbara Butera, Jean Chandy, Michael Curtis, Julie Davis, Nancy Jo Derby, Deborah Edward, Clifford Katz, Suzanna Maxwell, Lynn Roney, and Michael Tebeleff—and to Marcia Collins, William Erchul, Deana Graham, Karen Herndon, Rollie Lee, Vicky Martin, Phyllis Sager, Maryann Santos, Thomas Washington, Sidney Winicki, and to Jane MacDonald, who helped me crystallize my conceptions of the consultant role and the nineteenth-century conditions that led to its emergence. Encouragement from colleagues, including Gordon Anderson, Jackson Reid, and Beeman Phillips, helped me create this book; and Karen Kirkhart and Alfred McAlister contributed needed case study material. My thanks go to David Gallessich for help in compiling bibliographic references. A special kind of appreciation goes to my husband, Robert Reiff, for his wise counsel and support.

San Francisco, California   June Gallessich
July 1982

Contents

The Author

June Gallessich is professor of educational psychology and director of the counseling psychology program at the University of Texas at Austin. She was awarded the bachelor of arts degree in English with summa cum laude honors from Texas Christian University in 1952. She received the master of education degree with a major in counseling psychology from the University of Texas at Austin in 1965, where in 1967 she received the Ph.D. degree in educational psychology with majors in counseling and school psychology. She completed internships as a counseling psychologist at the Counseling-Psychological Services Center at the University of Texas and as a school psychologist in the Austin Independent School District. She later received additional training in human relations and consultation through National Training Laboratories Institute programs.

Gallessich is past president of both the Texas Psychological Association and the Southwestern Psychological Association. She is a fellow in the American Psychological Association (APA) and has been a member of the APA Council of Representatives. She was on the executive committee of the Southwest

Group Psychotherapy Society for many years. Gallessich holds a diplomate from the American Board of Professional Psychology. Her major professional interests are consultation and group processes. For the past twelve years she has taught a year-long course in consultation for doctoral students from professional psychology programs and from other fields, including communications, educational administration, and management. She also teaches courses in organization development, the social psychology of organizations, and group therapy. She has led many continuing education and in-service training programs for professionals moving into consultation in mid-career and has presented papers and workshops in various conferences in the continental United States and in Hawaii, Puerto Rico, Australia, and Israel. Her research has been reported in such journals as the *Journal of School Psychology, Professional Psychology,* and *Counselor Education and Supervision.*

Gallessich has been a practicing consultant for fifteen years and specializes in work with human services organizations.

To my husband and colleague, Robert Reiff,
and our children, Alfred, Gail, David, and Mark

The Profession and Practice of Consultation

A Handbook for Consultants,
Trainers of Consultants,
and Consumers of
Consultation Services

 # Part I

The Emerging
Profession

The needs of modern work organizations are creating a new profession and practice, consultation. Professionals from most fields—for instance, nursing, public administration, psychology, and management—find themselves consulting with various organizations to help them solve a wide array of problems. Many consultants, however, are not fully prepared to serve in this role. Their professional training has not equipped them to understand either the organizations in which they work or the unique functions and boundaries of the consultant role. Consequently, their services are often ineffectual. One purpose of this book is to bring together in one volume the body of knowledge needed for effective work in this new field. A second purpose is to examine consultation as an emergent and socially important profession.

Part One lays the foundation for later parts of the book by defining consultation and by examining its roots, its growth, and the milieu in which it evolved and is currently practiced. Consulting, an ancient and universal practice, encompasses many kinds of activities. Chapter One highlights the major varieties of consultation and then defines—within this diversity—the basic roles, functions, and boundaries of the modern consultant.

1

Since consultation is often confused with other helping services, it is contrasted to familiar roles, such as supervisor and teacher. This chapter also reviews the motives that draw professionals into consulting work.

Chapter Two is concerned with the relationship between the evolving profession and its social context. It first examines the prototypical helping forms and traditions that contributed to modern consultation practices and then reviews the social conditions and expanding technology that led to the creation and institutionalization of modern forms of consultation. In recent years practitioners have begun to professionalize. Chapter Two reviews typical professionalization processes and criteria for determining the degree to which an occupation has achieved professional status. It then charts the progress of consultation through three early developmental stages and points out that, on the whole, this field is being professionalized as a subspecialty of established professions. Some individuals and groups are, however, now practicing consultation as an independent or quasi-independent field. This chapter raises questions about peer association leadership and societal needs.

The consultant's workplace, human services agencies, is the topic of Chapter Three, which describes several organizational theories and illustrates their usefulness in analyzing these institutions. This chapter serves two purposes. It illuminates the organizational tensions that are creating and shaping the profession and practice of consultation, and it provides guidelines to assist the practitioner in understanding complicated agency phenomena and the milieu in which they are working. Consultants need such an understanding in order to make accurate diagnoses and formulate realistic recommendations—even when their work is limited to a "case" level or to a narrowly defined task such as teaching staff members to use word processing. For broader interventions (such as those involving team relationships, the redesign of jobs, or program planning), a sophisticated background in organizations is imperative.

1

New Social Roles for Human Services Professionals

Until a hundred fifty years ago, families and neighbors were responsible for maintaining the fabric of American society. They preserved the social order by educating and socializing the young, ministering to the sick and weak, and controlling antisocial behavior. Little specialized help was available, but little was wanted by our independence-minded ancestors. However, changes accompanying the industrial revolution weakened these primary institutions and, at the same time, created many new needs. Consequently, local and state governments and private organizations began to build secondary institutions, such as schools, clinics, welfare agencies, and probation courts, and assigned them the responsibility for providing helping services. In turn, changing and expanding demands overwhelmed these agencies at times. They looked to outside specialists, consultants, for help. Consultation eventually became a routine service and is today an important social role, a *tertiary institution* that helps the secondary ones serve society.

This book is written primarily for the practitioners of this emergent profession—individuals from such diverse fields as health, education, management, and the social and behavioral sciences—who shift from their original roles and functions to consult with the agencies that provide human services. The scope of the book, however, extends to concerns relevant to all who are involved in the practice of consultation—including those who work in business and industrial organizations. One purpose of the book, as stated earlier, is to bring together and systematize concepts, principles, and practices that are now scattered across the literature of a number of fields. The assumption is that an integrated and comprehensive body of knowledge will enable practitioners to deliver more competent services. The second purpose is to examine consultation from a sociological perspective by analyzing its origins as a social institution and its context, functions, and development. The hope is that this analysis will foster in widely dispersed practitioners a sense of their commonalities and promote the cross-disciplinary bonding needed for a new specialty to grow (Moore, 1970).

At present, the consultant role is characterized by diversity. Individuals who practice consultation come from many different professions and bring to the role varied specialized perspectives and methods. For instance, mental health professionals bring a diagnostic and treatment orientation. Organizational specialists—individuals with backgrounds in sociology, management, and communications, for example—approach the role with their distinctive concepts and methods. Specialists in agency technologies—experts in such areas as law enforcement, health care, education, and transportation—add further to the diversity of consultation practices.

These wide-ranging specialties enable consultants to serve many agency needs. But specialized technologies, though vital, tend to narrow practitioners' perspectives and are seldom sufficient for effectiveness in the consultant role. Consequently, consultants' efforts often fail—because the consultants are unaware of the effects of invisible norms and conflicts on agencies' use of new technologies, because consultants do not understand change processes and the powerful influence of individual and organizational resistance, because consultants are unclear about the boundaries of their role and become involved in unproductive conflicts over authority and responsibility, or because the consultant relies on a narrow set of techniques without evaluating their relevance to a particular situation. Thus, consultants' services may be irrelevant, ineffective, or harmful.

A major goal of this book is to reduce the gap between agency needs and the capacities of consultants to satisfy those needs. It begins with the assumption that consultants have much in common. They serve a common purpose—helping agencies function more effectively. They share a common role—all are technical specialists. They share a common workplace—human services agencies. They need a common body of knowledge—specialized concepts, principles, and practices—to fit this new role.

Consultants need an understanding of the workplace not only as a technological system but also as a complex social organization. They need to be familiar with the special features and problems of human services agencies and the pressures exerted on those agencies by a rapidly pulsating, pluralistic environment. They need to know the unique strengths and weaknesses of the consultant role and its generic principles, processes, and boundaries. They need alternative models for conceptualizing agency problems and alternative methods for solving them. This book meets these needs by clarifying the functions and boundaries of the consultant role, by providing a comprehensive description of its generic concepts, principles, and practices, and by delineating its specialized models. The text carries forward work begun more than a decade ago by consultants from many fields who recognized the need for knowledge and skills beyond their professional specialties and who began, by trial and error, to find this expertise and integrate it into their practices.

In examining consultation from a sociological perspective, the book has an even more ambitious goal. Because consultation is evolving from diverse professions, its practitioners—their perspectives limited to the confines of their particular fields—are generally unaware of the phenomenal growth of this practice and the implications of this growth. By focusing on consultation as an emergent social institution, the book seeks to foster practitioners' awareness of their commonalities and to promote the bonding needed to accomplish crucial professional tasks—such as development of standards of competence and ethics, a strong sense of social responsibility, and high quality programs for education and training—that must be achieved if consultants are to fulfill their potential to serve society.

Definitions

The word *consultation* has a number of meanings. Used colloquially, it refers to any kind of advice-giving or advice-seeking. Young parents "consult" relatives and friends about child-rearing practices. Next-door neighbors consult about building a fence. Business executives consult their spouses before planning an out-of-town conference. According to this usage, anyone can be a consultant, and the basis for the consultant's expertise comes from experience or from an intimate relationship to a particular issue rather than from specialized training. In contrast, *consultation* may also be defined as advising by occupational experts, persons with specialized training. A person consults an attorney about a will, a physician about a stomach problem, and a minister about a family crisis. In this book, however, *consultation* has a more restricted definition. It means tripartite interactions in human services agencies. The consultant (a specialized professional) assists consultees (agency employees who are also professionals) with work-related concerns (the third component).* In contrast to the situations in which a professional serves a client directly, consultation as defined here is an indirect service to clients. It may focus on many different levels of work problems. The problem may be described in

*Consultants face a dilemma in deciding whether to call the persons with whom they work "consultees" or "clients." Consultants to business and industrial organizations prefer to use the word *client*. However, *consultee*, a term traditionally used by mental health professionals, appears more suitable for human services consultation. It allows *client* to be reserved for the persons these agencies serve, thereby preserving their terminology, avoiding confusion, and, at the same time, underscoring the central mission of these organizations.

terms of agency clients, and the consultant may focus on a single client, following the clinical tradition of observing symptoms, making a diagnosis, and recommending treatment. Thus, a first-grade teacher consults a psychiatric nurse about a youngster who cries constantly. The consultation might be concerned with groups of clients or potential clients. A consultant might, for example, survey a community's characteristics and needs for a Planned Parenthood center. In some consultations, the problem may be defined in terms of consultees' needs, such as the knowledge and skills necessary to perform a particular task. A communications specialist, for instance, teaches a staff how to conduct more effective conferences. A mental health consultant helps a minister increase his abilities to recognize and respond to the social and psychological needs of his parishioners. The focus of consultation may extend beyond clients and consultees to organizational structures, processes, programs, or policies. A program evaluation specialist helps the head of a women's center design a new program. A management consultant helps the director of a probation office resolve a staff conflict. A computer scientist provides technical advice to the director of a public transportation system who is considering computerizing operations. Finally, agency difficulties might be defined in terms of environmental factors—such as community relations, governmental policies, or liaison between agencies—and the consultation focus would then shift accordingly. To illustrate, the head of a victim assistance center asks advice from a sociologist about the effects of neighborhood change on the incidence of crime. The head of a low-cost clinic asks a community psychologist for help in identifying neighborhood resources for referral purposes. Frequently, consultation focuses on several of these areas simultaneously.

For the purposes of this book, human services agencies are defined as those institutions that serve the needs of individual members of society and in so doing maintain and protect the social structure (Hasenfeld and English, 1975). These organizations offer an almost infinite array of human services for citizens, from the rich to the poor, from birth to death. They provide health care, education, material assistance, control and rehabilitation of offenders, employment advice, and family counseling. Human services agencies also make life safer, more enjoyable, and more convenient through public services such as pollution control, public transportation, recreational facilities, and information dissemination. The individual services provided by these institutions are indispensable to the survival of modern society. They socialize its members, integrate them into the social structure, and protect their general health and well-being. They preserve law and order. Without these agencies, society would disintegrate. Most of the institutions operate on public funds, but some are supported by private endowments or by nonprofit fee schedules. Still others are profit-making businesses that operate on client fees and/or contracts with federal, state, or local governments. Some childcare and health facilities, for example, are run by business corporations on federal funds, supplemented by modest client fees.

Basic Roles and Functions

Human services agencies call on consultants for a wide range of services, but most services are delivered through one or two basic roles. The major role of the consultant is that of *technological expert or adviser,* whose function is to introduce new elements—information, concepts, perspectives, values, and skills —into the agency to help it keep abreast of changing conditions. Most consultants' services are variations of this function, which links two systems—the consultant's specialty and a service delivery system. Service organizations can be seen as systems that are "born" at some point in time in response to certain needs and conditions. At their inception, they are permeable. They are in close interaction with and responsive to salient environmental forces, such as social needs and values, client characteristics, contemporary technology, and legal, political, and economic conditions. Over time, however, agency boundaries tend to thicken. Interaction with the environment becomes less immediate. Gaps appear between agency goals, structures, and operations and changing social conditions and needs. Figure 1 illustrates the tendency of systems to become closed and obso-

Figure 1. Agency Boundaries Across Time

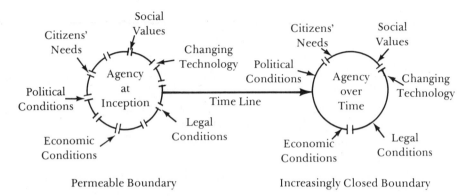

lete. To counteract this tendency, agencies need to update their perspectives, goals, services, and operations continually. Consultants can bring in elements from the outside world to help agencies stay up-to-date. This input function is especially critical for older agencies and in times of turbulence, when all agencies need to quicken their rate of change. For example, although service technology quickly becomes obsolete, agency staff members are often too busy to attend classes and workshops or read the trade journals that would enable them to keep up with new developments. Consultants can help plug the gaps between staff members' competencies and current job requirements by offering seminars, workshops, individual training, and group conferences. Similarly, governmental funding policies may demand sudden shifts in the target populations and in agencies' goals. Changes in services may then be needed. Consultants' expertise may help the staff identify the needs of the new clients and develop new programs for them. Consultants may help agencies examine their structures, staffing patterns, and technological and human processes in relation to environmental changes. For example, changes in services may require closer supervision and more frequent staff communication. Often the consultant's crucial function is to bring a fresh, outside view to internal problems, because insiders are either too close to the problems or too polarized to assess them objectively. For instance, an administrator may seek assistance in breaking out of an unproductive leadership style or in resolving a conflict between the junior staff and the "old guard." Sometimes agencies need certain technological skills, yet their needs do not justify the hiring of a full-time employee. Hiring a consultant to work for a few hours each week or month may be the most economical solution. For example, probation officers may meet regularly with a mental health consultant who helps them understand and counsel their clients. Occasionally, they may refer particularly baffling cases to the consultant for psychological interviews and diagnoses.

The second basic consultant role is *to help agencies cope with stress.* Agencies are sometimes so overwhelmed by changes and demands that they have difficulty maintaining minimal operations. External pressures may be so severe that they are disabling. Acute internal problems may similarly disrupt services and threaten agency stability. In such cases the consultant's primary service may be to help the system recover and maintain its equilibrium, so that it can continue to provide necessary services. To illustrate, the staff members of a welfare department may feel "burned out" by an overload of clients or demoralized by budget slashes that force personnel layoffs and eliminate crucial services. They may seek to ameliorate their problems through consultation with an outsider who can help them—either as individuals or as a group—to manage the stress and reintegrate their system (Hirschowitz, 1977; Levinson, 1972). In this role the consultant's services go beyond technological input to include emotional support and guidance.

Role Boundaries

Within the two basic roles, the methods used by consultants vary greatly. For instance, an agency might ask a consultant to make a diagnosis and recommendations, lead a seminar or workshop, help an administrator obtain feedback through surveys, or meet with a team of workers to help them resolve con-

flicts and set goals. But across these different approaches, certain common characteristics appear that apply to most consultation:

1. Consultants are professionals who are experts in specialized
    bodies of knowledge. Many are also experts in the process
    of helping peers (other professionals) solve problems.
2. Consultants work with consultees, staff members of human
    service organizations, to help them with their work-related
    concerns. Consultants do not focus on consultees' personal
    concerns except as they relate directly to the work situa-
    tion.
3. Consultation is an indirect service. In working with an agen-
    cy's staff, consultants serve a third party, the agency's cli-
    ents, indirectly. Exceptions may occur, however; for exam-
    ple, a consulting clinician may, at times, directly examine
    the consultees' clients. Further client contact ordinarily
    moves the consultant into direct services and outside the
    consultant role.
4. Consultants are outsiders. The consultation relationship is a
    temporary one. Consultants come from external bases, such
    as private practice or agencies that are independent of the
    consultee. Sometimes, however, consultants belong to the
    same agency as their consultees; in these situations, the
    consultant role is significantly modified by the consultant's
    membership in the agency's authority structure and social
    life.
5. The consultation relationship is between peers whose areas
    of responsibility and expertise differ. The relationship is
    voluntary for both parties, and each maintains control over
    her or his involvement. When the agency and the consultant
    agree to a contract, the consultant is authorized to enter
    the consultee's work domain; barring a binding contractual
    provision, the consultee may withdraw this permission at
    any time. Similarly, the consultant may elect to terminate
    the relationship. Consultees determine the concerns to be
    discussed. Both consultant and consultee may introduce
    ideas or questions they perceive to be important and screen

out irrelevant or inappropriate topics. To illustrate, a consultee might decline to discuss certain work topics even though the consultant perceived them to be related to the focal problem; or a consultant might decline to discuss a consultee's family problems. A consultant might also choose either to introduce or to withhold theories, research findings, or principles pertinent to the problem under discussion.

6. The consultee retains responsibility and authority for any action and is free to accept or reject the consultant's advice. However, two assumptions underlying the relationship are that consultees (1) will seriously consider the input of the consultant and (2) have the power to mobilize resources to effect improvements in their work situation.

The consultant role often seems similar to such familiar roles as teacher, supervisor, and therapist. Both the persons who deliver consultation services and the recipients often confuse consultation with these and other better-known roles. Certain overlaps in function are apparent, but the consultant role differs in significant respects.

Teachers are responsible for selecting topics for their students to learn and the teaching method to be used. Teachers also evaluate their students' progress. In contrast, consultees determine the topics to be discussed and the ways their consultants are to be used. Consultants do not ordinarily evaluate consultees' learning, except on request and for the consultees' benefit.

Supervisors are responsible for their employees' work and have the authority to insist on compliance. They direct and evaluate their employees and initiate and pursue discussion of any areas that they perceive to need attention. Consultants, however, as outsiders and as peers, have neither the responsibility nor the authority to direct their consultees' actions. Consultants may introduce topics they consider relevant but cannot pursue them without the consultees' consent. Consultees may reject any consultant suggestions and services. In some organizations, however, in-house consultants have both consultative and supervisory responsibilities; in these situations the contradictory functions of the two roles often lead to confusion about who has the ultimate authority and responsibility.

The therapist or counselor diagnoses and treats clients' personal problems. Consultants, however, work with other professionals as peers and focus on only their work-related problems. Unlike the therapist, who may penetrate defenses and bare a client's deepest anxieties, consultants preserve their consultees' defenses. Even when consultees are highly stressed, consultants usually focus on problem identification and solving and on strengthening coping skills. Nevertheless, while consultants do not "treat" consultees or invade their private worlds, consultation might help consultees examine the effects of their personal styles on their work or help them explore more effective ways of managing work-related stress. Moreover, consultants often assist their consultees in making changes in work-related attitudes and behaviors that, in turn, lead to changes in their personal lives. So, although consultants do not function as therapists, their impact may be therapeutic, and the skills that therapists use in direct services are often helpful to consultants for understanding consultees and establishing effective work relationships with them.

Program *evaluators* are sometimes hired by funding organizations to assess the effectiveness of a recipient agency in delivering services. These professionals are responsible to the funding institution and are its employees (or consultants), rather than the consultants of the service agency. *Researchers* enter agencies to gather data to answer basic research questions. Their primary goal is to contribute to bodies of knowledge. In contrast, the consultant is responsible to the staff of the consultee agency. Agencies often hire consultants to plan or conduct evaluations or to carry out research, however. Consultants working under these conditions are governed by agency needs and are concerned mainly with helping the staff answer questions.

The consultant role and the role of *advocate* are often confused, but their goals and boundaries are different. Consultants operate within agency values. Their orientation is to help agencies achieve their goals. Consultants may at times disagree with agency policies and operations, but they seek to change them only in the direction and at the tempo chosen by the administration. If consultants decide, for professional or personal reasons, that they cannot support an agency's practices, they are obligated to make their views known to their consultees. Both parties are then free to decide whether and in what ways the consultant can be useful. In consultation, any adversarial elements are minimized or eliminated. Advocates, in contrast, are committed not only to advise their clients (individuals, groups, or organizations) but also to implement adversarial actions in the clients' behalf. For instance, an attorney joins a minority coalition to exert pressure on the administrator of a welfare department accused of racist hiring practices. A psychiatrist confronts a high school principal over the expulsion of a patient. Whereas consultants enter organizations only with the administrators' permission, advocates sometimes force entry into an organization. To illustrate, a physician representing parents of retarded children may obtain a court order to examine records of a state institution in which several of the children mysteriously died.

Motivations of Practitioners

Agencies seek out individuals who possess the expertise to meet agency needs. As most professionals move through their careers, they experience strong pressures to spend more and more time in consultation. But responding to these pressures ordinarily requires them to give up some of their commitment to basic professional activities. Why, then, do professionals decide to practice consultation? Their motives are varied. Many turn to consultation to further their professional development, seeking growth through new forms of practice. As consultants, they find opportunities to move beyond the boundaries of their previous training and experiences, to conceptualize problems in new ways, to try new ideas and strategies, to work with different types of people and at different levels. Academicians find that applying their knowledge in consultation expands and deepens their grasp of their fields. Clinicians discover that the shift in focus from individuals to programs and systems is challenging and stimulating. Professionals also turn to consultation because of altruistic concern over the limited impact of their services. They discover that the practice of their basic profession benefits relatively few persons, and they look for new roles and methods to increase their impact on social problems. Through consultation they hope to effect changes in the quality and direction of service delivery systems. Thus, a sociologist moves from teaching to full-time consultation with state agencies that are developing programs for rural disadvantaged populations. A social worker whose regular job involves casework with juvenile defenders spends a portion of her time consulting with a national foundation that is studying the influence of government policies on juvenile offenders. A clinical psychologist who once worked full-time as a therapist now spends a day each week consulting with the staff of a hospice for quadriplegics, helping the staff members to find ways of ameliorating the distress of these clients and their families. Some practitioners consult to escape from what has been called the dirty work (Hughes, 1958), the routine services that may seem repetitive and boring after years of experience. Helping professionals may also turn to consultation because of the burnout syndrome: Wearied by years of work with recalcitrant, disturbed, and needy clients whose problems seem never to be fully resolved and, in fact, often worsen, these professionals seek to increase their contact with less needy populations or with peers. Professional advancement may be an incentive also. The consultant role is traditionally a prestigious one. In England, for example, the title of consultant is reserved for the highest-ranking physicians. Since the fees are typically higher than those for other professional services, practitioners can often substantially increase their incomes by consulting. Professionals from many fields now spend a significant proportion of their time working as consultants.

Annotated Bibliography

Altrocchi, J. "Mental Health Consultation." In S. E. Golann and C. Eisdorfer (Eds.), *Handbook of Community Mental Health*. New York: Appleton-Century-Crofts, 1972. Altrocchi reviews and contrasts different conceptions of the consultant role. He outlines the parameters of mental health consultation and differentiates it from other helping relationships, such as teacher/student and supervisor/supervisee.

Argyris, C. *Intervention Theory and Method: A Behavioral Science View.* Reading, Mass.: Addison-Wesley, 1970. In chap. 1, "The Primary Tasks of Intervention Activities," Argyris discusses his views of the purposes and boundaries of the consultant (interventionist). A primary tenet of Argyris's theory is that consultants should seek, above all, to increase their clients' autonomy. Consultants should be careful, therefore, not to allow their own values and beliefs to determine clients' decisions.

Conoley, J. C. "Advocacy Consultation: Promises and Problems." In J. C. Conoley (Ed.), *Consultation in Schools: Theory, Research, Procedures.* New York: Academic Press, 1981. Conoley takes the position that consultant and advocate roles can be combined. She points out, however, some of the difficulties in integrating the two roles. Her views offer an interesting counterpoint to those expressed in this chapter.

2

Evolution: The Social Context

Like all social roles, the consultant role evolved as a result of two conditions: (1) existing patterns were no longer adequate to meet crucial societal needs, and (2) knowledge was available that could meet those needs. This chapter examines the emergent role from a sociological perspective. It focuses on the relationship between the social context—including helping traditions, cultural changes, and technological developments—and the birth, growth, and characteristics of a helping institution. The evolution of the consultant role is traced from ancient prototypes to recent steps toward professionalization.

Origins

Prototypes. Primitive societies meet their members' needs directly and personally within the intimacy of family and community. Members of the tribe teach the young social and productive skills, inculcate cultural values and traditions, care for the sick and needy, and restrain the antisocial. In the most primitive groups, roles are not well differentiated; they can be filled by most adult members. But as the body of knowledge grows and group numbers increase, even the simplest cultures develop role specialists—hunters, shamans, and weavers, for example—to provide more highly skilled services. The evolution of roles is related to social needs. We find, for example, that in societies concerned with life after death, religious specialists, such as priests, sacred artists, and teachers, appear. When changes disturb familiar patterns of living, new specialties arise to ensure the continuity of society. For instance, cultures at war develop specialized military technologies and corresponding roles.

Three prototypical helping roles emerged in most primitive groups: the technological adviser, the healer, and the sage. Each served a specialized function and evolved a characteristic form and features. Modern consultation is derived from two of these prototypes and is often confused with the third.

The *technological adviser,* the major precursor of all professions, taught other members of the society specialized skills such as how to find and prepare food or how to construct tools, clothing, and shelter. Technological advisers were not doers. They helped others learn new techniques and solve problems. This role transmitted the knowledge and skills needed for societal survival and advancement (Znaniecki, 1965). All societies depend on skilled technicians for this function. In the modern world, the role of technological adviser is exceedingly important, since both social needs and technology are changing faster than the preparation and training of workers. From a few rudimentary specialties, technological helping roles have exploded into thousands of distinctive forms. Among them are technological consultants, whose specialized scientific expertise enables human services agencies to update and improve their services and adapt to changes in environmental conditions.

Another prototypical helper, the *healer,* evolved in all primitive cultures to attend to the sick and injured (Moore, 1970). The healer, whose expertise came both from medical technology and from the supernatural, was both a physician and a priest or sorcerer (Sigerist, 1965). Healers usually treated visible illnesses—such as wounds and fractures—by rational methods, since their origins and the necessary services were obvious. But when symptoms were internal or of uncertain origin, healers turned to religious prayers and sacrifices or to tools of sorcery, such as amulets and potions. Thus society came to associate healing with the supernatural. Although the importance of non-rational elements in treatment declined with the growth of medical technology, vestiges of ancient beliefs frequently appear. For instance, people—particularly those in crisis—sometimes assume that doctors possess esoteric insights and curative powers. This attribution is at times extended to modern consultants. In any case, consultants often find themselves in a healing or ameliorative role.

The third helping prototype was the *sage,* a person who conceptualized central issues in societal conflicts and made judgments about what was right or wrong from a moral or political point of view (Znaniecki, 1965). Ancient leaders, when faced with contradictory demands, sometimes sought the sage's help in making decisions; a sage might also initiate hearings for the purpose of persuading rulers that a particular value judgment was right or wrong. The sage and the modern consultant differ in important respects. Administrators of modern agencies might seek consultants' views about the effects of policies on particular clients or client groups; but consultants are usually sought for their technical or professional expertise, not for their moral or political judgments. Furthermore, consultants, because of the role boundaries discussed in Chapter One, are careful not to impose their values on their consultees. However, the sage is the prototype of the modern advocate, a role frequently confused with that of the consultant. Differentiation of these two roles is essential for successful consultation. Consultation and advocacy are contrasted later in this chapter, and the consequences of confusing these two social functions are discussed in Chapter 16.

Professionalization. With advances in civilization, the bodies of useful technologies expand. Social roles multiply and become increasingly specialized. Cultural mores reinforce and formalize them. Social contracts develop through which essential role specialists provide the public with needed knowledge and skills and in return receive certain privileges. Holders of a common role organize guilds or professions that further protect, stabilize, and elaborate their roles and social power. Most evolve standards and ethical codes to prevent exploitation; for instance, the Hippocratic oath, developed by a medical fraternity in ancient Greece, admonished physicians to protect their patients from exploitation and to disseminate socially useful knowledge.

Historical Conceptions. Another approach to understanding the consultant role is to examine the characteristics historically associated with the larger group to which it belongs—professionals in general. Thus we can identify societal conceptions of the essential characteristics of the professional and learn what behaviors are expected.

Medieval Germany contributed the first and most enduring concept, *freir beruf.* The professional is an independent, self-employed, and learned person who declares and practices a certain expertise (Hughes, 1966). From the *noblesse oblige* conception of the golden age came a tradition with extensive implications for the client/professional relationship: The professional is an aristocrat with a broad classical education, a person who assumes responsibility for protecting the public welfare, and one to whose wisdom and goodness all citizens should defer. Thus, professionals are viewed as superior persons whose power and authority extend beyond their technical specialty to encompass all social and moral concerns. Old World physicians introduced this image of the professional into America. They assumed a parent role and required their clients to behave with childlike obedience and dependence. The American Medical Association Code of Ethics, adopted in 1847, institutionalized this concept, admonishing physicians "to unite tenderness with firmness, and condescension with authority, so as to inspire the minds of their patients with gratitude, respect, and confidence" (Rothstein, 1972, p. 173). Patients were expected to obey their physicians' directions without question. Furthermore, after recovery, a patient should "entertain a just and enduring sense of the value of the services rendered him by his physician; for these are of such a character that no mere pecuniary acknowledgment can repay or cancel them" (King, 1958, p. 255).

This aristocratic concept influenced the development of all professions. But it was incompatible with American dreams of equality (Tocqueville, 1835-1840/1945). In the middle of the nineteenth century, sentiments against elitism swelled into a massive movement that—abetted by scientific discoveries that undermined the technical credibility of the professions—weakened professionals' authority (Haber, 1974). "There was a widespread arraignment of classical education as both exclusive and useless. It was surely not essential in the training of a gentleman, for that rank was being redefined to mean all well-behaved citizens. Also, the importance of the technical training of the professions was belittled. The professional, it was said, increased the difficulty of his work by design. Almost everything that he need know could be learned by any ambitious fellow with a natural bent for the subject; much of the rest was mistaken and even harmful" (pp. 246-248). Thus, a change in ideology, along with scientific advances, led the American public to challenge professional power and authority. Some extremists came to view the professional as a useless pedant. Although a professionalism movement in the 1880s eventually reinstated much of the professional's earlier status, more recent conceptions of the professional—the benevolent family friend and adviser, the objective scientist, the entrepreneurial capitalist, and the salaried bureaucrat—lack the grandeur of the *noblesse oblige* tradition.

The current public images of consultants, like those of all contemporary professionals, are pluralistic and include all those mentioned here. The core attribute is the possession of specialized knowledge and skill. But some consultants, especially those from health care professions, are invested with aristocratic qualities, such as benevolence and authority on a broad range of social and moral issues (Rodin and Janis, 1979).

Breakdown of Helping Traditions

Because of their belief in self-reliance, preindustrial Americans required very little in the way of specialized helping roles. The scarcity of professionals and other helping specialists reinforced the prevailing ideology. Institutionalized services were considered generally unnecessary and were rare indeed. However, the coming of the industrial revolution, the major social changes accompanying it, the disruption following the Civil War, and the subsequent waves of immigration to the United States resulted in a breakdown of folk culture and a failure of its helping functions. The new factories required a large, mobile labor force and recruited masses of rural people into the cities. Thus, the stability and shared values of the community were lost. Urban-dwellers seldom knew each other. Heterogeneity was introduced not only by movement from farm communities to industrial centers but also by masses of immigrants who brought ethnic, cultural, and language differences. These new-comers were usually poor, unskilled, and unable to speak English. Moreover, the family structure lost much of its power. Urban living and industrial jobs were especially attractive to the young, who could obtain wages that made them economically superior to their parents. As individuals moved to the cities, they left their families behind. Physical separation weakened adult authority and family social and emotional ties. Breaches between children and parents were especially severe in immigrant families, as children assimilated much faster in the new country and became alienated from their parents' life-style and language. With extended kinship ties thus weakened, the nuclear family became the basic family unit. Separated from traditional social support systems, this new unit had relatively little strength and influence over the behavior of its members. In addition, the structure of the nuclear family changed. Many women took positions in factories and offices that required them to be away from home for twelve or more hours, six days a week. Divorce increased. With both mother and father away from home, care of the young and elderly became more difficult. City children did not have the clear role and economic value they had in farm life. To "earn their keep," children often went to work for extremely long hours in industrial sweatshops and were thus further removed from family influence. The family unit provided a weak base and no longer could offer the services necessary to sustain society.

Thus, industrialization and its social consequences severely weakened the effectiveness of community and family ties and

brought great increases in poverty, crime, and mental and physical illnesses.

Institutionalization of Human Services

By the latter half of the nineteenth century, the helping
traditions of the folk society were strained past the bursting
point and could no longer meet societal needs. Social impera-
tives thus forced transfer of responsibility for human services
from primary relationships to specialized secondary institutions.
The values, structures, and goals of these new institutions were
shaped by a variety of factors, including the dominant social
ideology, technological changes, and the traditions and values of
emerging professions.

The prevailing attitude in the early years of the republic
was that social problems were caused by moral deficiencies; by
good example and moral exhortation, the poor might be turned
into contributing citizens. After the Civil War, however, beliefs
changed. Social Darwinism and the survival of the fittest became the dominant tenets and shaped the values and assumptions of the new agencies. The belief was that the social problems of the individual were due not so much to circumstance or
moral weakness as to inborn or genetic inferiority. To interfere
with nature by sacrificing the resources of the able to help those
who by "nature" were incompetent, lazy, or immoral would be
harmful to society and probably would not help the genetic un-
fortunates either. Social Darwinism complemented the economic climate in the era of the robber barons, who believed in
individual initiative, free enterprise, and profit making with
little or no government interference. The genetic assumptions
also fit with the general reaction to the gigantic influx of immigrants, who swelled the urban centers with impoverished, unskilled masses. Thus, human services organizations of this era
emphasized the welfare of well-socialized members of society
over the needs of those who were in one way or another unfit
or deviant, the undeserving poor. The goals were control and
containment rather than support or rehabilitation, a philosophy
that continues to influence some service agencies. Certain indi-

viduals and groups, however, contended that poverty, ignorance, and unemployment were the basic causes of human misery. Reform movements, antithetical to the dominant sentiments, appeared throughout the machine age. Leaders of the "social justice movement" gathered data on the severe problems of the poor and brought empirical evidence to state and federal legislatures in hopes of bringing about social reform (Levine and Levine, 1970). Today, human services agencies are frequently the battlefields in which proponents of these contradictory philosophies vie to control the shape and direction of services.

The expansion of technology in the middle and late 1880s was another important factor influencing the movement of the helping services to secondary institutions and setting the tenor of the new agencies. Changes in the conduct of medicine provide one clear example. At the beginning of the nineteenth century, the great preponderance of medical care was given in the home. The physician visited with black bag, giving the patient healing skill, caring, and whatever limited tools were portable in the bag. In the 1840s, however, with the introduction of ether and chloroform, the first effective anesthetics, surgery became more feasible. Increasingly, this became a treatment of choice and required large amounts of equipment and a group of supporting workers. The technology of medicine no longer fit into the black bag. Impersonal hospitals and clinics replaced the home visit. Another technological change that affected the practice of medicine was the development of high-power microscopes in the middle 1880s. These led to formulation of the germ theory of disease—that diseases are caused by microbes, not by moral failings. The germ theory led to the conception of medicine as a scientific endeavor, one that implicitly demanded its own laboratory and white-coated practitioners. Again, the office or hospital seemed a much more suitable setting than the home. Further, with a better understanding of the need for cleanliness and the ways in which infections are transmitted, hospitals became safer places than they once had been. But in hospitals, as in other care-giving institutions, relationships between staff and clients were typically impersonal and narrowly focused on specific needs.

The expansion of knowledge and societal needs increased the power of professionals, who further enhanced their status by organizing professional associations and guilds. The professionalization movement increased the social distance between helper and client. Professionals of the 1880s, unlike those of the golden age, were from the middle class. They were squeezed economically from above by the robber barons and from below by labor unions and increasingly assertive workers. Professions, therefore, sought a secure niche with a clear identity. They began to collect symbols, such as admissions criteria and ethical codes, to demonstrate their right to special privileges and prestige, thus accentuating their superiority to their clients and to the general public. The medical profession was the exemplar that the new professions sought to imitate, hoping they could obtain such benefits as exclusive rights to practice, privileged communication, and authority over clients. A primary means of enhancement was to stress the unique and esoteric nature of the profession's knowledge, to maintain secrecy over the exact procedures and knowledge involved in the diagnosis and intervention, thus fostering client credulity. "The physician uses mysterious procedures in diagnosis and therapy; the engineer uses elaborate formulas in calculating stresses; the chemist or physicist performs experiments of mystifying complexity; attorneys produce writs, briefs, and bases of appeal from a trial court judgment that could not be derived from 'common sense'; and social scientists, perhaps most vulnerable to the charge of deliberate mysticism, are at considerable pains to demonstrate the sophistication of their results and not simply of their procedures" (Moore, 1970, pp. 226-227). The drive for professionalism affected even the choice of technology. For instance, social workers displayed an early interest in community organizational strategies to solve social and individual problems, but they moved in the direction of casework and individual treatment to enhance their professional status (Lubove, 1965).

Many new structures arose to cushion the shock of a society in transition. Local and state governments assumed increased responsibility for education, social control, and certain health needs. Cities created departments to control fires and to provide public transportation. Public schools, opened to comply with new compulsory school laws, were soon flooded with students, many of whom were immigrants with different languages and customs. Welfare services were established. The rudimentary criminal justice system expanded to control the tremendous increases in rioting and crime that followed social disintegration. Public medical facilities increased to care for inhabitants of the new industrial centers. Richard Cabot, physician to patients at Massachusetts General Hospital in 1898, was astonished by the great masses of needy patients who came through like "shooting stars—out of darkness and into darkness" (Lubove, 1965, p. 26). Massive institutions, "bedlams," were built to isolate and control the mentally ill, thus removing them from society. A scientific basis for their treatment had been laid a century earlier, but a society in the throes of industrialization was not able to organize effective treatment. Furthermore, the prevalent societal belief in genetic premises for mental illness mandated control rather than treatment. But many new agencies, primarily those arising from private initiative, reflected humanitarian sentiments. Judge Benjamin Lindsey created a humanitarian Juvenile and Family Relations Court in Denver for the purpose of helping youngsters, rather than simply punishing them. Educated, wealthy young people established settlement houses to bring educational opportunities to the youths whom industrialization, urbanization, and immigration had dumped in the slums. Religious organizations created numerous institutions to help solve social problems. The Salvation Army and the YMCA are products of this era, as well as the Catholic church's educational and social systems. Workers organized unions to prevent exploitation and to negotiate for improved work conditions and fair wages.

Beginnings of a New Social Role:
Consultant to Helping Institutions

Secondary institutions arose to ameliorate social problems, restore order, and provide support for an industrial society. They are now an integral part of the social structure, although they wax and wane according to shifts in the dominant ideology. These agencies frequently turn to outside specialists for help, thus creating a new social role, the consultant to caregiving institutions. Six distinctive consultation models have evolved. All perpetuate practices of their prototype, the technological adviser; in some, the traditions of ancient and modern healers appear. The dimensions, beginnings, and unique contributions of these six models are briefly described next, along with the role of advocate.

Consultant as Educator and Trainer. An information-centered model, characterized by its didactic method, is the most basic form of consultation. The primary function is educational. The consultant takes the role of adviser, educator, or trainer to present knowledge related to some facet of agency life—for example, client characteristics, administrative styles, service technology, or evaluation procedures. The focus is on transmission of the consultant's knowledge rather than on a particular agency problem. The method involves a logical, cognitive process. It assumes that consultees will be able to apply the new information to agency needs. The consultant's role may appear to be similar to that of the classroom teacher, but it differs in that the "student," or consultee, is in charge and determines what is to be taught, when, and how.

Direct evidence of the origin of this consultation model is scarce, although scholarly papers written by nineteenth-century experts to educate their less knowledgeable peers about techniques for alleviating individual and social problems suggest that these experts did, in fact, visit agencies to advise, teach, and train staff members. Moreover, a few records of actual "consultant" visits exist. For instance, nineteenth-century superintendents of mental hospitals visited the staffs of medical facilities to lecture on the diagnosis and treatment of the insane (Caplan, 1969). Child psychologist Lightner Witmer taught the faculty of the University of Pennsylvania and the staff of the public school system of Philadelphia effective methods for working with handicapped children (Wallin and Ferguson, 1967). Educators G. Stanley Hall, William James, and E. Thorndike lectured teachers on principles of learning and individual differences, concepts from the new field of psychology (Cremin, 1961).

The educational model is a basic component of the contemporary consultant's repertoire. It offers a convenient method through which professionals, with little or no modification of their usual practices, convey needed technical expertise to agencies. Its strategies are economical in their use of time and money, since one consultant can disseminate information to an entire staff. The model also provides a low-risk mechanism for agency and consultant to get acquainted and, as such, can be a valuable first step toward a more extensive relationship. Because of the twentieth-century explosion of technology, this particular model is especially useful in contemporary agencies. Agencies often systematize arrangements for use of this model under such nomenclatures as staff development, in-service training, and human resource development.

Clinical Consultant. Several consultation models reflect healing traditions in their focus on pathology, their functions of diagnosis and treatment, and the esoteric nature of their knowledge. The earliest to evolve was clinical consultation, a client-focused centuries-old model, which physicians brought to nineteenth-century hospitals and clinics. The clinical consultant examines the consultee's client in order to make a diagnosis and recommend a treatment for the consultee to carry out. Amelioration of the client's illness is the primary goal; education and growth of the consultee are of secondary importance.

Consultation had been a common medical practice since the thirteenth century, and so physicians had well-established rules to follow (Kutzik, 1977a). Physicians practiced two different types—collegial and hierarchical consultation. They consulted in a collegial mode with less experienced peers about their patients. These consultees regarded the opinions of their consultant-colleagues highly but were free to accept or reject their advice. Still, consultation often strained professional relationships; disputes arose over diagnosis or treatment decisions, and the consultant sometimes competed with the consultee (the attending physician) for the patient's patronage (Rothstein, 1972). Physicians followed a hierarchical pattern when they consulted with apothecaries—unlicensed, independent practitioners who lacked formal training. The apothecaries, "doctors" for the poor who could not afford physicians, far exceeded licensed physicians in number. In England, because it was a felony when a patient treated by an unlicensed practitioner died, apothecaries regularly consulted physicians. This practice was only nominally a form of consultation, however. More accurately, it was supervision, a relationship between a superior and an inferior, consistent with the aristocratic concepts of the golden age (King, 1958).

As medicine in England and America became more professionalized, physicians began to restrict their consultative services to peers (licensed members of their own profession), refusing to consult with graduates of "inferior" schools and those without formal medical school training, such as apothecaries. Apparently physicians feared that consultation would legitimize the practice of unqualified persons. "By keeping irregular practitioners out of all consultations, the regular physicians hoped to destroy public confidence in them, deprive them of their clientele, and increase the gulf between them and the regular profession" (Rothstein, 1972, p. 171). By 1780 the code of the 400 physicians in the United States educated in medical schools specifically excluded nonphysicians from consultation. The American Medical Association Code of Ethics, established in 1847, called for physicians to consult only with physicians with regular medical education. Although exclusion enhanced the power of the medical profession and benefited well-to-do patients, it undoubtedly lowered the quality of service to patients who were treated by nonphysicians. Restriction of consultation to peers eliminated unqualified practitioners from the support and intellectual stimulation of physicians.

Early clinical consultation traditions contributed three major elements to contemporary consultation practices. These traditions assured social and professional sanction for "clinical," or "case," consultation, in which a second expert opinion is obtained to give an additional perspective and specialized knowledge for the benefit of the client. Moreover, consultation was accepted as a means for continuing education and professional development. According to the 1847 American Medical Association Code of Ethics, "consultations should be promoted in difficult or protracted cases, as they give rise to confidence, energy, and more enlarged views in practice" (Rothstein, 1972, p. 83). Medical practices also stressed the peer nature of the consultation relationship, in this case a restrictive practice that explicitly prevented noncolleagues from increasing their knowledge of professional "mysteries." The elitist tradition dominated early professional practices and continues to define who is eligible to receive consultation, in many cases. Physicians often consult only with other physicians, for example.

Clinically trained professionals—not only physicians but also psychiatrists, psychologists, social workers, and other health care providers—practiced the collegial model of medical or clinical consultation in early human services agencies and continue to do so today. They diagnose difficult cases and recommend appropriate treatment. These consultants also diagnose and treat organizational ills. When consulting with nonclinicians, the clinical consultant is likely to follow the hierarchical pattern described earlier.

Mental Health Consultant. The second medical model to evolve was consultee-focused and was created by mental health professionals. The psychiatrists who consulted with general practitioners in hospitals and clinics and the newer mental health professionals—social workers and clinical psychologists— were greatly influenced by medicine, the dominant profession, and therefore consulted in the clinical model. However, these practitioners found that the traditional approach touched only a fraction of the mental health problems they discovered. Eventually, their concern over the disparities between needs and services led them to construct the mental health model of consultation. The goal of this model is to increase the skills of agency staff in both preventing and ameliorating mental illness. Diagnosis of a particular case is a secondary goal. The consultants, then, are not just "doctors." Their primary function is educational. Their focus shifts from the client to the consultees' problems and needs.

A "spread of effect" concept is central to this theory. Consultation is viewed as a pyramid arrangement in which the mental health professional, at the apex, consults with and educates the consultees, in the middle of the pyramid, who work in social agencies such as police departments and schools. Through consultation, agency staff members acquire some of the professional's knowledge and skill. They thereby increase their ability to help their clients—the broad base of society at the bottom of the pyramid. A crisis theory of change, which assumes that services are most effective when either the consultee or the client is in crisis, is another important concept.

The beginning of the mental health consultation movement is set in the 1940s, but early in this century social workers operating out of child guidance clinics consulted regularly in this model with teachers, visiting teachers, probation officers, and child welfare workers. In a Minneapolis demonstration clinic in the 1920s, open case conferences were initiated to change teachers' attitudes toward the children being discussed and toward all their other pupils as well (Levine and Levine, 1970). The conferences were also expected to change principals' attitudes toward the pupils and teachers. The overall objective of a Cleveland demonstration clinic of the same era was to build the mental health service capacities of other agencies to the utmost by consultation and lectures to juvenile courts, child welfare agencies, probation officers, and the staffs of summer camps and residential treatment homes. This early movement failed, because it was not generally accepted by the professionals or by the public. The deviant professionals rejoined the traditional mainstream, conducting clinical examinations and developing treatment plans for agency staff members to implement. By the middle of the century, however, a changing ethos, including increased public awareness of the extent of mental illness, led to the reappearance of mental health consultation concepts and practices.

Caplan, the major spokesperson for mental health consultation, describes the experience from which his psychodynamic theory—with its emphasis on the consultee's perceptions—evolved (1970). In 1949 he worked in a Jerusalem mental hygiene and child guidance center with a small team of psychologists and social workers and about a hundred residential institutional staff members, primarily nonprofessional childcare workers and educators, who were responsible for 16,000 immigrant children.

Situational demands forced the professionals to increase the time spent in "counseling" staff members such as instructors and housemothers, rather than working directly with children. The professionals discovered significant differences among their consultees' perceptions of client symptoms, and the consultants began to concentrate on consultees' perceptions and formulations of problems. They identified negative stereotypic perceptions of clients, which they called *theme interference,* deriving the notion of theme from Murray (1938). Caplan and the other professional staff members then worked to discover methods for reducing or dissipating the "themes" that blocked consultees from effective problem solving. Lindemann and his associates in Wellesley, Massachusetts, developed a similar consultation strategy as a by-product of their research (Caplan, 1970). Psychologists observing grammar school classes for research purposes found that teachers were eager to talk with them about problems and discovered that they could increase teachers' understanding of children simply by discussing these problems. Subsequently the psychologists made a formal agreement for systematic consultation with teachers (Klein and Lindemann, 1961).

This model is traditional in its concepts of illness; it is innovative in its method for utilizing the mental health professional's expertise. Above all, the model contributes a comprehensive theory and guiding principles for the consultative relationship. Problems become the means for educative interventions in which the consultee is taught rather than the patient "cured." The consultant no longer examines the patient or client but relies on the consultee to describe aspects of the client that are essential to an understanding of the problem. Moreover, consultant and consultee relate as peers. Rather than seeking to mystify their expertise, consultants seek to demystify and popularize it. The model also stresses the importance of the consultees' emotions for their work and provides guidelines for ameliorating the effects of negative feelings.

Mental health consultation gained considerable government support because its pyramid theory calls for parsimonious use of scarce resources. It is now widely practiced by mental

health and other professionals, such as special educators, counselors, and ministers. Today's practitioners add cognitive and
behavioral concepts and interventions to the psychodynamic
concepts favored by the first mental health consultants and expand their focus from clients and consultees to include institutions, the community, and government policies.

Behavioral Consultant. Behavioral consultation differs
from other models in its adherence to the concepts and principles of learning theory. It merges technological and healing traditions. This model follows the medical model in its focus on a
problem case or situation involving some sort of dysfunctional
behavior and in its diagnostic and prescriptive functions. But
dysfunctions are assumed to be learned responses to environmental stimuli rather than manifestations of disease. Moreover,
the behavioral consultant often assumes a directive role—monitoring the consultee's implementation of a prescription, for
example. Some behavioral consultants, however, take an educative role, teaching consultees behavioral management skills.
This approach conforms to the pyramid concept of mental
health consultation, with its goal of prevention. The major assumption of behavioral approaches is that since human behavior
is learned, it can be modified by application of empirically derived learning principles. The emphasis is on the contemporary
environment and the subject's current, observable behavior.
Most behavioral consultants deemphasize the role of intrapsychic variables, believing that behavior is shaped by antecedents and consequences. Some, however, view cognitive and
affective variables as important determinants of behavior (Thoresen and Mahoney, 1974). The behavioral model places a high
value on control of behavior, including client self-control and
control of clients by agency staff members. Some behavioral
consultants stress control of consultees by assuming a relatively
high degree of responsibility for their work (Bergan, 1977).

Although only recently systematized, learning theory has
been known for centuries and used to change behavior. For instance, in the twelfth century, religious teachers encouraged students to read the Torah by rewards such as fruit and honey. A
sixteenth-century teacher, instead of following the common

practice of punishing by hitting students with a cane, offered fruit and sweets as incentives for learning Greek and Latin (O'Leary and Drabman, 1971). More recently, clinicians discovered that learning principles derived from laboratory experiments are useful in changing behavior. Many clinicians were attracted to learning theory because of its empirical base and its break with traditional intrapsychic approaches (Heller and Monahan, 1977). However, they found that real-life outcomes were often different from those predicted on the basis of laboratory experiments. In real life, the experimenter could not control all the contingencies necessary to obtain and maintain the desired behavior; the natural environment could nullify the changes made in restrictive settings. The focus of behaviorists thus shifted to the patient's natural setting and to key persons in that setting who could control the patient's reinforcement contingencies (Tharp and Wetzel, 1969). Behaviorists became consultants to agency staff members—such as teachers and wardens—usually with the intermediate goal of modifying staff behavior in order to change that of the agency's clients.

The behavioral model contributes three major elements to the consultant's range of options: (1) learning theory as a means of understanding the behavior of individuals, groups, and organizations, (2) a source of techniques to change behaviors of both consultees and their clients, and (3) an intervention model with a built-in paradigm for evaluating change.

Behavioral consultants are in great demand in the human services agencies that require a high degree of client conformity, such as certain schools and penal institutions. The staffs of these organizations often find that their clients do not comply with the necessary helping procedures and that behavioral technology allows the agency to exercise greater control over clients. In addition, behavioral consultants often help agencies cope with program and organizational problems.

Organizational Consultant. One consultation model has evolved that is distinguished by its focus on organizational phenomena. The organizational consultant is a technical specialist in some aspect of agency work—for example, management, communications, or a particular type of agency service. The consultant may take a variety of roles, including technical adviser, teacher, trainer, administrative coach, action researcher, and facilitator.

Toward the end of the nineteenth century, as the needs of expanding industries grew, the body of knowledge concerning work organizations advanced rapidly. Consultation based on the new technology began in the industrial sector and spread to the new human services institutions. Several focuses emerged. Some consultants, scientific management specialists, were empiricists who carefully measured the properties of tools and worker time and motion in their search for the most efficient work processes and equipment (Taylor, 1911). A second group of consultants focused on management of the new organizations. They emphasized the need for a hierarchical authority structure and specialization of tasks. The assumption was that logical bureaucratic structures and distributions of responsibility would reduce human irrationality and increase productivity (Weber, 1947).

These first approaches to organizations ignored workers' personal and social needs or treated them as constant. Eventually, however, a body of knowledge emerged that focused on the human processes within the workplace and brought new content, values, and functions to the consultant role. The shift of focus from tools and structure to people was made not for humanitarian reasons but because of the discovery that productivity can be increased when workers' social and psychological needs are met. Social scientists discovered the importance of motivation (Roethlisberger and Dickson, 1939), leadership style (White and Lippitt, 1960), and informal social groupings (Homans, 1950; Miller and Rice, 1967) on productivity and morale. Regularities in intragroup processes were found. Two crucial work-group processes—task and maintenance (socioemotional) functions—were identified (Bales, 1950). The National Training Laboratories and the Institute for Social Research of the University of Michigan developed laboratory methods for interpersonal skills training and led the way in applying laboratory findings and methods to business and to human services agencies (Bradford, Gibb, and Benne, 1964). Methods of surveying attitudes and giving data feedback were developed and refined.

Scientist-practitioners eventually developed guidelines for human process consultants (Argyris, 1970; Beckhard, 1969; Bennis, 1969). *Organization development,* the use of a variety of human process and structural interventions to improve both morale and productivity, became popular in the private sector and subsequently in human services agencies. By midcentury, managers were frequently using consultants to assist in such interpersonal processes as leadership, communications, group relations, and conflict.

The new bodies of knowledge uncovered a new arena for consultants, the workplace itself. The technological, social, and psychological processes of organizations became accepted domains for consultation. The image of the consultant as an empiricist and a theoretician was strengthened. The consultant's repertoire expanded to include active participation with staff members in their work and in laboratory training. New roles included systems analyst, administrative coach, and action researcher.

Modern agency administrators are acutely aware of the importance of organizational variables in the effective delivery of services and recognize that a broad range of technological expertise is available. Because of their increasing demands for assistance, organizational consultation is widely used.

Program Consultant. Agencies often hire program consultants to provide technological assistance to a particular program. Programs are defined here as services that receive earmarked funds for a target population. The assumption underlying programmatic approaches is that services that are coordinated and channeled to reach narrowly defined goals are likely to be more effective in meeting social needs than more diffuse services.

Program consultation differs from other forms of consultation in its close affiliation with and limitation to program goals. The responsibilities of the program consultant vary greatly. Sometimes consultants participate in the initial stages of program development and therefore influence the assessment of needs, definition of goals, choice of methods to reach goals, identification of resources, refining of administrative procedures, and integration of the new program with other agency programs (Glaser, 1978). Program consultants may help agencies design and implement evaluation procedures. They might, for example, be asked to advise the detoxification staff of a community mental health center in developing a design to assess the outcomes of a group counseling program. Sometimes the responsibilities of program consultants deviate from the usual consultant role. A program consultation contract might (explicitly or, more likely, implicitly) call for a consultant to supervise consultees or to "sell" staff members on the need to change their usual activities to incorporate the behaviors needed to carry out the program. For example, a consultant in the computerization of a welfare department's operations might monitor and supervise consultees to facilitate their switch to computer technology. A special education consultant, working out of a mainstreaming demonstration project sponsored by a college of education, may monitor the teachers' progress in integrating children from special education classrooms into regular ones. The contract would call for her to provide school administrators with her evaluations on the progress of individual teachers and on the faculty as a whole.

Programmatic approaches are not new, although the degree to which modern services are programmed is new. Many of the agencies established around the turn of the century attacked social problems through programs of coordinated activities. The settlement house movement, typical of this approach, addressed the problem of social disintegration by bringing together people from different social classes in a variety of activities, such as educational lectures, reading parties, social problem research, and personal services of all kinds. Another example of early programs was the nineteenth-century design for "moral treatment" of the mentally ill through regimes of work and play in wholesome environments (Bockoven, 1972).

The programmatic approach to social problems reached an all-time high in the 1960s, when a wave of humanitarianism led to demands for public funding of a huge variety of services. Consequently, today many human services agencies deliver all their services through programs. A Planned Parenthood center, for example, offers several discrete programs, each with a separate budget and delivery system and a narrowly defined target population: a clinic program for birth control services, a counseling program for low-income couples, and an educational program for high school students.

Although the program model adds nothing new to the consultant's repertoire, it does highlight the roles consultants may take in helping agencies sharpen their goals and deliver services consistent with carefully defined objectives.

Today the impetus for most human services programs comes from federal funding priorities, which give funds only to services that address specific needs and which are evaluated according to stringent criteria. Consultants are frequently asked to participate in all stages of program development to ensure that evaluative criteria are met (Anderson and Ball, 1978; Matuzek, 1981).

Consultation and Advocacy. Some professionals choose to be advocates rather than consultants. Finding that some institutions fail to provide certain clients with needed services, these professionals pressure administrators and government officials to reform and to expand services. Among the early advocates was Philippe Pinel, an eighteenth-century French physician who in his writings pressed for more humane treatment of the mentally ill and was appointed superintendent of an asylum at Bicêtre. Samuel Howe, an American physician and philanthropist, used political pressures to force the Massachusetts legislature to establish educational and training programs for the retarded (Kanner, 1964). Also in Massachusetts, Dorothea Dix, an educator and writer concerned over the treatment of the pauper insane, addressed the state legislature, demanding that mentally disturbed patients be removed from almshouses and jails to mental hospitals (Bockoven, 1972). Since the 1960s many professionals have turned to advocacy as a means of serving the needs of particular individuals or groups.

Sometimes consultants mix advocacy and consultation activities inappropriately. For example, a psychologist consulting with a police department observed that agency promotion practices discriminated against minorities. He confronted the chief about a particular case and eventually asked the city coun-

cil to intervene. In advocating for minority staff members, this
professional stepped out of the consultant role and the contractual boundaries described in Chapter One. Of course, it is appropriate for consultants to express their opinions and values.
Moreover, agency staff members sometimes solicit a consultant's judgment about the moral or social consequences of a
particular policy or practice. But consultants do not allow their
actions to deviate from agency policies and values, while advocates, acting according to their own views of justice, bring pressures to bear against agency practices that they view as discriminatory or harmful to clients. All agencies are committed to
and supportive of particular social values that, although often
obscure, shape their services. Most agencies support the status
quo; some seek to bring about social change. Consultants by
definition support their agencies' mission, while advocates, as
defined here, may take an adversarial stance regarding certain
agency practices.

Professionalization

During the past twenty years, human services agencies
have greatly expanded in number, scope, and complexity. Their
needs have stimulated tremendous growth in the practice of
consultation. It is now the major occupation of many individuals. Its practitioners are building and systematizing its body of
knowledge and principles, organizing its professional associations, and teaching others how to consult. The practice of consultation is being professionalized.

Processes and Criteria. What are the processes through
which professions evolve? Some professions are created by up-
wardly mobile members of occupations who are seeking social
recognition and greater financial rewards. Bookkeeping, for
example, accumulated sufficient accoutrements to become the
profession of accounting. Other professions evolve through specialization spin-offs, the process of interest here. The impetus
comes when changes in social conditions demand new services.
At first, members of established professions attempt to satisfy
the new needs. They eventually discover that their basic con-

cepts and skills are insufficient, and so they experiment with modifications of their usual practices. Through trial and error, they increase their effectiveness by adapting their basic body of knowledge to the new situation, often adding new concepts and methods. Subspecialties then evolve that become so massive and differentiated over time that they balloon out from their traditional cores. If the new practices continue to be relevant to social needs, spin-offs occur, creating independent fields with their own normative patterns and principles. Psychiatry, for example, split off specialized areas from medicine, psychology, and philosophy and synthesized them into an independent new discipline. Society reinforces the growth of new practices by rewarding the individuals who deliver them with social recognition, prestige, and relatively high incomes. Practitioners organize and accelerate the professionalization process by developing structures for training and socialization and by establishing standards to improve practice and to protect the public.

What factors determine whether professional status has been achieved? This is a difficult question to answer. Criteria for fully developed professions have been suggested (Greenwood, 1966; Hughes, 1958; Moore, 1970). However, few professions have attained all the criteria. Moore proposed a scale of professionalization that provides a checklist for evaluating a profession's status. This scale, from the lowest level to the highest, proceeds as follows:

1. *Full-time.* The first criterion separates professionals from amateurs and from ancillary members of a field. Professions are full-time occupations and the principal source of their members' incomes. Professions are neither subordinate to other professions nor stepping stones to them.

2. *A calling.* Members of a profession make lifelong commitments to its activities, values, and principles. The profession represents a primary and enduring identification. "The bond established by shared mysteries, exemplified in technical language and common styles of work and often even common attire, bespeaks a consciousness of being set apart, and insisting on it" (p. 9).

3. *Organization.* Members of professions organize asso-

ciations to protect and enhance their interests and to establish standards to protect the public.

4. *Education.* Professions possess "esoteric but useful knowledge and skills, based on specialized training or education of exceptional duration and perhaps of exceptional difficulty" (p. 6).

5. *Service orientation.* Professions are committed to serve the interests and to protect the welfare of their clients and society through rules of competence and ethical and conscientious performance.

6. *Autonomy.* The ultimate goal of professionals is autonomy and the prestige that goes with it. Attainment of this criterion is made possible by specialization. "The specialist in his field must be supreme, for who, other than another similarly qualified specialist, can challenge him?" (pp. 15-16). Autonomy is also attained through the salience of a profession's specialty to important societal needs. The members of autonomous professions are free of lay evaluation and control. They are entrusted to receive and protect privileged information. They are self-governing in determining their standards of education and training. They are influential in shaping the legislation that regulates their practices. The members of autonomous professions are usually self-employed and work for fees.

Consultation as an Emergent Profession. Consultation has just begun to professionalize. The process thus far has been marked by three developmental stages, which differ in the degree to which practitioners are involved in and committed to the consultant role and in the degree to which this role is differentiated from others. Consultants today are practicing at all three levels.

The first stage is a preliminary one in which consultation is practiced as an occasional or vaguely defined extension of the roles and functions of other professions. Thus, many professionals consult as a peripheral activity. This level of consultation will undoubtedly continue to meet important needs of human services institutions, and many professionals will prefer to practice consultation at this level. In this stage, consultants typically explain some facet of their fields or perform one of its functions for agency staff. They become bridges for conveying knowledge and services from their professions to agencies. Figure 2 depicts this early developmental stage. For example, a

Figure 2. First Stage in the Evolution of the Profession of Consultation

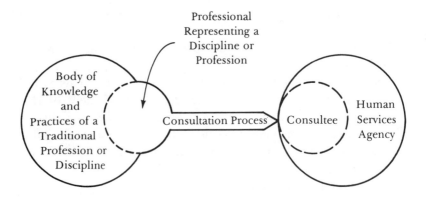

sociologist, a specialist in population control, may present a lecture on fertility research to the staff of a Planned Parenthood center; a communications specialist may lead a workshop on conflict management for administrators of a state welfare department; or a speech pathologist, acting in response to a teacher's request, may examine a pupil and write a report of the diagnosis and recommendations. These consultative services require little or no modification of the professional's basic practices. The familiar concepts and skills are usually adequate. In some situations, however, additional competencies, such as skills in teaching or in communication with peers, may be needed. Tensions arise if the consultant lacks these skills.

As human services agencies expand in number, scope, and complexity, so do their problems and their demands for consultation. Consequently, many professionals find themselves drawn into frequent consultation activities and spending large proportions of their time in them. Role tensions soon arise. These individuals often find that their usual practices do not fit agency needs. They begin to adapt them and to borrow elements from other fields. Their work leads to the development of consultation subspecialties and the second stage in the professionalization process. This stage features a new and clearly defined role. The individuals who practice in this role are committed to it, although it remains subordinate to their primary occupations. Consultant practitioners, on the whole, are at this level of professionalization, delineated in Figure 3. At this level, distinctive

Figure 3. Second Stage in the Evolution of the Profession of Consultation

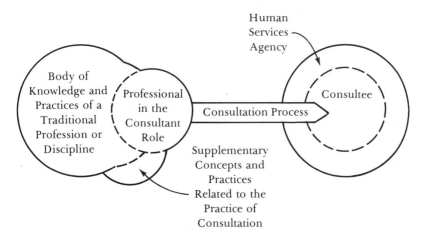

new roles evolve that enable professionals to meet agency demands and yet maintain the integrity of their professions. The consultants' participation in ongoing agency processes and problems increases. Figure 3 depicts the penetration into the agency's life.

This early stage in the evolution of consultation is characterized by tension, frustration, and creativity. Shifting from the primary practices of a professional field to consultation practice can be a disappointing and frustrating experience. Consultation may initially only increase the problems of the hiring agency. Tensions arise from many sources. Helping others with *their* work is a more intricate process than working directly on one's own task. Moreover, clear feedback is usually difficult to obtain, since the goal is often far removed from the helper's scrutiny. The presenting problem and the helping process are confounded by complex organizational phenomena. Maintaining the detachment necessary to understand organizational behavior is sometimes difficult. Consultants may become ensnared in agency politics and lose their precious objectivity. Familiar patterns of practicing, of thinking about clients, and of viewing the professional role often interfere with the new role. Levine (1972) noted, for instance, that mental health consultants' labels, such as "psychopathic personality," leave agency staff with no direction and are, therefore, useless to consultees, if not actually destructive to their relationships with clients.

Thus, consultants often find that the knowledge and skills in their basic discipline are not adequate to help other professionals with their work. When consultants' work expands beyond well-learned tasks—such as constructing a survey form or giving expert information—to deeper and broader involvement in agency work, they must develop a new role, new concepts, and new practices. Yet, professional training rarely includes preparation for this role, and many consultants do not have a clear conception of the differences between the expertise needed to practice their basic disciplines and that needed for the more advanced forms of consultation. Consequently, much consultation practice is atheoretical. Hamilton (1978), for example, in investigating the conceptual underpinnings of campus consultants, found that only 20 percent followed a model. They are their own guides, a heavy responsibility (Levinson, 1972). Finding individuals with whom they can discuss their experiences and conceptualize their roles and functions is difficult. Professionals who become engaged in consultation typically develop different concerns than their colleagues who remain in the practices for which they were originally trained. Consultants often experience a loss of identification with professional peers. Troubled over both the ambiguities of the consultant role and their isolation from peers, many feel compelled to return to their original roles and practices.

A major barrier to the evolution of a new role comes from established professions. Professions, like other systems, resist changes that might threaten their status quo. They are slow to lead their members in learning new specialties. Although professions seek to expand their ranges of influence, they usually extend their traditional practices to new territories rather than revising them or acquiring new ones. "New knowledge or innovations in techniques and practice threaten the very basis upon which the established professionals rest their claims to expert competence" (Moore, 1970, p. 44). Thus, new practices—and the colleagues who introduce them—are certain to arouse anxieties (Hughes, 1958). Training for new roles, such as consultation, receives a low priority. To illustrate, mental health consultation theory and principles have been known for sixty years but have only slowly gained acceptance by mental health professions, because their traditions are built around direct services.

Social needs supply the energy to overcome professional barriers. Support for the development of consultation as a professional subspecialty has come from the federal government in the form of conferences, publications, and training grants sponsored by the National Institute of Mental Health. In developing the consultation role, practitioners first sharpen its boundaries and differentiate it from their traditional activities. They alter their professional practices to fit the new role and borrow elements from other fields. Sometimes full-fledged models evolve that adapt a profession's basic content and form to fit the consultant role. Thus, new specialties have ballooned out from traditional disciplines. Several examples illustrate the process. The earliest is the clinical model of consultation, which evolved as a subspecialty of medicine. The more elaborate mental health consultation model emerged as a subspecialty of mental health professions. This model borrowed elements from such fields as organizational and communications theories. The consultation model described by Levinson (1972) adds open-systems theory to a core consisting of psychoanalytic theory and methods.

The individuals who lead the practice of consultation into this second stage are largely self-taught by on-the-job experience and self-directed study. But as they clarify the new specialties and as their expertise increases, they begin to disseminate their knowledge to professional colleagues through workshops, presentation of papers at professional conferences, and publications that describe case studies, research, theory, and principles. Their ideas and methods become the basis for courses in professional training programs.

Some individuals and professional groups are leading the practice of consultation into a third stage of professionalization. Specialties that ballooned out from a number of traditional core areas are beginning to spin off and form a new, loosely integrated, quasi-independent body of knowledge and practices consisting of elements from several parent professions. Figure 4 pre-

Figure 4. Third Stage in the Evolution of the Profession of Consultation

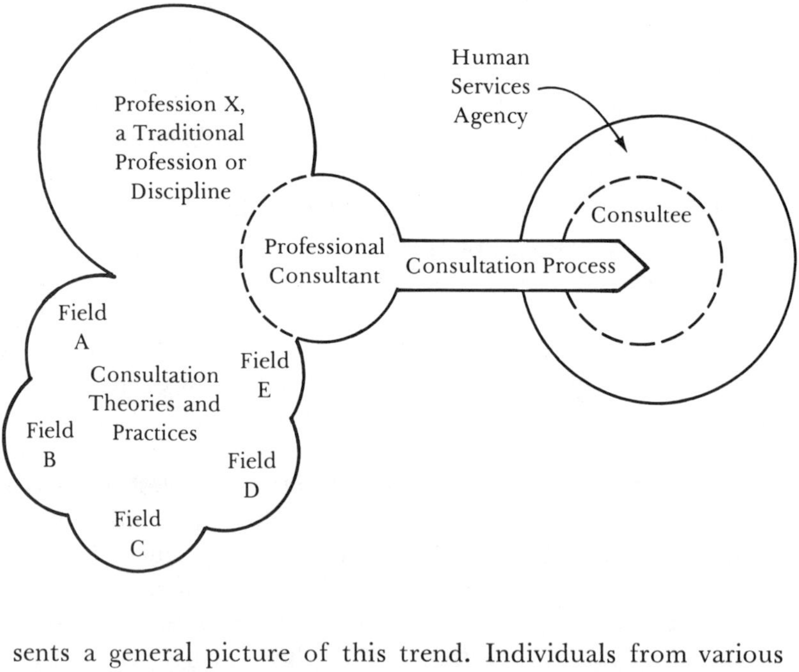

sents a general picture of this trend. Individuals from various professions (shown as Profession X in Figure 4) are spending a large proportion of their time in the practice of consultation. At the same time, they are drawing extensively on the knowledge of other fields, A, B, C, D, and E. For example, imagine that the professional consultant in Figure 4 is a member of the profession of psychiatry. Earlier in her career, she practiced consultation in a traditional form—perhaps the mental health consultation model—as a subspecialty of psychiatry. Eventually, she began to consult full-time. Her identity as a consultant has now become as important as her identity as a psychiatrist. Her central concepts and principles come not just from her traditional core but also from other disciplines—such as communications theory, sociology, and education. Her primary activities now bear little resemblance to her original practices. This process is being replicated by members of a number of professions. They are achieving the first two criteria on the ladder of professionalization. They spend a significant portion of their time (sometimes 100 percent) in consultation, and they are committed to its activities, principles, and values. Their consultation commitment has become equal to or greater than their commitment to their original fields. The third stage of professionalization is also being achieved by another route: A few academic programs are beginning to produce graduates whose primary identification is the role of consultant. (See Chapter 18 for a discussion of this trend.)

Professionalization and Social Needs

In order for occupants of new roles to reach their potential to serve society, they need to work together—to organize. Organizations are essential for professions to develop standards of performance and ethical practice, to systematize the new body of knowledge, and to create institutions and procedures for training and socialization. The nature of the organizations that evolve and lead in professionalizing consultation will be crucial in determining the profession's identity, standards, and role in society. (Professionalization issues are discussed in Chapter Sixteen.)

Annotated Bibliography

Greenwood, E. "The Elements of Professionalism." In H. M. Vollmer and D. L. Mills (Eds.), *Professionalization*. Englewood Cliffs, N.J.: Prentice-Hall, 1966. The author points out that as an occupation begins to professionalize, important changes occur both internally and in the relationship of the practitioners to society. His descriptions of these changes and of the essential characteristics of the "ideal" profession illuminate developments within consultation and between its practitioners and society.

Hughes, E. C. *Men and Their Work.* New York: Free Press, 1958. This book, a landmark contribution to the sociology of work, is concerned with the social-psychological aspects of work and especially with collective attempts by members of occupations to control the terms through which they relate to society. Its provocative ideas are especially important for consultants to consider at this early stage in the professionalization of their occupation—while their values, principles, and purposes are still being formed.

Levine, M., and Levine, A. *A Social History of Helping Services.* New York: Appleton-Century-Crofts, 1970. The authors describe the institutionalization of helping services for children at the turn of the century and the ways in which social beliefs and conditions influenced these institutions. The book is particularly helpful in understanding the continuing struggle between political conservatives and liberals for control of the direction and form of helping services.

Moore, W. E. *The Professions: Role and Rules.* New York: Russell Sage Foundation, 1970. Moore outlines the evolution of contemporary professions from the medicine men and priests of ancient cultures. He describes the characteristics and attributes of modern professions and the professional's relationships to clients, peers, and society at large. His conceptions of the professional's role and functions and his professionalization scale provide a foundation for analysis of the modern role of consultant.

Znaniecki, F. *The Social Role of the Man of Knowledge.* New York: Octagon Books, 1965. This book describes the evolution of social roles and the relationship between role holders (members of particular systems of knowledge) and society. Znaniecki's discussions of two prototypical social roles, the technological adviser and the sage, are helpful in clarifying the specialized functions of contemporary consultants and the differences between the consultant and advocate roles.

3

Understanding Organizational Structure, Processes, and Problems

   This chapter examines the consultant's workplace, the agencies that minister to individual and societal needs. The major goal of the chapter is to provide a conceptual framework to help consultants understand the special features and problems of human services agencies. Whether their focus is on staff, clients, programs, or organizational functioning, consultants need to understand the general nature and characteristics of these institutions. Otherwise, they are likely to miss or misinterpret important data, intervene in irrelevant or destructive ways, or become immobilized in political cross-fire. The second goal of the chapter is to clarify the needs that are creating and shaping the profession of consultation.

   The simple nineteenth-century human services agencies

that arose to meet the needs of a society in the throes of industrialization have metamorphosed into hundreds of complex organizations with specialized functions and diverse beneficiaries. Professions, like agencies, have splintered into specialties to staff expanding services. As the deterioration of the social structure that commenced with industrialization has continued (Lasch, 1977; Sennett, 1978), society has become increasingly dependent on secondary institutions. Agencies not only have taken over many of the basic functions of kin and neighbors but also supply a wide variety of highly specialized services demanded by a sophisticated public. For example, in addition to the traditional general hospitals and clinics, most communities have health facilities designed to prevent illnesses as well as to ameliorate them. Citizens can obtain assistance from clinics for well-baby care, pain and stress management, substance abuse, abortions, and maintenance of physical fitness. Visiting nurses bring treatment and meals to the homebound. Hospices minister to the dying. State hospitals continue to treat the mentally ill; however, many of their patients have been discharged and now receive sheltered care and rehabilitation from community facilities, such as halfway houses and daycare centers. In addition, community mental health centers supply a wide range of remedial and preventive services to individuals, groups, and organizations. In the educational field, regional service centers provide training and consultation to faculties of public and private schools. Regional laboratories generate and disseminate information to educational institutions. University-based research and development centers aid schools in implementing and evaluating new programs. Alternative schools both inside and outside public systems offer new curricula taught by new methods. Schools for special populations, such as deaf, blind, retarded, and developmentally disabled students, offer specialized educational and training programs. Community colleges with wide-ranging curricula attract students of all ages. Agencies and professions in the criminal justice field provide a wide array of programs and specialists to control crime, to detect offenders and rehabilitate them, and to serve their victims. Services for the poor—welfare assistance, low-cost housing, educational and training programs—have proliferated. All kinds of public services

—including mass transit systems, public information centers, park and recreation departments, and pollution control agencies —make life easier, safer, more convenient, and more enjoyable.

The study of human services agencies is a recent development. Its literature as yet offers meager guidance to consultants. However, the older and broader field of organizational studies has produced a rich and useful body of literature. Major directions of this field and some of the concepts most valuable to human services consultants are therefore discussed next.

The explicit purpose of organizations is to produce, and the focal issue in organizational studies is *productivity*. Most approaches focus on particular areas assumed (often tacitly) to be crucial to productivity. "The clinical psychologist catches the executive in a closeup, exploring the tensions of his aggressive personality. The social psychologist cuts from the executive to the members of his staff, illuminating the uncertainties of status and the waning cohesion of the group as the time approaches to choose a new president. The administrative theorist stands back and coolly assesses the discrepancy between the responsibilities and the authority of a subordinate, a gap never calculated by an executive who has cluttered up his communication channels. The economist inserts a wide-angle lens and comments that the market has dropped, while the political scientist notes that labor is in control of the legislature" (Perrow, 1970, p. 1). Consultants come from varied disciplines and may be primarily concerned with any one of these perspectives; most are people-oriented and are likely to focus on such areas as leadership or morale. However, since the source or the solution to any problem—including a human one—is often found in another domain, consultants need a broad framework to help them understand an agency's general nature and processes as well as the area of particular interest.

Sociotechnical Theory

The first organic, or systemic, approach to understanding organizations, a sociotechnical theory, came from efforts by the Tavistock Institute to increase productivity in English coal mines (Miller and Rice, 1967; Trist and Bamforth, 1951). Out of these benchmark experiments came clear recommendations for alleviating inherent tensions between human and organizational needs. Introduction of new machinery had led to the reorganization of work and human relationships. The longwall method of mining, in which work was fractionated and each worker performed a simple, repetitive task, replaced small, cohesive, self-contained teams. Work groups were then larger and less personal; pay was given on an individual rather than a team basis. As a result of these changes, morale and productivity declined, while absenteeism and accidents increased. Tavistock researchers found that some mines had not completely adopted the new method but rather had devised a "composite" longwall system, which retained much of the job continuity and team cohesiveness of the earlier method. They found striking differences between the two systems. The composite longwall method was superior in its lower rate of absenteeism and in its higher level of productivity.

These experiments led the Tavistock group to theorize that organizations are tools that have two purposes: (1) performing a task and (2) meeting members' needs for satisfaction and alleviation of the anxiety that inevitably results from working in organized groups. The inherent conflict between human needs and the performance of work leads to two kinds of organizations, the formal and the informal. The formal organization coordinates activities for task performance; for example, it includes administrative structures and technological procedures. The informal organization, or "sentient" system, coordinates the relationships that meet emotional and social needs. Discrepancies between the formal and informal organizations lead to lowered morale and productivity. In a university, for instance, imagine that the president and three lower-ranking administrators compose a long-standing social group. They play bridge and golf together, they lunch together frequently, and the president discusses work problems with these three far more openly than with his vice-presidents. The feelings of jealousy and exclusion engendered in other officers lower their sense of loyalty and commitment and diminish their productivity.

Most informal systems have mixed effects. To illustrate,

the individuals who work in a small hospital separate into three professionally defined social groups that are vividly revealed in their cafeteria behavior. Physicians eat in one room, nurses in another, and nonprofessionals in a third. Within these groups, members enjoy high levels of social and work-related interaction. However, the close relations within these occupationally defined social groups are more salient than relationships within the hospital's formal structure, and this prevents the cohesiveness across occupations that is needed for communication and maximum productivity. Ideally, the sociotechnical approach asserts, social and technical subsystems are integrated in primary work groups that satisfy social needs while carrying out organizational tasks. The sociotechnical approach also assumes that worker satisfaction increases with greater decision-making responsibility and involvement in meaningful units or cycles of work rather than in single, repetitive tasks.

Appropriate boundary control is a related concern of this theory. Without a firm boundary between the agency and its environment, the organization is too permeable for cohesion; members do not develop a strong sense of agency identity, and external stressors may overload agency operations. However, with a relatively closed boundary, the agency becomes isolated from the environment and lacks the external input needed to keep up to date. Internal boundaries pose similar difficulties; the lines of separation between units may be too sharply differentiated for coordination or so diffuse that worker responsibilities are not adequately distinguished.

Open-Systems Theory

An even more comprehensive approach to organizations, open-systems theory, came from efforts to understand biological phenomena (von Bertalanffy, 1950) and was subsequently applied to social sciences. This theory provides a dynamic model for examining every facet of organizational life. All processes, events, and structures are considered within the context of the entire system and its interactions with the environment (Katz and Kahn, 1978). Open-systems theory emphasizes the cyclical and dynamic nature of organizational events. In human services agencies, for example, intake, processing, and output of clients constitute the primary cycle, supported by interlocking cycles of tasks such as budgeting and personnel management (hiring, evaluation, and termination).

Open-systems theory includes a number of postulates. One concerns entropy, the universal law under which all organisms tend to run down and die; the theory holds that social systems, unlike biological organisms, may arrest the entropic process by importing excess energy from the environment and storing it to build a reserve. Agencies thus achieve negative entropy by acquiring extra staff, funds, and materials. They add to their stored energy when they build good relations with the public, key politicians, and grant-giving institutions.

Another postulate is that open systems move toward increased differentiation and elaboration. Agencies tend to grow more specialized. Workers divide into specialized subgroups that serve different types of client needs. Specialization sets up distinct immediate goals and methods and eventually requires particular types of training. Each specialized group develops its own processes and technology and tends to develop autonomy. However, these subsystems are in fact interdependent; thus, in a compensatory movement, systems develop coordination functions to integrate subsystems. In human services agencies, unity is achieved through common values, priorities, routines such as intake procedures and staff conferences, and cycles such as funding and recruitment.

A third principle is that open systems move in the direction of growth and expansion, while maintaining a dynamic homeostasis. Organizations seek to swallow up external systems, incorporating whatever external resources they need to survive and expand. To illustrate, low-cost housing projects expand their primary services to include educational, recreational, and vocational training programs; universities go beyond their educative function to offer health care, student housing, and many other services. But these systems maintain their steady state by mobilizing energies to restore balance and continue their essential nature, cycles of events, and relationship to the environment.

Open systems are also characterized by equifinality; this principle holds that agencies can reach the same final state by varying paths. Thus, there are alternative methods by which an agency might reach the same goal.

An open-systems analysis includes a review of salient environmental systems and internal subsystems. Five major subsystems have been identified (Katz and Kahn, 1978). Most important is the technological subsystem that is responsible for such primary cycle activities as education or treatment. Closely associated with this subsystem are supportive subsystems that procure input (such as staff members, funds for operation, and equipment) and dispose of output (such as money to buy needed materials and expertise, reports to funding organizations, and public relations information). Maintenance subsystems ensure that human and other resources carry out the primary task; these structures recruit, train, socialize, reward, and punish staff members. The management subsystem regulates and directs all subsystems. Adaptive subsystems—such as research and development departments—monitor the environment and assess the effects of impending changes on the organization.

The following sections apply open-systems theory to an examination of (1) the environmental systems that most profoundly affect human services agencies and (2) the characteristics and inherent problems of technological subsystems.

Environmental Interactions. Open-systems concepts are especially useful in analyzing the *interplay between human services agencies and their environments.* As open systems, agencies are continuously affected by systems outside their boundaries—dominant social values, government regulations and funding policies, consumers, professional organizations, technological changes, other helping organizations, and mass media. It is useful to examine each of these in turn.

A major shift in *social values* and in the *funding* of human services began fifty years ago. The first helping institutions were largely financed by local agencies and philanthropic societies, but the federal government, beginning with relief programs in the wake of the depression of the 1930s, took over major responsibility for the role of "helper." For half a century, the dominant ideology held that society itself, not genetic inferiority, is the cause of many human problems and should therefore be responsible for their amelioration. Public services, moreover, should not be limited to the indigent or to dire crises but should extend to the everyday problems and needs of all citizens. Agency staff became accustomed to expanding budgets and programs and to federal control as well, evidenced in governmental domination of policies and operations in all areas of service, including health, education, welfare, and the criminal justice system. But a reversal of this pattern appeared with the 1980s. Government funding and controls at all levels—federal, state, and local—are being cut back. Many agencies and programs have been eliminated. These changes reflect both a diminution of resources and a sweeping shift in social values.

The *role of client* has changed over the past century. Clients tend to reject the *noblesse oblige* conception of the professional; they have become less compliant and more demanding. Consumerism—the organized power of individual clients—has weakened the power of the professions and brought changes in services and policies. Clients organized on the basis of common needs pressure agencies to change current services and to add new ones to benefit their particular groups; some also insist on internal changes such as elimination of racial and sexual discrimination in agency staffing. The federal government is responsive to consumer lobbies, and agencies that do not comply with consumer demands risk loss of vital federal subsidies. The open-records law and funding contingencies that require client participation exemplify the increased influence of consumers.

Some consumers, unwilling to wait for agencies to change, have organized alternatives to mainstream institutions. "Third sector" agencies such as free schools and universities, law collectives, communes, and a wide variety of services for women, the poor, and the unemployed proliferated in the 1960s and 1970s. Their idealistic creators hoped that these institutions would serve as humanized exemplars of service delivery. "Technology, bureaucracy, and 'professionalism' would go by the board. Relationships in work would be personal and open. Members would participate directly in the affairs of the collectivity—one person, one vote. They would seek equality in other ways, too, notably by rotating jobs and sharing the dirty work. The new organizations would provide goods and services cheaply, help stimulate political reforms, and restore feelings of community, purpose, and satisfaction in their members. Thus would the social services be restructured and nonhierarchical, humane organizations be created, all at once" (Case and Taylor, 1979, p. 7). Many of these alternative, or third-sector, agencies survive in the 1980s. Some, such as consumer agencies, have earned mainstream status. Some have been incorporated by mainstream institutions; for instance, most large school districts include alternative campuses, and abortions are now available in some community hospitals and clinics. Thus, changes in client attitudes and actions often dramatically affect agency policies and practices. Consumer groups remind agencies of the needs of underserved members of society, thus providing important feedback; at the same time, they force agencies to contend with demands from multiple, conflicting constituencies.

To a greater extent than ever before, agencies are dependent on professionals and on *professional organizations.* The rights of agencies to work with particular clients and to provide services may be based in part on licensure of their professional staffs. Some technologies are by law within the exclusive domain of certain professions—medical treatment and psychotherapy, for example. Furthermore, an agency may seek to legitimize itself and its operations through its staff's professional prestige and expertise; professional staff members can protect an agency's autonomy by buffering and insulating it from external forces. The professions influence agencies in several ways. Guild training standards largely determine the supply of competent professionals; guild practice standards affect the content, quality, and direction of agency services and therefore the benefits to clients. Tensions frequently arise between professional and agency values; consequently, professionals may struggle with administrators or boards of trustees over policies, goals, and services (Kouzes and Mico, 1979). However, public skepticism toward all authority, including professionals, has grown (Nisbet, 1970), and guilds have lost some of their power and prestige. Professionals have also lost some of their traditional control over their work. General dissemination of certain knowledge formerly reserved by professionals, along with mass media coverage of unethical practices, have dispelled some of the traditional mystique of the professional. Consumerism and the federal government have taken away other areas of professionals' power. Federal grants influence training priorities and employment opportunities. Many professionals no longer practice autonomously but rather are salaried employees of agencies and dependent on federal funding priorities. Since decisions by the government, along with changes in social conditions and technology, can either eliminate or accelerate demands for particular services, the marketability of professional specialties becomes uncertain. To counter these forces, professionals are organizing more tightly to protect their status and security; they are increasing their lobbying activities to influence government policies. Their guilds, rather than agency needs, often determine their priorities.

Technological change also influences the structure and processes of the helping services. New procedures and tools continually appear that are useful in helping people cope with modern stresses and with age-old social and individual problems. Hoping to increase their effectiveness, agencies adopt innovative methods; for example, cancer treatment centers use biofeedback, visual imagery, and cognitive restructuring to control clients' pain, and elementary schools use computers to teach a wide range of subjects. New technologies usually call for revamping of established operations and lead to new structures—more specialized programs or departments. New technology also requires more expensive equipment and more specialized and expensive labor (Drucker, 1980). The proliferation of technology leads to increased specialization, and specialization intensifies interdependence and the need for intra- and interagency coordination and collaboration.

Other agencies determine many aspects of an agency's operations, such as the numbers and characteristics of entering clients and the methods of service delivery. The actions and policies of other agencies can result in both overloads and underutilization of resources. Interagency dependence is illustrated in the criminal justice system's lack of control over incoming clients. "A public defender service, for example, finds that the flow of clients will be determined by the arrest practices of the police, the practices of prosecutors, constraints on plea bargaining, the legislative mandates that determine client eligibility for service, the judges' assessment of the likelihood that a client will be incarcerated, and the courts' expectation concerning case flow" (Hirschhorn, 1979, p. 165). Some organizations create problems that others are trying to solve; for example, agencies that provide low-cost housing often create "ghettos" that generate enormous social problems for neighboring agencies (Demone and Harshbarger, 1974).

In addition to the environmental pressures enumerated above, the *mass media* play a role. Service organizations—most of which operate on public funds—are under continual surveillance by reporters and news analysts representing newspapers, radio, and television.

These environmental systems—prevailing social values, government funding and control, consumers, professional groups, technological change, other helping agencies, and mass media—impose enormous demands and constraints on agencies. An organization's staff must maintain liaison with influential public officials, such as legislators, heads of funding organizations, state and local planning officers, city councils, and others who control funds. Agencies must also maintain contact with unions, professional associations, and licensure boards. They must consider the agendas of consumers, including special-interest groups such as minorities, women, and the handicapped, when making policy or program decisions. Agencies must also operate within the dominant values of their communities. Some schools cannot teach courses in social skills or human sexuality or use corporal punishment; in some communities doctors face social censure and litigation if they perform abortions. Agencies need to stay abreast of advances in technology to judge the promise of new techniques. Agencies must depend on mass media to inform the public of available services and to present a positive public image. Moreover, since external forces often push and pull in different directions, agencies must somehow cope with contradictory demands.

An open-systems analysis of these environmental forces

illuminates the problems associated with *goal setting*. The purpose of these agencies is to respond to social needs; but since our pluralistic society makes contradictory demands, deciding whose needs will be served is often a complex and value-laden process. The dilemma is illustrated in the abortion centers, which are lauded by many citizens and condemned by certain others, such as "right to life" groups. Staffs and clients of these centers may thus feel threatened and ambivalent about their services. Similarly, schools struggle to fulfill their primary role of teaching while responding to conflicting consumer needs. The federal government, certain professional groups, and some parents press for inclusion of handicapped children in mainstream classrooms. Other parents (and some teachers) demand that these children be placed in special classes. Whose needs should prevail? Juvenile courts must contend with conflicting requests from police, public schools, professional and humanitarian citizen groups, legislators, and parents. Should courts incarcerate an offender to protect society or respond to the offender's need for freedom and new opportunities? Powerful administrators or politicians may even establish nonclient goals for agencies. Agency operations may be manipulated to improve the prestige or image of the agency, of local or state officials, or of a professional group. Agencies are at times the means for creating jobs and shoring up a depressed economy (Gartner and Riessman, 1974).

Constrained by conflicting demands, social institutions must serve multiple goals. The administrator's task is no longer to provide one primary service but rather to produce the minimum acceptable results for several constituencies in a "satisfice" policy (Drucker, 1980, citing Simon, 1947). For example, in schools undergoing desegregation, academic education might become—for the moment, at least—a secondary goal. Agencies may resolve conflict by stating their goals in abstract terms acceptable to all constituencies; to illustrate, schools announce that their objective is to educate the young to participate as good citizens in a democratic society (Hasenfeld and English, 1975). Another way agencies may settle disputes is by setting goals consistent with their most powerful interest groups; for example, state agencies typically align their goals with the agenda of the current governor.

Environmental tensions are the impetus for creating human services institutions. At the same time, these tensions greatly complicate the task of delivering services. To obtain help in clarifying these forces and deciding how to respond to them while maintaining internal equilibrium, administrators often turn to consultants—not only for their expertise but also for the objectivity that outsiders can bring.

The Technological Subsystem. The primary function of human services agencies, delivery of helping services, is accomplished through their *technological subsystems.* Open-systems theory envisions this domain in terms of stable cycles of events, patterned and interrelated activities that repeat themselves and that import, transform, and export energy from and to the environment, initiating a renewal of the cycle. Cycles fall into two major categories. The primary cycle is concerned with the delivery of the essential services; secondary cycles provide support for the primary one. The primary cycle begins with the *input* of clients into the agency—patients entering a dental clinic, patrons coming to a library, or riders using a mass transit system. In the *throughput,* clients receive services, such as treatment, information, or transportation. Clients are thus processed and transformed in some way and then *output,* or exported back into the environment. Outputs can usually be described in both individual and societal terms. Prisons strive to produce more socially responsible individuals and safer communities. Mental health centers work to produce emotionally strengthened individuals and a healthier society. Schools seek to educate individuals who will be knowledgeable participants in public affairs. The cycle begins anew as other clients enter the agency for services.

The supportive cycles enable agencies to carry out primary activities. To illustrate, community mental health centers annually recruit new staff members and terminate others; purchase, use, and discard equipment; negotiate with federal and local governments for funds; and confer with consumers, politicians, and professional groups. They also receive and export information about environmental conditions, public expectations, and their own performance—through news media, other agencies, and funding organizations.

Human services agencies must contend with several unique technological problems. First, the multiple constituencies described earlier create conflicts in setting goals and priorities; yet agency goals must be defined before the operations to achieve them can be selected. Moreover, the knowledge base of most human services gives little clear direction for making technological decisions. Cause-and-effect relationships are not well-established; therefore, precise standards and routines are lacking (Miringoff, 1980; Perrow, 1970). Input characteristics also pose special problems. Clients—the raw materials—vary widely and present inconsistencies that complicate the throughput process. Clients are reactive, and their values, attitudes, and behaviors may either enhance or constrain agency services. Patients may refuse to follow physician-prescribed regimes; penitentiary inmates may riot. To ensure that their treatments or change technologies are not undermined, agencies develop compliance mechanisms such as monitoring and examinations. The major vehicle for both achieving change and eliciting compliance is the staff/client relationship. The greater the degree of change sought, the more critical this relationship becomes. Quality control of these complex interactions is limited by clients' rights to privacy and by the autonomy of the professional staff.

Measuring outputs of service organizations is a complex task. Traditionally, simple records such as numbers of people served sufficed to evaluate an agency's performance. Today, demands for accountability—including funding contingencies—are forcing agencies to search for ways to define and measure their outputs more accurately and to make cost/benefit analyses of the merits of alternative services. Yet many broadly defined goals, such as social adjustment or good citizenship, are not amenable to precise operational definitions. Moreover, effectiveness can sometimes be measured in contradictory terms—for instance, the effectiveness of a welfare agency could be measured by the number of clients served or the number taken off the rolls. The services themselves are typically both complex and inexact, and they elude measurement. Many forces other than the agency also impinge on clients, and their effects cannot be measured or separated from agency effects. Clients are influenced by family, friends, various service agencies (clinics, churches, schools), their work organizations, and life events such as illness, new job opportunities, maturation, and neighborhood changes. Furthermore, the kinds of data available for evaluation are generally quite limited because of financial, ethical, and practical constraints. Few agencies are able to make cost analyses of different methods for dealing with a given problem (MacLennan, 1979).

Despite these problems, agencies must evaluate their output in order to receive funding. They must often be content to measure their services in terms of efficiency (costs per client or speed of service), amount of research done, numbers of new programs installed, or subjective evaluations by staff and clients. In some situations, however, even complex service goals can be defined in ways that permit criterion measures at input, output, and follow-up stages, and comparison groups can sometimes be found. Agencies often reach out to external professionals for specialized assistance in the complex task of evaluation.

Management Concepts

In addition to broad theories of organizations, consultants need conceptual frameworks to help them understand particular agency domains. Because of the importance of management in organizing and delivering human services, this domain deserves careful study.

The task of management is to ensure that the agency fulfills its social role. To this end, managers regulate internal activities and the interaction between the agency and its environment. The internal task includes responsibility for setting goals, procuring and maintaining material and human resources, maintaining efficiency and quality in services, coordinating and regulating various subsystems, reconciling organizational and human needs, and administering rewards and sanctions. The external tasks are similarly formidable. Managers must monitor the environment and adapt agency operations to keep them congruent with changes in social needs and conditions; at the same time, managers must maintain agency stability and keep stress on staff members below disruptive levels.

Because of their pivotal position in social and political conflicts of interest and because of the high visibility of their operations and outputs, human services administrators are often subjected to a great deal of scrutiny and criticism. Critics contend that agencies dehumanize clients (Gartner and Riessman, 1974); agency structures and technology are said to be rigid and deteriorating (Argyris, 1970; Illich, 1972). However, the task of these administrators is difficult. They must cope with uncertain budgets and pluralistic constituencies. Rapid environmental changes sometimes force administrators to adapt so frequently—to redirect their services, to reorganize and restaff their operations—that they cannot stabilize internal structures and processes sufficiently to analyze how best to deliver services. Moreover, agency administrators often have little actual authority. A number of groups, including superordinate boards and agencies, funding organizations, employee unions, and consumer groups, wield considerable influence over them.

Perhaps the major challenge of the administrator is to reconcile organizational and human needs. To achieve optimum productivity, all organizations need workers who are willing—at least at times—to subordinate their own needs to those of the organization. The first two approaches to obtaining this conformity came from the scientific management perspective, in which humans were perceived as cogs in machines. One model assumed that workers would be productive if they were technically competent, used the proper tools, and followed carefully specified mechanical procedures (Taylor, 1911). The second model viewed the bureaucratic structure as the key to productivity (Weber, 1947). It outlined distributions of authority based on theories about how to achieve the highest levels of efficiency. It offered well-defined pyramids and chains of command, carefully specified procedures and rules, and division of labor according to specialized functions.

The nature and needs of the human beings carrying out tasks became the object of research and theory building only when experiments on the effects of different physical conditions on worker productivity yielded erratic results. The startled investigators then discovered the Hawthorne effect: that recognition, prestige, and social contact influence worker productivity more than physical conditions of work (Roethlisberger and Dickson, 1939). Consequently, "individual motives, goals, and aspirations, which had no place in the Weberian conceptualization of organization, were put at the center of things. Organizational success was explained in terms of individual motivation and interpersonal relationships, particularly in the relationship between the supervisor and the subordinate" (Katz and Kahn, 1978, p. 278).

With the shift to human motivation as the key to productivity, *leadership* became a crucial concern. What kind of leadership would elicit the highest levels of productivity? Seminal concepts came from McGregor (1960), who contrasted Theory X, the machine view of the worker as an inert cog, with Theory Y, a humanistic conception of the worker as potentially growth-oriented, curious, and trustworthy. Theory X assumes that workers are inherently lazy. Economic incentives and threats of punishment are needed to induce them to perform, and good leadership requires a great deal of control, including close supervision and structuring of work. McGregor's Theory Y was in part based on Maslow's (1954) hierarchy of needs, which holds that once a worker's lower-order needs (such as the need for physical comfort and a sense of social belonging) are satisfied, higher-order needs can be activated. Theory Y leadership assumes that control is unnecessary. Instead, the leader's task is to unleash the worker's potential by providing challenging situations. The Theory Y leader progressively exposes employees to work situations with less external control, in which they can satisfy needs for affiliation, esteem, and self-actualization.

Likert (1961, 1967) constructed a similar but more highly developed management theory, which includes a continuum of four styles. System 1, like Theory X, is task-oriented, highly structured, and *authoritarian*. System 2 is *paternalistic*; leaders make all decisions but extend to their subordinates limited opportunities to participate in decisions. In System 3, the leader retains decision-making power but solicits subordinates' ideas and reactions through a *consultative* style. System 4, a *participative* style, is based—like Theory Y—on mutual trust and teamwork.

A related theory is reflected in the managerial grid constructed by Blake and Mouton (1964), who identified five leadership styles in terms of concern for the task and concern for people. The degrees of concern range from 1 to 9. Concern for the task or production is represented by the horizontal axis; a rating of 9 on this axis indicates a maximum concern for production. The vertical axis represents concern for people; a rating of 9 on this dimension indicates maximum concern for people. The "impoverished"·leader uses the 1/1 style and exerts minimal effort in regard to task and people. The "country club," or 1/9, style shows a high level of concern for satisfying relationships and creates a friendly and comfortable work climate; organizational needs are secondary. In contrast, the 9/1 leader strives for optimal efficiency but minimizes human needs—such as the need for satisfying work relationships and participation in decision making. The 5/5 style, a middle-of-the-road approach, seeks to balance the needs of the organization and those of its employees through a give-and-take strategy. Leaders in the integrative 9/9 style find that such compromises are not always necessary. Through attention to both human needs and organizational tasks, the highest levels of productivity can often be achieved.

Following these theories, a consultant might first administer surveys to assess employees' perceptions of existing decision-making and conflict management styles. The consultant could then lead training sessions to help managers understand the different leadership styles and their consequences and to choose and lead in the style best suited for each particular situation. The effectiveness of participative management styles (such as Theory Y, System 4, or 9/9) in eliciting high levels of morale and productivity has been demonstrated (Likert, 1961; Tannenbaum, 1968).

One of the most recent approaches to human relations management comes from Japan. In this model, called Theory Z to indicate its expansion of McGregor's X and Y concepts (Ouchi, 1981), organizations make lifelong commitments to their employees and involve them in all decisions affecting them and their work. The concern for employees is evident in the great care given to all decisions about employee welfare and in the high status of personnel managers. The socialization of the individual into the organization is nearly total. Consequently, conflict between human and organizational needs is diminished, and employees are more likely to be loyal, committed, and productive (Pascale and Athos, 1981).

An entirely different approach to the leader's dilemma of meshing individual and organizational needs is *management by objectives* (MBO). Worker behavior and conformity to organizational needs are controlled by written goals. The top administrator meets periodically with each subordinate manager to identify common goals and each person's major responsibility in terms of expected results. The emphasis is on a mutual commitment that satisfies both organizational and individual needs. Out of these meetings come agreements that serve as operational guides for a specified period of time and that provide evaluation criteria (Odiorne, 1965). Periodic reviews evaluate the achievement of objectives and individual performance; discrepancies are identified and analyzed, and these set the stage for the next period's objectives.

Increasing evidence of the complexity of motivation and of the interactions between individual and organizational variables has led to a contingency theory, which argues that the most effective leadership style depends on a number of variables, such as the nature of the work and the workers' educational level (Bass, 1976; Bass and Barrett, 1972; Fiedler, 1967; Hunt and Larson, 1974; Vroom and Yetton, 1973). To be effective, heads of human services agencies need an understanding of the various contingencies associated with motivation and productivity. Yet, many of these administrators, trained in a particular type of service rather than in management, lack a theoretical basis for this understanding and for making a choice of leadership style. As helping professionals, many prefer and rely on humanistic leadership styles that emphasize openness, good will, trust, and collaborative decision making (Bennis, 1969b; Harrison, 1972). However, some of the tensions in human services arise from irreconcilable conflicts of interest that require the use of hierarchical power or conflict negotiation strategies. Consultants can often help administrators expand their theoretical backgrounds and their range of leadership options.

Human Relations Perspectives

Human relations concepts are needed to guide in-depth studies of the social subsystem, the primary concern of most consultants. Management and leadership are, of course, central aspects of this subsystem. Intragroup and intergroup processes are also important in understanding organizations (Schein, 1969). Six types of group processes are crucial to organizational productivity: (1) development of norms, (2) communications, (3) defining member roles and functions, (4) problem solving and decision making, (5) intergroup cooperation and competition, and (6) handling conflict and stress.

Understanding *norms* is especially important, since norms evolve in all human relations and exert powerful controls over behavior. Norms exist when staff members share expectations that certain behaviors will be either rewarded or punished. Norms are often carried into agencies through workers' past experiences, especially through those of dominant members. New norms are created when an individual or group behaves in ways that violate the accepted standards and yet are accepted—for example, when a member disagrees with the boss or introduces innovative attitudes or techniques and these behaviors are allowed to stand. Norms provide tacit rules that reduce ambiguity and conflict. They shape and stabilize behavior and are very resistant to change. They govern attitudes and behaviors related to authority, to clients, to work, to professional identity, and to staff relations. Although norms are ordinarily implicit rather than explicit, staff members are keenly aware of them and can articulate them. For example, the norms of one agency include: (1) members always get to work and meetings on time; (2) staff members never question the boss about decisions; (3)

only individuals who work in the same division eat lunch together; and (4) no one talks about the big crisis that disrupted
operations last year.

Employees of human services agencies typically evolve
norms that reduce the high levels of stress inherent in their
work. The normative attitude of nurses in a ghetto clinic may
be that their clients' life situations are irremediable, so that low
levels of staff involvement, which reduce staff frustration and
psychological fatigue, are justified. Individuals who take a more
positive attitude toward clients' situations and make strong efforts to help them solve problems violate this norm and are
likely to be ostracized by their colleagues. Though reducing
stress to some extent, this norm is, of course, counterproductive
to the agency's mission. Given a similar client population, some
agencies develop norms that benefit both the staff and clients—
for example, the norm of opening up work problems for group
psychological and technological support and the norm of offering extra encouragement to staff members who are under stress
because of work or personal difficulties.

Communications processes provide a fertile source of
data for understanding organizational behavior. Measures can
be made of dimensions such as the relative frequency and length
of communications by different persons, facial expressions and
body movements, who talks to whom, and who is involved in
interruptions. Content analyses can also be useful. For example,
what topics receive the most attention, and which ones are
avoided? To what extent are problems and feelings discussed or
hidden? From studies of these processes, consultants can learn a
great deal about how people perceive themselves, their roles,
and one another as well as about the organization's effectiveness. Some theorists analyze communications to identify metaphors, contending that metaphors capture members' construc-
tions of the social realities of their organizations (Manning,
1979; Pondy and Mitroff, 1979; Weick, 1969). Workers in a
computer center, for instance, reveal certain perceptions of
their relationships through such terms as "bottlenecks" and
"tooling up" and their apparently incongruous reference to the
computer as "mother." In an agency under stress, members re-

flect their vulnerable feelings through phrases such as "going down the tubes," "bottomless pit of problems," and "over my dead body." A warmer yet controlling ambience is portrayed in a female administrator's references to her staff as "ducklings" and her constant admonishment "Check it out with me first." Usually consultants find multiple metaphors and must analyze them carefully to understand their implications.

Before people can feel sufficiently comfortable to work productively together, they must satisfy certain human needs. In initial interactions, they will be striving to answer questions about their *role and function.* "What will be my identity in this group? Will I take a listening role or be an active speaker? How will power be distributed? Will I have influence? To what degree will my goals and needs be included? Will members of this group like and accept me? How close and intimate will our relationships be?" These personal concerns create tensions and generally lead to one of three types of coping: (1) tough behaviors, such as fighting for control and resisting authority, (2) tender behaviors, such as creating alliances, helping others, and looking to others for support, or (3) withdrawal behaviors, including indifference and passivity (Bion, 1961; Schein, 1969). Work groups need to provide ways for members to satisfy the need for role definition. In addition, various task and maintenance *functions* are needed to get jobs done and to keep members of the group working well together. Work groups need task functions such as information seeking, giving, clarifying, and summarizing, as well as maintenance functions such as harmonizing, encouraging, and gatekeeping (ensuring that persons who have information to contribute have the opportunity to do so).

Schein (1969) proposes a useful model for *problem-solving and decision-making processes* that involves two cycles: (1) formulating the problem, generating suggestions for its solution, and predicting and evaluating the consequences of each proposed solution, (2) planning action steps, implementing them, evaluating their outcomes, and feeding the evaluation information back into the system. Crucial decisions are made at each step—for instance, the decision to discuss a problem and the choice of how to manage the discussion. The most visible decision is the one about which action to take to solve the problem. Decisions may be made by consensus, by default, by a ruling authority, by majority vote, by an aggressive minority, or by other means. Each method may be appropriate and effective under certain circumstances.

Most human services agencies are composed of several units differentiated according to their particular tasks. A hospital has an emergency clinic, a general ward, several specialized units, a laboratory, dietary and housekeeping departments, and a central administration. *Intergroup relations* are crucial determinants of organizational productivity. Units may be cohesive and effective in reaching their goals; yet they may be so insular and competitive that they subvert overall goals.

Conflict between individuals and groups is inherent in all human relations, including those in work organizations. The prototypical conflict is the clash between the organization's needs and the needs of the individual worker. Other conflicts arise from personality differences, from differences in professional, political, and personal values, or from competition for resources, power, and opportunities.

Tensions associated with conflict can be used in constructive and creative ways. Conflict can promote needed change, broaden perspectives, and increase energy. However, it can also be extremely destructive to individuals and organizations, especially when it is both long-standing and covert. The norms for managing conflict are of particular interest in human services agencies. To a greater extent than employees in business and industry, staff members of public-sector agencies characteristically fear conflict and deny its existence because it goes against their ideals of helping and politeness and their religious and professional traditions (Chesler, Bryant, and Crowfoot, 1975). Consequently, conflict in these organizations often appears in attenuated forms. It is hard to diagnose and even harder to confront and resolve. Hidden conflicts increase staff tension and stress and sap energies.

People working in human services agencies, especially the front-line workers directly engage in service delivery, must cope with certain uniquely stressful conditions. Studies of the *stress levels* of staff members offer a recent approach to understanding these agencies. The focus of stress research is usually individual rather than organizational health, but individual stress is, of course, related to agency health and development. Agency work requires employee interaction with clients whose reactive behaviors sometimes greatly complicate the successful delivery of services. Client problems also affect staff morale. For example, when clients are chronically ill or powerless, agency staff members are likely to be infected with feelings of depression and helplessness. They become highly stressed and demonstrate "burnout" symptoms, including emotional and physical exhaustion, negative attitudes, and lowered self-esteem (Douglas, 1977; McGrath, 1976; Pines and Maslach, 1978). Staff burnout is especially common in agencies requiring complex and intensive interactions with clients—such as family counseling centers —and in agencies seeking significant changes—such as half-way houses and alcoholism treatment centers (Cooper and Marshall, 1980). Burnout is aggravated by environmental turbulence. The reactions of paraprofessionals in a victim referral service illustrate the burnout phenomenon: "We found that, despite high enthusiasm at the beginning, within a few months the counselors absorbed and reflected the hopeless, frustrated, and apathetic attitudes of the victims" (Reiff, 1979, p. 66).

Traditional conceptions of the professional role—such as the aristocrat and the objective scientist—provided rules of practice that constructed an "armor," enabling professionals to maintain social and psychological distance. This distance was considered not only appropriate but also necessary for objective and effective assessment and intervention. Armor also protected professionals against stress and burnout. For many professions, however, the crisis of the 1960s undermined these traditions and their underlying assumptions. The loss of the armor of psychological distance places professionals in a poignant position. "If they identify with their clients . . . they are soon burned out by the complexity and stress of mutual interdependence and emotional interchange" (Hirschhorn, 1979, p. 177). If they try to maintain a classical detachment, they may lose their effectiveness. The unfortunate effects of depersonalization were dramatically illustrated in a recent case of mistaken identity in the operating rooms of a Philadelphia hospital. Surgeons performed gland surgery on one patient and began disc surgery on another, only to find they were operating on the wrong persons. Hospital employees had failed to check patients' identification wristbands and had placed them in the wrong operating rooms. None of the surgeons, nurses, or aides working with these patients—in what could have been a life-or-death situation—knew them well enough to identify them with their particular ailments.

Some theories apply organic, or unifying, concepts to the human relations domain in efforts to explain behavior. Studies of the *organizational climate* represent one such unifying approach. This perspective holds that organizations evolve unique and pervasive properties that exert control over workers' attitudes and behaviors (Taylor and Bowers, 1972). Other approaches interpret organizational behavior through a work-*family* framework. Transactional analysis, for instance, based on the theory constructed by Berne (1964) for use in individual psychotherapy, views agency employees as members of a family whose behaviors conform to certain "scripts," which reflect unspoken and spoken rules and expectations (Jongeward, 1973). The script often dates back to the member's personal script. It may, for example, mirror her or his attitude toward authority, sex roles, and ethnic differences. "Corporate parent" sacred traditions evolve—status symbols, rules governing relationships, and rituals such as company picnics and Christmas parties.

Structural Approaches

In order to carry out organizational tasks, labor must be divided and coordinated. In a hospital, for example, work must be distributed into individual and group tasks. Contemporary technologies generally demand highly specialized assignments; yet work activities must be integrated. Hospital admissions must be consistent with available space and staff; someone must order the specialized supplies essential to the work of the various departments. Most organizations, too large to permit face-to-face communication and coordination, require integrative mechanisms. Consultants need to understand the formal system through which labor is divided, authority and responsibility are assigned, and activities are coordinated.

The mechanistic, or bureaucratic, model is the simplest approach to organizing; it specifies rules and procedures to ensure coordination for all predictable events (Weber, 1947). Labor is divided according to specialized functions. Rules reduce the need for communication and decision making and at the same time provide continuity. Unexpected events are referred upward through the hierarchy to administrators, who then decide what responses will be made and who thus create new rules. When environments are stable and tasks are relatively undifferentiated, this type of structure is often satisfactory. Exceptions to rules are infrequent; little information exchange or coordination is needed.

In most contemporary human services agencies, the bureaucratic model does not provide adequate mechanisms for coordination. Uncertainties created by environmental changes or by relatively diverse services produce frequent exceptions; the need for information processing and decision making increases, and the hierarchy becomes overloaded. Delays then occur that interfere with productivity. There are several ways to improve communication and coordination when exceptions are frequent (Galbraith, 1973). One approach is simply to reduce the output level so as to allow more time for information processing. This method, of course, adds to the institution's costs. An alternative method is to organize workers by products or programs. Each work group then has its own specialists; for example, the staff of an emergency room may compose a separate unit with its own administrator, professionals, and support crew. The need for information and coordination diminishes because of the reduction in diversity and the decrease in worker specialization. Emergency room employees serve broader functions, working across specialty areas when needs arise, than they would if they were assigned to highly specialized roles to serve the entire hospital. Another approach is to set up more extensive vertical information-processing systems, perhaps through more frequent and elaborate conferences, interviews, and surveys and the use of computers to process data. Still another solution is to establish lateral mechanisms, which cut across hierarchical authority lines, to decentralize decisions. These arrangements may be informal and short-term or formal, continuing mechanisms such as interdepartmental task forces. The matrix design is a commonly used integrative structure involving dual reporting arrangements. Individuals, usually key persons such as administrators or technical specialists, are assigned to two (or more) departments or programs to provide closer coordination between units.

Contingency theory applies to structure as well as to leadership style. It contends that there is no one best way to organize; the optimal design depends on the diversity and uncertainty of the tasks being performed (Burns and Stalker, 1961; Galbraith, 1973; Lawrence and Lorsch, 1967). Consultants need familiarity with various structural theories and related research to increase their potential for helping administrators analyze the needs of particular situations.

Developmental Theory

A new approach to the study of organizations holds particular promise for understanding current problems in human services agencies. The developmental approach views organizational life as cyclical. Organizations evolve, develop, expand, contract, and decline (Kimberly and others, 1980). The assumption is that an agency's current functioning, problems, and needs can be understood only by studying its history, trajectory, and prospects. The implication is that interventions should be designed to fit each agency's particular developmental stage and future. Already, the literature from this new perspective offers valuable concepts to consultants.

Currently, in response to diminishing resources, many organizations are in a state of decline. This phenomenon is particularly pervasive in the public sector, owing to the tax revolt and a shift toward conservatism. Signs of decline such as cutbacks in budgets, programs, and staffs—and even some cuts of entire agencies—have become routine. Agencies, like society in general, are finding it difficult to accept the reality of declining resources. Retrenchment is contradictory to their experience and values. These organizations emerged in and adapted to conditions that support rapid growth (Whetten, 1980). Their staffs are unprepared to function under conditions of scarcity. The literature in the field of management (and organizational studies in general) offers few descriptions of retrenchment conditions and experiences or prescriptions for coping with them. Moreover, it is questionable how rational and creative administrators can be, when faced with the crises associated with cutbacks. Under these conditions, administrators are likely to react emotionally or in well-established but outmoded patterns. They may, at times, be incapable of accurately perceiving and interpreting changing conditions and rational actions. Faced with crises, administrators are likely to become less innovative and more conservative. Their decision making is likely to be more autocratic and less participative.

Because consultants have experience with numbers of agencies and have a relatively detached perspective, they may be able to help agencies realistically appraise their developmental status. They may use their expertise and objectivity to help administrators find the most constructive ways of responding to cutbacks. They may also add to the body of knowledge of this important new field by generating studies of cyclical processes and reports of different methods for managing decline and other developmental stages.

Closely related to the developmental perspective are concepts regarding organizations' state of health. Healthy organizations are said to be characterized by (1) realistic interactions with the environment, (2) basic staff agreement on goals and values, (3) self-awareness and understanding, (4) optimum use of resources, and (5) the capacity to learn from experience, to absorb new information, and to respond flexibly to changing conditions (Beckhard, 1975; Fordyce and Weil, 1971; Schein, 1965, 1969). Healthy organizations have also been described in terms of growth. They are "forward-pushing, growing, striving, learning, becoming" (Clark, 1969, p. 282). They may be characterized by the capacity to react to trauma by recovering and revitalizing. In an era of decline, this latter characteristic may be the crucial index of health.

Other Approaches

The scope of organizational studies continues to expand; this field offers consultants a variety of perspectives for understanding agencies. Some investigators focus on sociophysical factors (Hall, 1966; Holahan, 1977; Sommer, 1969; Steele, 1973). From this approach has come an understanding of the effect of physical features (such as floor plans, lighting, and color) on human relations, motivation, and performance. A number of theorists focus on external conditions (such as political, economic, and social forces) that affect the direction and processes of organizations (Bass and Barrett, 1972; Bass and Valenzi, 1974; Burns and Stalker, 1961; Drucker, 1980; Lawrence and Lorsch, 1967). Other dimensions that have received considerable attention include the flow and transformation of information (Knight and McDaniel, 1979), decision-making conflicts and choices (Janis and Mann, 1977), and the correlates of political power (Bacharach and Lawler, 1980).

Comparative studies that differentiate and classify organizations according to key variables offer another means for understanding agencies (Eldridge and Crombie, 1974). From these studies have come typologies based on dimensions such as technological complexity (Woodward, 1965), technological constraints (Thompson, 1967), and compliance strategies or methods for controlling employees' behavior (Etzioni, 1961). One particularly fruitful classification, proposed by Katz and Kahn (1978), groups organizations according to genotypic social functions: (1) production of goods, (2) adaptive functions, such as generation of knowledge for solving problems, (3) managerial or political functions, including legislative structures, and (4) maintenance functions. Maintenance organizations integrate society; all human services, including those that nurture, educate, socialize, and control deviant behavior, fall into this classification. By differentiating society's maintenance or human services institutions from other organizations, this typology makes more refined descriptions possible. Maintenance organizations can be subclassified; for instance, Hasenfeld and English (1975) differentiated human services agencies according to two major functions, processing people and changing them. The authors theorized that the two types of agencies differ systematically.

Some investigators seek to describe the unique characteristics of particular types of human services agencies. Educational systems have received considerable attention (Bidwell, 1965; Brookover and Erickson, 1975; Guskin and Guskin, 1970; Meyer and Rowan, 1978). It has been noted that they are "loosely coupled"; their technological activities are not connected to the formal authority system (Weick, 1976). To illustrate, the traditional autonomy of classroom teachers militates against quality control of teaching technology. Instead, administrators control nontechnical areas such as scheduling and hiring. Loose coupling appears to serve educational systems by reducing tensions associated with the inconsistencies that are created by conflicting environmental and internal demands.

Some of the most vivid descriptions of particular types of agencies come from consultants, whose close contacts with different types of agencies give them unique vantage points for in-depth comparison. Mann (1973), for instance, pointed out that the prevailing philosophy in police organizations—consistent with their role and function of maintaining order—is authoritarian and moralistic. Sensitivity to the personal problems of the people they apprehend interferes with their task and is therefore suppressed. Problems stay in-house. The rules are, "Take care of your own" and "Never discuss internal problems with outsiders" (Brodsky, 1977, p. 137). Another characteristic is the high attrition rate of well-qualified staff. Because opportunities for promotions and other rewards are limited, the most competent police officers are likely to leave for other jobs or moonlight in a second job. Caplan (1970) described the culture and characteristics of the nursing staff of public health agencies. Since these nurses often work with patients in extremely painful and apparently irremediable situations, they tend to feel helpless and depressed. Attrition is often higher than 50 percent. Furthermore, authority is a salient issue; because of their relatively low status, nurses tend to use covert methods of relating to their bosses, usually physicians.

The study of particular types of human services organizations is in its infancy. Expanded knowledge in this field would be very helpful both to persons working in agencies and to their consultants. The perspectives that sociologists might bring to the relationship between people and their work would be especially valuable.

Organizational Needs for Adaptation and Planned Change

The field of organizational studies reveals the dynamic and complex nature of modern human services agencies. Two major sources of tension are apparent: (1) an inherent conflict between requirements of the organization and the needs of the people who carry out the organization's tasks and (2) discontinuities induced by a rapidly changing environment that is characterized by periodic shifts in political power, by competing constituencies, and by technological innovation. These tensions are a continual source of stress and are especially acute in times of declining resources.

Although the tensions can never be fully resolved, they can be reduced through adaptive mechanisms. Structures and processes can be created to anticipate or identify environmental changes, to detect internal inconsistencies, to recognize gaps between external forces and agency operations, and to recommend, plan, and implement necessary changes. Agencies approach the task of adaptation and change in various ways. One organization may establish a special position or unit to gather and analyze data and recommend needed changes (Roeber, 1973). A manager may regularly set aside a significant amount of time for liaison with external systems for the purpose of gathering information (Drucker, 1980). A part of all regular staff meetings may be used to review current events and to brainstorm possible reactions or actions. Frequently, specialized expertise is needed to gather and interpret data and to generate solutions to identified problems. In such cases, agencies may send their staff members to training programs or recruit new employees who will bring in the knowledge and skills. They may also form federations to pool and share specialized resources.

Consultation with outside professionals is another means of obtaining the assistance needed to reduce tensions and make necessary changes. Agencies often find that consultants' detached perspectives are uniquely helpful in examining complex data. Moreover, hiring consultants is often a cheaper way to obtain specialized expertise than hiring new employees, and it gives the employer greater flexibility in stretching a budget. Sometimes the cost of consultation is defrayed by line items in grants. Agencies often call on consultants for these reasons, which has led to the tremendous growth of the consultant role.

Annotated Bibliography

Demone, H. W., and Harshbarger, D. (Eds.). *A Handbook of Human Service Organizations.* New York: Behavioral Publications, 1974. This is a collection of readings about human services agencies. It includes discussions of the environmental forces affecting these systems and internal issues such as roles, management, and evaluation.

Drucker, P. F. *Managing in Turbulent Times.* New York: Harper & Row, 1980. Drucker describes the "sea changes" taking place in contemporary society. He identifies some of the environmental forces impinging on human services and suggests innovative strategies for contending with them.

Hasenfeld, Y., and English, R. A. (Eds.). *Human Service Organizations.* Ann Arbor: University of Michigan Press, 1975. The articles in this volume describe many of the characteristics and problems of organizations that provide human services. Consultants will find it a useful reference in understanding public-sector agencies.

Katz, D., and Kahn, R. L. *The Social Psychology of Organizations.* New York: Wiley, 1978. This comprehensive book reviews the major approaches to the study of organizations and examines each aspect of organizations from an open-systems framework. It includes a thorough review of organizational research and provides a valuable framework to guide consultants in collecting and interpreting organizational phenomena.

Kimberly, J. R., Miles, R. H., and Associates. *The Organizational Life Cycle: Issues in the Creation, Transformation, and Decline of Organizations.* San Francisco: Jossey-Bass, 1980. This is a collection of articles concerned with the cyclical nature of organizational life. The concepts and empirical data presented by the authors will help consultants understand organizations and increase their awareness of the need to select interventions that fit a particular organization's stage of development.

Kotter, J. P. *Organizational Dynamics: Diagnosis and Intervention.* Reading, Mass.: Addison-Wesley, 1978. In chap. 5, "Long-Run Dynamics," Kotter discusses the need for organizations to adapt to constantly changing conditions. He identifies the conditions that support and impede adaptation and notes their implications for consultants.

Meyer, M. W., and Associates. *Environments and Organizations: Theoretical and Empirical Perspectives.* San Francisco: Jossey-Bass, 1978. The articles in this book are based on the assumption that environmental forces, such as economic, technological, and political conditions, largely determine the goals, structures, and processes of organizations. The theories and research findings presented will help consultants diagnose organizations and formulate realistic recommendations for the solution of organizational problems.

Miller, E. J., and Rice, A. K. *Systems of Organization.* New York: Tavistock, 1967. In this classic study, the authors draw on both open-systems and psychoanalytic concepts to construct and illustrate a sociotechnical theory of organizations. Their descriptions of the conflicts between task requirements and human needs and of internal and external boundary tensions illuminate basic problems consultants encounter in working with organizations.

Miringoff, M. L. *Management in Human Service Organizations.* New York: Macmillan, 1980. Following an open-systems perspective, Miringoff examines forces affecting the organization and delivery of human services. He then discusses the functions and processes of management and illustrates them with case studies. He describes such tasks as budgeting, accounting, and program evaluation. The insights presented will help consultants understand the tasks of administrators and the force field in which they operate.

Zander, A. *Groups at Work: Unresolved Issues in the Study of Organizations.* San Francisco: Jossey-Bass, 1977. Zander discusses group processes as they relate to a number of facets of organizational life. He covers a wide range of topics—for instance, hiring, firing, secrecy, embarrassment, harmony, and conference procedures—from the perspective of groups. This book will help consultants understand the pervasive influence of group processes on organizational functioning.

 *Part II*

Models
for Practice

Diversity, the subject of Part Two, is a key feature of consultation. Since agency needs fluctuate greatly and since consultants bring diverse professional backgrounds to their work, wide variations appear in consultation practice. The purpose of Part Two is to help consultants understand these variations and increase their awareness of the broad array of alternatives to consider in deciding how agencies' needs can best be met.

Chapter Four reviews some of the efforts to classify the variables giving rise to differences in practices. From this review, five major dimensions on which consultation varies are identified: the conceptualization of problems, goals, strategies, consultant role, and values. This chapter lays the basis for the remaining chapters in Part Two, which discuss and illustrate the conceptual and methodological bases of six distinctive consultation models.

Chapter Five describes an information-centered approach to consultation. Many consultants practice exclusively in this model, and most use it at some time. Often, educational and training services are the first step through which consultants build a broader relationship with an agency. Chapter Five describes the methods used in this model and the characteristics of successful workshop designs. Common problems—for instance, staying within the limits of the contract, managing the dynamics in workshops that include "family" groups, and coping with disruptive participants—are discussed. To illustrate the use of this model, the chapter presents and discusses the design and processes of a workshop on supervisory skills.

Several consultation models have evolved from the work of health professionals in human services agencies. The oldest of these is the clinical, or medical, model, in which consultants help consultees in their work with clients. Chapter Six describes the concepts and methods of this model and its applications to problems at both client and organizational levels. As mental health professionals moved out of their offices and into agency settings, they found the traditional clinical model ineffectual in alleviating widespread mental illness and suffering. To better respond to social needs, these professionals created a new model, mental health consultation, that seeks to increase consultees' knowledge and skills so that they can be more competent in preventing mental illness in their clients. Chapter Seven discusses conceptual and methodological foundations of this model and clarifies its unique features, such as the pyramid concept and theme interference. Applications of this model to groups, programs, and administrative problems are discussed. The third model to derive from clinical traditions is the behavioral consultation model, the subject of Chapter Eight. This approach, which can be applied to problems at all organizational levels—from clients to the entire system—is based on learning theory. Chapter Eight describes its basic concepts and the techniques derived from the paradigm of laboratory experimentation.

Organizational consultation, the topic of Chapter Nine, is an extremely diverse field. Organizational consultants may focus on problems in one or more domains—for instance, on an agency's technology, structure, management, or human relations. They may focus on an agency's interaction with its environment or on its physical plant. Organizational consultants' methods are even more varied than their focuses. They might use any of a number of methods, such as data feedback, processing of staff meetings, or laboratory training. Chapter Nine highlights major developments in this model, with case studies illustrating the increasing sophistication of strategies for organizational diagnosis and intervention.

During the past two decades a large proportion of the public funds granted to human services agencies has been earmarked for programs to address narrowly defined goals. Consequently, program-centered consultation has become a major model. The targets of these programs are varied, but usually they are designated by the federal government as high priority in terms of social needs—for instance, groups that are disadvantaged because of educational or physical handicaps. Consultation practices in this model cannot be neatly categorized, because they vary according to the programs themselves. However, Chapter Ten discusses issues in program consultation and presents three cases to illustrate this model. One is a study of successful consultation with a public health program in Finland. Additional case studies depict the more common situation in which program consultants find their work complicated by administrative conflicts or misunderstandings.

4

Diverse
Approaches to
Consultation

Consultation practices are similar in many ways. Consultants share a common social role and function. All are technical experts who bring specialized bodies of knowledge to agencies to help them serve society. Their activities fit within the boundaries of a generic definition. For example, they focus on consultees' work-related concerns, and they are independent of their consultees' organizational hierarchy. Their work involves the common processes of entry, diagnosis, intervention, evaluation, and termination. But the practices that fall under the rubric of consultation also vary in many ways—for example, in focus, in goals, and in certain dimensions of the consultant's role. This chapter describes the diversity within the realm of consultation. It reviews and summarizes attempts to classify the dimensions on which pivotal differences occur. Thus, it lays the foundation for later discussions of specialized models.

This chapter addresses one of the major weaknesses in consultation practice. Practitioners are, in general, unaware of the variations in consultation. Consequently, as they begin and carry out a consultation, they consider few alternatives. Yet, each consultation entails many choices. Obviously, the nature of the presenting problems and consultees' expectations set certain boundaries for decisions. The approach of a consultant called in for the specific purpose of helping a consultee understand and cope with a disruptive client will differ from the approach of a consultant asked to design a new service or resolve a staff conflict. But these bounds leave the consultant with considerable freedom of choice. Given the same presenting problem —for instance, a disruptive client—one consultant conceptualizes the problem in terms of the client's personality, another in terms of the consultee's coping capacities. Presented with a staff conflict, one consultant analyzes job descriptions and recommends structural changes; another consultant's approach is to get acquainted with the members of the staff and diagnose psychological and social factors underlying the conflict. Most consultant decisions, especially early ones such as conceptualizing the problem and setting goals, are crucial to the welfare of the agencies consultants serve. Obviously, the best decisions are based on a careful study of alternatives. But because consultants are unaware that viable alternatives exist, decisions are often made implicitly or within a narrow range of options. The major purpose of this chapter and of the others in Part Two is to expand consultants' awareness of their options.

Classification Efforts

What are the major varieties within the realm of consultation? Numerous classifications have attempted to map this realm by identifying the dimensions on which pivotal differences appear. Representative classifications from three major perspectives—social sciences, mental health, and political values —are described here.

Social Science. Social scientists have identified and classified a number of important variables, including conceptualization of the problem and goals, method of intervention, and consultant role.

Argyris (1970) found significant variations in the *depth*

with which problems and goals are formulated. He contrasted
interventions aimed at phenotypic (superficial) phenomena with
those directed to their roots—the underlying, or genotypic,
problems. To illustrate, a consultant working with the head of a
national park on supervisor/supervisee conflicts might, in a
phenotypic diagnosis, formulate the problem as a lack of supervisory skills, whereas a genotypic diagnosis would identify more
fundamental problems. Over a period of years, rangers' duties
slowly changed from educational activities to "policing" of park
visitors; yet job descriptions, selection criteria, and training of
recruits did not change. Consequently, conflicts arose because
supervisees were expected to perform tasks for which they were
not prepared. Argyris contends that genotypic diagnoses, by
creating constructs at the highest possible level of abstraction,
capture "the essence of phenomena that may appear dissimilar
to the eye" and are more likely to lead to permanent solutions
(p. 279).

Several classifications have been concerned with the *focus*
of problems. An important distinction has been made between
problems conceived in terms of human processes and those conceived in terms of technology (French and Bell, 1973; Friedlander and Brown, 1974). Blake and Mouton (1976) classified
consultation focuses into four categories—power/authority,
morale/cohesion, norms/standards, and goals/objectives; they
also identified variations in the *target or unit to be changed*—
ranging from a single individual to an entire system.

Blake and Mouton were also concerned with differences
in *strategy*, a dimension that requires further discussion. They
assumed that most problems are caused by "habitual but ineffective cycles of behavior" in individuals and in organizations
(p. 4). These cycles are often dysfunctional, but being habitual,
they are at times beyond the conscious control of agency staff.
The consultant may use various strategies to help consultees
identify and break out of damaging cycles. But before deciding
which strategy to use, a consultant must determine the source
of the damaging cycle; hence Blake and Mouton also classified
sources of problems. Their strategies are based on different assumptions about these sources. "Acceptant" interventions

assume that negative emotions block effective problem solving. The consultant offers support such as empathic listening to help consultees become more objective. The "catalytic" intervention assumes that dysfunctional behavior is caused by lack of factual information and seeks to broaden consultees' perspectives by providing new information or verifying existing information. "Confrontative" interventions assume that inappropriate or unjustified beliefs or values block consultees from effective actions. The goal is to aid them in identifying these values and beliefs and in understanding their implications. "Prescriptive" interventions assume that the consultees lack the skills needed to diagnose and solve problems. The consultant seeks to give consultees an expert diagnosis and a recommendation for appropriate action. The assumption underlying "theories and principles" interventions is that consultees lack concepts or principles to guide them in solving problems. The consultant helps the consultee acquire and integrate the needed knowledge. In classifying strategies, Blake and Mouton also identified a variety of *consultant functions*: acceptance of consultees' feelings (as a means of facilitating problem solving), dissemination of information and knowledge, facilitating the clarification of values and beliefs, helping the consultee verify existing information, and diagnosis and prescription.

Variations in methods are the subject of other classifications. Miles and Schmuck (1971), for instance, identified eight *strategies* an OD consultant might use: training/education, process consultation, confrontation, data feedback, problem solving, planning, establishment of OD task forces, and technostructural activities.

Chin and Benne (1969), were also interested in intervention strategies, but their approach was to categorize strategies according to their underlying *assumptions* about how change can be effected. Their concepts are particularly important in understanding fundamental differences between strategies. Chin and Benne's empirical-rational approach—which is similar to the theories-and-principles strategy and the catalytic strategy discussed earlier—presents consultees with knowledge; the assumption is that changes in cognition will lead to behavioral changes.

The consultant functions as an educator. To illustrate, a police chief asks a consultant how to reduce the aggressive behavior of his officers in handling suspects. The consultant (1) presents the officers with research evidence that police aggressiveness exacerbates violent reactions and (2) demonstrates nonviolent techniques. Similarly, in working with an administrator on morale problems, this approach would assume that if the administrator is given (1) evidence that employees will be more satisfied if they participate in decisions and (2) information and skills training related to participative decision-making processes, she will change her decision-making style accordingly. Thus, the consultant's function is to transmit needed information and knowledge, including a rationale for making changes. The prescriptive approach described by Blake and Mouton also seems to be based on empirical-rational assumptions; but, rather than providing knowledge with which consultees can decide exactly what changes should be made (an educative mode), the consultant in the prescriptive mode diagnoses the problem and prescribes a solution. The assumption is that the authoritative judgments of the consultant will effect changes in consultees' cognitions and thereby change their behavior.

Normative-reeducative strategies acknowledge that people are usually rational, but they also recognize the importance of noncognitive factors in supporting or preventing change. The assumption is that, for people to make lasting changes, they need to change old norms (established attitudes and patterns of behavior) and develop emotional commitments to new ones. Returning to the cases just described, in the normative-reeducative approach, consultants would help consultees explore the validity of their attitudes, processes, and values in relation to their problems. This strategy calls for the consultant to function not only as a disseminator of knowledge and skills but also as a facilitator, perhaps leading human relations and communications skills laboratories or workshops to clarify values, ideas, and feelings, and providing process feedback on staff meetings.

Power-coercive strategies may also be used to change behavior. The underlying assumption is that externally imposed sanctions are needed for behavioral change. Examples of this approach include use of administrative authority, political and economic power, and "moral" power, which elicits compliance through feelings of "shame" or "guilt" (Chin and Benne, 1969, p. 52). These strategies are outside the boundaries of the consultant role but may at times be recommended to administrators as means of achieving agency goals. A consultant might suggest to the police chief that he establish a policy of nonaggressive language and behavior and back it up with sanctions; for instance, he might fire or put on probation officers who continued to use pejorative language. The administrator might offer pay incentives and advancement opportunities to unit directors who switched to participative decision making.

The social bases of power described by French and Raven (1960) are useful in clarifying differences in the *sources of consultants' power* and in *relating their strategies to these sources*. Presumably all consultants possess expert power because their particular knowledge is valued by their consultees. Expert power is most evident in empirical-rational strategies (such as presentations of workshops or diagnoses of problems). However, it is the primary basis for all consultative strategies. A consultant may also influence consultees through referent power, the power that exists when one person likes, admires, and identifies with another and wants to emulate him or her. The use of referent power assumes that affective variables are instrumental in making changes, whether the desired changes are cognitive, emotional, or behavioral. Referent power is manifest in rapport, the presence of friendliness and trust in a relationship (Martin, 1978; Rodin and Janis, 1979). Referent power is often valuable in helping consultees make substantial and difficult changes—such as in their work norms. Thus, a consultant's referent power might be the impetus for consultees to learn a complex technique or to modify their attitudes and behavior toward each other. Sometimes consultees attribute legitimate power—the right to influence or prescribe behavior—to a consultant because of valued nontechnological characteristics, such as social status or seniority in age. A well-known, middle-aged consultant exerts influence on a young and inexperienced consultee that is unrelated to technical expertise (Caplan, 1970). The remaining types of power described by French and Raven, reward power and coercive power, like the power-coercive strategies discussed earlier, are derived from administrative authority and are outside the consultant's range of influence; but consultants may help agency administrators assess the advantages and disadvantages of these types of power in achieving agency goals.

Schein (1969) expressed interest in the degree to which consultants possess and use power when he differentiated models according to the *extent to which the consultant participates in the diagnosis.* In the "purchase" model, the consultee or agency defines a need and purchases specific consultative services to satisfy that need. The expert power of the consultee, rather than that of the consultant, determines the service. In the "doctor-patient" model, executives of an organization request a consultant to make a diagnosis of troubles that they do not understand; thus, the consultees rely on the consultant's expert power. Schein believes that the "process" model, in which consultees and consultant collaborate in the diagnosis, leads to more productive and satisfying outcomes. The assumption is that "the extent to which a change agent is successful (that is, influential) is dependent on the degree to which he is perceived as susceptible to influence by the client. In other words, the more transactional the influence, the more durable and genuine the change" (Bennis, Benne, and Chin, 1969, p. 148). A *facilitative strategy,* in which consultants help consultees expand and mobilize their problem-solving resources, is central to this model.

Mental Health. Like social scientists, mental health professionals have classified consultation problems and goals, methods, and roles. Caplan's (1970) well-known classification contrasts consultation on two dimensions: (1) the *problem focus,* or point of interaction at which consultant and consultee meet, such as a case or a program, and (2) the *target*—the person or unit to be changed. The four cells of this two-by-two classification identify different models of consultation. In client-centered case consultation (sometimes called the medical model), the focus is on a client and the target is the client; the consultant's goal is to ameliorate the client's problem by providing the consultee with a diagnosis and recommendations for treatment. For example, a client, a first-grader, exhibits symptoms of school phobia, and the consultant meets with the teacher to pinpoint the problem and recommend a plan of action. In consultee-centered case consultation, the focus is also on the client, but the primary target is the consultee; the goal is to increase this person's coping skills. In the example just mentioned, the consultant would seek to improve the teacher's understanding of school phobia and related disorders. Program-centered administrative consultation focuses on a program or project of concern to an administrator. For example, the consultation might focus on planning, implementing, and evaluating a new service. The primary target is the program, and the goal is to improve it by bringing the consultant's expertise to the administrator's assistance. In consultee-centered administrative consultation, the focus is also on a program or on the staff; the major target, however, is the administrator, and the goal is development of this person's knowledge and skills so that she or he can function more efficiently in future work. In the models that seek to change the consultee (the two consultee-centered models), the consultant/consultee relationship is crucial; the consultant, therefore, seeks to establish rapport (referent power) with the consultee. In the other two models, the consultant's strategy is more prescriptive and appears to rely on the consultant's expert (and legitimate) power.

In one of the first efforts to point out differences in consultants' *values,* Gouldner (1964) contrasted the engineering and clinical conceptualizations of problems. The engineering consultant accepts the client-administrator's definition of the problem (thus supporting the status quo), whereas the clinical consultant takes the consultee's problem definition as important data but recognizes that this definition reflects a biased perspective and, therefore, seeks to help the consultee clarify her or his values and their effects on perceptions and behavior. This classification of problem formulation appears similar to Argyris's differentiation of the phenotypic and genotypic levels of diagnosis.

McClung and Stunden (1972), using data collected from structured interviews between consultants and consultees, identified seven models of mental health consultation, which differ according to the *target of change*—ranging from individual clients to national and international concerns. They then collapsed these models into a typology consisting of three basic models with contrasting assumptions regarding the *source of the problem* and the *consultant's primary task*. The treatment model assumes that pathological behavior stems primarily from individual causes, especially from intrapsychic factors; the consultant's task is to make a diagnosis and prescribe a remedy. The prevention model assumes that certain environmental conditions often produce psychopathology and that through educational strategies consultants can assist caregivers in their task of helping clients cope more effectively with their milieu—thus reducing the incidence of mental illness. The basic assumption of the enhancement model breaks out of the clinical mold; it holds that the environment is the primary cause of mental illness and suggests that the consultant's task involves social change. The "individual and all aspects of his environment should be modified so that he will have knowledge of and freedom to choose those behaviors which are most congruent with the gratification of his needs and the realization of his potential" (p. 40).

Clinicians have always recognized the importance of the *helping relationship* in mediating clients' emotions and behavior. Three types of doctor/patient relationships described by Szasz and Hollender (1956) are analogous to those between consultant and consultee and, like Schein's classification, illuminate variations in the relative power of the two parties. In the active-passive relationship, the "doctor," or consultant assumes authority and responsibility for the "patient," or consultee, assuming that the latter is unable to help in formulating the diagnosis or the solution. This relationship is similar to Schein's doctor-patient model and is reminiscent of the aristocratic concept of the professional described in Chapter Two. In the guidance-cooperative relationship, the consultant guides the consultee, who is assumed to be able to follow the consultant's directions and cooperate with him or her. In the mutual participation relationship, the consultant helps consultees help themselves; the assumption is that both consultee and consultant have valuable and relevant knowledge and should participate fully in the diagnosis and intervention decisions. This relationship seems to parallel the process, or collaborative, model described by Schein.

Political Values. Individuals committed to social change have classified consultation approaches according to their political or ideological bases. Chesler and Arnstein (1970) emphasized political values in their comparison of the manager-engineer and the partisan-advocate models of consultation. The engineer-manager approach stresses a "technocentric" orientation to change. While claiming neutrality, the consultant identifies with the manager's interests and desires, thus implicitly advocating the status quo. The partisan-advocate explicitly uses a "value-centric" approach and consciously identifies with the "people who seem to him to need help most or whose growth he values most" (p. 22). Thus, in this model (and in some others to be described), the consultant is likely to step out of the boundaries of the role by supporting individuals or groups in conflict with the agency administrator. This classification was further elaborated by Pearl (1974), who distinguished four "consultative" approaches along a continuum of ideological orientation. At one pole he placed those consultants wishing to perpetuate the status quo; in this position he included organization men, efficiency experts, and behaviorists. Next come the "facilitative process consultant" and the "organizer of the powerless." At the other end of the continuum are the "visionary" yet "politically realistic" change agents who consider our world malignant and who lead efforts to eliminate malignancies. According to Pearl, consultants working in all but the last model are essentially technicians whose ideological assumptions are unarticulated.

Social values also define the boundaries between three approaches to change—professional-technical, political, and countercultural—described by Crowfoot and Chesler (1974). Although this typology refers to broadly defined change efforts, it also differentiates consultation practices. The professional-technical approach views society as basically sound and values the status quo; tacitly, at least, the consultant in this model supports the right of the "elites" (such as agency administrators) to make decisions and plans for others. Intervention efforts stress rational and systemic management of change processes and expansions of technology and productivity. This perspective contrasts sharply with the political approach, which views conflict as ubiquitous; since resources are finite, different interest groups will always compete for control over them. Hence, consultants cannot be neutral; their interventions will favor one group more and another less. Their strategies include using legitimate office and authority and mobilizing and organizing individuals with similar interests—whether they are the "elites" or the "oppressed" (such as parents of retarded children and unemployed minorities). According to the countercultural approach, overdeveloped technologies and proliferating bureaucracies have alienated and dehumanized our society. Individuals must be helped to lead more integrated and creative lives. Consultants might follow this perspective by working with staff members of alternative organizations; an example of this type of consultation is the work of Gordon (1979) with nontraditional youth programs.

A Social Role Classification

Historical perspectives are useful in identifying important variations in modern helping practices. For instance, Friedlander (1977) found that the philosophies and values of three often incompatible "grandparents"—rationalism, pragmatism, and existentialism—create significant differences in the practices of organizational development consultants. Variations in contemporary approaches to healing are attributed to differences between ancient, prescientific conceptions of illness and the conceptions of modern science (Frank, 1973; Rappaport and Rappaport, 1981). For example, the scientific model focuses on the problem or its symptoms, whereas the prescientific model focuses on the anxiety associated with the affliction.

The prototypical roles described in Chapter Two, the technical adviser and the healer, are the source of diversity in modern consultation practices and provide the basis for a heuristic classification. It should be noted that the sage, a prototype of the modern advocate, is not included in this classification since it is often incompatible with the consultant role. The social role of the technical adviser is to disseminate technical knowledge and skills to others for their use. Therefore, the consultant in this role formulates problems in terms of consultees' technical deficits. The goal is to fill these gaps. The social role of the healer is to diagnose and treat disease. Consultants who assume this role conceptualize problems and goals from complicated perspectives. The primary source of problems may be a disease or dysfunction in the client (defined as the organization or some division in it *or* as one or more of the clients for whom a consultee is responsible). However, it is also possible that consultees, because of emotional difficulties, are behaving in dysfunctional ways that are either creating or exacerbating the clients' problems. The analysis of the problem, therefore, involves two levels: (1) the client and (2) the consultee. The primary goal is to cure the client, but the intermediate goal may be to treat impaired consultees so they can function more effectively.

The power base of the healer is also relatively complex. People in both roles possess expert power, but healers typically have two additional and highly significant sources of influence: legitimate power and referent power. Therefore, the healer has a broader range of influence than the technical adviser and can use a wider range of strategies. From prehistoric times, laypersons have attributed legitimate power to members of the healing professions. Today the two traditional bases of legitimate power have eroded. Contemporary health professionals lack the status of either their priestly or aristocratic forebears, and modern media have demystified much of what was once an esoteric body of knowledge. However, contemporary society institutionalizes the legitimate power of healing professions in assigning them legal authority and responsibility for the diagnosis and treatment of persons who are either mentally disturbed or incompetent. Moreover, certain individuals continue to attribute legitimate power to certain healing professionals (Caplan, 1970; McWhirter, 1968; Rodin and Janis, 1979), a phenomenon that is amplified in times of uncertainty and crisis and when problems are emotional in nature. Anxiety associated with these circumstances appears to arouse primitive dependency needs that impel consultees to lean on their consultants for solving apparently insoluble problems. The consultant/consultee relationship appears to "tap into some deep archetypal layer of belief" in the consultant's esoteric insights and "magical" powers (Levine, 1972, p. 17). Consultants sometimes deliberately reinforce this dependency for therapeutic purposes, assuming that to inspire confidence that the "doctor knows best" will renew consultees' hopes and energies.* From this perspective, consultants' effectiveness will be related to consultees' dependency. Transference is highly desirable (Levinson, 1978). Consultants may reinforce their legitimate power by mystifying their knowledge—for instance, by sharing only very limited aspects of their diagnoses and the bases underlying them. They reinforce their legitimate power through conspicuous display of esoteric symbols, such as diplomas and licenses, and by use of status symbols, such as luxurious offices and other signs of affluence (Rappaport and Rappaport, 1981). Consequently, the gap between the power of the consultee and that of the consultant is widened. The relationship resembles the active-passive model described by Szasz and Hollender (1956) and contrasts with the relationships characteristic of the technical adviser, who is more likely to prefer the more egalitarian mutual-participative model (Szasz and Hollender).

Referent power may be developed by technical advisers, but it is most often associated with the role of healer, who from prehistoric times has found the "bedside manner" efficacious in promoting healing. Consultants in the healer role may seek to augment their influence through building referent power, assuming that a relationship of friendliness and trust will increase consultees' strength in attacking problems and help them internalize the "doctor's" prescriptions, attitudes, and values (Argy-

*Healers may also reinforce consultees' dependency for self-serving reasons, using their specialized knowledge to maintain or increase their expert power. Therefore, "there are built-in negative incentives for professionals to share the mysteries of their craft and to explain reasons for their information in less mysterious ways" (Rodin and Janis, 1979, p. 61).

ris, 1970; Caplan, 1970; Meyers, Parsons, and Martin, 1979). Consultants increase their referent power by communicating acceptance and support, demonstrating genuine caring and regard, and explicating and making salient similarities between themselves and consultees—especially values, beliefs, and attitudes (Blake and Mouton, 1976; Rodin and Janis, 1979).

The major strategy of the technical adviser is educational. It is based on empirical-rational assumptions: that consultees have sufficient power to cope with their problems and to make decisions in a logical and rational manner and that they are able to absorb and adapt new information, knowledge, and skills to fit their particular situations. The healer's major strategy is diagnosis—followed by treatment and/or prescription. If the diagnosis reveals that the primary source of the problem is the client, the consultant prescribes a treatment through which the consultee can remedy the problem. Underlying this strategy is the assumption that the consultant's expertise is crucial in establishing a valid diagnosis and in formulating an effective treatment plan. If, however, the diagnosis reveals that the consultee is impaired, the strategy involves treatment of the consultee; the assumption here is that consultees cannot fully understand either the nature of their problems or how to remedy them. Therefore, the "doctor's" wisdom and skill are essential. The healer's strategies depend on his or her ability to influence consultees' emotions and cognitions through the exercise of legitimate and/or referent power.

Basic Variables: The Consultant's Choice Points

Efforts to map the realm of consultation have produced a lengthy list of variables. However, considerable overlap is apparent. Five dimensions capture the major sources of diversity.

Conceptualization of the Problem. Consultation approaches differ in their conceptualizations of problems. Differences appear in the breadth and depth with which problems are defined. They may be formulated in terms of an individual, a group, a department, or an entire system and in terms of a single issue or many. Diagnosis may be based on readily apparent phenomena or on an analysis of their underlying roots. The primary sources of the problem may be viewed as lack of knowledge or skills, lack of access to social or economic power, or the presence of emotional problems. The problem focus varies across a number of domains, including human and technological processes and structures. The conceptualization of the problem determines to a large extent the decisions on the other dimensions.

Goals. The overall goal of consultation is to improve agencies' performance in delivering services. However, goals differ according to the target in which change is to be effected—for example, in people, processes, policies, services, or structures. The size of the target may be set at a micro- or macrolevel or somewhere in between. The nature of desired outcomes varies. For example, a consultation might seek to increase employees' technical skills or change their attitudes, cognitions, or affect; institute a new policy; or change communications processes. Goals vary also according to their ultimate beneficiaries; the beneficiary may be the whole of society or some segment of it or a particular client or client group.

Methods and Assumptions. Methods for reaching goals vary on several dimensions. The most important variables are the locus, the agent(s) responsible for carrying out the intervention, and the strategy for bringing about needed changes. The *locus* may be identical to the change target, but often an intervening link is needed to effect a change; the link might be an administrator, a policy, or a process. To illustrate, a target might be staff morale, but the locus might be the chief administrator and, in particular, that person's leadership style. Most of the classifications reviewed earlier implied that the consultant is the agent for the intervention; but the consultant's involvement might end with a diagnosis or a recommendation, and agency staff might implement any needed changes.

Before discussion of *strategies,* it must be noted that consultative interventions are likely to involve two levels: (1) the strategy used by the consultant to effect changes in consultees and (2) strategies through which consultees subsequently effect changes in their work. The strategies used at these two levels may be similar; for instance, a consultant uses a facilitative strategy to help consultees discuss conflict openly; subsequently, they adopt facilitative strategies to help one another maintain openness in managing conflict. More often, the methods used at the two levels are different. For example, a consultant might use an acceptant strategy to help a consultee manage negative feelings more successfully, but the strategy actually used by a consultee to solve his or her problem might involve coercive processes and cognitive skills. A consultant may use educative strategies to help an administrator acquire a broader understanding of employee motivation; the administrator may solve a particular problem through increased use of reward power—for instance, more generous use of praise and other forms of social recognition.

The choice of strategy is usually derived from assumptions about how change can best be effected (Chin and Benne, 1969) and is related to the power base of the change agent— whether the agent is the consultant or consultee. (Consultees, especially administrators, possess multiple bases of power. Legitimate, coercive, and reward power are inherent in hierarchical positions. Most consultees possess expert and referent power. These varied sources of influence permit consultees to choose from a wider range of strategies than consultants, whose influence is often limited to expert power. Consultants' influence may also be relatively weak because it is transient.) Consultants' methods may involve any one or a combination of educative, diagnostic, prescriptive, treatment, directive, emotionally supportive (affective), or facilitative strategies.

Educative strategies include formal and informal methods of disseminating information and teaching skills. They are based on the empirical-rational assumption that behaviors can be changed through logical, cognitive processes. Consultants may use a diagnostic strategy—collecting and interpreting data —and/or a prescriptive strategy—telling consultees what they must do to solve problems. These approaches assume (1) that the consultant's knowledge is the critical factor in understanding and solving problems and (2) that consultees' cognitions of the diagnosis and prescription will lead to the necessary behavioral changes. For these three strategies, the consultant needs only expert power. Consultants who use treatment strategies, however, are usually attributed legitimate power and regarded as healers. The choice of a treatment strategy typically assumes that consultees cannot fully understand either the problem or the steps needed to remedy it; therefore, the consultant may not explain the diagnosis and intervention. For instance, a consultant decides that an administrator's stress level has reached a crisis stage and treats this individual with carefully structured cathartic interviews and with relaxation techniques. In using a directive strategy, the consultant takes on responsibility for supervising some of the consultee's work. (Occasionally a consultant actually performs some of the consultee's tasks.) The consultant's supervision is assumed to be necessary for the implementation of crucial techniques, such as procedures to carry out a behavior modification program or to computerize agency records. (This type of monitoring by consultants differs from line supervision in that it is limited to certain specific technical procedures.) Use of this strategy requires only expert power. Emotionally supportive strategies are based on referent power and recognize the importance of noncognitive factors in making changes. The assumption is that needed changes will occur if consultees recognize, accept, and/or deal with emotions related to problems or their solutions. Consultants' interventions include empathic listening, nonjudgmental acceptance of feelings, and communication of ideas in a friendly, encouraging manner designed to counteract negative emotions that might prevent the absorption of new information.

Consultants may use facilitative strategies to stimulate consultees in generating ideas, clarifying feelings and/or values, and mobilizing resources for identifying and solving problems. In facilitative strategies—in contrast to supportive strategies—the consultant's goals and methods are explicit. Underlying facilitative strategies are these assumptions: (1) consultees' expertise is essential to achieve valid diagnoses and to plan effective solutions, (2) consultees will be more motivated to follow through on intervention plans that they help design, and (3) the facilitative approach is most likely to increase consultees' effectiveness in solving future problems. Consultants' facilitative strategies may include cognitive and/or affective components and may seek to bring about changes in consultees' cognitions, emotions, attitudes, and/or behaviors. Referent power is essential.

Consultant Role. The basic role of the consultant is that of technical adviser; consultants may or may not assume the role of healer. Their power base varies. All consultants possess expert power. However, some are also accorded legitimate power —because they possess certain valued nontechnical characteristics such as social status or physical attractiveness—and some develop referent power. The degree of decision-making power exercised by consultants is variable. It may be shared equitably with the consultee or either of the two parties may assume greater authority for decisions. Consultants also differ in the degree to which they are involved in consultees' actual work activities.

Values. Choices on most dimensions described above reflect differences in professional values. Some of the classifications reviewed earlier referred to differences in ideological values, particularly in regard to social change. But as the role is defined here, consultants support the social role and values of the agencies they serve, even though they may personally disagree with certain policies or practices. Variations in consultants' values may, however, be expressed in their choices of client-agencies. To illustrate the range of possibilities, consultants may choose or refuse to work with such divergent organizations as a state medical association, a Moral Majority coalition, a public school system, an environmental conservation society, and a civil rights union.

Consultation Models:
Clusters of Related Choices

A choice on one of the dimensions just described is usually related to certain choices on others. For instance, the choice of goals is closely related to problem conceptualizations. The choice of strategy is related to assumptions about change. Clusters of related choices are the basis for consultation models. Most begin with a characteristic assumption about the source of the presenting problem and proceed to make related choices on other dimensions. Table 1 delineates these patterns. Chapters Five through Ten will discuss models in detail.

Factors Influencing Consultants' Choices

Although the unique features of each consultation situation and the expectations of agency staff impose certain boundaries on consultants' choices, consultants make many decisions. Hence their predispositions become important. Why does a consultant choose one method or role rather than another? The factor that most influences consultants' choices is the "set" produced by their professional training and experiences. Consultants tend to follow the "law of the hammer," which holds that professionals tend to interpret problems in terms of their particular tools or skills: to a person with a hammer, everything looks like a nail. Consultants trained in conflict management are likely to diagnose problems in terms of staff conflicts. Health professionals are likely to diagnose problems in terms of their particular treatment specialties. Consultants may skip the diagnostic process and move immediately into their prepackaged intervention programs without checking first on the degree to which their "tools" fit the problem at hand (Lorsch and Lawrence, 1972). Personal and social values and motives also influence consultants' decisions. In consultation with a court, a psychiatrist's judgments regarding a child custody case will be affected by his own involvement as a litigant in a child custody dispute. The recommendations of a psychiatrist consulting on criminal issues will be influenced by his attitude toward common practices of the criminal justice system (Pollack, 1968). Consultants sometimes "act out" their problems—such as problems with authority figures—in their diagnoses and interventions (Walton and Warrick, 1973). Chapter Two pointed out the ways in which the prevailing ethos shapes helping roles. Certain roles become salient and others temporarily recede in importance, only to reemerge in another *Zeitgeist*. Consultation practices are also re-

Table 1. Consultation Models: Variations in Concepts and Methods

Dimension	Education and Training	Clinical	Mental Health	Behavioral	Organizational	Program
Formulation of the problem	Consultees' lack of technology: knowledge, information, skills	Disease or dysfunction in client; consultee's lack of technical expertise	Emotional problems and/or technological deficits in client and/or consultee	Dysfunctional behavior—the result of learning; consultees' lack of technological expertise	Variable: often lack of technology related to organizational problems and health	Lack of varied types of technical expertise needed for a program
Broad goal of consultant	Transmission of needed knowledge, information, skills	Diagnosis and alleviation of problem; restoration of normal functioning	Increase in consultees' coping effectiveness	Reduction of frequency of undesirable behavior; increase in frequency of desired behavior	Increase in organizational productivity and morale	Development, implementation, evaluation of programs
Major method used by consultant	Education	Diagnosis (based on clinical analysis of data); prescription; treatment	Education; facilitation; support	Diagnosis; prescription; direction	Variable: often facilitation; education; diagnosis; support	Variable
Consultant's major assumption about change	Empirical/rational (behavior can be changed through logical, cognitive processes)	Empirical/rational; the clinician's expertise is essential	Normative/reeducative; empirical/rational	Empirical rational; expertise of the consultant is essential	Variable: empirical/rational; normative/reeducative	Empirical/rational
Consultant's primary source of power	Expert	Expert; legitimate	Expert; referent; legitimate	Expert; legitimate	Variable: expert, referent, legitimate	Expert
Consultant's primary underlying values	Technology	Health care from a medical orientation	Diffusion of mental health concepts, principles, information, skills	Technology and the scientific method	Variable: typically either humanism or technology	Technology and/or values related to the particular program

lated to social conditions. To illustrate, the mental health consultant role was introduced in the 1920s but quickly faded when the milieu grew conservative. It reappeared and grew in popularity in the spirited 1960s, as did the role of advocate. In the explosion of knowledge of the 1970s, technologically oriented consultation flourished. In the 1980s, federal cuts are creating crises in care-giving institutions. Consequently, consultants are finding themselves drawn into crisis-oriented, ameliorative roles.

Annotated Bibliography

Blake, R. R., and Mouton, J. S. *Consultation.* Reading, Mass.: Addison-Wesley, 1976. Organized to explain and illustrate the consulcube, this book describes five major intervention strategies—acceptant, catalytic, confrontational, prescriptive, and theories and principles—that may be directed toward one or more focal issues (power/authority, morale/cohesion, norms/ standards, and goals/objectives) to bring about change at one or more levels (individual, group, intergroup, organizational, and larger social system). The detailed cases illustrate diverse consultation strategies applied in a wide range of organizational settings.

Caplan, G. *The Theory and Practice of Mental Health Consultation.* New York: Basic Books, 1970. Principles governing four types of mental health consultation are described and illustrated: client-centered case consultation, consultee-centered case consultation, program-centered administrative consultation, and consultee-centered administrative consultation. The author's explanations of the psychoanalytic theories from which these models were derived are especially thorough and clarify some of their little-understood nuances.

Dworkin, A. L., and Dworkin, E. P. "A Conceptual Overview of Selected Consultation Models." *American Journal of Community Psychology,* 1975, *3* (2), 151-159. These authors describe and compare four consultation models: consultee-centered, group process, social action, and ecological. They briefly discuss criteria for selection of models and the importance of fitting the model to the particular needs of the client organization. The framework presented here typifies efforts by consultants to differentiate the major types of consultation and to clarify the dimensions on which they differ.

French, J. R., and Raven, B. H. "The Bases of Social Power." In D. Cartwright and A. Zander (Eds.), *Group Dynamics: Research and Theory.* (2nd ed.) New York: Harper & Row, 1960. This classic essay identifies five bases of social power—reward, coercive, legitimate, referent, and expert—and describes the ways social power can be used to change cognitions, behavior, and attitudes. This typology can help consultants understand their own and their consultees' diverse sources of influence.

Schein, E. *Process Consultation: Its Role in Organization Development.* Reading, Mass.: Addison-Wesley, 1969. Schein describes three basic types of consultation that differ according to the relative influence of the consultee or consultant in the decision-making processes. These models are the purchase, doctor/patient, and process approaches to consultation. Schein points out the advantages of the process approach and discusses ways it can be implemented.

Szasz, T. S., and Hollender, M. H. "A Contribution to the Philosophy of Medicine: The Basic Models of the Doctor-Patient Relationship." *Archives of Internal Medicine,* 1956, *97,* 585-592. These authors differentiate three fundamental models of doctor/patient relationships and their underlying concepts in regard to disease, treatment, and cure: (1) active-passive, (2) guidance-cooperative, and (3) mutual-participative. Although each is necessary and appropriate under certain conditions, the authors contend that helpers' (and helpees') personal needs often strongly influence the choice of model. Although this paper is concerned with the medical profession, it is directly relevant to consultant/consultee relationships. It is an important contribution to the understanding of commonly held but often tacit assumptions regarding helping roles.

5

Education
and Training
Approaches

Teaching and training are the most common of all consultative activities. Consultant-led lectures, seminars, and workshops help agencies keep their services updated and functioning smoothly. The following examples illustrate the wide range of services in this model. A psychometrist presents a workshop for the personnel department of a large hospital on the use of tests to screen prospective employees. A physician discusses stress management techniques with the staff of a center for battered women. An environmental specialist reviews research on the effects of various physical conditions on prisoners' attitudes and behavior for a state legislative committee on prison reform. A communications expert advises the staff of an advocate organization on effective uses of mass media.

As defined in this book, the education and training model of consultation is limited to prearranged, organized services, in contrast to the impromptu educational and training activities that are incidental to most forms of consultation. This model, an exemplar of the technological approach to consultation, is *in-*

formation-centered and emphasizes the dissemination of concepts, information, and skills rather than the formulation of a diagnosis. However, a formal or informal diagnosis or needs assessment—by the agency and/or the consultant—usually precedes and initiates services in this model. Education and training activities are often a separate element in a larger consultation contract. They may be a prelude or sequel to other types of consultation. For instance, university-based consultants prepared patrolmen to staff a new family crisis motor patrol through a month of full-time on-campus educational activities that included lectures, human relations laboratory training, and demonstrations of family crisis interventions (Bard and Berkowitz, 1969). Later these patrolmen received weekly consultation on problems arising in their new jobs.

Many factors contribute to the demand for educational and training activities. Ongoing training activities are necessary for most agencies to respond to technological, political, legislative, and social changes. Moreover, some professional staff members must present evidence of updating of competencies to professional regulatory boards in order to renew their licenses. In human services agencies, special training for professional staff members who move into middle management positions is especially important because these persons are often unprepared for administrative responsibilities. Changing views of learning and of adult and career development have also added to the interest in training. Learning—for professional and personal growth—is now regarded as a lifelong activity.

Agencies use a variety of training mechanisms. They often provide informal, on-the-job training along with periodic in-house workshops and seminars. Increasingly popular are special internal structures—such as personnel development, in-service training departments, and human resource development (HRD) departments—that systematically program training for all units within their organizations. These departments often call on external consultants to assist in ongoing educational activities. For instance, they may ask one consultant to lead a workshop on time management, another to train secretaries in telephone communication skills, and still another for a seminar on word processing. For the past fifteen or twenty years, grant funds have often been available to help agencies pay for workshops. Agencies also provide financial support for their staff to attend outside training programs, such as those offered by certain universities, professional organizations, and consultant firms. Since the primary focus of the education and training model is on the dissemination of the consultant's specialized information or skills rather than on problems unique to a particular agency, the practices described in this chapter include these externally organized and conducted seminars and workshops that provide training for staff members from a number of agencies.

Concepts

The education and training model conceptualizes problems in terms of deficits in knowledge and skills. The consultant's goal is to bring whatever information, knowledge, or skills are needed. The criterion of success is staff acquisition of needed competencies. The consultant's strategy is educational. It is based on expert power and on a collegial relationship. The assumptions are that (1) cognitive processes will bring about needed changes in the consultees' performance, (2) consultees have the necessary ability and motivation to learn new concepts, attitudes, or skills and apply them in their jobs, (3) the organization will support the acquisition and incorporation of the new technology, and (4) subsequently the agency will become more effective.

Open-systems and developmental concepts of organizations provide the rationale for educational and training activities. If organizations are viewed as open systems, continuously interacting with and influenced by a rapidly changing environment, adaptation and development must also be continuous. Therefore, agencies require constant updating of technology related to all facets of the organization. Equally compelling arguments come from changing concepts of adult and career development (Super and Hall, 1978). No longer is it assumed that the person who completes a professional or technical training program is prepared for a lifelong career. Instead, it is expected

that there will be shifts in the career field itself and in job requirements and that additional training will be needed to maintain competency in one's field. Continuous training can be the
means by which agencies prevent arrested development of employees. Training also enables people whose interests change to
make career movements in both lateral and vertical directions.

Stimulated by these increasing demands, the field of instructional technology is growing rapidly in size and sophistication. The trend is toward a systems approach that includes a
needs assessment, specification of objectives, creation of unique
learning experiences that are carefully defined and controlled to
achieve these objectives, feedback loops, and coordination with
all parts of the organization (Goldstein, 1980). The needs assessment phase requires analyses of three elements: the organization, the operations or task, and the persons who are to be the
learners (McGehee and Thayer, 1961). The organization's future
as well as immediate goals and needs should be considered. The
organizational analysis also assesses the degree to which the organizational values, climate, norms, and incentives can be predicted to accept and incorporate the changes sought through
training. In the task analysis, the operations needed for a particular job are determined, and the concepts and behaviors needed
are compared against those already present. In the person analysis, the relationship between the learning task and the prospective
learners' personalities, abilities, learning rates, and life history is
analyzed (Cronbach and Snow, 1977). From these assessments,
goals of the educational and training activities are established
and criterion-referenced (Scandura, 1977). An instructional design is selected to accomplish the goals. Seminars and lectures
are widely used, as well as cognitive-behavioral approaches in
which didactic presentations are combined with opportunities
to observe and practice the target behaviors. Game simulations
and other laboratory-based methods are also popular.

The evaluation of training is progressing from simple
methods such as use of anecdotal reactions of trainers and
trainees to methods of greater precision and complexity. Evaluations often include measures of several outcomes taken on a
temporal continuum before, during, and after training to provide
feedback loops for continuous modification of the instructional

system; evaluation designs are constructed to gauge the impact of the instruction on the learner and on the organization. Criteria based on performance standards are replacing norm-referenced measures of achievement. Qualitative variables such as training processes are documented. Organizational constraints on the incorporation of new behaviors and costs (in terms of time and money) and benefits are assessed.

Methods

A wide range of educational and training methods are available. The following pages describe the major methods. Each offers relative advantages for certain objectives. Many designs include several of these methods.

1. *Lectures.* For most training objectives, lectures are the most effective means of presenting the initial theoretical framework and for conveying essential information and illustrations. Lectures providing cognitive "maps" probably should be included as at least a brief part of each element of a training design since some consultees learn best through a didactic, auditory approach.

2. *Media and materials.* Film, videotapes, readings, programmed materials with self-guiding instructions, and computerized instructional programs can be very helpful as alternatives or supplements to lectures. These materials can be especially valuable in allowing trainees to proceed at their own pace and to the depth and breadth that suit individual needs. For those who learn best through visual media, printed materials are essential.

3. *Structured laboratory experiences.* Acquisition of new behaviors is greatly facilitated by simulations in which trainees learn new concepts and skills through experiences. In this category are leader demonstrations, role-play exercises, games, and other laboratory activities. Structured experiences can also be used to help trainees get acquainted and to establish positive norms. Sometimes trainers prefer to use a structured laboratory (rather than cognitive input) to evoke trainees' awareness of needs for the information and skills to be offered.

4. *Small-group discussions.* For most instructional pur-

poses, small-group discussions following both didactic presentations and laboratory experiences are needed to help trainees assimilate new information and relate it to their particular work situations. Group discussions help trainees discover and appreciate different perspectives. The small group can also provide cognitive guidance and affective support for members to experiment with new attitudes, theories, and behaviors. Sometimes small-group discussions are listless, off-target, or otherwise unproductive; clear goals, an agenda, and suggestions from the trainer on how best to structure the work can then be useful.

5. *Behavioral role modeling.* A training method that systematically integrates the principles of observation, modeling, and vicarious reinforcement can be used to teach complex skills (Goldstein and Sorcher, 1974). Trainees are first introduced to new principles. Next, they observe a model (live or filmed) applying the principles. They then role-play application of the principles. Finally, the trainer and the group members reinforce the performance of new behaviors and provide feedback for further practice.

6. *Measurement and feedback.* Trainees' learnings can be measured through tests, surveys, or live or videotaped observations and then fed back to guide trainers and individual trainees in planning further activities.

Methodological Decisions. Taxonomies have been constructed suggesting the methods appropriate for each category of learning sought (Gagné and Briggs, 1974; Schindler-Rainman and Lippitt, 1975). But empirical studies as yet offer little guidance for decision making (Herbert and Yost, 1978). Choices of which methods to use in a particular situation are usually based simply on the trainer's judgment. In making decisions, in addition to considering the issues involved in all forms of consultation (such as objectives, time commitments, and evaluation responsibilities), the trainer needs to know the consultees' previous training experiences, the heterogeneity of their level of expertise, their relationships to one another (including supervisory linkages), the size of the training group, and any immediate events or concerns that are likely to spill into training discussions. Consultants also need advance information about any consultees who are likely to experience significant difficulties during training, thus creating problems for themselves or others.

Effective training designs have the following major characteristics:

1. *Collaborative planning.* The training goals and design are evolved through collaboration between trainees, agency administrators, and trainer.

2. *Relevance.* The planner derives training objectives from needs assessments, thus ensuring that the learning goals are relevant to the organization, to the persons involved in the training, and to their jobs.

3. *Uniqueness.* The content and training activities are designed to fit the needs of a particular agency and its staff. Prepackaged programs are modified to conform to unique needs and conditions.

4. *Flexibility.* Training designs are carefully planned but are sufficiently flexible that changes can be made in the content and method to meet important, unexpected needs.

5. *Alternative methods.* The design includes a variety of methods in order to accomplish varied objectives and to accommodate learner differences.

6. *Clarity.* Trainees are given accurate advance information. For each aspect of the training program, trainees are apprised of the relationship of topics and activities to subgoals and to overall goals. They are also aware of the different responsibilities of the trainees and the trainer.

7. *Voluntary participation.* Since involuntary participation ordinarily sets up resistance that is very difficult to overcome, trainees have the choice of whether to attend the training program and whether to participate in laboratory activities.

8. *Careful sequencing of learning tasks.* Activities build on basic and simple concepts and skills and move toward more complex ones. For example, before teaching feedback or conflict negotiation skills, trainers help trainees acquire listening skills.

9. *Pacing fits learners and material to be learned.* Pacing is often an extremely complex task, since the pace of individuals within and across groups varies. Trainers watch for direct

and indirect signs of fatigue, cognitive overload, boredom, emotional exhaustion—signs such as tardiness, talking during leader presentations, yawning, and impassive or negative facial expressions—and pace activities accordingly. Opening up pacing issues and problems for participant discussions usually provides the trainer with adequate information to pace activities satisfactorily.

10. *Learner comfort.* Moderate tension enhances learning, but ordinarily the learning tasks provide adequate tension. Trainees must be physically comfortable. Learning is inhibited if, for example, learners are hungry or are working in a room that is too cold or too crowded or in otherwise unfavorable conditions. Consultant-trainers ensure that physical conditions support the learning task. Trainees also need social and psychological comfort. Trainees need to feel reasonable compatibility with other trainees and to feel respected and accepted by them and by the trainer. Trainers can reduce participants' anxiety by providing icebreaking activities and by anticipating and alleviating common fears, such as fear of forced participation and fears of becoming overexposed or subjected to destructive criticism.

11. *Supportive group norms.* Trainers create positive learning climates by building group norms that provide social rewards for experimentation, for responsibility taking, for expressing differences, and for open discussion of the content and process of the training.

12. *Readiness.* The overall design and each step in it establish trainees' awareness of their need for skill and information before moving into actual educational activities.

13. *Learner activity.* Trainees are active. When the design calls for leader domination (as in lectures), trainees at least are active listeners. For example, they are encouraged to ask questions and to critically examine new ideas. Active participation facilitates learning and also gives the trainer valuable feedback on trainees' progress.

14. *Feedback loops.* Trainers obtain and share with trainees feedback on their learning and on the training design at all stages. Feedback on achievement of objectives and on the effectiveness of methods can be obtained through open discus-

sions, questionnaires, tests, and playback of videotapes. Final feedback on learning and on the design goes to organizational decision makers to guide future planning.

15. *Leader support.* As in all forms of consultation, trainers are more effective if they have competent and objective persons to whom they can turn when unusual problems arise. Cotrainers can add greatly to a consultant's effectiveness. By alternating as observers, cotrainers can obtain useful data to feed back into the ongoing planning. Trainees benefit from the expanded repertoire of expertise and from the additional role models. Chapter Thirteen discusses team issues in more detail.

Common Issues

Certain issues can be expected to arise in most training situations. Trainees always, for example, want to know the consultant's qualifications. (This question, of course, is a general one in consultation and is not limited to the education and training model). Until legitimacy is established, trainees are likely to be skeptical about the consultant's ideas and reluctant to accept them and to participate in activities. The underlying question, often politely hidden, is "What qualifies *you* to be an expert on *our* work?" Descriptions of credentials may help earn legitimacy, but usually consultees reserve acceptance until they see a demonstration of the consultant's competence. Trainers should be sensitive to indications that their legitimacy is being questioned. Sometimes the legitimization process can be accelerated through judicious use of illustrations and anecdotes relating one's expertise to trainees' work. Many consultants, however, prefer to make matter-of-fact statements to the effect that trainees naturally will need to see for themselves what the consultant has to offer and then move quickly ahead to demonstrate their competence and relevance.

One of the major drawbacks of this model is that the consultant may have no opportunity to contact the persons who are to attend and plan conference content and methods with them. Despite careful advance planning with agency representatives, trainers often discover that their planned design is incongruent with trainee needs. To illustrate, one training director arranged for a consultant to talk to administrative staff on legal aspects of hiring and firing. The consultant discovered that the staff were already sophisticated in this area and that she could bring little new to them. A rural community mental health center asked a consultant to present a seminar on use of biofeedback techniques, but the center had no feedback equipment. Federal funds originally promised for purchasing it had been wiped out by budget cuts. In some such situations, consultants can use an *emergent* design, produced by on-site discussions with trainees about their needs, to construct a more relevant workshop. The emergent approach is most useful when the training program allows sufficient time for interaction between trainer and trainees and when all involved are comfortable with ambiguity and a relatively high degree of trainee responsibility. Emergent designs also require trainer flexibility and a wide range of useful skills.

Keeping the focus within the limits of the contract is another common problem. Trainees may hope to obtain assistance on organizational problems, such as interpersonal conflicts within their group or between them and an administrator. Training topics frequently trigger associations with urgent work problems that are outside the bounds of the consultant's contract. For instance, a discussion with supervisors about theories of leadership precipitated comments about their director's unilateral decision-making style and expressions of their anger over a recent unexplained firing. Consultants who unwittingly hit such a "land mine" are likely to feel highly conflicted about what to do with it. They will probably feel empathic with the trainees and interested in their real-life problems; but if the contract is limited to education, consultants have no choice but to refuse to get into discussions of actual interpersonal conflicts. If the contract permits, trainers can use an academic approach with hypothetical examples to teach and demonstrate conflict management skills. They can help employees acquire broader perspectives through discussions of theories of conflict. The consultant may also suggest that work-family concerns be taken to the appropriate supervisors. The trainer may need to clarify repeatedly the differences between a skills-training contract and an organization-focused diagnosis and intervention and be consistently firm in maintaining limits. Trainers may then need to help disappointed consultees recognize the usefulness of the educational approach—despite its limits—as one important element in solving organizational problems. Trainers will usually want to make notes of pressures to move outside the contract and include them in feedback (though keeping the sources anonymous) to the administrator who arranged for the training.

The presence in training groups of members of work families creates special problems. Participation is often constrained because consultees are fearful that they may expose weaknesses that later will be used against them. For instance, in a workshop on leadership skills for employees of a large state agency, the trainer found the group surprisingly subdued. Questions were perfunctory and superficial. No one responded to the trainer's call for volunteers to role-play. One participant finally explained the passivity. The "big boss," the agency's director, was in the audience, and participants were fearful about how he might judge their words and behaviors. The director then spoke up and said he was present to learn, not to judge. But his staff, obviously skeptical of his motives, remained cautious.

Even when hierarchical relationships are not involved, members of family groups are often justifiably inhibited in workshops because they fear they might offend fellow employees and damage work relationships. Loyalties and antagonisms related to family alliances and schisms may override commitments to training activities. Stranger groups are often more comfortable with risk taking—asking questions that may expose ignorance, testing out new ideas, experimenting with new behaviors, and challenging others' ideas. Familial connections may have positive effects, however. If levels of trust and respect are high, family groups can provide valuable support for training activities and goals. Moreover, generalization of learning is more likely when all members of a staff are exposed to new information and learn new concepts and skills.

Individuals sometimes interfere with training activities. For example, a trainee may interrupt others, make long-winded or irrelevant "speeches," or interject hostile and sarcastic remarks. The leader is responsible for protecting the investment of the agency and the other trainees by controlling disruptive behavior. Experienced trainers learn to anticipate and minimize disruptive behaviors by clearly outlining the objectives and methods, the time allocated to each training element, and what is expected of the training group members. Frequent checkups on the progress of the training in relation to its goals help keep groups working productively. Leader monitoring of deviant behavior should be firm and businesslike but pleasant. If a trainer moves too swiftly in curtailing disruptive behaviors or is excessively punitive, other trainees may become resentful and sympathize with the deviant member. It is usually best to time any confrontations so as to (1) ascertain that the behavior is indeed inappropriate, persistent, and detrimental to goals, (2) delay confrontations until trainees become aware of the disruptiveness and its effects so they will understand the leader's actions, and (3) intervene before serious loss of time and energy occurs. The most potent antidote for disruptions, however, must come from trainees. Modeling of positive behaviors by highly regarded trainees and group verbal and nonverbal expressions of disapproval of disruptive members are essential to maintaining an effective work climate.

Occasionally participants inappropriately expose very personal feelings and problems. Sometimes they reveal disturbing experiences or illnesses. For example, a trainee spoke of traumatic wartime experiences and residual nightmares. In another situation, the grief of a recently widowed trainee dominated group discussions. Personal problems can become the focal point of a workshop and divert members' energies from goals. Such exposures leave those who disclose the problems in vulnerable positions. The leader is responsible for helping trainees keep their disclosures within proper bounds. Probably the most effective method is to remind the group, gently but firmly, of its goals and clearly differentiate the topics that are within and outside the parameters. Illustrations can help get the point across and eliminate any remaining ambiguity. This approach clarifies the contract and justifies any subsequent measures that are necessary to stay within it. If a member violates the parameters, the leader may first want to interrupt with a fresh reminder of the objectives. If this procedure does not work, it may be necessary to talk to the trainee outside the group and—in extreme cases—to ask her or him to leave the training session. Occasionally, inappropriate behavior in a training group is a sign of serious illness. In rare cases, the trainer may decide to notify agency authorities to ensure that a vulnerable person receives needed support and treatment.

Example of a Workshop Design

To illustrate the elements that go into a workshop, a design that has been used extensively to help nurses who are moving into middle management positions acquire supervisory skills will be described. Nurses experience a great deal of role tension when they move from direct services into middle management positions. Their training has not prepared them for supervisory responsibilities. Often they find it difficult to accept and to use legitimate power. The design to be described is constructed to help nurses learn the new concepts, attitudes, and skills needed for administrative responsibilities. The goals and instructional design for this workshop evolved from conferences between the consultant and continuing education specialists in the nursing field, from needs assessment surveys, and from evaluations and critiques of many earlier workshops.* Consultants can delete or add elements and emphasize different topics, according to participants' unique needs. The design can be used with large groups—up to a hundred—and with both "family" and "stranger" groups. In the former case, however, the leader should be alert to family issues that may complicate trainees' interactions and participation. The design incorporates the six methods described earlier: (1) lectures, (2) media and materials, (3) laboratory activities, (4) small-group discussions, (5) behavioral role modeling, and (6) measurement and feedback.

Announcement materials are distributed by the sponsor-

*The trainer was the author. The continuing education specialists were Dorothy Bloom and Joyce Hoover of the School of Nursing of the University of Texas at Austin. A second consultant-trainer, Earl Koile, contributed significantly to early versions of this design.

ing agency (such as hospitals, clinics, and the continuing education programs of schools of nursing and professional associations) to inform prospective trainees of the workshop's purposes, content, and methods. The announcement reads as
follows:

Supervisory Skills Workshop

The purpose of this workshop is to provide
R.N.s in supervisory positions an opportunity to improve their skills in communication and interpersonal
relationships. The content will focus on communication skills, interpersonal relations, interviewing techniques, conflict resolution, and group processes.

Learning activities will include lectures and discussions, small-group experiences, role playing, and
demonstration and practice of specific communication techniques. Upon completion of this program,
the participant will be able to:

1. Describe the process of establishing an effective
    working climate.
2. Identify communication barriers and demonstrate
    behaviors that create a climate of defensiveness
    or supportiveness.
3. Demonstrate strategies of interviewing in a simu-
    lated situation.
4. Describe different approaches for resolving con-
    flict.
5. Identify factors affecting group productivity.

The schedule and topics, also included in the announcement, are shown in Figure 5.

The design (Table 2) balances didactic and experiential
activities and work in groups of different sizes—large group,
small group, and triads (or dyads). The topics move from less to
more complex and from lower to higher risk. Although throughout there is an emphasis on application of new ideas, information, and techniques, in the last hours the emphasis on taking
learnings back to the trainees' agencies intensifies. This design

Figure 5. Supervisory Skills Workshop Schedule

First Day

8:00-8:30	Completion of Registration
8:30-9:00	Introduction and Overview of Workshop
9:00-11:30	Establishing an Effective Working Climate
11:30-1:00	Lunch
1:00-4:30	Communication Skills

Second Day

8:30-11:30	Interpersonal Relations
11:30-1:00	Lunch
1:00-4:30	Interviewing Techniques

Third Day

8:30-11:30	Conflict Resolution: Theories and Methods
11:30-1:30	Lunch
1:00-3:00	Group Processes
3:00-4:30	Applying Workshop Learning Back on the Job

includes a brief feedback discussion at the end of each half-day, in which the trainer seeks evaluative comments on content and activities. In addition, written feedback is obtained at the end of each day (see Figure 6). The mean scores, the range of responses, and a summary of comments are regularly reported back to the participants and discussed with them. A final, more comprehensive evaluation is conducted at the end, such as the one in Table 3.

In the first component, the Introduction and Overview, officers of the sponsoring agency greet trainees. Usually tea, coffee, soft drinks, and doughnuts are available. After trainees register and receive any materials they did not receive in advance, they seat themselves at tables arranged for six to eight persons. The tables underscore the workshop's task orientation

Table 2. A Workshop Design

Component	Primary Objectives	Content	Examples of Activities
1. Introduction and overview	To provide preliminary information	"Housekeeping" topics such as the schedule, and how to obtain continuing education credit	*Large group:* announcements, questions, discussion, dissemination of reading materials and bibliographies
2. Establishing an effective work climate	To provide a "cognitive map" for workshop with clear goals, structure, and responsibilities; To establish positive working relationships	Overview of workshop; Trainer's background; trainees' backgrounds, interests, goals; Characteristics of positive work climates; Feedback of initial perceptions; individual goal setting	*Large group:* leader-led discussion; *Laboratory:* getting-acquainted exercises, formation of triads and small groups of five or six to work together throughout the workshop
3. Communications	To teach trainees basic communication concepts and skills; To establish and reinforce positive group norms	Communications concepts, processes; different styles and their effects; guidelines for constructive feedback	*Laboratory:* new groups formed for listening exercises with feedback on listening behavior; *Large group:* discussion to relate experiences to theory; *Small group:* return to original group to discuss and integrate learnings, practice skills
4. Interpersonal relations	To teach trainees basic concepts related to management positions	Middle management roles, issues; Organizational roles, relationships; Role shifts; Leadership styles; Motivation of employees; Stereotypes	*Large group:* leader presents concepts, leads discussion; *Small group:* discussion and integration of concepts; *Triads:* helping members identify strengths and problem areas for focus in workshop

Module	Objectives	Content	Methods
5. Interviewing techniques	To teach trainees interviewing principles and skills	Interviewing purposes, principles, techniques, structure, problems	*Laboratory:* leader demonstration of interview and discussion of issues. Trainees observe and discuss the demonstrations. Trainees practice in new groups. *Small groups:* Return to original small groups for further discussion and identification of individual needs
6. Conflict resolution	To teach trainees basic concepts of conflict and different styles of conflict management. To teach trainees how to receive and give feedback on perceived styles. To increase trainees' self awareness	Social, organizational, and personal bases of conflict. Variable management styles	*Large group:* leader-led demonstration of styles, lecture, discussion. *Small group:* discussion of feedback on perceived conflict styles and of applications in own work
7. Group processes	To teach trainees basic group concepts, roles, processes, interventions. To increase trainees' self awareness. To give trainees practice in applying concepts and skills	Work group: roles, processes, norms	*Large group:* discussions of concepts and applications. *Small group:* structured exercises, discussions, participant-observer exercises. Trainees receive and give feedback on roles in groups
8. Applying workshop learning	To allow trainees to construct plans for transfer of workshop learnings to work settings, including behavioral contracts	Review of workshop learnings; relevance to work	*Large group:* discussion. *Small group:* work in triads

Figure 6. Session Evaluation

1.   How relevant were the topics covered?

      Of little relevance   1   2   3   4   5   6   7   Of great relevance

2.   How effective were the methods used?

      Not effective   1   2   3   4   5   6   7   Very effective

3.   How useful to your ongoing work was the session?

      Of little use   1   2   3   4   5   6   7   Very useful

4.   Comments:

and facilitate trainees' notetaking. Since nurses are on tight work schedules, the trainer is careful to accommodate their needs by beginning and ending promptly. The officer of the sponsoring agency begins the workshop with announcements on such matters as the schedule, materials, continuing education credit, and forthcoming workshops.

In the second component, Establishing an Effective Work Climate, the consultant briefly describes relevant aspects of her background and prepares trainees for the work to come by clarifying the contract, providing an overview of the workshop goals and strategies, establishing positive group norms, and helping participants get acquainted. Two ongoing groups are established: a dyad or triad and a small group in which two or three of these smaller groups are joined. These groups provide social and psychological support and help participants with cognitive tasks. These groups also provide their members with feedback, the most valued outcome of the training for many participants.

The Communications component uses an experiential activity to heighten members' awareness of salient communications processes—such as the style in which questions are asked and both verbal and nonverbal interaction patterns—and to help them begin to examine their own assumptions, values, and styles. Guidelines are established and the activities directed so as to reinforce positive group norms, such as the giving of responsible and constructive feedback, careful and active listening, and respect for different points of view. This session, like all others, ends with each trainee's making a self-assessment of strengths and problem areas to work on. At the end of the first day, in preparation for subsequent work, trainees indicate (through brief lists coming out of small-group discussions) the types of interviews they find to be most difficult.

The next day begins with a didactic module on Interpersonal Relations. The trainer presents theories, principles, and case studies related to management roles and functions. The group's understanding of this material and of its relevance is checked through large- and small-group discussions. In the Interviewing Techniques component, the leader uses the participants' lists to help them acquire principles and techniques for managing common interviews. Most frequently chosen by participants are interviews in which (1) they give negative evaluations to subordinates, (2) their boss expresses a closed attitude toward their points of view, and (3) they discuss a conflict with a peer. Also popular are employment screening interviews and interviews to guide the development of subordinates. From leader demonstrations and group discussions, interview principles and techniques are generated and summarized.

In the sixth component, Conflict Resolution, the leader first demonstrates and then discusses concepts underlying different approaches to conflict (Blake and Mouton, 1976; Likert and Likert, 1976). Members then give and receive feedback on their own styles from their small groups and discuss conflict problems back on their jobs.

The Group Processes component begins with a brief conceptual input in which participants' attention is focused on group roles and processes. To get discussions started, the leader assigns the small groups topics for discussion, and a volunteer in each group is designated to observe and periodically feed back observations on roles and processes. Members learn to differentiate behavioral observations from their inferences and interpretations.

The last session focuses on trainees' transfer of workshop learnings to work settings. Each person works out a plan that includes a diagnosis of personal and situational problems, a force-field analysis, and a behavioral contract. Objectives are estab-

Table 3. Workshop Evaluation[a]

INSTRUCTIONS: Please place an X under the heading that most closely agrees with *your* idea about each statement.

	Strongly Agree	Agree	Neither	Disagree	Stongly Disagree
1. Speaker(s) encouraged participant discussion.					
2. The program was too long.					
3. One or more members of my group monopolized the discussion.					
4. I accepted the responsibility of my learning in this program.					
5. The program's objectives were presented in a clear manner.					
6. The information was presented in a clear manner.					
7. I was reluctant to verbally participate in our group.					
8. I attempted to contribute regularly to this program.					
9. This program met my expectations.					
10. Learning materials such as handouts and audiovisuals were useful.					
11. The days of the program were convenient.					
12. Our group assignment was not clear.					
13. I would seriously consider attending another program like this one.					
14. I can use this information within the next week at work.					
15. Speaker(s) belabored the obvious.					
16. The sequencing of presentations and coffee breaks was about right.					
17. My understanding of the program content was enhanced by the group work.					
18. Compared with the effort I usually put into a program, my efforts in this program were below average.					
19. The program did not meet my personal learning needs.					
20. I was able to meet the stated program objectives.					
21. The group work helped me to use the program's information.					
22. Before this program I had no understanding of the ideas that were presented.					
23. The way this workshop was organized allowed me to make efficient use of my time.					

Table 3 (Continued)

	Strongly Agree	Agree	Neither	Disagree	Stongly Disagree
24. The hours of the program were convenient.					
25. The discussions helped to increase my learning.					
26. I could have prepared better for this program.					
27. I learned a lot.					
28. The speakers had an understanding of the presented content.					
29. I came to realize that I need to know more about this subject.					
30. The speaker(s) covered the stated objectives.					
31. I believe that I participated to my optimum in this program.					
32. I feel more confident in my ability to use the information presented in this program.					
33. Speaker(s)' mannerisms bothered me.					
34. This program was of practical use to me.					

35. What was the *One* major strength of this program?

36. What was the *One* major weakness of this program?

37. What do you want for future programs?

38. Were the room and facilities adequate?

[a]This instrument is used by the university of Texas System School of Nursing Continuing Education Program.

lished and an intervention plan, including criteria for success and a time line for achieving goals, is outlined.

Critique

Teaching and training are basic tools in the consultant's repertoire and provide an economical method for bringing specialized expertise to agencies. Information gained in lectures and workshops often enables consultees to solve work-related problems. Moreover, information acquired through training activities frequently stimulates staff members to seek further educational opportunities. Seminars and workshops are also ideal means for agencies to get acquainted with consultants. Through these short-term, low-risk activities, consultants and consultees can discover whether they want to continue their relationship. Often, a workshop or seminar is the first step in a long-term relationship between consultant and agency. Professionals who wish to begin to consult will find that this model is an ideal way to begin. It offers opportunities for them to acquire entry and contracting skills and to increase their understanding of organizational processes and problems.

The major disadvantages of this model are its limitations, which, if ignored, interfere with its usefulness. To be successful, an educational or training intervention must be based on an accurate assessment of needs and followed by supportive mechanisms. Unfortunately, training activities are often presented in prepackaged form without the benefit of an assessment. They may be based on a superficial assessment that ignores deep-rooted and complex organizational phenomena. The cognitive assumptions underlying this model are often valid. Consultees can and do acquire certain types of knowledge and skills through educational methods. They may be able to apply these learnings in their work. But internalization and application of new information and skills involve complex processes. Usually application of new competencies requires changes in organizational structures, incentives, and processes and in individuals' attitudes and habits. Trainees, although motivated and knowledgeable, may lack the power to make necessary changes. Attitudinal or emotional barriers may prevent trainees from learning or applying new skills. Consultants can help agencies use this model more effectively by pointing out the need for it to be connected to a careful assessment of needs and supported through organizational structures.

Consultant Preparation

Most professionals acquire considerable skill in leading educational and training activities early in their careers. They can increase their expertise in this model through experiences as members of training and educational programs led by other consultants, by working as apprentices or coleaders with more experienced consultants, and by studying videotapes of their own performance and that of others. They can add to their knowledge and skills by reading some of the excellent publications on this topic.

Annotated Bibliography

Benne, K. D., Bradford, L. P., Gibb, J. R., and Lippitt, R. O. (Eds.). *The Laboratory Method of Changing and Learning.* Palo Alto, Calif.: Science and Behavior Books, 1975. This book provides an overview of current laboratory concepts and methods. Chapters such as Leland Bradford's "Creating a Learning Environment" and "Designing for Participative Learning and Changing" by Ronald Lippitt are helpful in expanding a consultant-trainer's abilities to plan and implement successful workshops.

Gagné, R. M., and Briggs, L. J. *Principles of Instructional Design.* New York: Holt, Rinehart and Winston, 1974. This book, a basic text of instructional theory and technology, lays out the parameters of this field. It is packed with information that trainers will find valuable in designing effective programs.

Goldstein, I. L. "Training in Work Organizations." *Annual Review of Psychology,* 1980, *31,* 229-272. This publication is a comprehensive review of issues related to training in work settings, including those related to needs assessment, evaluation, and instructional strategies. The author critiques the developments in this field and identifies the major problem areas.

Jones, J. E., and Pfeiffer, J. W. *Annual Handbook for Group Facilitators.* San Diego, Calif.: University Associates. Yearly publications include sections on structured experiences, instrumentation, lecturettes, theory and practice, and resources. These practical handbooks are valuable resources for planning and conducting workshops.

Pfeiffer, J. W., Heslin, R., and Jones, J. E. *Instrumentation in Human Relations Training.* (2nd ed.) San Diego, Calif.: University Associates, 1976. This book describes a wide range of instruments that are useful for training groups. Positive and negative features are discussed, and the costs and sources where they can be ordered are listed. Trainers will find the listings helpful in locating instruments for diagnostic and evaluative purposes.

Training and Development Journal. Published monthly by the American Society for Training and Development, this journal features pragmatic "how to do it" articles by trainers and organizational consultants.

6

Clinical
Approaches

Human services agencies sometimes need an expert diagnosis of a client's mental or emotional condition and an authoritative recommendation as to how staff should treat the client. They may need a referral to an outside specialist. The clinical model of consultation responds to this type of problem. The early exemplar was the highly skilled nineteenth-century physician, a high-status expert among experts who was called in by other physicians for consultation on particularly difficult cases. The specialty of psychiatry adopted the clinical model of its parent profession along with the white coat and black bag (Brosin, 1968). Later, the newer mental health professions, including social work and psychology, patterned their practices after psychiatry and adopted its mode when consulting with colleagues about their clients' problems. Today, health professionals take this model outside traditional clinical settings to consult with staff of other human services agencies. To illustrate, a clinical psychologist in private practice responds to a call from the head of a juvenile probation department to examine a puzzling probationer. The consultant confers with staff, observes and tests the youngster, and studies all available case records. Her analysis reveals a negative self-concept, poorly developed social skills, and above-average intellectual abilities. In a report to the probation office, she describes her diagnosis in lay terms and outlines corrective procedures, including referrals to a personal counselor, a social-skills group, and vocational testing and advising.

Schools, nursing homes, and many other types of human services agencies ask clinicians for similar services. Increasingly, mental health professionals are asked to provide clinical consultation to courts (Howard, 1971; Kaslow, 1979; Pollack, 1968). For instance, a judge may want an expert opinion—either in courtroom testimony or in a written report—on whether a person is mentally competent to stand trial or to be a witness. A judge may need a recommendation about the living arrangements that would be in the best interests of children who are the object of a custody battle. A request may be for an assessment of the mental state of persons before and during accidents, including judgments about the presence of drugs, alcohol, or fatigue and the effects of personality traits.

Some clinicians follow this model in consultation with organizations (Halliday, 1948; Jacques, 1951; Levinson, 1968, 1972). Their consultees are administrators or supervisors. The "patient" is a program, team, or entire organization. These consultants may screen prospective employees with tests and interviews or assess the potential of middle-level managers for high-level positions. They may analyze personnel policies and recommend changes. They may perform global diagnoses. For example, the director of a senior citizens' center calls on a clinical psychologist for help in figuring out why staff attrition is high and client use of services is decreasing. After discussions with all staff members, the consultant diagnoses the core problems as a serious personal crisis in the director's life, which prevents him from focusing on his job, and a well-concealed but destructive conflict between two staff members. The consultant recommends that one of these two persons be dismissed. He also contracts to treat the director in brief therapy to help him work through the crisis.

Although the clinical model is indigenous to the medical profession and is frequently used in health-related consultation, professionals from fields other than health care often use this model of consultation. A teacher in a school for the retarded asks an educational consultant, a specialist in learning problems, to examine a puzzling case. The consultant observes the student's current performance in the classroom, gathers background data from school records, and examines the student's responses to a battery of tests. She eventually writes a report on her diagnosis of the learning disorder, including recommendations to the teacher for its remediation. The director of a legal assistance center asks a management consultant to diagnose what appears to be a staff morale problem. The consultant administers a survey to all units, assessing job satisfaction and organizational climate. He analyzes the responses and presents the director with a summary of employee attitudes and recommendations for improving morale. The director of a low-cost housing complex hires an ecological engineer to analyze present space utilization and recommend a plan for improved use.

Concepts

The clinical model conceives problems in terms of patients' diseases or dysfunctions. The patient may be a client of the agency, the organization itself, or some part of it. The primary goals are to diagnose and ameliorate the problem. The criteria for success are remediation of symptoms and restoration of normal functioning. The consultant's strategies include diagnosis, treatment, and prescription. In addition to expert power, the consultant often possesses and uses legitimate or—less frequently—referent power. Since an accurate diagnosis is crucial to success, the consultant's specialized technical expertise is essential both for the collection of valid data and for an authoritative interpretation. Hence the diagnosis is assumed to lie outside the consultee's range of competencies. Because of these assumptions, the consultee takes a passive role. The consultant assumes responsibility for the case and determines the data to be gathered and how to gather them. The consultant directly examines the patient, focusing on such variables as history, present functioning, and environmental interaction. The consultant

may treat the client directly or prescribe treatment for the consultee to administer. In some cases, consultants may observe
that the consultee is exacerbating the client's problems and may
use their influence (through legitimate, expert, or referent power)
to change or treat the consultee.

Generally, the goals are limited to the case. The consultant does not seek to educate the consultee or change the consultee's behavior in relation to other cases. Often it is assumed
that the diagnosis is too technical for the consultee to understand. The client's problem may be judged to be an unusual one
that the consultee is not likely to encounter in the future, so
that he or she has little reason to acquire an in-depth understanding of it. In many cases, opportunities for education of the
consultee are limited, since most of the consultant's time is
spent in observing and gathering data on the client. Contact
with consultees may be limited to a telephone call, a brief interview, and a written report.

As Chapter Two noted, the relationship between clinical
consultants and their consultees varies according to the latter's
professional status. When clinical consultants and their consultees
belong to the same profession, the relationship is likely to be
collegial. The consultative process is interactive, and the consultant shares much of the diagnostic data and processes. For
example, a consultation between a clinical psychologist (the
consultee) and a neurological psychologist (the consultant) regarding the former's patient would likely be collegial. Because
consultees from different professional backgrounds are unable
to understand the technical aspects of difficult cases, the consultant is more likely to take a directive rather than a collegial
role. This type of relationship is exemplified in the consultation
between a classroom teacher and the school district's neurolo-
gist concerning a student's eye-hand-coordination problems.

Method

Client as Patient. Many human services agencies—such as
probation offices, childcare centers, halfway houses, schools,
and nursing homes—have standing contracts with mental health

professionals for clinical case consultation. Staff members may then contact their consultant directly or through intermediaries, such as secretaries or program officers. In each referred case, the consultant checks to determine that the contract is appropriate and that there is a clear agreement with the consultee about the nature of the contract and their different responsibilities. The method involves the collection of data, a diagnosis and recommendations for treatment, and a report to the consultee. Often it includes a follow-up conference.

Assessment of clients usually begins with the consultee's report of symptoms and an examination of any records related to the case. The consultant then examines and assesses the client's functioning through such methods as psychological and educational tests, interviews, and behavioral observations. Interviews and tests may take place in the consultant's office. However, interviews with the client in the consultee's office yield valuable information about the setting and the consultee/client relationship. They may increase rapport and communication between consultant and consultee. On the basis of the available data, the consultant determines the nature of the client's problem, whether a referral for more extensive diagnostic work is needed, and the potential of the consultee and the agency to either ameliorate or exacerbate the client's problems. The consultant then prescribes a treatment plan, which may call for a referral to a specialist and/or procedures for the consultee to follow. Sometimes the consultant assumes responsibility for treatment.

The report to the consultee includes the diagnosis and recommendations. The purpose of the recommendation is to help agency staff members understand the practical implications of the client's problems and to mobilize their helping capacities. Ideally the report is presented in written form as well as in a conference. The written report provides a tangible guide to which the consultee can refer from time to time and is a valuable addition to the case folder. The conference allows the consultee to clarify any unanswered questions. The interview and the report should also make it easier for consultees to make future referrals by increasing their understanding of the usefulness and limitations of the consultant and by reducing any barriers to communication. In both written and oral communication, the consultant should avoid professional jargon and abstruse concepts, restricting the content to concise, diagnostic information that is relevant and useful to the consultee. Recommendations should be oriented to the capacities of the consultee, the agency, and community resources. If the consultant is available for further assistance, the report should make this availability clear.

Ideally, the consultant and consultee have later opportunities to discuss the client's progress. Often a follow-up conference is held to evaluate the effectiveness of the treatment and to provide new data with which to formulate a more precise diagnosis and treatment plan.

Agency as Patient. Agency staff members sometimes turn to clinical consultants for assistance with organizational ills. The approach of these consultants differs from that of most organizational consultants (described in Chapter Nine) in its adherence to the healing traditions that emphasize disease, the salience of the clinician's expertise, and the corresponding dependency of the staff. Narratives of consultation with organizations by clinically trained professionals provide rich illustrations of this model (Levinson, 1968, 1972, 1978; Caplan, 1970). Levinson (1978) describes the helpless feelings that lead administrators to call on a "doctor." His first question is "Where do you hurt?" He points out that the pain may not be where the problem is, but the consultant's first step in diagnosis is to identify, label, and conceptualize the consultee's pain. He views the consultant as a therapeutic and stable external anchor who helps consultees and/or the system reorient and stabilize. Caplan (1970) describes the clinical interviews and observations with which a clinician first captures a "birds-eye view" of the system. In a process similar to the analyst's unfocused attention to the patient's free-floating associations, the consultant avoids premature closure and allows a long period of "confusion." He then relies on his unconscious to integrate conflicting data into a Gestalt closure.

The organizational "patient" may be more complex than one of its clients, but the method of diagnosis is similar to that in case-centered clinical consultation. Again, the assessment is twofold: What are the nature and extent of the problem? Does the agency staff have the capacities to solve the problem, or will it need interventions by specialists? The consultant enters the organization, studies its problems, assesses the significance of relevant factors, and presents a report containing the appraisal of the situation and recommendations for action.

Data collection typically includes formal and informal interviews with individuals and groups; on-the-job observations of the organization's culture and structure; observations of service delivery, management, and communications; and surveys. Some consultants prefer to rely completely on clinical observations and in-depth interviews. Levinson (1972), for instance, follows a comprehensive case-study outline that includes genetic data (organization type, size, history), a description of the organization as a whole, process data, interpretative data, and analyses and conclusions, including summary and recommendations. Other clinical consultants prefer to use one or more standard surveys such as those described in Chapter Fourteen. Data gathering and interpretation culminate in a report—usually presented both in writing and in a face-to-face conference with the administrator-consultee(s) who asked for the consultation. Just as in case-centered consultation, the consultant does not communicate in terms of psychiatric syndromes but in terms of behaviors that are dysfunctional to agency work.

In some instances agencies require clinical consultants to perform tasks that involve coercive power. For instance, they may be asked to certify legally that certain behavior is abnormal for the purpose of agency control. A psychiatrist, for example, is asked to diagnose a rebellious and disruptive teenager who, to his teacher, appears to be so emotionally disturbed that he is unable to benefit from normal classroom activities. Consultants may use coercive power not only in regard to the consultee's clients but in regard to agency staff as well. An administrator may ask a clinical consultant to examine a staff member to ascertain whether that person's behavior is "sick" enough to warrant reassignment or firing. Some of these requests, reflecting societal expectations that mental health professionals will relieve communities, agencies, and families of onerous burdens, pose complex dilemmas for clinical consultants, who ponder over their right to use their professional expertise for judgments that have significant moral, social, or political implications.

Illustrations

The case studies in the following pages illustrate the methods of clinical consultation.

A Classic Case. Grotjahn (1968) describes and illustrates the traditional clinical approach to consultation. He illustrates its disease orientation and the consultant's authoritative role in formulating the diagnosis and prescription. In this case, however, since consultant and consultee were both physicians, the relationship was collegial; Grotjahn shared technical aspects of the diagnosis with the attending physician.

Grotjahn, a psychiatrist, consults with internists about their patients' psychiatric problems, such as alcoholism, sexual dysfunction, depression, suicide threats, and juvenile delinquency. The purpose of these consultations is to bring a psychiatrist's perspective to help the family physician successfully treat patients. The consultations begin with a brief conference between the psychiatrist and the internist. Next, consultant and consultee meet with the patient and the patient's family. After the internist makes a short introduction, Grotjahn leads the interview, drawing the family into discussions that eventually reveal the underlying pathology. After each interview, the consultant gives a brief report to the attending physician. At the end of the series of interviews, he writes a summary of his impressions of patient and family dynamics and presents his recommendations.

In one consultation, the consultee explained that he thought a patient's obesity had psychiatric implications. The consultant, in describing the preliminary interview, reported, "Before the family entered, the doctor quickly related a warning: still living with the patient and her parents was the grandmother, who would not be present because the entire family said that they would not talk freely in the grandmother's presence. There is a deep secret about the grandmother which must not be mentioned: nobody knows the patient's mother was adopted by the grandmother many years ago. I felt somewhat handicapped in the spontaneity of my interviewing through this information, obsessively thinking: Don't mention the mother is an adopted child" (p. 183). The patient and her sister, women in their middle twenties, each weighed about 350 pounds. The interaction among the sisters, their mother, and their father soon led Grotjahn to diagnose them as an intensively hostile family in which overeating and overfeeding symbolized a cannibalistic act in which "everyone devoured everyone else" (p. 184). The hostility originated in the grandmother's desire to come between the mother and the granddaughters. When the sisters were babies, the grandmother had stuffed them with food and unconsciously hoped the mother would give them to her. The severity of the hostility was revealed in a dream. "During the consultation, one daughter told of her dreams where she, with her tremendous weight, brought down an airplane and her entire family was destroyed. Everybody in the family intuitively understood this dream when it was told: overfeeding and overeating can stand in the service of hostility" (p. 184).

Working through these dynamics might have effected a cure. However, the family had a firm pattern of denying their feelings and resisted interpretation of the hostility. This consultation concluded with Grotjahn's recommendation that the two sisters be removed from the family residence.

Case-Centered Clinical Consultation with Agency Impact. Even in a very brief consultation, clinical consultants can sometimes mobilize agency resources. The following case illustrates the impact of a few hours of clinical consultation in marshaling resources to benefit a client (Caplan, 1970). The crucial factors in the consultant's effectiveness were (1) his thorough knowledge of the agency and the community resources, (2) the staff's respect for his opinions, and (3) his ability to establish rapport with the client. Thus, the consultant's expert power was augmented by his legitimate and referent power.

A psychiatrist was asked to consult with a pediatrician who worked in the well-baby clinic of a large Northern city. The consultation involved a "head-banging" baby who appeared to be neglected by his mother, a black woman who had recently moved north from a Southern state and who was suspected of being mentally deficient. In interviewing the client, the consultant quickly gained her trust. She soon revealed a situationally induced depression and hitherto undisclosed events that had caused it. Her husband had lost his job. When insensitive and rigid welfare workers insisted that she take him to court for nonsupport, he ran away to avoid being jailed. The staff in the well-baby clinic had ignored the role these situational variables played in creating and exacerbating her problems. Consequently, she felt helpless, lonely, and isolated in the strange city.

The consultant briefly interviewed the pediatrician-consultee and the agency's public health nurses. He noted the consultee's cursory attitude toward the woman and his poor rapport with her. He found that the nurses were convinced low intelligence was the cause of the woman's neglect of her baby. The nurses also revealed some conflicts between them and the welfare workers over certain policies. In short, the consultant quickly discovered a cluster of agency difficulties affecting the client—communication blocks, conflicts between nurses and welfare workers, and stereotyped attitudes toward Southern blacks.

In his report the consultant stressed the client's normal intelligence and the situational factors involved in her depression and the neglect of her child. The consultant made a number of direct recommendations to the agency staff concerning ways it could assist the client and alleviate her distressing circumstances. For instance, he recommended that the husband be contacted, helped to find employment, and provided with legal aid to untangle the problems related to the nonsupport suit. He cited a number of community resources that could be mobilized, including an employment agency, a family guidance clinic, and a free legal aid center.

The consultant thus used his clinical expertise, referent power, and the authority inherent in the clinical model to build bridges between the professional resources, between them and the client and her family, and between the client and her husband. This case demonstrates that under certain conditions, clinical consultation can be a remarkably potent—yet economical—means of ameliorating agency patterns that prevent clients from receiving needed services.

Organization as Client. The following case illustrates the application of the clinical model to organizations (Levinson, 1968). In this particular case the client was a research laboratory, the smallest of several laboratories of an old manufacturing company. The director of the laboratory requested consultation to assist the staff in a self-study that was a part of the company's long-range planning. The laboratory director hoped that consultation would alleviate conflicts within the laboratory and increase cooperation among all the research staff members. "He saw the laboratory's long-range problems as the setting of comprehensive goals, decentralizing authority, and recruiting an imaginative new staff" (p. 170). The laboratory staff included ninety-three scientist-professionals, thirty semiprofessional assistants, and twenty clerks.

In the diagnostic stage, over a two-week period, the psychiatrist and a psychologist interviewed about half the people who worked in the plant. They discovered that morale was low because most of the leadership had been transferred in from other laboratories rather than being promoted from within. A major conflict within the organization came from a split in values. An older group preferred technical research, while the younger group preferred innovative and basic scientific research. The younger researchers were dissatisfied because much of their work concerned product and market research that they considered relatively unimportant. A former director had encouraged some of the younger scientists to become more innovative but had done nothing to protect them from the rigidities of their older supervisors. Thus, he intensified an internal conflict, and the innovative efforts were expensive failures. The consultants found other problems. Equipment was inadequate. Salaries were not competitive. Consequently, recruiting new staff was difficult. Some work had to be farmed out to other laboratories. Another problem came from communication failures. Although the director clearly was in charge of the laboratory and his office was necessarily the center of all communication, administrative work prevented his listening to his staff.

The consultants' diagnosis typifies the pathological orientation of the clinical model. "The members of the laboratory seemed to be heavily dependent men who had an intense, chronic preoccupation with their internal relationships and their organizational self-image, while simultaneously denying important aspects of reality. They tended to ignore their own traditions and history, to reduce their intake of information from the outside, and to expect magical results from consultants" (p. 173). The climate of the laboratory ranged from hostility to depression. Staff members felt angry and yet guilty over feeling angry. Their anger, hostility, and depression appeared in the interviews with the consultants. During the interviews, the scientists often referred to their laboratory as "schizophrenic." The consultants concluded that "the psychological conditions of the laboratory could be characterized as the organizational equivalent of a person who was suffering from a chronic depression" (p. 174).

The consultants recommended procedures for providing staff with needed support, for sharpening the organization's identity, and for strengthening the bond between staff and organizational goals: (1) The laboratory director should assume greater leadership responsibilities. (2) The director should establish and develop the nurturant functions of the organization. For example, he could expand the medical benefits to include comprehensive examination and preventive care for the staff. (3) The laboratory work should be reorganized to be consistent with the goals of the innovative subgroup—basic research. The staff should be encouraged to continue their academic work and to obtain more advanced degrees. (4) The laboratory's history, including its contributions, should be written and disseminated to the staff. The rationale was that such a history would help staff identify with the achievements of the laboratory and see their work more clearly in its historical context. (5) The director should continue to use a consultant and to have the consultant meet with some of the research groups and the management councils.

The manner in which these recommendations were presented illustrates the clinical consultant's authoritative stance and the active-passive relationship described by Szasz and Hollender (1956). The consultants prepared the recommendations and read them to the laboratory director. The director was invited to raise any questions about the report and was asked to study it overnight. The next day he discussed it with the consultants. They did not permit him to change the substance. However, they solicited his advice on how to word and present the report and his opinion of its probable impact on organizational politics. After this discussion, the consultants also permitted the director an opportunity to discuss his own feelings about the report. Subsequently, the report was presented to department heads and to the staff of the laboratory. The consultants invited comments and discussion by all. Later, the vice-president of the corporation visited the laboratory and expressed agreement with the consultants' recommendations. The vice-president gave the director support in the proposal for advanced training. His encouragement and support strengthened the director's position.

Consultation was successful. A few months after the recommendations were disseminated, the laboratory staff in general seemed less hostile and anxious. They were more open in discussing angry feelings. The director seemed more confident of his leadership competencies and of the direction in which he was leading. He was less disturbed by the emotional reactions of his staff. An impressive historical display was established. The executive council worked more effectively and devoted considerably more time to deliberations. The director appointed three assistants to assume responsibility for tasks that unnecessarily burdened him. A new research unit was established that became the pride of the entire laboratory staff.

Critique

The clinical consultation model is a basic part of the repertoire of most mental health professionals. It provides an essential tool for helping consultees in many fields—education, health, religion, and criminal justice—cope with their clients' needs. Probably this model is most useful (1) when the consultant is considerably more skilled than the consultee in both collection and analysis of data relevant to a particular problem

(Argyris, 1970) or (2) when a crisis exists that calls for an immediate, expert judgment—for example, when a minister needs a quick assessment of the suicidal probability of a troubled parishioner or when a judge needs expert information to make a decision about a child custody battle. In addition, clinical consultation provides a convenient, low-risk entry point for mental health professionals to begin to work with an agency or with an individual staff member. McWhirter (1968), for instance, recommends that consultants use the case-focused or client-focused model of consultation for initial contacts with clergy, since it involves less risk for the consultee. At the same time, this model offers an opportunity for consultees to become acquainted with the consultant and with the usefulness of behavioral science in solving their work problems.

    For a variety of reasons, however, the clinical approach may not achieve the desired goal of problem resolution. The assumption that the consultee will have the motivation and skill to use the consultant's advice is often ill founded. Consultees may lack the knowledge or skills to carry out the recommendations effectively. They may have the needed competencies but lack confidence to implement the consultant's advice. Consultees may reject recommendations because they react negatively to the authoritative stance of the consultant. Consultees may disagree with the diagnosis or recommendations and therefore ignore them. The consultant's knowledge of the agency's scope and the client's milieu may be inadequate for constructing appropriate recommendations. The recommendations may be antithetical to agency policies. The agency may lack the resources to carry them out. The source of the problem may lie in the client's life beyond the influence of the consultee. The diagnosis and recommendations may also fail to bring about needed changes because the consultee is emotionally overinvolved in the case and, as a result, has lost professional objectivity. The consultee may not want, for some reason, to solve the presenting problem. A consultee may want to be advised to give up on it or to transfer it to someone else. Another limitation of the clinical model is its restricted focus. The narrowly focused diagnostic set of the clinician is likely to lock problem-solving efforts into costly, nonproductive interventions. The common assumption that the locus of the problem is in the patient may not be valid—whether the patient is the organization or an individual client. The "patient" may not be diseased; the source of the difficulty may instead lie in the consultee or in the environment. The problem may stem from a discrepancy between the client's needs and available resources. In addition, there are two economic disadvantages to the clinical approach. First, the one-to-one method is costly. Second, the consultee's problem-solving skills do not expand; this model leaves the consultee no more knowledgeable than before the consultation. Dependency on the expert, a costly resource, continues.

Consultant Preparation

Client-centered clinical consultation requires no additional training for mental health professionals. However, their effectiveness is greatly enhanced if they have a background in organizational theories and are familiar with the milieu of the particular agency and clients with whom they are working. When the clinical consultant's focus shifts to *agency* problems, expertise in organizations is crucial. Knowledge from the fields of organizational theory, management, public administration, and social psychology is needed.

Annotated Bibliography

Caplan, G. *The Theory and Practice of Mental Health Consultation.* New York: Basic Books, 1970. Two chapters in this book are concerned with the clinical model of consultation, chap. 6, "Client-Centered Case Consultation," and chap. 10, "Program-Centered Administrative Consultation." The author clarifies theoretical underpinnings of this model and provides extensive, well-illustrated guidelines for their application.

Levinson, H. *Organizational Diagnosis.* Cambridge, Mass.: Harvard University Press, 1972. This volume describes a clinician's case-study approach to organizational diagnosis. Levinson offers detailed pragmatic advice and abundant illustrations that integrate open-systems theory with a clinical approach. Consultants will find Levinson's case-study outline particularly valuable.

Mendel, W. M., and Solomon, P. (Eds.). *The Psychiatric Consultation*. New York: Grune & Stratton, 1968. This collection of readings discusses principles of clinical and mental health models of consultation as applied to a wide range of individual and organizational clients.

7

Mental Health Approaches

Mental health consultation evolved as a reaction by clinicians to the limitations of the traditional model described in the preceding chapter. The goal of the mental health model is to expand consultees' knowledge and skill in preventing and remediating mental illness and in promoting mental health. Unlike clinical consultation, this is a collaborative approach in which consultant and consultee work together to identify problems and solutions. Like the clinical model, mental health consultation is case-centered. However, the problems presented by the consultee become leverage points for educational purposes. Mental health professionals consult with and educate agency staff—teachers, nurses, ministers, and police officers, for example—who can then capitalize on their new expertise and their strategic relationship to the public to prevent and ameliorate mental health problems.

A number of social and professional factors supplied the impetus for the development of this model. During the 1940s and 1950s, traditionally trained professionals began to move out of clinics into other types of agencies, such as schools and nursing homes, to diagnose referred clients. These clinicians found emotional problems so widespread that professional treatment of individuals was out of the question. The well-publicized outcomes of epidemiological research in the 1950s heightened public awareness of the discrepancies between needs and available services. Resources were not only scarce; they were costly. Low-income families, especially, could not obtain professional services because the fees were prohibitive. Moreover, investigations suggested that the traditional direct treatment of mental illness, psychotherapy, was often ineffective (Eysenck, 1952, 1961). The standard indirect service, the clinical model of consultation, seemed to have little impact on client welfare. At the same time, professionals became increasingly aware of the effect of social variables on mental illness and of the need to consider clients' context both in diagnosis and in treatment.

The mental health model of consultation was a response to many of these concerns and was eventually institutionalized by the federal government and by some professional groups. The Joint Commission on Mental Illness and Health (1961), created by Congress in 1955, called for mental health consultation to the caregivers of society. The Mental Health Centers Act (originally passed by Congress in 1963) identified mental health consultation as one of the essential services that the new community mental health centers must provide if they were to receive government funding. Leaders of the 1960s community mental health movement adopted mental health consultation as one of their basic strategies.

Today the staff from these centers—and from other caregiving institutions—consult with probation offices, police departments, schools, churches, welfare departments, and many other service agencies. Typically, the focus of these consultants is a "case," a client whom the consultee is unable to understand or help. To illustrate, a social worker consults with a juvenile probation officer about possible ways of modifying the harmful effects of a client's home environment. The consultant helps the consultee understand the family's pattern of interaction and its effects on the youngster. Together they locate community resources that could give the probationer counseling and educational and recreational services. Sometimes the focus of mental health consultation is on a program or on the organization or some aspect of it. In these consultations, the consultees are agency administrators.

Concepts

We can more easily understand mental health consultation by contrasting it to the traditional clinical, or medical, model described in the previous chapter. Caplan (1970), who most clearly articulated the theoretical principles of the mental health model, constructed a typology to clarify the differences between the two approaches. By crossing two axes, he identified four "mental health" consultation models. The axes are (1) *target*—the place in which change is sought (by implication, the target is the "problem") and (2) *focus*—the point of interaction at which consultant and consultee meet. From these two axes, four cells, or models, are created. *Client-centered case consultation,* the clinical model described in Chapter Six, focuses on cases; the goal is to diagnose the problem and recommend a solution. In *consultee-centered case consultation,* the focus is also on a case, but the primary goal is the increased competence of the consultee. Following this model, for example, the consultant might work with a nursing home director to increase her understanding of depression and of ways to ameliorate it. Thus, the consultant helps the consultee solve an immediate problem (the secondary goal) and similar ones in the future (the primary goal). *Program-centered administrative consultation* focuses on an agency program or project. The primary goal is to help the consultee with a particular program. The consultant might, for instance, assist in planning, implementation, and evaluation. In *consultee-centered administrative consultation,* the focus is also on a program or on some aspect of the organization. However, the primary goal is to help the administrator function more efficiently in future program development by increasing her or his expertise. Mental health consultation, as defined here, includes the two models from Caplan's typology that are primarily educative: consultee-centered case consultation and consultee-centered administrative consultation.

Mental health consultation formulates problems in terms

of consultee deficiencies—such as lack of knowledge, skill, or confidence—or personal overinvolvement in a particular case. For example, consultees may lack vital *information*; a probation officer does not understand the cause, symptoms, or effects of an adolescent's depression or vulnerability to peer pressures. Consultees may lack *skill*. A dormitory counselor may not know how to obtain information by interviewing or how to use incentives to improve the dormitory climate. The consultee may be overwhelmed with concrete and immediate details and may need help in conceptualizing and organizing an approach to the problem. Consultees often are competent but lack *confidence*. A unique feature of this model is the assumption that consultees' work problems often come from emotional involvement and consequent loss of objectivity. They are then unable to use their usual skills. Hence, additional information has little effect. Caplan pointed out some reasons that consultees become emotionally involved. They sometimes overidentify with a client, and consequently their perceptions both of the situation and of its implications for the client are distorted. Identification may lead to either systematically favoring or punishing the client and to anxious predictions of disaster. Transference also may occur. Consultees may project onto the client assumptions and expectations from their own experiences. A minister, for example, may have a negative transference with a member of his congregation. He may perceive that person to be worse off than he is. Consultee emotional overinvolvement and loss of objectivity are especially common in regard to sexual and aggressive behavior. In sixth- and seventh-grade teachers, for example, we sometimes find distortions because of their anxiety over their pupils' sudden assertiveness and sexualized manner.

Assumptions and Values. This model assumes that consultees have the capacity to solve most of their work problems and that consultants can help them increase their range of effectiveness. Moreover, the model assumes that consultees sometimes need emotional as well as cognitive support in order to solve problems (and that consultants can accurately assess these needs). In cases that create high levels of anxiety, affective support is especially valuable in helping the consultee realistically confront and assess the situation, gather data, decide on actions, and implement them. As a result of psychological support from the consultative relationship, the consultees' feelings about the client and about themselves change. They become less anxious and more willing to believe that the problem can be resolved with a scientific approach. They become more self-confident, more realistic, and more accepting of their strengths and limitations. At another level, the consultees begin to view the client more objectively and are less prone to emotionally laden biases or "themes." Stereotyping of the client and rigid expectancies of failure and catastrophe diminish. A most important assumption is that consultee attitudinal, cognitive, affective, and behavioral change achieved in management of one particular case will be generalized to future cases. Mental health consultation is conceptualized as a *pyramid approach* to mental illness, in which the mental health professionals (psychologists, psychiatrists, and social workers) at the apex of the pyramid provide indirect treatment to the mentally ill by consultation with the societal caregivers who have the greatest access to persons under stress. The model assumes that through consultation a relatively small number of professionals can extend their impact to the large base of society.

Crisis Concepts. A fundamental concept of mental health consultation is the strategic use of mental health resources in crisis situations, the stress points of life (Caplan, 1964; Klein and Lindemann, 1961; Lindemann, 1944; Parad, 1965). Intervention in crisis situations can both ameliorate an acute problem and prevent future ones from developing. There are two types of crisis. There are the normal developmental crises, such as entry into school, puberty, marriage, and retirement. And there are the unexpected crises, sudden and traumatic events such as accidents, death of a relative, or crippling illness. Either type of crisis leads to coping difficulties because the situation demands skills outside the person's usual repertoire. However, the theory holds that in times of crisis, when coping methods fail, people are most open to change. Crisis is, then, a pivotal point at which the potential for either growth or deterioration is heightened, and intervention at crisis points maximizes the possibilities of increasing the client's coping abilities. Mental health consultants, in adhering to this theory, determine an agency's readiness for change by assessing the degree to which it is experiencing crisis and thus is open to intervention. They give a high priority to the situations in which either the consultee or the client is facing a crisis. For example, a psychologist works with a consultee, a young minister, to help him with his first experience in consoling a family bereaved over the sudden death of a child. The consultant helps the minister help the *family* work through its grief and become more competent in coping with stress. But, more important, the intervention increases the *minister's* understanding and skills in regard to bereavement and family dynamics, so that his competence as a pastor increases. Consultation is also a means of preparing caregivers and their agencies to assist their clients in anticipating crisis situations and preparing to cope with them. For instance, a consultant might help first-grade teachers anticipate and prevent destructive parental behavior associated with children's entering school or help agency directors provide guidance to employees approaching retirement. Consultation with hospital staff can help staff members anticipate needs of patients and of their families and develop skills in reducing the harmful effects of crisis events.

Method

The criterion of success of this model is the degree to which consultation expands the consultee's capacities to diagnose and solve problems. Given the primary objective of increasing the consultee's effectiveness, the consultant seeks information about the source and nature of the work problem, the consultee's capacities for solving it, and the ways in which consultation might be useful. Therefore, the consultant is concerned simultaneously with a number of variables—the client (or work problem), the relationship between the consultee and the client, the consultee's coping abilities and difficulties, the organizational milieu, and the relationship between the consultant and the consultee. Throughout the consultation, the consultant continually scans these domains for information to formulate diagnoses of the work problem and of the consultee's difficulties in coping with this kind of problem. The diagnosis of the client is a collaborative activity. However, the consultant's diagnosis of the consultee's coping problems may be, at times, unilateral and covert. Consultants are likely to share assessments of the consultee's need for *cognitive* assistance. However, when an assessment concerns a consultee's *psychological* problems, the consultant may simply provide the services he or she believes are needed—for instance, encouragement or emotional support or reduction of distorted perceptions—without making the assessment explicit. Hence, the consultant may treat the consultee without explicating the diagnosis or the remedy. More recent versions of mental health consultation take for granted the egalitarian nature of the consultant/consultee relationship. They are likely to emphasize straightforward problem solving (Berlin, 1973) or a more outspoken, open discussion of perceptions and feelings (Signell and Scott, 1971).

The diagnosis of the consultee's needs—such as for expert information, concepts related to the problem, skills, or emotional support—guides the consultant's intervention. Consultants often begin with the assumption that the consultee's problem is lack of knowledge or skills and take a straightforward problem-solving approach unless signs of psychological difficulties appear. Then, depending on the consultee's needs, the consultant seeks to help by such means as increasing self-confidence or reducing distortions. To accomplish the goal of consultee growth, mental health consultants take a variety of roles, including model, teacher, resource, collaborator, and encourager.

This model assumes that consultees feel weak and threatened when they are unable to solve their problems and that they will not expose their difficulties and open themselves to new perspectives unless they feel safe. Consequently, the quality of the consultant/consultee *relationship* is considered critical. Establishing rapport and a relationship of trust is the consultant's first task. Because of the importance of the relationship to this model, this discussion will emphasize methods for establishing and maintaining a good working relationship.

The major strategy is to emphasize the *peer* nature of the

relationship. Consultant and consultee relate as experts from different fields, not as the expert to the inferior. The consultee is in charge of the decisions on the topic to be discussed and the direction of the discussion. The rationale is that only what makes sense to the consultee will be acceptable. The consultant has no authority over the consultee's interpretation and management of the problem. Although the consultant is likely to offer suggestions for gathering and interpreting data, the consultee makes the final decision about the diagnosis. Furthermore, although the consultant actively explores alternative actions with the consultee, the consultee retains responsibility for any intervention decisions. The assumption is that the consultant is a resource whom the consultee may or may not choose to use. The consultant's formulation of the problem, the solution, and the consultee's needs is considered subject to error because the consultant lacks certain vital information that only the consultee can provide. Therefore, the interdependent nature of the relationship is very real. The consultee depends on the consultant for cognitive guidance and, perhaps, for emotional support also. But the consultant depends on the consultee for information about environmental and role difficulties and about the presenting problem. Moreover, the assumption is that even if the consultant independently arrived at an accurate diagnosis and a sound recommendation, presenting these ideas from a unilateral perspective would endanger rapport. The consultee might feel intimidated and lose self-respect. Thus, mental health consultants stress the interdependent and coordinate nature of the relationship and their role as facilitator.

The consultant remains nonjudgmental, always respecting the consultee's opinions and management of the work situation. The consultant's confidence reinforces consultees' strengths and the peer nature of the relationship. What if a consultee behaves incompetently or destructively? The consultee's behavior is the responsibility of the agency administrator and, therefore, lies outside the consultant's domain. In an extreme case, a consultant might choose to violate relationship rules by discussing a consultee with his or her supervisor. However, this action involves a radical departure from basic principles of mental health

consultation and is usually taken only after first discussing concerns with the consultee in an effort to help her or him recognize the problem and seek assistance from the supervisor.

Getting an interactive, egalitarian dialogue started is
sometimes difficult. Consultees often expect to describe client
symptoms and then passively await the consultant's pronounce-
ment of the diagnosis and the recommended treatment. Consultants all too often find themselves in a complementary stance,
interrogating and prescribing in an expert mode, thus reinforcing consultees' passive role. Caplan's (1970) strategies for building relationships, although they reflect his traditional psychoanalytic training and his experiences as a prestigious consultant
working with lower-status consultees, apply to many consultative relationships. Caplan describes a selective, directed shaping
of the relationship, in which consultants sit *beside* their consultees and assert their presence by taking an active role. By
talking, interrupting, asking questions, and expressing their own
thoughts and attitudes, consultants reduce consultees' regression, transference, and dependency. The rationale is that when
consultants are silent, the consultee can only guess at their
thoughts and reactions, and thus fantasies are fostered. Moreover, the consultant can enrich the data by giving impressions of
the client and the situation throughout the interview. The consultant thus is supplying information and points of view as she
or he interacts. At the same time, the consultant welcomes and
listens attentively to the consultee's observations and opinions.
The consultant is careful to avoid putting consultees on the spot
by asking questions that might make them lose face if they do
not know the answer or if their answer reveals an obvious mis-
take. Consultants provide affective support by communicating
their own difficulties in understanding the case. The intent is to
let the consultee know that presenting problems are complex
and difficult for anyone to understand. The consultant's calm
view of the normality of the problem situation can strengthen
threatened consultees. When a consultee sees a vexing problem
as common or universal for persons working in similar settings,
some of the disabling pressures will be relieved and constructive
coping will be fostered. Rapport is maintained by keeping the

focus close to the consultee's phenomenological view. The consultant may threaten the consultee by abruptly shifting from the consultee's conceptualizations, especially when there is no explanation of the leap.

Thus, as consultation progresses, the consultee's thinking about the case gradually becomes richer and more complicated. Yet he or she feels supported by the consultant, who is also trying to make sense out of the confusing material. Consultation allows the consultee an opportunity to consider a work problem in greater depth and breadth, to consider alternative formulations of the difficulty, and to expand the range of potential interventions.

New consultants often misunderstand mental health consultation's deemphasis of the expert role. They fear that if they offer opinions, they are violating the guidelines of this model. To avoid giving their views, they often get locked into a questioning mode that destroys rapport and offers no help to the consultee. Yet knowledge-giving is as important as in the clinical model. The mental health consultant introduces expert information, points of view, experiences, or resources when they might be useful to the consultee. However, the way knowledge is given differs. Mental health consultants do not represent themselves as more authoritative than consultees in regard to the latter's particular problems. In addition, mental health consultants are skilled in helping processes and choose their content and timing to fit the consultee's needs.

What if consultees bring personal problems into consultation? The assumption is that if the consultant allows the consultee to expose personal problems, an inequity develops that might interfere with the peer status essential to mental health consultation. Therefore, the consultant keeps the focus on work-related problems, avoiding involvement in discussions of the consultee's personal life. If the consultee introduces personal problems, the consultant tactfully asks how these problems affect the work situation. If the consultee continues to focus on personal issues outside the job, the consultant may clarify the limits of the contract and perhaps suggest some community resources for personal counseling.

In the classical model, the mental health consultant relies on psychoanalytic theory. Today most mental health consultants approach problems without a predetermined theory or intervention technique. They take an open-ended approach to each case, introducing whatever concepts and methods appear relevant to the case and to the consultee's needs. They draw on a variety of theories—such as learning, personality, and social and developmental theories, psychopathology, group dynamics, and transactional analysis.

Theme Interference and Reduction

Concepts. One special type of emotional involvement that reduces consultee effectiveness is called "theme interference" and is based on concepts derived from Murray (1938). A theme reflects unsolved conflicts of the past, which even normal people displace onto present work situations. Themes result in decreased effectiveness in areas related to the conflict. Signs that a theme is interfering include (1) repetitive difficulty with a particular type of problem, (2) confusion, (3) anxious, emotional reactions, and (4) erratic and inappropriate responses. Since they are related to unsolved problems, themes represent failure and defeat and are negative in tone. Themes are syllogistic; the consultee sees an inevitable link between two elements. "A," the initial category, will lead to "B," the "inevitable" outcome —an expectation that can lead the consultee to panic and overreact. For example, a shy, retiring person (A) will be a social isolate (B). An artistic boy (A) is destined to become a homosexual (B). A child of divorced parents is doomed to be a maladjusted adult. The theory holds that the client's behavior arouses the anxiety of the consultee because he or she has unresolved conflicts in a similar domain. The consultee then becomes defensive; perceptions become more and more biased; constructive coping stops.

Indirect Methods of Theme Reduction. There are two ways—both indirect—of reducing a theme that is interfering with a consultee's work. *Unlinking* is one method of reduction. In unlinking, the consultee breaks the syllogism by taking the client out of the initial category, deciding that this is not a "true" case of A. The shy person is not really shy. The artistic boy is not really so artistic. As a result, the "inevitable" outcome, B, is no longer inevitable. The consultee's anxiety subsides and coping returns.

Unlinking helps free the consultee to work more effectively with one client but does not help with subsequent clients. The preferred way to relieve theme interference is to confirm the initial category and then *invalidate the inevitable outcome* by demonstrating authentic cases of A in which B does not occur. The consultant helps the consultee see that other outcomes are possible, even likely, thereby reducing her or his anxiety and restoring the usual coping. The assumption underlying this method is that through successful work with this case and with several similar cases the consultee's theme will be weakened. According to this position, the consultee must not become aware of the "theme" that is creating undue emotional involvement in the case. If the consultant connects the case to the consultee's personal conflict, anxiety and defensiveness will increase. Therefore, the consultant maintains the consultee's unconscious displacement. Caplan (1970) suggests several indirect techniques for theme reduction:

1. *Verbal focus on the client.* Using this approach, the consultant helps the consultee examine evidence, including the data that confirm the initial category and any disconfirming data.

2. *The parable.* The second method is to use a parable, a case far removed from the present situation. The consultant tells the consultee, through anecdotes, about experiences with authentic cases of A that led to satisfactory outcomes, not to B, the inevitable and dreaded outcome.

3. *Nonverbal focus on the case.* Using this method, consultants model a different view from that held by the consultee. Consultants demonstrate through their relaxed and confident manner that, though aware that a client fits into the initial category A, they are not anxious and clearly do not fear the future.

4. *Nonverbal focus on the consultation relationship.* The consultant demonstrates respect for the consultee and deference to the consultee's opinions and busy schedule. The consultant

communicates confidence in the consultee's ability to manage the problem case.

Working with Groups

Much mental health consultation takes place in groups composed of individuals who work together and share common client concerns (Altrocchi, Spielberger, and Eisdorfer, 1965; Beisser and Green, 1972). As in individual consultation, the goal is to increase the consultees' capacities to prevent and ameliorate mental health problems. Sometimes a consultant joins a group of consultees on a one-time basis to discuss a particular case, but often a consultant meets with a consultee group on a continuing basis over a period of months or years to discuss both specific cases and general issues. A council of ministers might, for instance, want to discuss ways of maintaining their own mental health, group counseling techniques, or stages of grief. To get such a group started, consultants may first present several informal lectures, such as discussions of client characteristics or methods by which consultees can screen their clients for "red flags," indicators of mental illness. The spotlight is on the consultant; when group members become comfortable talking about their work problems, the consultant assumes a lower profile and members take increased responsibility for the direction of discussion. They may also take turns presenting current cases. The consultation follows the collaborative style described earlier, with the consultees and consultant working interactively to understand work-related problems and to identify ways of solving them.

These groups, like others, go through phases and evolve norms that affect their productivity. Trust—of one another and of the consultant—is often an issue. Competitiveness and defensiveness sometimes develop and prevent productive work. Osterweil and Marom (n.d.) found a group of Israeli teachers so fearful of exposing their difficulties to colleagues that a case-study approach had to be abandoned. At the other extreme, these groups may get into personal problems or complaints about the organization. Therefore, ground rules are usually established to exclude discussions of personal and organizational problems. Any personal problems introduced by consultees can be reformulated in terms of the work situation, just as in individual consultation. Personal feelings about work with clients are, of course, appropriate topics for consultation, whether with individuals or groups. Organizational conditions affecting consultees' work may be germane and might be included in discussions unless administrative policies or behaviors are involved. The consultant who is engaged to help consultees with their work with clients cannot ethically allow discussions to move to their problems with their bosses. However, with the group's permission, a consultant might convey the members' general concerns to an administrator. But rather than being an intermediary, a consultant might serve the agency better by encouraging consultees to take these issues directly to their administrators. At any rate, changes in focus should never be made without explicit renegotiation with all group members and their administrator.

Case-centered group consultation offers certain advantages over individual consultation. It can be more economical, because a consultant can help an entire group in the same time that one consultee would be using. Group discussions can reduce feelings of isolation, anxiety, and inadequacy and lead to increased communication and cooperation outside the group meeting (Spielberger, 1967). Groups can also be much more effective than an individual consultee in counteracting any of the consultant's blind spots. Consultees also typically learn a great deal from one another through sharing their perspectives of problems and their methods for solving them. Where consultees share responsibility for a pool of clients, group consultation is especially helpful in diagnosing problems and in establishing systematic procedures for their solution. Usually, the client who is viewed as impossible by several consultees is no problem at all to one consultee. Thus, consultees' understanding of their individual differences and their impact on clients grows. Group members usually quickly learn to ask each other salient questions but, at the same time, provide support when needed. Consultees can take turns as coconsultants, reversing roles and increasing their learning through taking responsibility for the consultant's function (Caplan, 1977).

Consultants who work with groups of consultees need special skills in group processes. Although most mental health consultation groups do not include contracts to *discuss* group processes, unless the consultant-leader is highly skilled in anticipating, identifying, and managing these processes, they can block productive discussions. For example, some groups resist involvement in discussions that go beyond superficial levels. Some groups splinter into conflicted subgroups. Some react negatively to leadership. Positive norms can usually be established by leaders who are experienced in group leadership and in interpreting the subtle nuances of group behavior. To illustrate, in the last moments of an initial group conference and within a discussion of the need for self-awareness, one consultee turned to another and said, "Your beard probably scares a lot of children" (Davis and Sandoval, 1978, p. 375). The consultant, who was (besides the person addressed) the only bearded person in the group, interpreted the statement as an expression of the group's feeling somewhat vulnerable and uncertain whether he (as consultant leader) could be trusted, a common phenomenon in a new group. Consultants might respond directly or indirectly to group processes—just as they might to themes. For example, in the situation just described, the consultant might simply use this information: He might seek to make himself appear safer by telling the group more about himself; he might be more careful to clarify group rules or slow down the members' self-exposure until group trust was better established. The consultant might communicate in the group's metaphor and say, "After the children get used to him, they probably will accept the beard." Or the consultant might respond directly, "It will probably take some time and interaction for you to get used to me and feel comfortable with me. Are there any questions you want to ask about me to help break the ice?"

Focus on Programs and Organizations

The discussions of consultation discussed thus far in this chapter have been limited to concerns about clients. Many consultants apply the mental health model to program and organizational problems. The goal is the same as in case consultation:

to increase consultees' problem-solving abilities. The concepts and methods described earlier (including the clinical perspectives, the use of the presenting problem as a means for increasing consultees' knowledge and skill, the building of a supportive relationship, theme interference, and the crisis, pyramid, and prevention concepts) are equally applicable to program and organizational consultation.

To shift to a program focus, consultants need to be experts in some aspect of the particular type of program with which the consultee is concerned. Agency staff typically do not have all the expertise needed to plan and implement successful programs. Experienced consultants can help them avoid pitfalls (Budson, 1979). For instance, they can alert staff to the need for collecting data about the target population's characteristics and needs, community attitudes and resources, and funding possibilities. Often an experienced consultant can, in the planning stage, help consultees develop realistic and effective evaluation designs.

To work with organizational problems, mental health consultants need, in addition to their clinical expertise, a thorough understanding of organizations. They can apply familiar mental health and illness concepts to organizations. For example, healthy organizations are realistic; they are able to search out, assess, and interpret the real properties of their organization and its environment. Healthy organizations evolve mechanisms for anticipating problems and for instituting systematic procedures to solve them. Members of healthy organizations have a strong sense of identity with the organization. The tasks of individuals and of units are clearly differentiated yet coordinated. The organization is sufficiently stable to provide continuity and support but flexible enough to adapt to change.

In human services agencies, dysfunctions can usually be predicted in several areas (Gallessich, 1972). Often staff lack a clear and mutual understanding of the agency's priorities. Typically communication blockages and hidden conflicts prevent diagnosis of problems. Consequently, decisions are often based on inadequate information and made without participation by those who must implement them. Inertia—simple resistance to change—often is the biggest problem.

As the consultant examines the organizational problems, she or he also examines the consultees' needs. How can their capacities to diagnose and solve problems be strengthened? For example, do they need knowledge? If so, what kind? Do they need skills, emotional support, greater objectivity? The consultant uses the organizational case as a vehicle for increasing the consultees' ability to manage problems.

Illustrations

Theme Reduction. Because of the importance of theme reduction in this model and because of its unique method, several cases will be used to illustrate theme-reduction techniques. Following is an illustration of theme reduction using the *orthodox method* of invalidating the consultee's syllogism.

Miss Martin, a career teacher approaching retirement age, had become a recluse; her activities had shrunk so that little was left except her teaching. She ignored the school's new consultant, a clinical psychologist, for several weeks. Her first interactions were at a social level. Later she initiated discussions of professional concerns of a general nature. Finally she sought his help with a fifth-grade pupil, Miranda. This child, in her words, was "bad" and came from a "bad" family. She was a show-off, a sexy tease who disturbed the rest of the class. The teacher referred to Miranda's mother as a "disreputable" woman, several times divorced and currently living with a man not her husband. The theme was "This child is sexy; sexiness will lead to a life of promiscuity—perhaps prostitution."

Over several interviews, the consultant helped Miss Martin focus on the case. Miranda was indeed a flirt and disruptive at times. However, she was not completely "bad." For example, in prolonged discussions the teacher recounted events that indicated that the child was energetic, bright, good in math and art. She also had been helpful in some work, such as cleaning up the room and clearing bulletin boards. Occasionally she had helped other pupils with math. Obviously the youngster was strong and healthy in some ways. Her potential was both good and bad. Another important piece of information came to light in these discussions: a cousin raised in the same environment as Miranda held a decent job and lived a respectable life. The consultant told Miss Martin some "parables," true anecdotes of cases in which youngsters who were sexually provocative and disruptive in their preteen years became law-abiding and productive citizens.

Over a period of time Miss Martin's perceptions of Miranda changed. The teacher saw that, despite the youngster's sexual aggressiveness, she had talents and could be socially helpful. Miss Martin realized she could help Miranda to become a more responsible and competent person than the child would otherwise. The situation changed from an unsolvable problem to a developmental one with a positive prognosis. Future work with Miss Martin indicated greater acceptance of the flirtatious behavior of other fifth-grade girls, newly aware of their sexuality.

In this method of theme reduction consultants do not explain their analyses and strategies to their consultees. The assumption is that to tell consultees that they—not the client—are the source of the "problem" might damage their mental health and diminish their effectiveness. However, some mental health consultants believe that it is more appropriate to deal with themes directly (Altrocchi, Spielberger, and Eisdorfer, 1965; Parker, 1961, 1962). These consultants assume that consultees, who are, after all, professionals, do not need the protection that patients do. Therefore, if a consultant thinks a consultee's feelings and attitudes may be interfering with a client's welfare, the consultant brings this perception into the discussion to check it out. The following case illustrates this approach.

A psychologist, Winn, consulted with a college dormitory counselor, Mark, who was very concerned over the adjustment of a freshman. Jim, who came from a small town, felt overloaded by the college's academic demands. He feared he would flunk out. His expressions of anxiety worried Mark, who confided to Winn that this was the most anxious youngster he had seen in five years of residence hall experience. This last bit of information led the consultant to ask Mark to check on the extent of Jim's problems. Winn suggested that Mark find out whether Jim's eating, sleeping, and work patterns and social interactions were normal. As an interim strategy that might help Jim or at least furnish further data, Mark also decided to encourage the student to structure his study time and break heavy assignments down into smaller, more manageable bits. Mark also planned to develop a relationship with Jim and to foster friendships between Jim and other students in the dorm.

In the next interview Mark offered some important new information. Although Jim made average scores on standardized tests, he had been a high academic achiever in high school. Furthermore, he had been extremely popular and had won sports, academic, and citizenship awards. Within the dormitory, his work and social patterns appeared normal. Winn and Mark began to speculate that Jim was grieving over the loss of a positive self-image as an outstanding, successful student. Mark also reported that Jim's parents were distraught because of phone calls in which he discussed fears of failure and reported problems with sleep and loss of weight. They had called Mark to ask for his help. At this point, it seemed important to know more about Jim's background, including any history of depression and resources for dealing with stress. Winn suggested that Mark ask Jim whether he had experienced similar episodes of immobilization and, if so, how he had coped with them. At the same time, they discussed the likelihood that, unless he improved, Jim should soon be referred to the counseling center for therapy.

The third week, Mark reported that Jim had confided that he indeed had suffered previous depressed periods but had always somehow been able to pull his resources together in time to prevent failure. Mark also noted that the boy seemed to like the opportunity to talk not just about confronting his problems but also about his feelings of depression and anxiety. The two were spending a lot of time together. However, at the same time, the parents were considering withdrawing Jim from school.

During this third interview Winn began to realize that Mark was inordinately involved in the case. Obviously Jim was getting a message from his adviser as well as his parents that he was the object of extreme concern. The underlying message seemed to be "You're fragile. You're not able to manage this stressful situation." The theme was "Heavy academic pressures will lead to a mental breakdown." Winn broached these perceptions to Mark, who quickly recognized his identification with

Jim's feelings of being overwhelmed and his fear of an impending "breakdown." Mark then "connected" Jim's situation with his own painful experiences as a freshman and with similar problems currently faced by a younger brother in a distant university. Mark decided to change his "message." He would try to communicate, "It's tough, of course, to make the transition from a small school to a university. The demands are considerably greater than you've had before. It's going to take a while to learn how to meet these new demands. You will have to settle for lower standards at times. But I'm confident you're going to make it." The counselor also planned to tell Jim about his own experience and about successful methods for coping with anxiety.

Two weeks later Mark happily reported that Jim seemed less tense. Soon his grades began to climb; he completed the year with satisfactory grades and was the center of social activities on his floor.

In the following case, a consultant *reinforced* a consultee's theme until a second consultant reformulated the problem. Wayne, a high school teacher, came to a consultant because he was very disturbed over one of his students, Peter, who had come to school with a black eye. When Wayne asked him how he got it, Peter became embarrassed and stuttered, "I, uh, I got it from playing football yesterday." The astute teacher persisted, "Hey, I know there's only one way to get a 'mouse' like that. Did your father hit you?" The youngster tearfully acknowledged that his father had indeed hit him the night before during an argument over the use of the family car.

The teacher was very upset and wanted the consultant to tell him what to do. He was afraid the boy might suffer serious physical and psychological damage. The consultant was very concerned, too, and suggested that they confer with the principal. They made an appointment for the next day. That night the consultant's colleague, another psychologist, called him to ask whether he knew Peter. This psychologist, Zack, was working with Peter's family and wondered whether some family "problems" had come into discussion at the school. The consultant told him they had and explained the situation. Zack then asked for permission to attend the meeting the next day. The consultant checked with the principal, who obtained permission from Peter's parents for the therapist to attend the conference.

At the meeting, the principal, the teacher, and the consultant expressed great concern about the youngster. Child abuse was foremost in their minds. The theme was "A child whose father hits him in this way will suffer permanent psychological damage." After listening to the discussion for a while, Zack, the family therapist, leaned back and began to talk in a relaxed way about other cases in which parents had hit their children: A mother had spanked her child harder than she had meant to; a father had slapped a son in anger. Zack also reminisced about the times he had been struck by his own father during heated arguments. Over a period of a half-hour, Zack changed the group's perceptions: The black eye, though unfortunate, resulted from a fit of temper that was within the range of normal behavior. The family was indeed a "good family." The incident of the black eye began to recede in importance. Eventually the principal, teacher, and consultant began to view it as one unusual, negative incident in a normal family. The new formulation became "This is a normal father, with a good batting average. In a fit of anger he struck his child in a degrading way. Yet he will probably continue to be a warm, decent, caring father the majority of the time, and Peter is likely to become a normal, healthy adult."

Organization and Program Consultation. In the following case, a community psychiatrist used the mental health model of consultation to help the staff of a radio station increase skills in organizational problem-solving (Bernstein and MacLennan, 1971). He also helped staff members design and implement on- and off-the-air programs to benefit the mental health of their communities. The consultant, a staff member of the Mental Health Study Center of the National Institute of Mental Health, initiated this consultation as a pilot project to explore the potential for improving community mental health through consultation with a public communications agency. The consultant's purpose, therefore, was to test out the "multiplier" concept—the pyramid principle described earlier—through which a professional brings mental health expertise to bear on a large population.

The psychiatrist began by writing to a number of radio station program directors to offer consultation in regard to programming, community services, and liaison with mental health specialists. He did not, at this point, offer staff-focused consultation, because he thought prospective consultees would find the suggestion of interventions in the interpersonal areas so threatening they would not respond. A progressive radio station whose general manager responded to the exploratory letter became the client agency. This station was community-oriented and had a reputation for its documentaries and its influence on legislators. It served a large metropolitan area with a listenership estimated to be as high as 60,000. In the initial meeting between the consultant and the agency administrator, the consultant explained his purpose of exploring (1) the ways a radio station could affect community mental health and bring about social change and (2) the ways a mental health specialist might aid the station in reaching these goals. He offered services for a number of areas, including organizational issues, staff relationships, mental health programming, and community service projects outside radio broadcasts. The manager expressed concerns about his own effectiveness and about staff relationships and his hope that consultation might increase both his own managerial competencies and those of his administrative staff. He was also interested in strengthening the station's educational and community-action programs. The consultee set as his general goal the increase in his leadership skills and the reduction of hostility between department heads. He set as an initial goal making the consultant available to his administrative staff—the heads of the news, AM programming, FM programming, community activities, sales, business management, and engineering departments. The two agreed that more specific goals would be evolved as the relationship developed.

During the initial phase of the contract, the consultant and the general manager met weekly. The consultant was introduced to the seven department heads as a management consultant. He met with them in their monthly meetings and conferred with each individually. He clarified the contractual provision that any issues discussed in consultation with individuals would be held confidential.

The consultant soon found a major staff problem. "There was a general feeling of anxiety, anger, and insecurity. This was partly due to the recent loss of a charismatic general manager who had been promoted to a position in a different city. The current general manager, who had been his program director, was himself involved in the feeling of loss. These feelings were also manifested as a division between several older, more established department heads and the newer, younger ones, who were in conflict over philosophical goals in broadcasting, program orientation, and the amount of community involvement of the station. The department heads were involved in a group-dynamic situation that did not allow them to have a primary identity with the goals of the station but forced them to deal with their own insecurity by building their departments into private empires, competing with other departments. The acting out of these feelings took the form of inefficient interdepartmental communication, resulting in such problems as advertisements being put on the air late and contracts being misplaced" (p. 724). Although the consultant apparently made this diagnosis unilaterally, he used the dynamics of this particular situation as an educational vehicle to help the general manager increase his understanding of staff interactions and his skill in future assessments of staff problems.

From this early phase, the consultant and consultee sharpened the goals of the consultation: to increase staff members' communications skills and to strengthen their identification with the agency as a whole rather than with their separate departments. At first, progress was slow because department heads seldom sought consultation. Apparently they feared loss of control over their own departments and their relationship to the general manager. However, over time, because of the consultant's availability, the usefulness of his expertise, and his discreet handling of confidential material, they gradually sought more and more consultation. Consultees at times brought problems with conflict and competition into discussions. The consultant tried to help them reduce distortions and become more objective. For instance, he suggested trying to understand the other side's perspectives and pointed out the ways people block communication when angry by selectively listening and tuning out. The department heads progressively became more trusting of the consultant and more aware of the relevance of his expertise to their problems. A major breakthrough came when "one of the older (and certainly more aggressive) department heads, who was at first quite unsympathetic to the need for consultation, suggested that in addition to the once-a-month department head meeting, a second, less structured meeting be added to help 'increase communication.' The acknowledgement of the need for such meetings by the department heads, the successful leadership of the meetings by the general manager, and the resulting cohesion of the group brought the consultant closer to the group and made them more able to ask for his advice regarding the work of their individual departments" (p. 725). The consultation expanded to other areas. For instance, the consultant helped news staff members understand the motivation of persons threatening violent acts. He also helped them locate professionals for interviews in documentary projects.

After six months, the consultation had achieved its major goals. The staff members had increased their understanding of their own organizational dynamics and of the destructive effects of competitive and hostile behavior. They learned ways to communicate more effectively and increased their identification with the agency as a whole. The following episode, four months after consultation began, demonstrates the increase in cohesiveness and commonality of goals. The department heads joined together to ask the general manager to redecorate the station. "When told by him that economic circumstances would make it necessary to put off the redecoration, they banded together to work out arrangements whereby they could reduce their own department budgets sufficiently to make the redecoration of the station feasible. This was seen, both by the consultant and the consultee, as a definite sign of staff unification and identification with the station as a whole. Although at times there were reversions to previous miscommunications and hostilities, these were of short duration and were easily dealt with" (pp. 725-726).

The consultant's services were expanded to programs—the territory that (because of staff rivalries) had been most jealously guarded. The consultant worked with the staff on programs addressing drug abuse, including broadcasts of a documentary series, publication of a resource book, establishment of a hotline, and work with other agencies to establish community houses for drug-related information services. The cooperation among the staff members in carrying out these projects was further evidence of their decreased hostility and increased organizational effectiveness.

Critique

In theory at least, the mental health approach makes more efficient use of expensive professional resources than the clinical model. The mental health model seeks to increase the capacities of agency staff members to prevent some mental illness from developing, to detect early signs of problems, and to make more appropriate referrals in serious cases. Staff members are in a more strategic position than mental health professionals to prevent mental illness. They have the obvious advantage of relatively frequent contact with members of the general public, many of whom, for one reason or another, are unlikely to come in direct contact with a psychiatrist or psychologist. Moreover, these caregivers are often more able than mental health professionals to formulate feasible interventions because of their extensive knowledge of their clients' circumstances and milieu.

From the mental health professional's perspective, this model is also appealing because it provides a means of coping with social systems as they are now—without waiting for them to change. It promotes changes from inside and acts as an internal "lubricant" to help agencies adjust to a turbulent environment (Beisser and Green, 1972, p. 6). Since this approach is based on traditional professional concepts of illness and on well-learned traditional practices, the professional can understand it and apply it to the huge caseload that human services agencies tend to accumulate.

However, mental health consultation is very time-consuming, at least in the initial stages. The relationships on which success depends often take a long time to build and maintain. Consultees accustomed to the clinical model often prefer to continue to turn to the expert for a diagnosis and recommendations. Moreover, working with consultees who are emotionally involved in cases without moving into a therapist role requires considerable skill. Consultants can easily fall into the more familiar role of therapist or adviser. Clinically trained professionals sometimes find it difficult to collaborate as peers with clinically unsophisticated agency staff members. However, consultees today are usually less intimidated by professional status than thirty years ago. Professional elitism is not so prevalent as at the time mental health consultation was conceived. Moreover, the status gap between consultants and consultees is often negligible. Many mental health consultants are not "doctors"; they are neither M.D.s nor Ph.D.s but master's-level practitioners. Their consultees are often well educated in their own fields and in mental health as well.

Critics have noted flaws in this model's conceptual foundations. The "spread of effect" by which a consultee generalizes learnings from one case to others has received little support in empirical investigations (Rogawski, 1979). Critics frequently attack the concepts of theme interference and reduction. Zusman (1972), for instance, although he believes that themes are easily identified and that consultees can recognize them with little help, questions the ability of the consultant to see the consultee often enough to reduce theme interference.

Perhaps a more serious problem is the inconsistency between the principle of the consultant as a peer and the *covert* analysis of the consultee's psyche. The assumption that the consultant can make an accurate assessment of consultees' needs without an open discussion seems to claim overmuch. To conceal and yet act on this assessment seems ethically questionable, since the consultee has not contracted with the consultant for such an analysis and intervention. These practices, which contradict the collegiality of this model, appear to be remnants of the traditional doctor/patient relationship. Several persons have attempted to free mental health consultation from this inconsistency. Signell and Scott (1971) expanded the concept of the coequal relationship. They recommend that consultants freely share their own feelings, attitudes, and experiences as they relate to the consultee's situation. Berlin (1973) described a revised mental health consultation model involving a systematic problem-solving method—a cognitive rather than a clinical approach. In their long-term work with groups of teachers, Osterweil and Marom (n.d.) encouraged expressions of theme-related emotions with the rationale that explicit emotions are more manageable than those that remain unexpressed. These consultants also strive to make explicit "initial categories" and "inevitable outcomes" and invite groups of consultees to suggest alternative outcomes.

Consultant Preparation

This model's core concepts—such as the emphasis on relationship building and on educational goals—can be acquired through readings and used by all consultants, including those from nonclinical backgrounds. However, supervised training is necessary to achieve a high level of competence in applying the model's complicated theories regarding professional power, consultee resistance, and theme interference. Supervision might be obtained through workshops offered by professional associations or through individual arrangements with practitioners or trainers.

Annotated Bibliography

Altrocchi, J. "Mental Health Consultation." In S. E. Golann and C. Eisdorfer (Eds.), *Handbook of Community Mental Health*. New York: Appleton-Century-Crofts, 1972. This chapter is exceptional in its clear and concise description of mental health consultation theory, the consultant's roles and functions, and the techniques for applying the model.

Beisser, A., and Green, R. *Mental Health Consultation and Education*. Palo Alto, Calif.: National Press Books, 1972. The authors aptly call this book a primer for mental health consultants. It is succinct; yet it covers major concepts and issues. Especially helpful are numerous exercises that suggest ways individuals or groups can integrate material presented in each chapter.

Caplan, G. *The Theory and Practice of Mental Health Consultation.* New York: Basic Books, 1970. This book is the bible of most mental health consultants. Caplan's delineation of the model's theoretical basis and his illustrations of its applications are comprehensive and rich in detail.

Grady, M. A., Gibson, M. J. S., and Trickett, E. J. (Eds.). *Mental Health Consultation Theory, Practice, and Research, 1973-1978: An Annotated Reference Guide.* Adelphi, Md.: Mental Health Study Center, National Institute of Mental Health, 1981. This book contains annotated references of mental health literature published between 1973 and 1978. The classification scheme organizes references by models, fields of practice, consultee settings, consultation processes, and research.

Rogawski, A. S. (Ed.). *New Directions for Mental Health Services: Mental Health Consultations in Community Settings,* no. 3. San Francisco: Jossey-Bass, 1979. The chapters in this volume describe contemporary versions of mental health consultation in various settings. The last three chapters examine funding and evaluation issues and recent trends in mental health consultation.

8

Behavioral
Approaches

Specialists in learning theory and techniques have created a consultation model that is based solely on the rapidly growing concepts and technology of this field. The model focuses primarily on behaviors. The goal is to eliminate or reduce the frequency of undesirable behaviors and replace them with more positive, appropriate ones. The method involves the systematic application of learning principles. The behavioral model blends traditions of the laboratory scientist with those of the medical profession. Behavioral consultants typically come from clinical backgrounds and often relate to consultees in the clinical traditions described in Chapter Six. Their technology, however, is derived directly from laboratory experiments. Diagnoses and interventions are empirically based. An experimental orientation pervades all interactions.

Behavioral consultation is most often case-centered. For instance, a consultation enabled a phobic first-grader to attend school full-time. The intervention method called for the child to be taken to school after hours and allowed to play. His parents changed their pattern of rewards and punishments to make staying home more aversive than attending school. Natural reinforcers, such as playing with friends and playing outdoors, were used as incentives for staying in school. Sometimes the goal of this model is to change group behavior. For example, consultants improve the academic and social behavior of entire classrooms through reinforcement schedules in which rewards are contingent on group behaviors. Behavioral strategies have been used to change behaviors of organizations and communities (Glenwick and Jason, 1980). Some large industries now use behavioral programs to increase productivity. One company found that a positive reinforcement schedule—including smiles, encouraging nods, and friendly visits over coffee—resulted in significant savings (Huse, 1975). Behavioral interventions have increased use of public transportation, thus conserving energy (Everett, Hayward, and Meyers, 1974). They have been used to decrease energy consumption in homes (Winett, 1980) and reduce littering (Geller, 1980).

Behavioral consultation is most frequently practiced in agencies that require high degrees of client control, such as educational and corrective institutions. Some organizations, such as large school systems and state schools for the retarded, include behavioral consultants on their staff. In other agencies, contractual arrangements provide behavioral consultants on an as-needed basis. Some consultants specialize in this model. Most consultants, whatever their background and theoretical preferences, find some of its concepts and techniques useful at times.

Concepts

Learning theory breaks with traditional conceptions of mental illness in its assumption that all behavior—normal as well as "abnormal"—is learned through external patterns of reinforcement. The basic principle is that behaviors that are rewarded are repeated and behaviors that are punished are inhibited (Thorndike, 1911). Behavior that is dysfunctional and undesirable, therefore, is not symptomatic of disease. It is simply the means by which a person has learned to cope with life events. Therefore, labels such as "psychopathic" and "hysterical" are irrelevant. Problems may be conceived in terms of unwanted behaviors—behaviors that are inappropriate, disruptive, or destructive. Or they may be formulated as a lack of desired behaviors; a nursing home resident does not leave his room, for instance. The assumption is that since these behaviors are learned and are shaped by external forces, they can be changed. But first, the precise relations between target behaviors and the salient environmental reinforcers must be determined and changed. "Reinforcers are the environmental consequences which strengthen or weaken behaviors. Reinforcers lie within the environment of the individual, and are embedded within his social nexus" (Tharp and Wetzel, 1969, p. 3). A reinforcer might be a new toy or a slap, a promotion or the loss of a job. Reinforcers are administered by the people in one's environment. "If the environment is the hospital, these people are the nurses, doctors, or other patients; if the environment is the school, they are the principal, teachers, or other pupils; if it is the family, they are siblings, the spouse, or the parents. These people control reinforcers, in that they may either administer them or withhold them. Depending upon the pattern of control, they may modify the behavior of the individual by strengthening it or weakening it" (Tharp and Wetzel, 1969, p. 3).

The behavioral consultant assumes that consultees—as members of the client's environment—are key sources of reinforcers. The consultant's task is to find the reinforcement contingencies that have the potential to alter the undesirable behaviors. To reach this goal, the consultant must formulate a situation-specific diagnosis and treatment plan (Keller, 1981). Target behaviors are defined in measurable terms, such as frequency of arriving at work on time or quantity of acceptable work produced. Interventions, too, are operationally defined, such as ignoring certain behaviors, frowning, smiling, or saying, "That's good." Carefully defined measures taken before and after interventions are an intrinsic part of the behavioral model.

To achieve the desired changes in a client, the consultant functions as an expert, diagnosing the contingencies related to a client's behavior and prescribing a treatment plan through which the consultee can modify that behavior. The consultant may also direct or monitor the consultee in carrying out the intervention. In some behavioral consultation the goal of changing the client is secondary to the goal of increasing the consultee's skills. The consultant may then use the educative methods described in Chapter Five. Or, like the mental health consultant, the behaviorist may take the role of facilitator and use presented cases as a means for increasing the consultee's expertise. Some behavioral consultants use behavioral techniques to treat or shape the consultee's behavior (Bergan, 1977).

Typically, behavioral consultants rely on learning theory. They emphasize contemporary, observable, public phenomena and deemphasize internal processes and historical events or experiences. However, many behaviorists expand their repertoire to include other theories that, like learning theory, are derived from laboratory studies and call for measures of target behaviors but also involve internal processes. For example, they use cognitive theories that emphasize the importance of private cognitions as mediators of behavior as the basis for certain interventions—such as visual imagery and cognitive restructuring methods and such techniques as "self-talk" (Mahoney and Thoresen, 1974; Meichenbaum, 1975). Social learning theory, which differs from learning theory in its emphasis on the importance of social variables as reinforcements and which draws on concepts from theories of modeling and interpersonal attraction, is frequently combined with learning theory in interventions (Bandura, 1977). Some behaviorists also apply ecological theories in their diagnoses and interventions (Winett, 1980).

Method

Case-focused behavioral consultation generally begins with a consultee's request that a consultant observe the behavior of a client or a group of clients. Typically such requests involve behavior that is regarded as flagrantly antisocial or self-destructive. The consultation often begins with an interview in which the consultant seeks to obtain a precise definition of the problem behavior and the desired behavior. Often the consultant must help a consultee give up evaluative labels and descriptions of internal states, such as poor attitudes, laziness, and stubbornness, before he or she is able to define the problem in terms of behavior. The consultant's interventions go through several well-established steps (Bergan, 1977; Bergan and Tombari, 1976; Tharp and Wetzel, 1969):

1. First, the problem is defined in behavioral terms; thus, the problem consists of public and measurable events. For instance, a probation officer might define a probationer's problem as absences from scheduled conferences. An attendant in a state school might define a client's problem as appearing in the wards and classrooms without shirt or pants.

2. Provisions are made for observing and recording behaviors to obtain an objective record of the frequency of target behaviors. Behavioral measures establish baseline frequencies essential for detecting any changes associated with modifications in reinforcement schedules. The observations may be taken by the consultant, the consultee, or anyone who can accurately observe and record behaviors.

3. The consultant analyzes the behavior, its antecedents, and its consequences and selects reinforcement contingencies that appear likely to change the behavior. The consultant reviews the available agents and selects one who can maintain the needed reinforcements. Ordinarily, the consultee is the primary reinforcement agent.

4. The consultant then designs a program for changing the behavior. This program calls for the establishment and maintenance of systematic contingencies between the target behaviors and reinforcers. Typically, the consultee implements the program under the consultant's guidance or supervision and the two evaluate the results, using pre- and posttreatment measures. They then reevaluate the program and, according to the outcome data, make decisions about continuing with the program or redesigning it.

5. The consultation usually concludes with a systematic withdrawal of the consultant's involvement and the consultee's assumption of full responsibility for the client's behavior.

Depending on the contract, the consultant may take the role of adviser, analyst, program designer, teacher, supervisor, or evaluator or some combination of these roles. In most situations, the behavioral consultant takes a rather directive role because a high level of expertise is needed for an accurate behavioral analysis and for designing a successful program and because a high degree of control is needed to implement such programs. To effect changes in consultees' behavior, consultants may use such techniques as modeling, positive reinforcement, stimulus-control techniques, and role play (Russell, 1978). In modeling, the consultant describes and then demonstrates the behaviors that will bring about desired changes in the client. Positive reinforcement techniques include verbal and nonverbal expressions of encouragement and praise. Stimulus-control methods involve placing artificial cues or reminders into the consultee's environment to elicit new behavors. If cues are consistently offered and if consultees consistently respond to them, the likelihood that consultees will perform the new behaviors without assistance is increased. Eventually cues are no longer needed. In using role-play techniques, the consultant guides the consultee in discriminating significant antecedent events and performing the new behaviors. Bergan and Tombari (1976) describe ways consultants may control interviews with consultees through elicitors (messages that request action or information) and emitters (messages that give information).

Organization-focused behavioral consultation is growing in popularity. Administrators of both private- and public-sector organizations contract with behavioral specialists to diagnose and solve organizational problems. The procedures are similar to those outlined earlier for interventions with individuals. The following steps are recommended for industrial organizations but are applicable to human services agencies as well (Huse, 1975).

1. *Needs assessment and baseline data.* The first step is to conduct a performance inventory to find the areas in which change is most needed. In many organizations, quantitative data on performance are difficult to obtain. But quantified measures are essential to obtain baseline information for making decisions such as where to intervene and for comparison against posttreatment performance. The data can come from the employee's own observations and records. A neutral presentation of data, such as through a computer printout, reduces staff members' resistance to examining and discussing measures of their behaviors.

2. *Establishing performance goals.* From the performance inventory, standards and goals for each worker are developed and defined in measurable terms. Employees should be involved in setting their own goals.

3. *Tracking performance.* Workers are provided with their baseline data and with structures and guidance for recording their own performance in relation to established goals. Thus, each receives immediate self-guided feedback from his or her own records. This feedback constitutes a continuous reinforcement schedule that allows workers to determine immediately the degree to which they are or are not improving.

4. *Reinforcement.* Supervisors use supervisees' reports and any other records—such as attendance—as the basis for feedback. They may use social reinforcement (for example, recognition in staff meetings, praise and encouragement) as well. Other resources for reinforcement include raises, bonuses, and other financial incentives. Reinforcement is as immediate and specific as possible. At first it should be frequent, perhaps as often as twice weekly. Later, reinforcements are put on a random schedule with a readily decreased rate of frequency.

Illustrations

A Client-Centered Case. An example of client-centered behavioral consultation is described below (Meyers, Parsons, and Martin, 1979). The consultant used a reinforcement program to help an inexperienced teacher decrease a pupil's disruptive behavior. This case is particularly interesting in that the consultant subsequently shifted into a consultee-centered model, a shift that apparently changed the teacher's management of the entire class and resulted in a significant classwide decrease in disruptive behavior.

A third-grade teacher asked a psychologist to help her manage a classroom and identified two children, Donna and Frank, who appeared to be creating the most problems. Behavioral observations were made on both children, and Donna was selected for the first intervention. Her program included four conditions: (1) pretreatment, (2) treatment, (3) reversal—discontinuation of treatment—and (4) reinstatement of treatment.

Behavioral observations were made for each condition. In this case, disruptive behavior was defined as out-of-seat or talking (when these behaviors were contrary to classroom assignments). Observers took baseline measures of twelve periods of ten minutes each, indicating the presence of disruptive behavior by checkmarks on a time chart. In the baseline condition, disruptive behavior occurred 27 percent of the time.

The consultant then designed a treatment plan for Donna. Observers' notes helped him identify reinforcers. While recording baseline data, observers noted that when Donna received attention from the teacher, she often smiled and stopped behaving disruptively. The consultant instructed the teacher to reward Donna for nondisruptive behaviors. Positive reinforcement consisted of verbal interventions in which the teacher made comments conveying praise and encouragement. Nonverbal reinforcers by the teacher included making positive contact by such physical means as touching Donna or by smiling at her. The consultant also instructed the teacher to ignore disruptive behavior as much as possible. Should she find it necessary to react to it, she was told to use nonemotional discipline. Observations were made (ten periods of ten minutes each) during four days of treatment. The consultant conferred with the teacher during this period and gave her written notes describing both her successful implementations and her failures as well. The treatment led to a decline in disruptive behavior to 17 percent.

Next came a reversal condition in which the teacher was instructed to discontinue the treatment. The observations included ten periods during four days of reversal conditions. Disruptive behavior rose to 44 percent. The treatment was then reinstated, and twenty observations of ten-minute periods were made over eight days. After reinstatement of the reinforcement program, disruptive behavior decreased to 27 percent. However, further analyses indicated that the reversal condition had resulted in persistence of the disruptive behavior. Only after two days of reinstatement of the program did the disruptive behavior subside. A statistical analysis revealed a significant treatment effect ($p < .05$).

While Donna's program was being designed and implemented, observers monitored Frank's behavior. Throughout Donna's reinforcement program, Frank's behavior remained unchanged. Moreover, although the reinforcement program had modified Donna's behavior, the disruptive behavior of the rest of the class persisted. School officials were seriously concerned over the teacher's lack of control. An intervention with the entire classroom was needed.

The consultant found that observers had noted that the teacher seemed ambivalent about being an authority. He initiated a consultee-centered conference by reporting these observations to the teacher and asking for her reactions. The two discussed the role of the teacher. The consultant stressed that teachers are, of necessity, authority figures. Consultee-centered discussions, focused on the teacher's role conflict, extended over three conferences (held during the first two days of the reinstatement period of Donna's plan). Following this consultee-centered consultation, Frank's disruptive behavior decreased dramatically. Further, anecdotal evidence indicated that the disruptive behavior of the entire class declined. "This general decrease in disruptive behavior included less inappropriate talking, more in-seat behavior, and fewer fights. For the first time, the students would respond to the teacher's directions consistently" (Meyers, Parsons, and Martin, 1979, p. 141).

The consultant hypothesized that the consultee-centered consultation was responsible for the changes. The consultee-focused consultation helped the novice teacher conceptualize role-appropriate and inappropriate teacher behaviors. However, the client-focused behavioral consultation had given the teacher clear and easily implemented strategies for control of disruptive behavior. Consequently, she was able to connect the behavioral treatment to the role requirements of her position. The consultant's flexibility and openness to new data were key factors in the success of this intervention.

Organizational Intervention. Industrial organizations have found behavioral technology useful in increasing productivity. Often the intervention is aimed directly at actual performance behaviors. Because private-sector, profit-making organizations have greater control over reinforcements than do public-sector organizations, they can more easily implement behavioral programs. In the case described, an industrial organization was the setting for a behavioral intervention aimed at decreasing absenteeism of hourly employees (Pedalino and Gamboa, 1974). The technique, an intermittent reinforcement schedule using monetary rewards, could be used in human services agencies.

The client organization was a manufacturing and distributing industry composed of four relatively autonomous plants. The hierarchy of each plant consisted of the plant manager, superintendents, foremen, and employees. The employees, whose attendance was the object of the intervention, were unionized blue-collar workers. Each employee was allowed, in addition to certain holidays, six days of annual sick leave. The intervention took place in one plant, and the other plants were used for comparison purposes. The plant chosen had, before the intervention, a significantly lower absenteeism rate than the other three plants. It was selected because the plant manager asked for help in reducing absenteeism; thus the usual entry problems were minimized.

The procedure consisted of four phases:

1. *Baseline One.* The problem was identified and described in measurable terms.
2. *Phase Two.* The behavior modification program was implemented for six consecutive weeks.
3. *Phase Three.* A "fading" procedure reduced the program reinforcement to every other week for ten weeks.
4. *Baseline Two.* The program was discontinued.

In Baseline One, consultants studied the absenteeism records of all employees to obtain baseline information about attendance. Absenteeism rates were calculated on a weekly basis by ascertaining the proportion of absences in relation to the number of days when attendance was expected. Absences due to vacations, jury duty, bereavement periods, and paid holidays were excused. Baseline measures were obtained for thirty-two weeks for all four plants. The baseline absenteeism rate for the 215 employees of the target plant was 3.01 percent. The goal was set as 2.31 percent, a rate that could be achieved if employees were absent for no more than the six days that were authorized for sick leave.

For Phases Two and Three, in accordance with the principles of shaping behavior and stretching the reinforcement schedule, a lottery incentive system was devised that involved a poker-game strategy. Before implementation, the consultants discussed the plan with plant managers, who agreed that it would probably work. The plan increased in the following manner the incentive for workers to come to the plant each day: "Each day an employee comes to work and is on time, he is allowed to choose a card from a deck of playing cards. At the end of the five-day week, he will have five cards or a normal poker hand. The highest hand wins $20. There will be eight winners, one for approximately each department" (p. 635). The foreman gave each employee who arrived at work on time a card from a poker deck and recorded the card on a master game chart, posted to arouse interest. This program continued for six weeks. For the next ten weeks (Phase Three), in a "fading" procedure, the frequency of the lottery was decreased to biweekly. The purpose of the fading technique was to stretch the reinforcement interval, with the hope that attendance would be maintained while lowering the reinforcement contingencies.

After sixteen weeks the program was removed. Absenteeism of the experimental group was monitored for twenty-two more weeks (Baseline Two). Outcomes indicated that the program significantly reduced absenteeism. From the baseline rate (3.01 percent), absenteeism dropped below 2 percent for some weeks (below the goal of 2.31 percent). Overall, the sixteen weeks of intervention produced an average absenteeism rate of 2.46 percent, an 18.27 percent decrease in absenteeism—a significant reduction ($p < .05$). However, the twenty-two-week follow-up indicated that absenteeism rose once more to the original level (3.02 percent), evidence of the program's effectiveness. Further evidence came from an unplanned change in the schedule. Following the eighth week of the program, owing to unexpected circumstances, no incentive was offered for three weeks in a row. Absenteeism then jumped from 2.3 to 3.9 percent. The reinforcement interval had been stretched so far that it was no longer effective in maintaining attendance. A comparison of the weekly reinforcement schedule with the stretched schedule showed that attendance did not drop significantly when the interval was lengthened (the Phase Two rate was 2.38 percent and the Phase Three rate was 2.51 percent, a nonsignificant change). Over the sixteen-week period, the absenteeism rate at the comparison plants rose 13.79 percent.

This intervention demonstrated that an incentive system can significantly reduce absenteeism and that when the schedule of reinforcement is stretched from one- to two-week intervals, the improved rate does not deteriorate significantly. Moreover, since employees had to be on time to participate, tardiness was also decreased.

This case shows that a *specific* dysfunctional behavior can be altered through a carefully designed and implemented behavioral intervention. The capacity of the organization to control reinforcers and the attractiveness of those reinforcers to the employees were key factors in the plan's success. The relation between the target behavior and organizational productivity was not demonstrated. However, it could be assumed that improved attendance will increase productivity.

Institutional and Societal Constraints. Because behavioral consultation requires consistency in reinforcement patterns, it requires a high degree of consultee cooperation and control over contingencies. Large-scale interventions obviously require large-scale control. They often fail because of lack of flexibility and cooperation among reinforcement agents, a problem that is greater in public-sector agencies than in business and industry. Consultants involved in efforts to bring about systemic changes need to be alert to the organizational and societal factors that are likely to block their efforts. They need to acquire competencies in diagnosing and solving systemic barriers. The following case describes an agencywide intervention that succeeded despite institutional and societal constraints (Reppucci and Saunders, 1974). First, the intervention itself will be briefly described; then the barriers that threatened to undermine it will be discussed.

The consultants in this case were faculty members and graduate students from Yale University. The agency was the Connecticut Training School, a large state institution that trained male juvenile delinquents. The consultants were invited to intervene by a new superintendent who had been appointed to reform the institution after violent shooting had created a strong public reaction. The school had no treatment program. Brutality was widespread. Staff members were divided into warring camps, and morale was very low. The consultants discussed the problems and alternative interventions with the staff. "It was decided that the entire institution would be the focus of change efforts based on behavior modification techniques and an orientation to community involvement. Furthermore, it was decided that the program would be developed and implemented by the staff who were there at the time, and that the change effort would receive little special funding outside of the normal school budget. These decisions reflected the two primary goals of the consultation: (a) The consultation should bring about total institutional change; and (b) the method of change should have the potential for applicability to other institutions and, therefore, should not be based on specially recruited staff or an abundance of funds" (Reppucci and Saunders, 1974, p. 650). A number of organizational changes ensured that staff and residents participated in decision making. The entire staff was trained in behavioral techniques. The residential cottages converted to twenty-four-hour token economies in which points were used in order to purchase a variety of goods and privileges on the campus. The outcomes of the program in the boys' school were so successful that when the school was later merged with a girls' school, the behavioral techniques were adopted by the girls' cottages.

Four constraints that threatened the success of this intervention—and that are commonly encountered by behavioral consultants—will be described: (1) difficulties in communication of technical concepts, (2) limited resources, (3) lack of systemwide cooperation, and (4) negative community reactions.

The support of all staff members, including many who

are relatively untrained in behavioral science, is essential to a
successful intervention. Therefore "there is a need to develop a
common vocabulary for both the general guiding philosophy
and the more specific aspects of the program. This process is
usually begun at staff training sessions at which basic principles
and concepts are taught, for example, positive reinforcement,
immediacy, specific behavior, stimulus, response. At the conclusion of such training programs, most staff members know the
words, what they mean, and can use them in talking with each
other about a particular situation" (pp. 652-653). However, the
understanding of behavioral terminology may be superficial.
Consultants in the case described here found that implementation of the program was weakened because consultees lacked
full understanding of the concepts expressed in technical
terms.

Money, human resources, and time are usually quite limited in human services agencies. Resources may be inadequate to
implement or evaluate an intervention. "Since all of the operations normally performed by elaborate equipment or skilled research assistants in the laboratory must be left to indigenous
staff in most natural settings, the precise measurement of behavior necessary for optimal behavioral modification cannot be obtained" (p. 655). The intervention in the training school was
continually short on resources in every domain—from personnel to potato chips and underwear. For example, a sleeping alcove was needed for boys who wanted more privacy than was
available in the usual dormitory sleeping arrangement. No money or materials were available from the training school because
other needs were given higher priorities. Finally the local Jay-
cees volunteered to help. But because of changes in the officers
of the Jaycee group, it took more than a year and a half to complete the alcove.

Lack of cooperation from key staff is probably the most
frequent cause of failures in behavioral interventions, since such
interventions require systemwide consistency. In this case the
consultants noted that they needed to include all "available reinforcers on campus within the framework of a single exchange
system that would employ points as currency. One obviously

powerful reinforcer that we were eager to incorporate in the token economy point system was the work-for-pay program. The work-for-pay program paid youngsters 15 cents an hour for performing such jobs as washing dishes, serving food, gardening, sewing, cleaning, and delivering messages" (p. 651). The consultants wanted to change this cash-based system to a point system and to use reinforcers for the teaching of useful skills. Because of resistances within the organization, however, the work-for-pay program continued in its cash payment mode. One top administrator accepted the idea of the plan but found that it was impossible to change, since "any changes in the allocation of work-for-pay money would require approval by the state legislature—a task outside the realm of political possibility" (p. 651). The business office head, at the middle level of administration, was sympathetic with the goals, but he insisted that his office could not participate in the plan of exchanging points for money. At the lowest level, staff members who were supervisors in the work-for-pay program refused to teach skills, on the basis that teaching would interfere with their work, would impair their effectiveness, and might possibly be dangerous. Thus, constraints at all levels of the institution blocked changes in the work-for-pay program.

External forces often counteract agency interventions. Chapter Three described the contradictory demands that our pluralistic society places on human services agencies. Attempts to make changes to benefit one constituency typically mobilize powerful resistances from other constituencies. The intervention in the Connecticut Training School called for a reduction in constraints that, in turn, increased the number of runaways and provoked negative reactions from the community. Politicians, the police, schools, and the media pressured the school for tight restrictions on runaways. These pressures led to the use of maximum security units—a coercive response that decreased the effects of the treatment plan. The public's demand for custodial goals interfered with the intervention's rehabilitation goals.

The constraints described here are, of course, likely to be encountered in any consultative intervention. They are most formidable when a high degree of behavioral precision and consistency are needed, when systemwide changes are required, and when the intervention's underlying values antagonize the status quo.

Critique

Behavioral technology offers powerful tools for changing behavior. Behavioral approaches have been particularly successful in treatment of conduct disorders such as delinquency, sexual irregularities, and alcohol and drug abuse (Davison and Stuart, 1975). Moreover, behavioral consultation can be particularly valuable as an entry model in work with consultees who are in crisis because of uncontrolled, disruptive clients. Its focus on specific, measurable behaviors and on causal relations can have the effect of calming anxious consultees. The discovery that they have the power to control certain undesirable behaviors strengthens consultees' sense of adequacy and self-confidence. An important by-product of behavioral consultation is the effect of the consultant's modeling on consultees' skills in observation and in taking a scientific approach to problems. Moreover, although the targets of this model are typically narrow, success in making small changes often encourages consultees to continue to apply learning techniques or other methods to broader and more complex client behaviors. A major strength of the behavioral approach is its technological precision. In contrast to most consultative approaches, problems, interventions, and outcomes are always operationally defined. Therefore, the effectiveness of this type of consultation is much more easily evaluated than most, and valuable feedback is provided to decision makers.

A frequent criticism of this model is that its practitioners often ignore the difficulties involved in taking behavioral techniques out of the laboratory into natural settings. "Most of the academic literature in the field leaves one with the impression that implementation of an effective behavior modification program is a straightforward, trouble-free affair, and all one really requires for success is an understanding of learning theory and the techniques of behavioral analysis" (Reppucci and Saunders, 1974, p. 650). Yet, most organizations will not conform to the necessary procedures. Professionals applying behavioral approaches in natural settings face many practical problems absent in the laboratory situation, in which the professional has almost complete control over contingencies. In the laboratory, behavior modification involves a two-component relationship —the behavior modifier and the subject. In natural settings, the agency staff must carry out the behavior technology. These persons become the "natural" behavioral engineers. Some consultees do not understand the concepts involved and the need for a systematic reinforcement schedule. Some reject the idea of rewards because they view them as bribes. Many consultees reject the notion of determinism that underlies the behavioral approach (Heller and Monahan, 1977). Others contend that all clients should be treated alike and no special rewards should be offered. Some constraints come from red tape—institutional policies, procedures, and practices that can be overcome only by considerable effort from either the consultants or a high-level administrator. One of these constraints is the unwillingness of agencies to make exceptions in order to deal with problems with individual clients. Behavioral consultants may overlook these real-life barriers to interventions because of their heavy emphasis on technology (Heller and Monahan, 1977; Tharp and Wetzel, 1969). The ready availability of techniques to control behaviors tends to limit consultants' perspectives and prevents them from considering the whole environment (Fine, 1970).

Behavioral consultation is sometimes used for ethically questionable purposes. Consultants may help consultees exercise undue—even destructive—control over clients. Winett and Winkler (1972) noted that schools use behavior modification to exert unnecessary and ethically questionable control over pupils who get out of their seats, rattle papers, sing, cry, laugh, or simply do something different from what they are supposed to be doing. "Reducing disruptiveness can be important if classroom learning is to move forward. The disruptive child impedes his or her academic performance and has a similar effect on the progress of other class members. Still, when does reducing classroom disruption become fostering docility? The danger is greatest in those settings in which obedience and order are valued much more highly than learning and creativity. If there already exists a preoccupation with order and control, there is a high likelihood that behavior modification techniques will be abused" (Heller and Monahan, 1977, p. 241). An especially critical ethical problem arises in behavioral programs in institutions where the residents or clients are involuntarily held, such as prisons and closed wards of mental hospitals (Davison and Stuart, 1975; Stolz, Wienckowski, and Bracon, 1975). Behavioral consultants may also exercise inappropriate control over consultees' behavior, disregarding their need for autonomy. This tendency is, of course, not restricted to the behavioral model; however, behavioral consultants are especially prone to dominate the decision-making and case management processes. Behaviorists may use persuasion to get a consultee to behave in accordance with their values and views of what is appropriate (Heller and Monahan). Some use covert techniques to control consultees. For instance, Bergan (1977) apparently assumes the consultant has the responsibility for controlling consultees' behaviors and describes techniques for doing so. According to this view, the consultee's function is to provide specific information to the consultant and to implement the plan the consultant designs and directs.

Consultant Preparation

Most consultants, no matter what their background, can learn the fundamentals of the behavioral approach to consultation from self-guided reading. To achieve competence in systematic use of behavioral techniques, however, instruction and supervision are needed. Consultants who wish to acquire skills in this model may find people who can help them by contacting local mental health centers and psychology departments of universities. Numerous professional organizations also offer workshops on behavioral approaches.

Annotated Bibliography

Bergan, J. R. *Behavioral Consultation*. Columbus, Ohio: Charles E. Merrill, 1977. Bergan describes in detail his unique behavioral consultation model. He clearly states the model's principles and rationale and illustrates them with case studies and empirical data. This book is a useful reference for organizing behaviorally oriented training programs and for self-guided instruction as well.

Glenwick, D., and Jason, L. (Eds.). *Behavioral Community Psychology: Progress and Prospects*. New York: Praeger, 1980. Chapters review and critique recent advances in the use of behavioral interventions to solve problems at five levels: individual, group, organizational, community, and society. In the final chapter, the editors highlight the promise of behavioral technology for preventing problems and bringing about environmental changes. They also comment on some of the limits of this approach.

Keller, H. R. "Behavioral Consultation." In J. C. Conoley (Ed.), *Consultation in Schools: Theory, Research, Procedures*. New York: Academic Press, 1981. Although the focus of this article is behavioral consultation in schools, it is a useful reference for behavioral consultation in any setting because it synthesizes a broad body of literature. Keller presents a wide range of perspectives, analyzes the unique strengths of the behavioral model, and suggests directions for future research and development.

O'Brien, R. M., Dickinson, A. M., and Rosow, M. (Eds.). *Industrial Behavior Modification: A Learning Based Approach to Industrial-Organizational Problems*. New York: Pergamon Press, 1982. This book describes methods for applying behavioral analysis techniques to industrial settings. Case studies demonstrate methods for motivating workers, increasing productivity, managing stress, and evaluating performance.

Reppucci, N. D., and Saunders, J. T. "Social Psychology of Behavior Modification: Problems of Implementation in Natural Settings." *American Psychologist*, 1974, *29*, 649-660. The authors discuss common barriers to successful implementation of behavior modification techniques in natural settings such as prisons, mental hospitals, and public schools. They suggest ways consultants can mitigate these constraints.

Tharp, R. G., and Wetzel, R. J. *Behavior Modification in the Natural Environment.* New York: Academic Press, 1969. This much-quoted work describes a behavioral consultation model that the authors evolved from experiences in a research project. The conceptualization of the model, the methods by which it is applied in real-life situations, environmental constraints, and evaluation issues are fully and clearly described.

9

Organizational
Approaches

Much of the consultation to human services agencies is concerned with some aspect of the organization itself. The major focuses of the organizational consultant are the domains described in Chapter Three: the technical, structural, managerial, and human relations subsystems. Consultants might, for example, help the staff of an emergency clinic learn how to use new lifesaving equipment or reorganize their staffing patterns. A consultant might help the clinic director develop a more effective leadership style or resolve a conflict between two employees. The focus of the consultant might be on the physical domain—for instance, a specialist in use of space might help the staff relocate equipment so as to improve efficiency. The focus might be on the organization's environment and include an analysis of discrepancies between the clinic's resources and those needed by its changing community. Obviously, these organizational interventions vary greatly not only in their focuses but in their conceptual bases and methods. This chapter highlights major developments in the broad field of organizational consultation by briefly reviewing its major domains, concepts, and methods and illustrating them with case studies.

Two major themes appear throughout this chapter: Effective interventions are often systemwide and use a variety of methods.

Major Domains and Concepts

Organizational consultation began with the advent of machines, and the first organizational consultants conceptualized the new industries as work machines. Their focus was the *technological domain*. Their task was to find the work procedures and equipment with the most favorable input/output ratios. Taking the role of the scientist-technician, they used strategies such as time and motion studies and analyses of the properties of tools. Today business, industry, and military organizations continue to make extensive use of a wide array of technical consultants to improve the quality of their products or services, to make their operations more cost-effective, and to improve conditions for their workers. To a lesser extent, human services institutions also seek consultation concerning technological problems. For instance, computer specialists work with a welfare department on a system for storing information about clients and resources in order to build a data bank that will enhance caseworkers' effectiveness and efficiency. These same consultants help a staff of physicians design a computer program to strengthen their diagnostic capacities, thus increasing the benefits of their services while reducing their costs. Agencies' technological consultation needs vary with shifts in ideology, professional trends, and the availability of funds. For example, a hospital adds or takes away abortion services, depending on the dominant sentiment in the surrounding community. Treatment modalities in mental health centers change according to professionals' interests. Reductions in public funds for social services are currently shifting attention away from technological innovation and diversity and toward concerns for technological cost-effectiveness. Thus, human services administrators are becoming more like their private-sector counterparts in their concern with economy. They are seeking consultants' assistance in comparing the cost/benefit ratios of alternative technologies, a formidable task because of their "softness" (Miringoff, 1980).

Another early group of consultants also viewed organizations as machines, but their area of interest was the *structure* through which labor is divided and supervised. These consultants were concerned with such issues as lines of authority, spans of control, and the proper distributions of tasks. The assumption was that rational assignments of responsibility and authority would increase organizational productivity. Contemporary organizational consultants continue to help administrators establish rational lines of authority and work assignments. But because of the highly specialized nature of most contemporary human services technologies and the shifting demands from the environment, traditional bureaucratic structures seldom provide adequate information exchange and coordination of activities. Consultants are often called on to help agencies establish new structures—such as the matrix organizations described in Chapter Three—to provide the needed integration of highly specialized services and to provide the flexibility for rapid responses to environmental changes.

Since the discovery fifty years ago that productivity can be increased by satisfying workers' social and psychological needs, organizations have called on consultants for assistance in the *managerial and human relations* domains described in Chapter Three. For instance, consultants may help administrators reconcile organizational and human needs by expanding their understanding of motivation and of managerial theories. They may help administrators expand their leadership range and make more discriminating choices of which style to use in various situations. Through administering and interpreting surveys, consultants help administrators understand their organizations' cultures. Consultants help teams of workers examine their coalitions, schisms, and norms and make changes that increase productivity and morale. Often a consultant's major task is to help staff members confront and manage conflict constructively and find ways to keep stress to tolerable levels.

Few consultants focus exclusively on the external *environment,* although this domain is at least an implicit consideration in most interventions in organizations. The need for continuous environmental monitoring is especially urgent in today's turbulent conditions. Without mechanisms for sensing changes and trends, organizations can quickly become anachronistic (Roeber, 1973). As outsiders, consultants are often especially helpful in assessing environmental changes and their implications for agencies' services.

Some consultants specialize in the *physical environment* of the work organization—the setting (building, spatial arrangements, furniture, and lighting), its properties, and their effects on staff performance and client services. The famous Hawthorne studies experimented with the effects of physical variables on productivity, but the discovery of the importance of social variables blurred the importance of physical factors for years afterward. In fact, Hall (1966) named his book on the physical factors affecting human behavior *The Hidden Dimension* because of the tendency to ignore the impact of this domain. But the physical environment is a dynamic influence on the behavior of workers and clients (Holahan, 1977, 1978; Proshansky, Ittelson, and Rivlin, 1970; Sommer, 1969). Several distinct consultative approaches to this domain can be identified (Steele, 1973). Some consultants assist organizations in locating new plants and offices. They analyze such factors as the cost of living, availability of personnel, and congruence between the community and organizational values. A second type of specialist focuses on the efficiency of the plant or office layout in facilitating the flow of work. Another kind of environmental consultant specializes in more general space planning—offering economic analyses, interior design, and engineering assistance. A new specialty, organizational design, is emerging from the integration of the fields of behavioral science, architecture, and engineering.

An Effort to Unify Interventions:
Organization Development

In the late 1950s, organizational consultants began to realize they could be more effective if their efforts were directed to multiple domains. They sought to create a more unified and systemic approach to organizational problem solving through organization development (OD), a broad spectrum of human process and structural interventions that are, by definition, systemwide (Beckhard, 1969). The OD movement incorporated open-systems theory—with its emphasis on the interrelationship of all parts of the organization and its environment and the need for renewal mechanisms through which agency staff can regularly adapt to current and anticipated environmental changes and avoid the "dry rot" that tends to engulf organizations (Gardner, cited in Argyris, 1970). However, the centerpiece of the OD approach consists of the human relations and managerial concepts described earlier and the concepts, values, and techniques of the fields of group dynamics and action research. In its early days, the OD movement was characterized by a humanistic assumption, the belief that, through building a climate of trust, people's inherent "goodness" will emerge, thereby solving many problems. This assumption was later tempered by practitioners who recognized the inevitability of conflicts of interest and added conflict management concepts and techniques to their repertoire (Leavitt, 1965; Likert and Likert, 1976; Walton, 1965).

The number of OD practitioners in the United States has increased tremendously over the past twenty years and is estimated to be 5,000 (Burke, 1980). Publication of a number of books on organization development in the late 1960s stimulated the growth of this field. Especially influential were the early books in Addison-Wesley's OD series (particularly Schein's *Process Consultation,* 1969, which presents a clear and pragmatic description of major organizational processes and relevant interventions) and the publication of numerous survey instruments. Blake and Mouton (1964) added to the popularity of OD by packaging training programs and disseminating them throughout the world. However, the OD approach has not fulfilled its early promise to integrate or systematize interventions. In actuality, most OD consultants focus almost exclusively on interpersonal processes and administrative structures (Burke, 1980). The OD practitioner typically works in such areas as communications, decision making, leadership, team relations, and conflict. OD interventions are usually directed toward administrators or small work groups. Some, however, involve interdepartmental relations or an entire organization. The most frequently used methods are process observation and consultation, laboratory training, coaching and counseling, survey feedback, team building, and conflict management.

Like other forms of organizational consultation, OD is rooted in, and most frequently used in, private-sector organizations. Human services organizations are less open to acknowledging the interpersonal problems in which OD specializes (Goodstein, 1978). Moreover, in applying OD techniques to these institutions, most consultants find they must modify them because of the distinctive characteristics described in Chapter Three (Golembiewski, 1969; Rubin, Plovnik, and Fry, 1974).

Methods

The methods used by organizational consultants are as diverse as their focuses and concepts. The following pages briefly describe the most commonly used methods.

Laboratory Training. Laboratory training typically addresses problems in the human relations and managerial domains. Unlike the laboratory training described in Chapter Five, an organizationally focused laboratory not only offers opportunities for staff to learn concepts and skills; the consultant's contract is likely to include diagnosis and intervention in actual problems. Often a laboratory begins with training, shifts to diagnosis, and moves back to training in areas related to the diagnosis. Whereas the earliest laboratories were concerned with general problems in group dynamics, today they are often used to address specific interpersonal areas such as power and conflict (Oshry, 1976) and team building (Boss, 1979). Human relations laboratories are usually conducted in retreat settings—"cultural islands" away from work interruptions. Training strategies include those described in Chapter Five (simulations, lecturettes, and group discussions). As the laboratory moves toward diagnosis and intervention, the consultant's role shifts from teacher and trainer to such roles as facilitator, process analyst, conflict manager, and coach. Variations of a training model based on the T-group (training group) developed in 1947 in Bethel, Maine, by the National Training Laboratories are widely used (Bradford, Gibb, and Benne, 1964). The basic T-group is composed of ten to fifteen persons. Its objectives are to discover how groups function and how group processes and roles evolve and influence morale, learning, and productivity. The lack of structure and direction from the leader and the lack of defined roles produce tension that results in emotionally charged reactions, which, in turn, accentuate and exaggerate common group processes. Nonevaluative, descriptive feedback from leaders on these processes stimulates participants' learning. Generalization of laboratory learning is facilitated by individual and group consultation and by role playing of salient back-home problems, diagnosis of their basic sources and issues, and development of plans for solving them.

Process Consultation. Often laboratory training proves ineffectual in bringing about the enduring changes needed to solve the back-home problems. Many consultants prefer on-site process consultation, in which the consultant helps consultees "perceive, understand, and act upon process events" that occur in their work and affect their morale and productivity (Schein, 1969, p. 9). The assumption underlying this approach is that agency staff are often unaware of recurrent processes—as in supervision or decision making—that significantly affect outcomes. Through increased awareness of these patterns, it is assumed, staff members can change them and increase their effectiveness. The major processes of interest include patterns of communication, intergroup relations, individual roles and functions, decision making, leadership, supervision, and conflict. Most process consultants take a facilitative role with the goal of increasing their consultees' abilities to diagnose and intervene in processes. Some, however, prefer to take a directive role, especially in the early stages of an intervention.

Process consultation is often used to help committees or boards increase their effectiveness. Consultants typically begin by defining the term *process* and discussing the purposes of process consultation and their roles. Subsequently, during the meeting, the consultant may interrupt to point out certain processes—such as frequent interruptions or changes in subject—for the group to study and interpret. The consultant provides opportunities for consultees to take the lead in identifying their ongoing processes and to pinpoint the implications of these processes. For example, consultants may suggest stopping a meeting at regular intervals to discuss processes or adding a process discussion at the end of each meeting. Members may take turns observing ongoing meetings and providing their groups with data for self-study. The use of audiotapes and videotapes and of instruments that survey consultees' perceptions of processes and feelings about them are helpful. Staff members can easily learn how to make objective records of such processes as the duration of monologues, the length of time spent on various topics, and patterns through which members support or ignore one another.

A brief vignette of process consultation with a VISTA staff will illustrate this method. In this case the consultant helped the staff identify obstructive processes and the feelings and attitudes that precipitated them. Moreover, staff discussions revealed a "dominant coalition" that established and controlled group norms. Carlos, the director and a newcomer to the agency, led the meetings. The consultant's responsibility was to help the group identify and examine their processes. In the first meeting, communication was generally lively and productive; however, occasionally participation declined and energy appeared to ebb. When these subdued processes reappeared in the second meeting, the consultant pointed them out and asked the group whether they could find a relation between process and content. Two major issues quickly came to light in an energy-charged, emotional discussion of feelings related to two topics. One topic involved a decision about who would be assigned to a coveted new position. One individual, Rico, had asked for permission to take the assignment. Two persons had pleasantly agreed, but the remaining eight members remained silent. Focus on this process opened up angry charges that Rico was not committed to his work. Edwardo, an energetic, dedicated worker and a senior member of the group, led the challenge. He accused Rico of not fitting into the agency practice. He did not attend certain night meetings, for example, and had recently missed a weekend workshop. However, the focus shifted from Rico to a more general issue of commitment. The underlying question was how much deviance from the norms of the highly dedicated senior members of the group would be tolerated. (Eventually the group established rules setting forth the minimum acceptable level of participation.)

The second major issue surfaced in a discussion of staff resistance to an apparently innocuous decision made by Carlos, the director. In this case, the salient process was a challenge of Carlos's authority. The issue was his legitimacy as group leader. Carlos belonged to the same ethnic minority as the other staff members—but, unlike them, he came from a well-educated, affluent family. The senior staff members were acutely sensitive of the gap between their socioeconomic status and his. They were skeptical of his motives and commitment to VISTA and withheld their full support for many months until a crisis arose in which he demonstrated that he shared their values and their devotion to VISTA's mission.

Similar process methods are used to observe staff in their daily routines, interdepartmental coordination, community relationships, and recruitment and orientation of new staff.

Action Research and Survey Feedback. Consultants collect or help agency staff collect data to provide feedback to the system about its functioning and needed changes, a method that can be used in any domain. The feedback concept comes from the cybernetics field (Wiener, 1954). The assumption is that continuous and accurate feedback is essential to keep systems on their courses. Consultants conduct action research (Lewin, 1951) by collecting data to help consultees answer questions and guide problem solving. Closely related is the survey feedback method (Mann, 1957), through which consultants survey employee opinions on such topics as morale, organizational climate, and job satisfaction and report their findings back to the respondents to generate problem-identification and problem-solving discussions. Data may be collected for use in each stage of a consultation—to obtain a preliminary orientation at the entry stage, to formulate a diagnosis, to plan an intervention, to motivate staff to begin to take action, and to evaluate the intervention (Nadler, 1977).

Ideally, survey feedback methods involve close interaction

between consultant and consultees from the beginning. "Optimally, participants themselves define the kinds of data needed and plan for the data collection. Characteristically, the instruments deal with 'soft' data: employee satisfaction, concern about problems, perceived influence of self and superiors in decision making, perception of norms and goals, and the like. It is very desirable to get 'hard' data as well—that is, information on goal achievement, turnover, and cost—which let the members of the system see how well they are doing. Ordinarily, the data are fed back to an intact work 'family'—people who report to a common superior, and whose jobs are interlocked in a meaningful way. The group members and their superior then begin examining and interpreting the data, start problem-solving in relation to the diagnoses they make from the data, and begin to bring about changes in both their own relationships and the home organization. Characteristically, this process then trickles further down through the organization, so that the people who were subordinates in the first meeting then lead meetings with *their* subordinates around the same set of data, and the process continues" (McElvaney and Miles, 1971, pp. 115-116). Survey feedback is generally used in conjunction with other strategies led by internal and external consultants, including administrative coaching, process observation and feedback, theory sessions, and ad hoc task forces that discuss and analyze data and make recommendations.

Survey feedback is a powerful consultant tool when wisely used (Bowers, 1973; Halpin and Croft, 1963; Mann, 1951, 1957; Miles and Schmuck, 1971; Moos, 1973). However, consultants often use survey methods inappropriately (Nadler, 1977). Administrators and their staff are then understandably wary of their use. They often fear that the results will make them appear incompetent, that they may be irrelevant or difficult to interpret, and that the entire survey activities may only stir up problems or be an unproductive extravagance.

Focus on Goals and Objectives. Many consultants prefer to focus on goals not just as the starting point but as a continuing reference point and guide for all consultation activities. The best known of the goal-focused consultation methods is based on *management by objectives* (MBO), a management strategy originated by Drucker in 1954 in which supervisors agree on specific and measurable job objectives for the subordinate. MBO is essentially a method of controlling employees' behavior through highly specific and concrete organizational objectives.

Most MBO consultants prefer to begin at the top. The MBO consultant helps the executive:

1. Analyze the environment in which the organization operates.
2. Evaluate the organization's present operating capabilities.
3. Identify opportunities and problems, both short-term and long-term.
4. Design programs that take into account existing opportunities and problems.
5. Analyze program alternatives on the basis of their resource needs.
6. Select appropriate program alternatives with feasible, desirable, and timely objectives.

Next, the consultant or the administrator replicates these steps for each level of the organization. The result is a set of objectives that are concrete, measurable, and time-limited for each unit and each staff member. These objectives are divided into two types: (1) performance objectives, such as number of client interviews per week, and (2) personal development objectives, such as development of proficiency in new skills relevant to the job.

Among the strengths of this approach are (1) its strong production emphasis—task completion, not task activity, is the focus; (2) its rational allocation of authority and responsibility; and (3) its potential for improving the quality of planning and of increasing worker satisfaction through realistic, finishable, and concrete goals. However, staff often complain that MBO techniques take too much time and paperwork. Full implementation may take years. Moreover, it is not suitable for some human services settings because of their nonroutine and complex nature.

Team Development. Douglas McGregor, in a systematic

OD approach at Union Carbide, was among the first to use team-building techniques. He administered a team development rating scale to the management group to assess members' opinions about their work processes and about interpersonal variables such as trust and conflict. Consultees' responses to the scale were pooled, and the resulting profile of scores provided the diagnosis for a team intervention. The objective of team development is "the removal of immediate barriers to group effectiveness and the development of self-sufficiency in managing group processes and problems in the future" (Beer, 1976). The consultant's focus might include leadership, communications, roles, trust, and conflict. Methods for team development are central in the repertoire of most organizational consultants (Alderfer, 1977; French and Bell, 1978; Merry and Allerhand, 1977). They include education and training, survey feedback, conflict confrontation and resolution, analysis and intervention in members' roles and processes, and goal-setting activities. Team development methods are most effective when used as a bridge to integrate technological and social domains (Woodman and Sherwood, 1980).

Structural Revisions. Some consultants specialize in the analysis and revision of structures through which labor is divided, coordinated, and supervised. Consultants may help agencies revise structures to better meet human needs. The techniques include job enlargement (a horizontal rearrangement in which related tasks are combined into one job so as to give the worker a better sense of the whole) or job enrichment (a vertical rearrangement of duties in which employees are given greater responsibility and discretion over a larger portion of their work). Changes involving greatly expanded worker authority and responsibility have resulted in significant increases in productivity (Ford, 1969; Friedlander and Brown, 1974; Kahn, 1974; Katz and Kahn, 1978). Another promising approach to the distribution of work does not change the assignment of tasks but allows workers greater flexibility in work hours by expanding their discretion over the particular hours they report for duty. These "flexi-time" interventions report positive outcomes in terms of worker morale, job satisfaction, productivity, and lowered absentee rates (Golembiewski, Hilles, and Kagno, 1974). Consultants may help agencies develop integrative structures that increase efficiency by improving the coordination between diverse units and activities. The structures of human services organizations—unlike those of profit-making organizations—tend to be disjunctive. Their formal control structures are disconnected from their policies and technology (Kouzes and Mico, 1979; Weick, 1976). Consultants may help agencies confront the underlying tensions and find ways to alleviate them.

Illustrations

The following case studies highlight the wide-ranging focuses and methods of the organizational consultant. The first illustrates use of the classic laboratory training method to improve human relations. The second describes use of a survey feedback method to diagnose problems in the sociotechnical domain. The third and fourth cases reflect the growing sophistication of organizational consultation and the trend toward multimodal and multidimensional interventions.

A Classic Human Relations Laboratory. The president of El Centro, the first campus of the sprawling Dallas County Junior College District, requested consultants to lead a series of four human relations laboratories with the goal of increasing both organizational and individual effectiveness (Koile and Gallessich, 1971). Like most interventions of this type, this one was more successful at identifying problems than at solving them, and it created new problems. It was more facilitative of individual than organizational growth.

The president invited all staff and faculty members to attend on a voluntary basis, stating that laboratory participation would provide opportunities for them to (1) learn how their behavior affected others and how others' behavior affected them, (2) gain some understanding of how individual behavior influences group functioning, and (3) learn more about the effect of group processes on goal achievement. The laboratories were held in a retreat setting. Each was three days long and included morning, afternoon, and evening meetings. A thirteen-member core group, including the college president and deans, constituted the initial laboratory. Each member of the core group later returned to participate in one of the subsequent labs and also in a follow-up conference to evaluate the outcomes of the laboratory and to plan further training. The second, third, and fourth laboratories included work in twelve- to fifteen-person T-groups and in large-group sessions attended by all laboratory participants, about thirty persons.

Eighty-two persons, a majority of the college staff, attended the laboratories. The intervention design was typical of human relations laboratories (Benne and others, 1975). Small- and large-group work included structured exercises to increase awareness of individual style and interpersonal processes; general sessions provided theoretical discussions about individual behaviors, group dynamics, and generalizations to back-home work situations. "Activities during general sessions included brief discussions in small cluster groups, roleplaying of problem situations, demonstration groups, and planned exercises on intergroup relations. Thus, the workshop experiences moved from general sessions to intensive small groups and back to general sessions to foster the development of individual members through their interpersonal relationships and to create a climate in which participants could discover greater freedom to explore relationships with others and to learn how to give, receive, and use feedback constructively" (Koile and Gallessich, 1970, p. 2). The general sessions in which two groups joined for structured exercises and discussions provided opportunities to experience and then study small-group cohesion and group conflict.

Two major "themes" emerged in the Dallas labs, concerns with authority and with people regarded as "different." The extreme sensitivity of faculty and staff to authority surprised administrators. Most participants felt vulnerable to those in authority and were intensely curious about administrators' thoughts and values; the laboratory experience dramatized the administrators' dilemma about how egalitarian and how open to be in the lab setting—as well as back at work. The "differences" theme came out of stereotypes related to personal characteristics such as sex, race, and age and out of role-related differences; for example, the presence of an administrator or counselor in a group composed mainly of faculty members brought out tendencies to stereotype and exclude the "deviant" member. Faculty subgroups appeared that stereotyped and separated those in humanities from those in the hard sciences and the college-preparatory faculty from technical-vocational faculty. Thus, the laboratories flushed out into the open issues affecting morale and productivity, such as dependent and counterdependent attitudes and stereotypes related to role and to personal characteristics.

Several follow-up events helped to evaluate the labs and to apply insights back at work. As in most laboratory interventions, the outcomes were mixed. At the institutional level, participants achieved greater cohesiveness; they felt more like a "family" group. However, a schism arose between those who participated in the labs and those who did not. Participants reported increased freedom in expressing ideas and feelings, greater trust of others, and more sensitivity to self and others but found it difficult to share with workers and families alike the experience and its impact. They also experienced problems in applying what they had learned; many found they made inappropriate use of such lab processes as confrontation and disclosure. The contrast in honesty and openness of communication of the lab and back at home and work was particularly painful to some participants. Generalization of newly acquired interpersonal sensitivity to classroom teaching was noted as one of the most important outcomes. Probably the participants had more power to change classroom processes than relations with peers and administrators.

Data Feedback. The following case illustrates use of data feedback methods to diagnose problems in social and technical domains (Nadler, 1977). It depicts a common consultation dilemma. Consultants were left with a great deal of frustration because the administrators did not accept the diagnosis and no intervention took place.

The client organization was Northeastern Hospital, a 300-bed hospital with a staff of 600. The hospital specializes in chronic diseases and rehabilitation; many of its patients are terminally ill. Rehabilitation patients undergo long-term treatment by physicians, occupational therapists, and physical therapists. Rettew, the hospital administrator, became concerned about a cluster of problems that were especially notable in the nursing service, including high turnover and absenteeism, difficulties in recruiting nursing staff, poor communication, low morale, and increasing staff interest in unionization. Rettew asked a consultant team to make a diagnosis of the organization, to serve as a basis for changes to improve its functioning. The team met with the executive committee, composed of the administrator and those who reported directly to him—such as the medical director, finance manager, and director of nursing. The purpose of the meeting was to clarify the goals of the consultation and the strategies through which data would be gathered and analyzed and a diagnosis fed back.

The consultants began with orientation meetings with each work group. They introduced themselves, described the goals and the data-gathering activities, and answered questions. The second step involved data collection. The consultants observed employees in staff meetings and examined hospital records. They held in-depth interviews of a random sample of 100 staff members and subsequently observed each at work for two hours. A short questionnaire was administered to all employees, including such items as "Supervisors listen to people as well as direct them" (Nadler, 1977, p. 31). Respondents chose one of five responses ranging from "always" to "never," and they also indicated how often they thought the activity indicated in the item should occur. Data collection took two months. During this period the head of the consultant team also met weekly with the hospital administrator to report on progress and obtain assistance in gathering data.

In the data analysis, two major problems appeared. First, members of the executive committee appeared confused about their roles and their authority to make decisions. Most believed that the hospital administrator made all decisions in secrecy prior to meetings. Some thought he made "side deals" with individuals, giving them special favors in return for support in committee meetings. Members of this committee felt confused, dissatisfied, and manipulated. Second, the nursing staff had feelings similar to those of the executive committee members. Their administrative structure and lines of authority were unclear. Supervisors complained about lack of authority. Staff nurses reported that they lacked direction and open communication from their administrator.

The team wrote a twenty-six-page report that included data-collection methods, major patterns and problems observed, conclusions, and recommendations for changes. The report did not directly address the hospital administrator's style but did suggest clarification of the roles of the members of the executive committee and changes in the decision-making style. The report included a complete discussion of the problems in the nursing staff. The consultants submitted the report to the executive committee and spent several hours discussing the findings, their implications, and recommended changes. Although the reactions of some members of the group were positive, others, including the director of nursing, appeared to become increasingly anxious during this meeting. In a subsequent meeting this person walked in "with a thick book on hospital administration under her arm and began attacking the consultant team, claiming that their knowledge about organizations was not really applicable to the hospital, because hospitals are different from other kinds of organizations" (pp. 32-33).

The consultants expected that the report would be available to all employees, but executive committee members refused to allow it to be disseminated outside their group. They insisted that the original agreement with the consultants, while guaranteeing that all would receive feedback, did not require that it be in written form. "Several of the committee members felt that the report could be a 'bombshell' and that to make the findings of the report public would create unrest and actually provide ammunition for those employees in nursing who were agitating for a union" (p. 33). At the same time, employees were expressing their eagerness to read and discuss the report. They hoped it would surface the problems that they felt must be faced and solved. Against the consultants' protests, the executive committee refused to allow the report to be circulated; instead, it was read aloud in meetings. The executive committee scheduled six feedback meetings. Each of these meetings included 60 to 100 people drawn from different units (the executive committee was unwilling to allow an entire unit to take time off from duties to attend a meeting). In each meeting, the consultants read the report, presenting graphs and charts with an overhead projector. They allowed questions and discussions; however, members of the executive committee were present at all times. In the first meetings, staff members asked questions about why the report was not disseminated and about the next steps to be taken. The members of the executive committee responded that they would consider the report and the recommendations included in it and would take whatever action appeared appropriate. In the later meetings, participation declined. "A rumor developed that people who spoke up at the meetings would 'pay' for it later, once the consultants had left" (p. 33). In a final meeting, the members of the executive committee thanked the consultants for their thorough work and assured them that their recommendations would receive serious consideration. The consultants later learned that the executive committee did not follow any of the recommendations. Moreover, some of the more outspoken nurses left this organization to work in other hospitals.

In this case, the top administrator apparently was not ready for a full-scale diagnosis. Perhaps Rettew had expected that the consultants would discover the problem to lie with lower-level employees or in some other domain outside himself. In retrospect, a period of education and of team building at the executive committee level might have been useful in preparing these administrators for the painful self-examination typically needed for an accurate diagnosis and productive intervention.

A Long-Term OD Intervention. Some consultations involve long-term relationships in which the consultant role and functions expand as the relationship develops. The following case study describes a four-year OD consultation with a sheriff's department (Boss, 1979). In this highly successful endeavor, a wide array of typical OD interventions were used, including confrontation of conflict, process consultation, education and training, survey feedback, team building, and changes in both the organizational structure and spatial arrangements.

The major consultee, the sheriff of Metro County, had been elected to this office three years before the consultation began. He made rapid changes, moving the department in a progressive direction and bringing in young, dedicated, educated new officers. He instituted an open-door policy, giving all employees immediate access to discuss any topic with him. However, many employees reacted negatively to his progressive orientation. They became hostile when, after two years, he suddenly changed his administrative style—directing that all communication must be filtered through the undersheriff, who was to settle as many matters as possible at that level. Top-level-staff anger and tension pervaded the department. A unionization movement began, fueled by staff frustrations.

The sheriff called in a consultant, who first attended staff meetings in the role of observer. He simultaneously held interviews with each member of the top administrative staff, including the sheriff, the undersheriff, and five division heads. Next the consultant obtained staff agreement for a six-day off-site meeting for the purposes of team building and solving human relations and departmental problems. In preparation for the off-site meeting, he held in-depth interviews with the seven top administrators. In these interviews, the consultant recorded responses to a number of questions on critical issues and explained to the interviewees that all responses would be written on large sheets of paper and posted during the coming retreat. The identity of respondents would not be given, but any participant who wished to could indicate which responses were his during the session.

The interviews revealed the following problems:

1. The staff thoroughly disapproved of the undersheriff's attitudes and his management style.
2. Lack of direct access to the sheriff was experienced not only as a loss in communication but as a loss of status.
3. The attrition rate was high—between 40 and 60 percent.
4. Staff members resented the sheriff's frequent absences to attend politically related community activities.
5. The atmosphere within the department was stiff, strained, and defensive; communication, therefore, was poor.

6. Staff members were furious over "bolts from the blue," arbitrary decisions made by the sheriff and undersheriff (p. 201).
7. The department finances were grossly mismanaged, with budgetary decisions often made capriciously.
8. The sheriff and the undersheriff were no longer trusted by the staff. Three division heads had written letters of resignation, and the other two were considering doing so.

The goal of the retreat was "to build this fragmented and hostile group of managers into an effectively functioning team. In effect, it gave participants the chance to work through the unresolved socioemotional 'garbage' that was not manifest in the interviews" (p. 201). An exercise in consensual decision making led participants to make critical comments on the sheriff's style; soon a torrent of anger burst out, releasing a buildup of three years. The consultant asked for a cooling-off period and then gave the staff his observations of the processes of the preceding period; he suggested reasons that might lie behind the explosion and outlined possible consequences of the conflict and alternative solutions. The group then evolved a temporary truce with a commitment to work on basic causes of the conflict rather than on symptoms.

The next two activities of the retreat called for confrontive feedback. In an organizational "mirror" exercise, the sheriff and undersheriff were placed in one organizational subgroup, and the five division heads formed another. The two top administrators were asked to write out answers to the following questions: "How do you see yourselves in relation to the staff? How do you see the staff? How do you think the staff sees you?" The five division heads responded to corresponding questions regarding their perceptions of the administrators and of themselves. The second confrontation activity encouraged participants to communicate directly about their individual responses to the questions mentioned earlier that had been asked in interviews before the retreat. The first confrontive exercise surfaced organizational issues, and the second brought out specific issues between individuals. Ground rules for both activities prevented defensiveness and arguments and encouraged clarification of perceptions with specific examples and nonjudgmental attitudes.

These confrontive experiences culminated in a list of priorities and led into a problem-solving phase. First, each participant created a two-way interpersonal contract: (1) He would behave in specific ways that would increase the organization's effectiveness—for example, "control my temper" and "speak in positives." (2) He would receive certain specified help from the group, such as "open communication" and "high trust" (p. 207). Next, and for the remainder of the session, the focus moved to organizational problems such as communication, decision making, and control processes.

Several instruments were used to measure the progress of the confrontation team-building retreat. Significantly, the mean trust level moved from a low of 1.5 the first evening to a high of 9.5 (on a 10-point scale) at the end of the session. Similar changes were manifest in the organizational climate and were maintained during the following four years of consultation.

Subsequently, the consultant assisted staff members in a number of interventions, including an organizational restructuring and settling of disputes over personnel reassignments and space allocations. Over the next four years, the consultant also led additional off-site retreats to solve interpersonal and organizational problems, trained supervisors in leadership skills, provided process consultation, and assisted in resolving conflicts.

The results of the consultation were striking. Periodic surveys indicated significant improvements in the effectiveness of all administrators and in the organizational climate. Many other positive changes occurred, including a marked decrease in employee attrition and in jailbreaks and a substantial improvement in the department's management of finances.

A Multimodal, Multidimensional Intervention. The next case highlights the growing sophistication of organizational consultation and an unusually close relationship between practice and theory. The intervention addressed problems in several domains: structural, human relations, environment, and technology. It employed a wide array of methods. In this case consultants often took a somewhat directive role in order to help this organization make rapid and systemic changes.

The intervention had two goals: (1) to improve the organization's ability to adapt to environmental and technological changes and (2) to improve employees' motivation (Stein and Kanter, 1980). Environmental turbulence requires organizations to respond rapidly and flexibly. At the same time, growing numbers of well-educated employees are demanding more opportunities for leadership and responsibility. The classic bureaucratic organization is unable to satisfy either of these demands; yet, this structure is well suited to some conditions and certain tasks. This intervention created a *parallel* organization (Miller, 1978), a structure designed to supplement the bureaucratic organization by managing change through "a set of externally and internally responsive, participatory, problem-solving structures alongside the conventional line organization that carries out routine tasks" (Stein and Kanter, 1980, p. 372). The parallel organization also provides power and advancement opportunities for persons who, within the bureaucratic structure, are relatively lacking in power and options for promotion. Thus, the parallel organization can enhance the quality of work and the satisfaction and effectiveness of these individuals.

The intervention described here is also based on the hypothesis that staff competencies are closely related to opportunities for growth and exercise of power (Kanter, 1977). The assumptions are these: (1) The structural characteristics of a job (as well as individual abilities) in part determine individual effectiveness. The key aspects of any position are the *opportunities* and *power* it offers its holder—for instance, the degree of access to promotions, chances to increase competencies and contribute to the organization, and degree of access to resources and ability to mobilize them. (2) To the extent that their jobs provide opportunities and power, people will be motivated to develop and use their abilities productively and will support the organization's goals. (3) People whose positions are low in opportunity and power will withdraw from involvement, devalue their skills, and resist change.

The client organization was a multiplant industry, the

Compu Corporation, a fast-growing producer of electrical equipment. The company had grown so large that it had become difficult to manage in the traditional mode. Market conditions demanded tighter control of operations. Technological changes required conversions of manufacturing processes. One plant, Chestnut Ridge, was particularly affected by these changes and was the cause of great concern, since its management regarded the staff as lacking the competence to make the necessary adaptations. The Chestnut Ridge personnel staff manager secured central office funding for a consultant team to help his plant address these problems. The goals of the consultants were (1) staff development, to increase the competencies and promotability of the lower-level production supervisors, and (2) organizational adaptability, to increase the organization's ability to make changes smoothly and effectively.

The intervention involved five overlapping stages (p. 375): (1) initial education and planning, (2) information gathering, structural diagnosis, and hypothesis testing, (3) action planning, (4) implementation, and (5) integration and diffusion of results within the system.

The purpose of Stage One, the educational and planning stage, was to obtain understanding and support from the corporate management and from the plant management and staff. The consultants held interviews, group discussions, and seminars to explain the concepts; with staff they explored the relevance of the theories described above to Chestnut Ridge. The consultants brought employees' doubts and anxieties out into the open and discussed them at length. One manager's approval came with difficulty: "He turned green, swallowed, clutched his heart, slid under the table, but said, 'Go ahead' " (p. 376). In this first stage, consultants also asked senior managers from inside and outside the Chestnut Ridge plant to be members of a project advisory group in order to provide authority and rewards for staff participation, counsel in regard to implementation, linkages to the plant and corporation, and dissemination of information about the project.

In Stage Two, the consultants gathered and analyzed data and fed them back to plant employees. In addition to informal observations and interviews, they used a questionnaire to assess staff perceptions of the information, opportunities, flexibility, and problems in their jobs. The data from this survey supported the initial hypothesis and differentiated by levels and by the seven separate production units the degree to which opportunity and power were available to staff members. Preliminary results were quickly disseminated and discussed in voluntary meetings.

In Stage Three, consultants began to construct the parallel organization, a structure independent of the internal hierarchy. First they formed a steering committee composed of the plant production managers and persons from other units. This committee became the management structure for the evolving parallel organization. Ultimately the new organization included—in addition to the steering committee and the project advisory group—three demonstration pilot groups, or parallel structures. All the pilot groups included employees from two or more levels. The volunteer members perceived that these structures offered opportunities to learn new skills and bypass bureaucratic blocks to problem solving. Each of the three pilot groups drew up proposals for action projects related to its particular unit and presented them to the corporate research and development committee, which enthusiastically endorsed them all. The members of these projects had access to, and became recognized by, influential persons with whom they ordinarily would have had no contact, and thus their opportunities and power increased. The projects responded to the earlier data analyses: (1) The first pilot group redesigned the organization of the assembly line in order to increase production and decrease isolation and loss of power. (2) The second group devised a mechanism for bringing new staff members into the organization more quickly and thoroughly. (3) The third pilot group had two projects: (a) development of a more carefully focused and timed supervisory training program and (b) a program to reduce troublesome inconsistencies between production groups.

In Stage Four, the pilot groups implemented their projects and completed them within six months. Working independently of the bureaucratic organization, they developed goals and strategies, gathered data, educated themselves, and coordinated with one another and with the steering committee. The results were reported to be highly successful.

The integration of the projects within Chestnut Ridge—Stage Five—was also successful. The products were applied to the units for which they were planned. The parallel organization became a permanent part of the plant, offering opportunities for all levels of employees to participate in the management of change. Project participation was included in new job descriptions and in performance evaluations. However, diffusion of the project into other plants within Compu was relatively weak.

The employees who had participated in the pilot groups made significant gains in skills, productivity, and job satisfaction. Their growth helped solve the problem of "incompetent" staff.

Critique

Organizational consultation is characterized by diversity and rapid growth. Increasingly sophisticated technology enables practitioners to offer more and more specialized assistance. Consequently, consultants are moving toward working in teams that include members of different specialty areas.

Many criticisms have been leveled against organizational consultants, particularly those in the OD field. They sometimes become so preoccupied with interpersonal processes that they neglect the relations between these processes and areas such as budgets, administration, and technology (Margulies and Raia, 1972). Their interventions are typically piecemeal responses to systemic illnesses and do little to remedy problems (Burke, 1980). More often, the organizational consultant's contribution is a "fine tuning" of the human relationships that make up the quality of life (Schein and Greiner, 1977). Organizational consultants have been accused of aiding managers in exploiting staff (Friedlander and Brown, 1974; Walton and Warrick, 1973). They have been said to introduce such overwhelming changes that they threaten the very survival of their consultee agencies (Klein, 1969).

Though well established in the private sector, organizational consultation is less often used in human services agencies. Administrators of these institutions are, on the whole, less ready to acknowledge internal difficulties, particularly those in interpersonal relations (Goodstein, 1978). Moreover, because of the distinctive characteristics described in Chapter Three, methods derived from business and industry often fail to fit the needs of human services agencies (Golembiewski, 1969; Rubin, Plovnik, and Fry, 1974). Perhaps the major task of organizational consultants is to help the staff of human services agencies confront and manage the tensions created by the disjunctive nature of their organizations (Kouzes and Mico, 1979, p. 462).

Consultant Preparation

Organizational consultation includes diverse theories and methods, but extensive publications are available to enable consultants to acquire knowledge in all areas of this broad field. Moreover, organizations such as the Organization Development Network, the National Training Laboratories Institute, and University Associates offer seminars and workshops and, in many cases, opportunities to obtain supervision. Most universities also include courses in topics related to organizational consultation, and a few university-based professional training programs include courses and supervised field experiences in this model. (See Chapter Eighteen for sources of training; also see the directory written by Campbell, 1978.)

Annotated Bibliography

Argyris, C. *Intervention Theory and Method: A Behavioral Science View*. Reading, Mass.: Addison-Wesley, 1970. This book, written by one of the most distinguished consultant scientist-practitioners, is notable for its synthesis of theory and practice, its humanistic approach to the consultation relationship, and its delineation of the complex dilemmas of the consultant. It begins with Argyris's original theories and methods and then goes on to illustrate them with case studies. The verbatim accounts of consultation interviews are especially helpful in understanding the author's orientation.

Goodstein, L. D. *Consulting with Human Service Systems.* Reading, Mass.: Addison-Wesley, 1978. This book is one of the first to focus exclusively on organizational consultation in human services institutions. Goodstein reviews a number of approaches to understanding both consultation processes and organizational phenomena.

Journal of Applied Behavioral Science. Published quarterly by the NTL Institute for Applied Behavioral Science, this journal regularly includes articles concerned with organizational consultation theory, practice, and research. All consultants who are interested in organizational consultation will find this journal extremely valuable in keeping up to date in this field.

Schein, E. H. *Process Consultation: Its Role in Organization Development.* Reading, Mass.: Addison-Wesley, 1969. Schein systematizes existing concepts and practices of process consultation. He describes major human processes in organizations and methods for studying and intervening in these processes. This book is a valuable addition to the library of all consultants.

Schmuck, R. A., and others. *Handbook of Organization Development in Schools.* Palo Alto, Calif.: National Press Books, 1972. Stressing the need for organizations to make continual adaptations to keep up with environmental changes, this book outlines ways consultants can help organizations increase their capacities to adapt. Theoretical issues are integrated with detailed suggestions and examples of how to conduct various interventions. This book is especially useful for new consultants because it offers a great deal of pragmatic advice, along with well-developed concepts and principles.

Steele, F. *Consulting for Organizational Change.* Amherst: University of Massachusetts Press, 1975. Steele writes about the difficulties inherent in the role of organizational consultant and ways of learning from experiences in this role. Readers will find an unusual depth of understanding of consultation processes beneath the author's humorous style.

10

Program
Approaches

Over the past two decades, most agencies have increased the proportion of services they deliver through programs —coordinated services geared to reach carefully defined goals and target populations. Consequently, consultants are frequently involved in helping agencies design, implement, and evaluate these programs. The concepts and methods of this model—like the programs themselves—are difficult to define because of their diversity.

Programs have been broadly defined to include all sponsored activities designed to alleviate social problems or improve social and economic conditions (Anderson and Ball, 1978; Perloff, Perloff, and Sussna, 1976). In this sense all human services are programs. In this book, however, the definition is limited to those agency services that receive earmarked funding from public or private sources and involve systematic and coordinated activities designed to benefit a particular target group in a particular way. Thus, in this definition, the broad spectrum of educational services offered by a public school system does not make up a program, but many of the system's projects are programmatic—for example, activities designed to desegregate teachers and pupils, a project to mainstream handicapped pupils, and an alternative high school designed to attract actual and potential dropouts and retain them through graduation. Although these illustrations refer to programs that primarily serve disadvantaged groups, programs serving more affluent populations would also come under this definition—for example, a continuing education program piloted by a professional association and a physical fitness program offered by a private health center.

Programming appears to be a stage in the evolution of human services and the result of technological specialization, increasing demands, and diminishing resources. Agencies that once offered general services now have the capacities to deliver highly specialized services and to fit them to the needs of particular client groups. It is often convenient—for public relations, grant application, and accounting purposes—to separate these specialized services into discrete programs. Programming also offers a means for ensuring that high priority needs are met.

Which needs are to be served? Which agencies and services are to be funded? Which client needs and agency requests are to be denied? Demands for services are ever increasing while resources—such as money, equipment, and professional staff—are limited and shrinking. Officials who control funds must make difficult decisions. Each consumer group insists that its needs are most urgent. Particularly strong appeals come from advocates of groups (for example, the aged, the mentally retarded, and minorities) not served by mainstream institutions. In the face of intensive competition, funding agencies must determine and make public their priorities. Agency requests characterized by programmatic specificity—such as clearly delineated goals, benefits, constituencies, and strategies that conform to funding guidelines—are most likely to receive support.

A further impetus to programming has come from increased pressures for financial accountability as we move into an era of declining resources. Agencies can no longer expect to receive funding unless they provide evidence of their effectiveness. Programmatic activities designed and coordinated to meet specific goals are more amenable to evaluation than broad-gauged, less precisely defined services. Programs may thus enhance agencies' chances for survival.

Agencies often lack internal resources for developing, implementing, and evaluating programs. They frequently turn to consultants for technical assistance. Typically, program grants include line items for these consultant services. Program consultation is here defined as consultant services that are directly related to and limited to a program. The consultant's functions differ according to the nature of the program and the agency's needs. Consultants may be globally involved, assisting in all aspects of a program, or limited to a highly specific task. They may be asked to add their expertise in the developmental stages, for instance, to help agency administrators plan a program and write a proposal for a grant to fund it. They may be asked to assist in the implementation stage—perhaps by helping staff learn and incorporate new concepts and technologies. In some cases, consultants are asked to step outside the usual boundaries of their role to act as supervisors or monitors to ensure incorporation of behaviors needed to support a program. Quite frequently, consultants are asked to assist in the evaluation of programs, to help administrators assess their impact (Anderson and Ball, 1978; Matuzek, 1981; Perloff, Perloff, and Sussna, 1976; Scriven, 1967).

The use of a variety of consultants for highly specialized functions related to a program is illustrated in a victims' assistance program developed by the staff of the Albert Einstein College of Medicine (Reiff, 1979; Reiff, personal communication, 1980). The program, funded by the Law Enforcement Assistance Administration, served citizens of the Bronx. Its major purposes were to explore victims' needs and to design a model program for meeting these needs. A specialist in community organization advised the staff on how to locate victims. A sociologist, a specialist in the criminal justice system, provided the staff with information on police processing of victims. A statistician assisted in the design, implementation, and analysis of an evaluation.

Illustrations

Three program consultations will serve to exemplify the diverse goals and activities of this model. The first case describes long-term consultation with a highly successful and well-supported program. The remaining cases illustrate the more common situation in which program consultation is hampered by lack of full administrative support.

Consultation with a Public Health Program. Prevention and amelioration of health problems are common program goals, but conflicting beliefs and values often dilute program impact. The following case study illustrates the way a consultant, in the role of technological and theoretical adviser, assisted in the continuing development of a strongly supported public health program in Finland. The North Karelia Project was formed by the Finnish government to reduce the incidence of cardiovascular diseases in a region of eastern Finland (McAlister and others, 1980). Historically, the province of North Karelia has had the highest rate of cardiovascular disease in Finland, and Finland's is the highest in the world. The government formed the project in response to citizen demand for some kind of preventive program. The objectives of the North Karelia Project are (1) to develop and implement disease prevention strategies in that province and (2) to develop and disseminate methods to be used throughout Finland for encouraging and assisting people to give up cigarette smoking. The consultant, a social psychologist from the Harvard University School of Public Health, is a specialist in theory and research concerning behavioral counseling and mass communication (McAlister, personal communication, 1981). The primary consultee, a physician trained in social and preventive medicine and in sociology, is the principal investigator in the North Karelia Project and a scientific officer of the Epidemiological Research Unit of the Finnish Ministry of Public Health.

The goals of the consultation are to develop methods through which the educational and counseling efforts that the North Karelia Project conducts can be extended to the greatest possible number of people in North Karelia and throughout Finland. Before the consultation began, the North Karelia Project had already conducted community educational and counseling programs intended to bring about improvements in eating habits (lowered fat and salt consumption), cessation of cigarette smoking, and better cooperation with health centers' programs to detect and control hypertension. But these classes and other community activities could not provide expert education and counseling to all the 200,000 adult residents of North Karelia, not to mention the several million residents of Finland as a whole. Hence, the consultation objective was to find ways in which the successes experienced in intensive group counseling could be produced among a larger portion of the population. This goal required a way to provide expert instruction on a large scale and to maximize active involvement in and social support for the process of behavior change and maintenance of achieved changes.

The role of the consultant to this ongoing program is to suggest ideas based on theory and research. The consultee contributes to those ideas, adapts them to existing conditions, and then executes them through his research team and the cooperating organizations, agencies, and individuals in Finland and North Karelia. The consultant and consultee meet several times a year and also consult by mail. The essential process of consultation involves the following steps: (1) The consultee clarifies goals and objectives. (2) The consultant proposes ideal, theoretical approaches to achieving those objectives. (3) The consultee explains organizational constraints and resources and any limitations relevant to the proposed ideas. (4) The two "brainstorm" to develop practical ways of implementing the ideal strategy within the existing setting. (5) Together they evolve a preliminary research and implementation plan, which they later refine through correspondence. (6) The consultee implements the plan.

The first outcome of the consultation was a series of television programs that were broadcast throughout Finland to help smokers who wished to give up their habit. The format of the programs was a pair of expert counselors assisting a studio group representing typical smokers attempting to achieve and maintain cessation. Before the broadcasts, a national campaign was conducted to recruit volunteers to lead self-help groups of community members who wished to give up smoking. Especially intensive recruitment and organization work was conducted in North Karelia. During the first broadcast series, about 40,000 Finns were actively involved in attempting cessation along with the program. About 10 percent of these were in a self-help program; most of the rest watched the television programs from their homes. Data suggest that about 10,000 of these people achieved at least a year of nonsmoking as a result of the program. A repeat broadcast was conducted about six months after the first one, and nearly twice as many Finnish smokers participated, with about the same rate of success. It appears that about 2 percent of all smokers before the series were broadcast have been helped to become permanent ex-smokers. This was about half of what was originally hoped for but is still considered a very useful result. As an outcome of this successful experience and through further consultation and discussion, a second broadcast series was produced to provide more general education and counseling about how to change behavior to improve health—for example, improved eating habits, stress management, smoking cessation. In the province of North Karelia (population 200,000 adults) about 1,000 volunteers organized self-help groups for the purpose of participating in the program and improving their health habits.

This illustration is noteworthy not only for its successful outcomes but as an exemplar of a consultant's long-term involvement in the conceptualization and design of an evolving program. His detailed knowledge of the program's goals, environment, and staff enable him to offer continuing assistance at a relatively low cost to the consultee. The consultant attributes the successful outcomes in this intervention to (1) the openness and trust in the consultation relationship, (2) the consultee's willingness and ability to translate ideas into action and to organize support for the program, and (3) social conditions, the eagerness of the Finnish population to participate in mass education and counseling (McAlister, personal communication, 1981). Finns are probably somewhat more likely than Americans to participate in organized activities. Moreover, the Finnish broadcasting system is publicly owned and thus more willing than commercial broadcasters to perform this kind of complicated public service.

Consultation with a Mainstreaming Program. In the 1970s, federal and state laws were enacted requiring public schools to normalize the education of handicapped children. Pupils with learning, emotional, behavioral, developmental, and physical impairments are no longer segregated for the entire school day but are integrated to the degree that their abilities permit them to learn through "mainstream" activities. Compliance with these laws demands many changes. Teachers and pupils must make difficult adjustments. Mainstream teachers must learn how to work with disabled pupils and modify their instructional designs and methods to meet the needs of more diverse classroom groups. Special education teachers, who previously were often as segregated as their pupils, must work closely with the mainstream. Many are designated as in-house consultants and are responsible for helping mainstream teachers understand the needs of handicapped children and learn techniques for managing them. This major shift in roles and relationships creates tensions for all concerned. Handicapped children, accustomed to the sheltered environments of special education classrooms, must adapt to mainstream distractions and pressures. The children in these rooms must learn to get along with classmates who have a wide range of disabilities. Resistance to these changes appears at all levels. Successful implementation requires systemic support. Consultants are called on to provide a variety of services (Robinowitz, 1979).

The following case involves a mainstream program in a small school district. To help teachers acquire competencies needed for mainstreaming, the district scheduled a series of inservice workshops on related topics—such as the nature of various disabilities and their implications for classroom management, human processes such as communications and team building, and uses of media in the instruction of heterogeneous groups. A grant provided funds for consultants and for teacher stipends. Teachers were allowed to select the workshops they wished to attend. The case described here concerns one of these workshops and illustrates a common consultation problem—one that is not unique to the program model. Consultants were hired to provide concepts and skills related to the implementation of a program that, though well funded by external sources, received only token support from within the organization, owing to serious conflicts about the timing and scope of the mainstream program. A poorly managed contract with the consultants was only one manifestation of these administrative problems and of the tenuous commitment to the program. Without the incentives associated with federal funding, this program and many like it would not have survived.

The director of staff development asked two out-of-state consultants to provide training in communication concepts and methods for teachers whose schools were participating in the mainstream program. Through letters and telephone conversations the consultants were told that the decision to offer this workshop topic was based on results of a survey of teachers' perceptions of their needs. The contract called for the consultants to meet in a two-day retreat with a group of twenty teachers (from nine schools within the district) who had requested this particular training. The goal was to help them increase their skills in communicating with other teachers, pupils, and parents. The workshop was to involve seminars, demonstrations, and opportunities for teachers to learn and practice new skills through role playing.

Arriving at the retreat site in late afternoon, the consultants found an unreceptive group. Only twelve of those scheduled to attend were present. A spokesperson for the members of the group announced that they had been assigned to this workshop. She also reported that a power struggle was going on in their district. The administrator who had arranged for the workshop had been fired. Another administrator—the director of curriculum and instruction—had announced his resignation. The mainstream program was foundering because these conflicts absorbed much of the time and energies of administrators and teachers and because official commitment to the program was uncertain.

The prospects for a successful consultation appeared dim. The teachers felt frustrated and pessimistic about implementation of the mainstream program. The workshop topic appeared apropos; however, the administrators who were the source of the communiations problems and the underlying conflicts were not present. The exact nature and scope of the problems could not be determined. Moreover, the consultants were not authorized to focus on administrative issues, much less attempt a diagnosis or intervention, although they were obviously more salient than teachers' communications problems and training. The contract between the director of staff development and the consultants was invalid. The teachers present had not participated in a needs assessment and had not volunteered for the conference. Justifiably, they were unhappy at being required to attend it. Finally, these discoveries came at 5:00 P.M. on a Friday, and the consultants' hurried efforts to reach the administrator who had arranged the workshop were fruitless. Several teachers commented that they would like to return home to their families, and the consultants considered canceling the conference. However, the district had made a sizable investment in travel expenses, lodgings, consultants' fees, and teachers' stipends. The consultants decided to try to work with the teachers to negotiate a new contract that would meet their needs without violating the terms or spirit of their original one.

In the opening session the first evening, the consultants discussed their views of the dilemma and their hope of reaching a mutually satisfactory agreement. The teachers agreed to negotiate with the provision that they would have the final say in the topics to be covered. The consultants then described their resources and limitations and the contractual boundaries. They could work on teachers' problems as long as they related to the program that was paying for the consultation. The consultants could not focus on the administrative conflicts that were exacerbating the teachers' problems. For example, they could not discuss the personalities and behaviors of the administrators involved. Outside these restrictions, the consultants offered to help teachers identify needs and to provide them with relevant concepts and skills for solving some of their problems. To make their discussions more productive, the consultants decided to perform an on-the-spot needs assessment. Using the group confrontation technique described in Chapter Fourteen, the teachers identified the four top-ranking problems: (1) How can we keep our cool and refrain from hitting the kids when we are so frustrated with our problems? (2) How can we teach our pupils self-control and self-respect? (3) How can we communicate and have impact? (4) How can we teach multiple levels of ability? Further analysis of this list revealed a control theme in several levels: the participants' control of pupils; their own self-control; their sense of being controlled by their bosses and the conflict situation.

The emergent goal was to help the teachers increase their understanding of the situations and dynamics that left them feeling helpless and to help them learn appropriate ways of managing these situations successfully. The consultants created a workshop design, including lectures and demonstrations, to reach these goals. Participants role-played typical stressful situations to identify their characteristics and interactive patterns. Consultants helped them explore principles and methods for gaining and maintaining control in these situations. Later, in additional role-playing exercises, teachers experimented with and critiqued alternative styles of conflict management.

The teachers' ratings of the workshop's usefulness were high. Although administration conflicts continued for many more months, the district contracted for the consultants to return to lead two similar workshops—one for teachers and one for junior administrators. Two years later the administrative conflicts were finally resolved, and the mainstreaming program was firmly incorporated in most of the district's schools.

Program Evaluation Consultation. As competition for funds intensifies and evaluation standards increase, administrators must give a high priority to planning and carrying out internal evaluations. They must include well-designed evaluation plans in their applications for funds. They must present evidence that the goals are being achieved in order to obtain renewals. Since agency staff members often lack skills in this area, administrators frequently turn to consultants for help. The next case describes an evaluation specialist's work as a program consultant to a mental health services center. It demonstrates two common phenomena: (1) resistance to the painstaking analyses and planning required for sound evaluations and (2) the hope that the consultant will provide a magical solution. Like the preceding case, this one illustrates the long-term effects of administrative problems on program development.

Edward Center is a not-for-profit corporation providing mental health services to a low-SES metropolitan community. The agency is funded by United Community Services, the county community mental health board, and the state department of mental health. The center began twenty-five years ago as a multipurpose center for the elderly but evolved over the years to serve all adults. With the advent of deinstitutionalization, Edward Center came to play an especially heavy role in providing services to adults returning to the community from state hospitals for the mentally ill. Edward Center consists of administrative offices and seven branches, each of which sponsors a number of direct service programs.

Mr. G., the assistant director of Edward Center, requested consultation from a community psychologist, a specialist in program evaluation, for the purpose of laying the foundations for an agencywide system for evaluation of programs. Five intermediate goals were identified:

1. To define program evaluation and to begin the process of formulating agencywide evaluation goals and plans.
2. To assess current evaluation procedures in one program (the Developmentally Disabled, or D.D., Program housed in one of the seven centers) in order to demonstrate an analytical approach to evaluation.
3. To outline a framework that the Edward Center administrative staff could use to assess its evaluation procedures and lay the groundwork for an agencywide system.
4. To help the administrative staff identify the information needed for evaluation.
5. To help the administrative staff begin to develop agencywide evaluation procedures.

The contract specified that the consultant would make a total of eight consultative visits to Edward Center.

After the circulation of the consultation contract, the consultant met with the consultees (Edward Center's administrative staff and the program committee members of its board) to clarify the consultation goals and the consultant's role and perspectives on program evaluation and to explore staff attitudes toward evaluation. The consultant introduced herself, described her role and answered questions, and made a brief formal presentation in which she defined program evaluation, discussed the kinds of skills necessary to carry out evaluation, and presented an overall "blueprint" of the evaluation process. Staff members discussed the evaluation model at some length and agreed that it was suited to Edward Center. However, they expressed much resistance to *applying* this model. A past evaluation within the agency had taken enormous effort and produced virtually no benefits. Moreover, staff members felt that using a specific program to demonstrate the evaluation process would make people feel "under fire" and threatened. They were also concerned about the time that evaluation would take away from services. On a positive note, staff members thought evaluation could shed new light on their programs, help the program committee of the board carry out its responsibility for monitoring effectiveness, and assist the agency in obtaining future funding. Although the resistance remained, the group agreed that the consultant would proceed with the next step, the analysis of the evaluation procedures in the D.D. Program.

The consultant met with the director of the D.D. Program to discuss her evaluation procedures. This administrator (who had not attended the original session) welcomed the consultant and showed no resistance to the analysis. (Perhaps one reason for the lack of resistance was the program director's imminent resignation. She left Edward Center several weeks later to take a higher-paying job.) She described the program's present data-collection procedures and how these data were (and were not) used in reports to various audiences to whom she was accountable. The program itself was in flux, having recently changed funding sources; reporting needs were changing as well. The consultant collected copies of all data-collection and reporting forms presently used by D.D. and made a detailed status analysis of this program's informational system, which she presented in writing to the D.D. director and, later, to the entire group of consultees.

In discussions of the consultant's analysis, it became evident that consultees were confused about the relation between routine program monitoring and program evaluation. They were also concerned about the amount of effort it would take to standardize evaluation procedures across the seven divisions. Therefore, before proceeding further with developing an evaluation model, the consultant prepared a second didactic session on the relation between evaluation and management information systems. She compiled a brief report on the many commonalities among the present data-collection forms and procedures in use across the seven centers. At this meeting, the consultant also raised the issue of what types of information were needed at various levels of administrative decision making, in an attempt to move the group ahead to the next intermediate goal. But this issue proved premature, and in response to resistance to taking this next step, the consultant proposed an intermediate step of essentially replicating the information-system status analysis previously performed for D.D. but this time on an agencywide basis, across all seven service centers. The consultees agreed to this proposal, and the general status analysis was performed by an administrative assistant in consultation with the consultant. In working with the managerial staff to develop this report, the administrative assistant also documented staff concerns and reactions to the process.

The impact of the consultant was evident in the consultees' increasing attention to the question "Just exactly what evaluation information does each level of administration need?" However, it became clear that the persons who most needed help in answering this question were the center director and the assistant director who had initiated consultation! Moreover, they appeared reluctant to take responsibility for identifying *their own* decision-making requirements (rather than continuing to simply react to whatever information was supplied from the service centers). Their lack of understanding and hesitancy created resentment among the other administrators, whose attitude was "Since the director and assistant director don't seem to know what they want, why should we go to the effort of making all these changes?" The consultant realized that the two top administrators needed to catch up with the staff before the agencywide evaluation planning could move ahead. Rather than continuing to work with the whole group, she scheduled two sessions with only the director and assistant director. She emphasized the importance of management decisions in guiding the entire evaluation process and helped them identify, clarify, and summarize their informational needs. Mr. G., the assistant director, grasped the concepts and their implications for action much more quickly than did the director. A basic conflict between the two came to light. The center director dealt with each program director on an individual basis, exemplifying a personalized but laissez faire management style. Up to this point, the individual programs and centers had been quite autonomous, and there had been no attempts to standardize any aspects of program management. Although the director acknowledged certain limitations of this style, she was reluctant to change. However, Mr. G. believed that changes were needed. He favored greater accountability of local programs to the central office and saw standardized program monitoring and evaluation as a means to this end. Hence, the consultation ended with an escalation of a basic conflict between the two administrators. Their confusion and hesitation had functioned to conceal this conflict.

The consultative process unfolded within the contractual guidelines and, to some extent, achieved its goal of laying the foundation for systemwide evaluation procedures. The agency staff members grew in their understanding of the complexity of evaluation procedures and in a beginning awareness of their own state of development and of the directions in which they needed to move. However, the top administrators' lack of readiness delayed the development of an integrated evaluation system. The director reacted against the evaluation to the extent that it forced her to articulate decision-making criteria and information needs; such specificity was contrary to her customary management style. The assistant director, though favoring the evaluation in principle, had never considered it from the viewpoint of his own information needs. He, too, had to begin that process of articulation "from scratch" rather than taking a leadership role. Despite repeated clarification by the consultant of the developmental nature of internal evaluation and of her role as adviser—not implementer—these administrators continued to seek quick and easy solutions and essentially wished the consultant would "make it happen" by putting evaluation procedures in place without the need for continual staff involvement. To the extent that center staff members continued to see themselves as spectators and not as major actors in the evaluation process, the consultation was a failure. Managerial staff members generally interacted pleasantly with the consultant. Their real agenda, however, seemed to be to slow the process down until they could discern the true motives and commitment of the director. The agency took no further steps in evaluation efforts during the next two years. Two years later, the director hired a second consultant to continue to develop an integrated evaluation system.

Critique

Programmatic consultation can help human services institutions in their efforts to bring about changes through innovative programs. However, as some of the cases discussed here suggest, the difficulties in incorporating and maintaining programs are myriad. Often programs are never fully internalized, and program behaviors fade out when the external support system leaves (Sarason, 1971). A basic factor in many failures is the lack of involvement in decision making and planning by the people who will be most affected—clients and staff. However, support may be difficult or impossible to obtain. Since new programs are usually proposed to meet the needs of special-interest groups, they can expect to meet resistance from the mainstream and from opposing interest groups. Efforts to obtain system-wide support may be fruitless and, at best, costly in time and energy. Yet, to survive, programs need this support. Although consultants do not always have the authority to initiate contacts with key staff members to obtain their support—and probably this responsibility should remain with the agency staff—consultants can help program administrators by alerting them to the need to obtain broad support before beginning a program.

From the consultant's perspective, consultation in this

model is frequently frustrating because of its typically narrow parameters. Program consultants often have little flexibility. Their role may be limited to a very small range of goals and activities. Program consultants sometimes find themselves in a bind because they discover serious differences between their own values and those of the program to which they are attached. To illustrate, a computer specialist hired to help an agency staff use expensive new equipment—paid for by a program's grant money —discovered that staff members could not use the equipment without extensive training and software. Yet, funds and time for training were not available. In working with mainstreaming programs such as the one described earlier, consultants have discovered that the quality of education received by children in a regular classroom dropped significantly. In these situations, consultants are usually torn between their commitment to the program's goals and their concern for persons who appear to be adversely affected by the program. Sometimes, resolution of these conflicts is not possible, and consultants may decide to break their contracts. But consultants' thoughtful, documented feedback to program administrators about a program's overall effects may enable these officers to ameliorate any undesirable consequences.

Consultant Preparation

The services needed by programs vary greatly and include a wide range of professional specialties. The only area in which all programs typically need help is evaluation. Competencies in this field can be acquired through reading (see Chapter Fifteen) and through workshops and seminars offered by numerous professional organizations and all universities.

Annotated Bibliography

Anderson, S. B., and Ball, S. *The Profession and Practice of Program Evaluation.* San Francisco: Jossey-Bass, 1978. This book is the first attempt to systematize the body of knowledge of an emerging profession. It also offers pragmatic guidelines in regard to everyday problems faced by program evaluators and is a valuable addition to the consultant's library.

Rogawski, A. S. (Ed.). *New Directions for Mental Health Services: Mental Health Consultations in Community Settings,* no. 3. San Francisco: Jossey-Bass, 1979. A number of the chapters in this volume describe mental health program-centered consultation. These readings are helpful in conveying the commonalities and differences between the practices of different consultants and between the needs and characteristics of different agencies.

Part III

Common Processes, Principles, and Practices 🔊🔊🔊

All consultants, no matter what model they are following, go through similar processes. Most consultation, for instance, involves a contract, an "entry," and an evaluation. The focus of Part Three shifts from descriptions of the different models of consultation to describe these generic processes and to suggest principles for effective consultation.

Chapter Eleven is written for the beginning consultant and answers basic questions about the establishment and conduct of a consultation practice. It includes information on such matters as contacting potential consultees and fee setting. To give new consultants an overview of consultation, this chapter also describes its typical phases—from preliminary explorations to termination. A variety of informal ways consultants can use their role and their relatively detached perspective to help consultees identify problems and expand their thinking about solutions are described.

Chapter Twelve discusses the steps through which consultants and agency representatives move toward the establishment of working relationships. The protocol and processes of the preliminary interview and the questions that both parties need to raise at this early point are reviewed. This chapter also describes the elements that should be included in a consultation contract and points out common flaws in contractual arrangements. When consultants "enter" agencies, they often find an atmosphere of ambivalence and resistance. Chapter Twelve discusses the entry process in detail; it explains agency dynamics that influence consultation and reasons that consultees may distrust and resist consultants. Guidelines for successful entry into the agency's social-psychological world are suggested.

Tensions inherent in the consultant role and discrepancies between consultant's and consultee's perspectives may interfere with the development of effective working relationships. Complications may arise as a result of individual characteristics, such as gender, age, and communication style, and be exacerbated by stereotypes held by either consultant or consultee. Consultation failures are often associated with conflicts over power. Chapter Thirteen identifies the major sources of tension in the consultant/consultee relationship and suggests ways consultants can reduce these tensions and establish effective working relationships.

Chapter Fourteen presents general guidelines for the central tasks of the consultant. The chapter stresses the value of collaboration between consultant and consultees and the use of a cyclical model in which data are continually fed into the diagnosis and into decisions about intervention goals and strategies. Methods and conceptual frameworks for gathering data, formulating diagnoses, and intervening are reviewed.

Evaluation and termination, the topics of Chapter Fifteen, are the most neglected aspects of consultation. Because of the complex nature of consultation and of agency processes, evaluation is an especially difficult task. This chapter presents a model for evaluation of consultation and discusses technical problems related to measurement and design. Guidelines for effective management of evaluation and termination processes are outlined.

11

Getting Started:
Basic Steps

How does a person get started as a consultant? Individuals who would like to begin to consult or to move from an occasional consultation into a more extensive practice may not be sure how to get started. They may be uncertain whether they have the necessary expertise and how to acquire needed competencies. They may wonder what would be involved in terms of time and money. Answers to questions such as these are difficult to find. The consultation literature, for example, has very little to say about fees. This chapter responds to the beginning consultant's need for basic information on how to go about establishing a consultation practice.

What competencies are needed to practice consultation? Most successful consulting requires (1) competencies in a professional specialty, such as instructional design or the sociology of organizations, and (2) competencies in consultation, including a thorough understanding of work organizations, an understanding of the nature and ethics of the consultant role, and skill in helping professional peers. (The technical-professional competencies most in demand in the 1980s are discussed in Chapter Sixteen. Minimal competencies for successful consultation are listed in Table 4 and discussed in Chapter Eighteen.)

For a few consultation services, professionals need little or no special skills beyond those of a primary field. For instance, specialized consultation training is not essential for the computer specialist to teach an agency staff word-processing skills or for a clinical psychologist to evaluate the mental status of one of the agency's clients. However, even these types of services are likely to be more effective if the consultant has acquired basic consultation skills.

How can minimal consultation competencies be achieved? A large proportion of the necessary knowledge can be obtained through reading. The chapters in this book cover basic concepts and principles, and annotated bibliographies at the end of each chapter can help readers locate additional information on all aspects of consultation. In addition, Table 7, in Chapter Eighteen, contains a conveniently arranged reading list. To become a skilled practitioner, however, laboratory training and supervised field experiences are essential. Suggestions on sources through which individuals can obtain laboratory training and field supervision are found in Chapter Eighteen.

How much time does a consultation practice require? Persons who are already involved in a full-time job—such as an academic position or a clinical practice—often have little time left over for other activities. They may wonder whether consultation would require more time than they have to give. The proportion of time practitioners spend in consultation varies widely. Although many people practice consultation full-time, others spend most of their time in some other occupation and consult on an occasional basis. Consultants can put as little or as much time into consultation as they like.

How much time does a consultation take? A consultation may be limited to a three-hour workshop. It may involve a single contact in regard to a client or a program. Consultation may, however, extend indefinitely. A consultant might work on a continuing basis over a long period—perhaps years—visiting an agency weekly or monthly or remaining on an on-call basis. Most consultants and consultees prefer to start a consultation on a limited basis and expand it if both parties are so inclined. Ongoing consultation should be regularly reviewed to provide both consultant and consultee the option of continuing with the same arrangement, modifying it, or terminating.

Where do consultants work? Consultants do practically all their work in their client agencies. Full-time consultants, therefore, are very mobile people. They might, in the course of a week, visit as many as four or five agencies—including one or two that require out-of-town trips.

What kinds of settings do consultants come from? How does their "home base" affect their work? The settings consultants come from are varied. However, most fit into one of two categories—public-sector agencies or private practice—and it is this dimension that most influences their work.

Many consultants are employees of public-sector institutions that, in addition to providing direct services, offer consultation to the staff of other community agencies. Among the best-known and largest sources of these consultation services are the community mental health centers established by the 1963 Mental Health Centers Act. The primary mission of these centers is provision of direct services, but they also offer "outreach" programs that include indirect services. They provide consultation and education services to local agencies, such as schools, juvenile courts, nursing homes, and women's centers. Providing consultative services to other organizations is the *sole* purpose of some publicly funded agencies. For example, regional educational service centers offer public and private schools consultation and training in such areas as teaching techniques, media utilization, and organization development. Sometimes the consultant's agency and the consultee's agency are parts of a larger organization. Child services departments of state human welfare departments provide consultative services to local and regional welfare agencies. University-based counseling centers provide consultation to residence hall staff members.

Consultants who work out of publicly funded agencies frequently find consultative activities to be a refreshing and rewarding shift from heavy client loads and administrative responsibilities. However, they may face certain problems. When an agency's primary responsibility is to provide direct services, support for consultation is often relatively weak. Agency structures, peer-group norms, and rewards are typically geared for direct services. Little time may be budgeted for consultation. Interested staff members sometimes find themselves consulting on their own time or on agency time set aside for professional development. Those who become deeply involved in consultation often begin to feel like peripheral members of their organization.

When the outreach staff member is a counselor or therapist, the shift to the consultant role often creates considerable discomfort. Kamerschen (1974, pp. 3-4) vividly described this shift and the accompanying feelings when a university counseling center began an outreach consultation service:

> The new role created an identity crisis. Where once the counselor sat responsively in her office, she now had to relinquish that security and move to unfamiliar territories. The role of coequal replaced that of authority figure or helper. Rewards that once came quickly and clearly from grateful clients yielded to slower, more ambiguous, and frequently ambivalent reinforcement patterns from hesitant, cautious consultees. Knowledge of personality development and psychodynamics no longer sufficed. New concepts and learnings regarding the theory and practice of consultation, the structure, function, politics, and interrelationships of campus and community agencies, organizational dynamics, techniques to facilitate social systems change, ecosystems, funding sources and patterns, interaction styles, and many others became imperative for those who dared to venture forth. Watching one's cherished doctoral training shrink alongside the immensity of newly emergent bodies of knowledge would readily cause a quiver in even the most secure. Experienced staff members with strong identities and actively engaged in the competent delivery of their skills were understandably reluctant to return to the frustrations and ambiguities of the student-learner role in their own organization.

Consultants working out of agencies whose primary mission is to provide consultation services may encounter a special type of problem. Away from their home base most of the time, they often lose their sense of identification with it. Their particular activities may take precedence over the agency's priorities. They may begin to operate like private practitioners. They may view their consultee agencies as their "turf" and compete with other consultants for client organizations. Their competitiveness can be energizing and productive—but it can interfere with agency goals. Rivalry can prevent consultants from reviewing problems with their peers and thus adversely affect their performance and reduce their opportunities for growth.

Successful outreach programs require not only administrative and budgetary support. Outreach consultants need cognitive support from "home" staff to help them examine their experiences and problems. Consultants also need emotional support from their peers. Otherwise, they may turn to consultees to satisfy social and psychological needs and, in so doing, lose the independence and objectivity that are crucial to successful consultation.

A large number of consultants work out of the private sector. Many are on the staff of private organizations, some of which specialize in consultation. Some consultants work alone in an independent practice. Consultation is frequently a sideline activity. Individuals who are full-time employees of either public- or private-sector organizations often conduct a small consultation practice. They may work alone—out of a home office—or be associated with a consulting firm. Consultants who operate out of the private sector often have certain advantages over public-sector consultants. Consultees tend to view private-practice consultants as more competent and more professional (Levinson, 1978). Furthermore, unlike public-agency consultants, private-sector consultants almost always work on a fee basis, and agencies that pay consultants are more likely to be highly motivated to work with them. Moreover, private-practice consultants, since their practices are not subject to the constraints imposed by most human services agencies, usually offer a broader range of services.

Training programs provide a third type of home base for consultants. Numerous professional training programs now offer students field experiences as consultants. The status of trainee affects consultation services and relationships in several ways. The range of services offered by trainees is usually limited by their relatively narrow repertoire of skills and because of the restrictions imposed by training programs. For example, trainees may be restricted to such tasks as administering and reporting results of surveys, leading workshops, or performing case-centered consultation. Legitimization may be difficult for these consultants to achieve, because consultees are likely to stereotype students as naive and inexperienced. Consultant interns may not be allowed into the inner circle and its concerns. However, consultees' attitudes toward consultant-trainees are influenced by their attitudes toward the training program and the trainees' supervisors and may be highly positive.

What does it mean to be an internal consultant? Are there any special advantages or disadvantages for the in-house consultant? In many agencies certain staff members are designated as "consultants" to other members of the same organization. For example, a large childcare agency employs a child development specialist who consults with staff members of the agency's twelve neighborhood centers. The head of staff development in a state hospital consults with the directors of the institution's five units. The internal, or "in-house," consultant has unique advantages and disadvantages. On the positive side, internal consultants ordinarily are much more knowledgeable about their agencies than outsiders. They know the context and background of problems and the resources that might help solve them. Their in-depth knowledge and continuity of experience give them important advantages. However, since the agency is the primary source of internal consultants' income, they are likely to be more cautious than external consultants. Their interventions may avoid issues that, if confronted, might threaten their job security. And, like the prophet in his own land, the internal consultant must often contend with legitimization difficulties. Staff members typically attribute greater expertise to outsiders. Moreover, hierarchical status is a sensitive issue for in-house consultants. In-house consultees are likely to discount the expertise of an internal consultant whose hierarchical position is lower than theirs.

Objectivity may be difficult for in-house consultants to achieve. Their consultees may be justifiably suspicious of "vested" interests. As members of agency subsystems that have their own unique goals and values and compete with other subsystems for funding and power, internal consultants will tend to perceive and interpret agency phenomena from biased perspectives. The common assumptions that consultants are objective and that they support their consultees' values may not hold in these situations. For example, the student-oriented perspective of consultants from a university counseling center may conflict with perspectives of faculty members and administrators. A university professional from a mental health center, in consultation with a faculty member about problems of a failing student, is likely to feel a strong concern for the student's welfare and personal and educational development. The consultee may be much more concerned about preserving academic standards. Similarly, consultees who are in administrative positions are, quite properly, more likely to be concerned about maintaining rules and regulations. Thus, internal consultants, although more knowledgeable and committed to the agency than external consultants, usually have an "agenda" reflecting their particular niche within the organization. They are less able to serve the important function of bringing fresh, objective points of view to consultees. In addition, consultant and consultee may have a dual relationship involving role conflict. Consultants may have "line power," including supervisory and evaluation responsibilities, over consultees. In these cases, it is especially important to define the boundaries of the consultant and consultee roles at the beginning of consultation to reduce ambiguity as much as possible (Pipes, 1981).

The implications of these conflicts for internal consultation are little understood. Candid discussions can help clarify the issues and resolve conflicts. However, hierarchical and political considerations often prevent the parties involved from bringing problems into the open. Sometimes periodic use of an external consultant is helpful in these situations, but often the sticky issues inherent in in-house consultation cannot be fully resolved.

External consultants, as well as internal, may find themselves involved in multiple relationships with consultees that create role conflicts. For instance, a consultant and consultee may serve on the same professional board or public service committee. Sometimes a consultant and consultee are former colleagues or business associates. They may be related through family ties. They may belong to the same social club or neighborhood organization. These multiple relations produce an enriched but sometimes biased body of information and attitudes. They involve some degree of role conflict and the potential to adversely affect the consultation relationship and its outcomes. For example, consultants' perceptions of a consultee's work performance may be colored by the positive feelings emanating from a friendship or by negative feelings associated with a previous unpleasant experience. In addition, role conflicts are likely to limit consultants' freedom of expression and action. A consultant, for instance, may be hesitant to refuse to perform an inappropriate service for fear of jeopardizing a personal relationship with a consultee.

Ideally, consultants should be financially, socially, and emotionally independent of the consultee system in order to take needed risks. Their relationship to consultees should be temporary. They should be free to turn down or terminate any contract should adverse conditions appear.

How about fees? Consultation by staff members of public-sector agencies usually does not involve a direct financial transaction. Consultation may be a free or low-cost service, paid for by a grant from a third party, such as a private foundation or the federal government. However, some of these agencies are now offering consultation to business and industrial organizations for fees that net modest profits (MacLennan, 1979). An agency may pay a consultant's agency or pay the consultant directly (Beisser and Green, 1972). The commitment to pay consultant fees is usually associated with relatively high levels of motivation. Paid consultants are almost inevitably more valued than those who are available free of charge.

In calculating fees, consultants may charge on an hourly or a daily basis (Frankenhuis, 1979). Consultant fees reflect not only contact time but also, for example, that spent in preparing for a visit or in writing a report. If the consultant comes from a consultant firm, the fee must be set so as to contribute to over-head expenses. Consultants may be hired on a retainer basis. The agency then pays the consultant a monthly fee, no matter whether and how much the consultant is used. The contract may provide for the consultant to be available on an "on-call" basis. In such cases, the consultant's fee varies according to the time spent. Consultants base their fees on their experience, specialization, and reputation. Currently, fees of $50 an hour and $200 a day are at the low end of a continuum that, at the high end, is $100 or more an hour and $800 to $1,000 a day. Human services agencies often cannot afford private-practice consultants, since agency grants frequently set low ceilings—such as $100 or $200 a day—on consultant services.

How do consultants contact potential consultees? Is it proper to take the initiative in seeking a contract with an agency? These questions touch on a basic consultant concern—the degree to which "promotional" activities are appropriate in consultation. The underlying issues are complex, and the questions are difficult to answer. Consultants' attitudes toward promotional activities are influenced by their training background, the degree to which they are known as consultants, the norms of their "home base," and the norms of the client organization. In the business world, the standard practice is to initiate contacts and to engage in other promotional activities, such as mailouts. Consultants from the private sector typically bring this tradition to their work with human services agencies (Ford, 1969; Lippitt and Lippitt, 1978). Consultants from academic settings and mental health professions are more likely to wait for agencies to make the first overture. Typically the direct service work of mental health professionals brings them into contact with a number of human service organizations. Requests for consultation evolve in the natural course of events. However, some mental health professionals do not wait for agency invitations. As a part of their agency's mission, professionals working in outreach programs—such as those based in Planned Parenthood centers, educational service centers, state hospitals, and university counseling centers—call on certain organizations to explain their services and solicit contracts (Pipes, 1981).

Many helping professionals feel ambivalent about promotional activities, especially when fees are involved. The ethical codes of some helping professions imply that promotional activities are contradictory to the goal of "helping." Actually, many professional activities are subtly entrepreneurial. Individuals may perform free or low-cost services (making speeches or presenting workshops, for instance) with the expectation that they will lead to fee-for-service contracts. Academicians and professionals sometimes secure grant money to provide consultation to human services agencies in order to, obtain research subjects or to promote copyrighted tests or materials. Similarly, state and federal agencies package and "sell" programs that include "consultation" services. These services increase the income and expand the territory of the providers, benefiting them as well as the "recipient" agencies.

Well-known and sought-after consultants have little reason to initiate contacts. Beginning consultants, even though they may prefer not to, may find they must initiate introductory contacts if they wish to get started in consultation. In any case, promotional activities that give consumers accurate information about consultants' services seem to be valid and useful. Calling on agencies to introduce oneself and to describe services such as workshops or seminars seems an appropriate way to contact potential consultees. An introductory interview can provide both consultees and consultant with opportunities to discover whether they are interested in further involvement.

Do consultants often work in teams? Because it makes a service much more costly, consultants do not work in teams as much as most would like. However, teams can add greatly to the productivity of consultation because they can offer a wider range of resources and because individual biases are more easily corrected by teams. Teams can also contribute to their members' personal and professional growth, although they are sometimes troubled by internal difficulties that require considerable time and effort to resolve (Khajavi, Broskowski, and Mermis, 1972; Steele, 1975). In the future, consultants will probably find themselves working more often in teams, as services—both those delivered by consultants and those delivered by agencies —become increasingly specialized.

What are the steps or phases of the consultation process? Like most other services, consultation proceeds through phases (Altrocchi, 1972; Lippitt and Lippitt, 1978):

1. Preliminary explorations.
2. Negotiation of a contract.
3. Entry.
4. Diagnosis of problems or needs.
5. Goal setting.
6. Exploration of intervention alternatives and selection of one or more intervention strategies.
7. Implementation of intervention.
8. Evaluation of outcomes.
9. Institutionalization of change.
10. Termination of consultation.

These phases are rarely sharply defined. Moreover, backward movements often occur. For instance, an intervention in the implementation stage uncovers new data that indicate the diagnosis was inaccurate. The unexpected information leads to a new diagnosis, which, in turn, calls for a review of agency needs and consultation goals. A new contract emerges that modifies the role of the original consultant and adds the services of another consultant in order to obtain skills in a different specialty. Awareness of the nature and sequence of these phases by all parties involved can help them keep discussions focused and productive. Some consultants suggest regular "stop sessions" in which they discuss with the consultees the progress of their work and the degree to which both parties are satisfied (Lippitt and Lippitt, 1978, p. 23).

Each of the ten phases listed has at least two distinctive elements: (1) the consultee's work and (2) the consultant's relationship to the consultee and the consultee's work.

1. *Preliminary explorations.* In this phase, the consultant and the consultee explore the agency's needs and the relevance of the consultant's competencies, interests, and values to those needs. The goal is to find out whether there is sufficient "fit" to justify working together.

2. *Contract negotiation.* The task of this phase is to evolve a tentative contract. Ordinarily, at this point problems and solutions can be defined only in general and tentative terms, because sufficient data for a conclusive diagnosis are lacking. Since the underlying problems are not yet clear, the usefulness of the consultant and his or her potential functions are also uncertain. However, consultant and consultee begin to discuss possible ways they might work together.

3. *Entry.* After the contractual agreement, the consultant officially enters the agency, begins to get acquainted, and begins to explore the problems and needs presented by the consultees—individuals or groups. The task is to get sufficiently inside the agency to understand its general nature and to establish open communication with the staff.

4. *Diagnosis of problems or needs.* The task of the diagnostic phase is to gather and interpret sufficient data to formulate a diagnosis. The diagnostic process includes scanning the context of the problem and examining the forces or systems affecting it. The degree to which consultant and consultee interact in this task varies greatly (see Chapter Four). Many consultants prefer an independent approach. Some, however, find it more satisfactory to collaborate with consultees in gathering data and formulating diagnoses. Achievement of a diagnosis that appears valid may take one or many interviews.

5. *Goal setting.* After the problems or needs are identified, the consultation moves into a goal-setting phase. Often consultant and consultees propose and weigh the merits of a number of goals. They may weigh alternative goals on the basis of such criteria as urgency and feasibility—for instance, availability of resources and staff interests. Sometimes at this point the conclusion is that there are no realistic solutions to the problem. Consequently, consultation may stop here. Or it may appear that the goals could be reached with the present staff resources (without further consultant help) or would require skills outside the range of the consultant's competencies.

6. *Exploration of intervention alternatives and selection of one or more intervention strategies.* The next task is to decide on the best method for reaching chosen goals. Alternative

solutions are generated and examined. In reviewing options, attention is given to the consultee's needs, the nature of the problem, the resources available, constraints, and the points most amenable to intervention. A force-field analysis is often used to identify the forces that are keeping the agency from moving closer to its target and the forces that are helping—or might help —it move toward the goal (Lewin, 1951). These forces are ranked in order of importance, and the alterable ones are identified. The intervention steps chosen should include a clear definition of the objectives, the actions to be used in reaching the objectives, any barriers or problems to be anticipated, and the persons responsible for any action. The consultant's role, functions, and responsibilities and those of consultees should be clarified. Criteria for evaluation of the success of the intervention are specified. Methods for evaluation are determined and a schedule for evaluation steps is established.

7. *Implementation of intervention.* Next, the chosen strategy is implemented. Implementation need not involve the consultant. The functions of consultants who continue into the implementation vary widely. They may range from suggestions and advising to teaching, training, and direct "hands-on" involvement.

8. *Evaluation of outcomes.* The evaluation of the degree to which goals have been achieved provides feedback for further decisions. The contract should have made clear whether evaluation is a part of the consultant's functions. Consultees often prefer to conduct their own evaluation. An assessment of the consultant's performance is often included in the evaluation.

9. *Institutionalization of change.* Institutionalization of changes involves incorporation and routinizing of any new procedures and behaviors that have been assessed as desirable. This is the phase that Lewin (1951) calls "refreezing," the stabilizing of the changed behaviors. Typically, agencies need to provide social and financial incentives, additional training, and special monitoring and feedback mechanisms to ensure that new behaviors are incorporated and maintained.

10. *Termination of consultation.* Termination of the consultant's involvement may come at any step. Often it comes

at a late stage, following refreezing (institutionalization). Termination might occur through a series of steps. First the consultant might reduce the intensity of the relationship by gradually reducing involvement in terms of time and activity level. Termination plans often include supportive follow-up structures, such as temporary task forces, an internal consultant, or telephone follow-up calls by the external consultant.

How can a consultant move from working with agencies on a limited basis—such as conducting surveys or leading workshops—to working with them on more basic problems and on a more long-term basis? Typically, the relationship between a consultant and an agency begins with a limited contract that—if outcomes are satisfactory—expands over time. Consultants usually move from a narrow role and focus toward broader functions that involve more diffuse organizational problems and more penetrating interventions. Sometimes the first stage in the development of a consultative relationship is a test of the consultant's competence, integrity, and willingness to conform to the parameters prescribed by the agency. "The initial request for assistance may conceal issues that at least to some extent want to keep hidden, even from the consultant. Success in the consultation may depend then on establishing trust so as to get down to basic problems and aims without threatening agency staff" (Glaser, 1978, p. 9).

Progressive changes in the roles and relationships of members of a large consulting firm illustrate the developmental nature of consultation. The psychologists who in the 1940s joined the engineering staff of the consultant firm of Roher, Hibler and Replogle at first served clinical functions ("The Work of RHR: Section I: A Brief Overview," 1976). They assessed employees under consideration for promotion to executive positions and screened prospective employees. During the second stage of development, these consultants began to help staff members increase their managerial and interpersonal skills. During the third phase, consultants' attention shifted to the "corpus." They began to analyze and intervene in organizational dynamics.

Caplan (1970) identified eight stages in the evolution of the relationship between mental health consultants and agencies. The consultant's functions progress in the following order:

1. Linkage for referrals from the agency to the consultant's own clinic.
2. Education and training for agency staff.
3. Screening and diagnosis of agency clients. Recommendations for their treatment.
4. Collaboration with agency staff in treatment.
5. Client-centered consultation to help agency staff with difficult cases.
6. Consultee-centered consultation to help staff increase their skills.
7. Program-centered consultation with agency administrators.
8. Consultee-centered consultation with agency administrators.

A case study of consultants' work with the Peace Corps illustrates in greater detail the evolution of the relationship from a restricted, client-centered model to the seventh stage described by Caplan, the program-centered model. The consultants in this case envisioned and hoped for a broad role from the beginning of their discussions with agency administrators (English, 1968). However, they found their activities restricted to narrow, clinical functions until they demonstrated their usefulness.

Peace Corps administrators knew volunteers would undergo emotional stress during their two-year stint in a foreign country. They would be speaking a new and difficult language, eating strange foods, living in primitive circumstances, and isolated from contact with Americans. These administrators hoped to reduce the number of casualties by careful psychiatric screening and hired mental health clinicians for this important task. The consultants' first assignment was to give applicants intensive medical screening and make recommendations for acceptance or rejection. The consultants were extremely successful in this work. Of the 20,000 volunteers—who, at that time, had served in fifty countries—the rate of premature return for psychiatric reasons was less than 1 percent. Legitimized through their success as clinical consultants, these professionals were then invited to consult in regard to the training processes. They helped in the psychological preparation of recruits by meeting with them in small groups to discuss potential overseas adjustment problems and ways of coping with them. Consultants also began to consult with the training teams. They helped members of these teams anticipate trainees' adjustment problems.

In the Peace Corps's second year, administrators faced the task of keeping volunteers overseas. They asked their consultants to visit volunteer programs overseas for the purpose of diagnosing problems and making recommendations for their resolution. The consultants discovered that volunteers' adjustment was delayed by the training design, which left them alone in their first months of service. Cut off from support staff and from one another, trainees felt isolated and abandoned. Each had a feeling that her or his problems were unique. The consultants' diagnosis led to changes that provided volunteers with more careful and specific preparation for the adjustment period and the opportunity to meet with support staff more frequently.

The agency faced new problems in the third year. There was evidence that the volunteers had changed as a result of their highly significant but disruptive experiences. A big question was how to get them returned to their homes and reintegrated into their communities as smoothly as possible. Consultants suggested that the staff hold "completion of service conferences" in the overseas country just before the end of the two-year tour of duty to prepare volunteers psychologically for their return. The consultants led small-group discussions to help volunteers conceptualize and integrate their experiences. In addition, consultants developed a questionnaire to survey volunteers' problems and satisfactions and used the results of the survey as the basis for two days of intensive discussions in small groups of volunteers who had been trained together before going overseas and who had served in the same country.

The consultants summarized and interpreted information gained through these discussions and surveys. Their findings provided valuable data for Peace Corps administrators. To illustrate, from survey data, the consultants found that an overall adjustment pattern characterized all volunteer experiences. Four major periods of psychological difficulty could be predicted to occur during the twenty-one months of overseas service. Consultants also identified variations in adjustment patterns related to the area of the world in which the volunteer served. The consultants' feedback was used as the basis for improvements in training volunteers, in assigning them and supporting them during their tours, and in the education and training of the support staff.

What do I have to offer? This question is commonly a source of concern to beginning consultants. Beyond clear-cut tasks in their specialty areas—such as administering and interpreting a survey or giving technical advice about a program—they may wonder whether they have anything to offer consultees. This chapter and the preceding ones have emphasized structured aspects of consultation. The discussions have focused on services involving carefully specified content (the consultant's specialty area) and processes (such as analyzing a job design, reviewing and critiquing a proposal for a new program, or coaching an administrator in how to motivate employees). Although structure is an essential feature of consultation, the picture conveyed through descriptions of predetermined and carefully defined consultant services is incomplete. Consultation often involves far more, and a consultant's most important contributions may not be mentioned in the contract. For instance, consultants may introduce a point of view that puts a problem in a new perspective and opens up new solutions. They may make an encouraging remark that gives a "burned-out" consultee the lift needed to keep working on a difficult task. They may ask a question that crystallizes the issues in a conflict situation. These helping processes are not dependent on expertise in a technical specialty. They depend on the consultant's more objective perspective and on problem-solving or interpersonal skills.

Typically, neither consultants nor consultees are aware of the many ways one person can help another solve problems (Lippitt and Lippitt, 1978). Therefore, although consultants may have the potential to make a number of contributions, they may not make full use of their resources. By making some of these informal helping services explicit, consultants may become more aware that they have many ways to help consultees. The following pages describe some of the more informal and spontaneous ways consultants can help consultees in any phase of consultation—from the initial interview to the termination.

Because they have different backgrounds of training and experience and because they are in a relatively detached position, consultants view agency phenomena differently than the staff does. Often consultants' most helpful service is bringing consultees different perspectives. New perspectives can dissipate consultees' attitudinal blocks (Beisser and Green, 1972; Caplan, 1970; Clark, 1977). New perspectives help consultees "reframe" their problems (Emery and Marholin, 1977; Hopper and Whitehead, 1979; McGreeny, 1978; Sills, 1976). Reframing lifts the problem out of one set of parameters—which, in some cases, may present unsolvable conditions—into a changed category and parameters. Reframing makes possible the introduction of new data into both the definition and solution of the problem.

To illustrate, a consultant conferring with the discipline committee of a high school was puzzled by the committee's unusually severe reactions until he realized that the student being discussed had, in an unrelated incident, angered one of the most influential members of the committee. The consultant introduced new perspectives into the discussion. He (1) noted some of the student's positive characteristics, (2) raised questions about the standard penalties for the violation being discussed, and (3) asked whether the student's developmental needs were relevant. These new perspectives led the committee to bring a much wider range of data and concepts to bear on the case and to reach a more appropriate and constructive recommendation. In a similar way, a consultant helped an administrator—whose judgments about a consultee were colored by anger—to weigh the employee's performance from a number of points of view and to decide how to handle the problem on the basis of a consideration of the entire agency and from a long-term perspective. Consultants often help consultees who are feeling inadequate or guilty over their failures through introducing a "normalizing" or "universalizing" perspective. By helping consultees see their difficulties from a broader and less subjective viewpoint, consultants can help consultees see that problems that seem unique are actually inherent aspects of their jobs.

Consultants can help a consultee or an entire staff conceptualize problems. Often perceptions of problems are unclear.

Consultees are so caught up in "doing" that they are unable to generalize. Consultants can help consultees explicate the feelings, thoughts, and incidents that are creating tensions and tie these data together with unifying concepts. For example, an administrator, perplexed by the destructive competition of two staff members, might find "sibling rivalry" a helpful concept in understanding and managing the situation. The administrator's individually oriented leadership style might be exacerbating competition. Generalizations such as these allow consultees a means of organizing discrete data into hypotheses that can then be confirmed or rejected through further data collection and analysis.

Consultants can help a consultee or an entire staff structure their problem-solving approaches. They can offer new models for problem solving and help consultees apply them to their particular situations (Schein, 1969). They can help consultees increase their options by testing out their assumptions about what can or cannot be changed. Through habit, consultees may be imposing unnecessarily narrow limits on their choices—for example, through overly restrictive interpretations of agency policies or of their roles. Consultants can help staff members generate a wide range of solutions and choose and plan action steps.

Staff members of human services agencies often feel overwhelmed or "burned out" by the stressful conditions under which they work. Consequently, they are unable to function effectively. In some cases, just the awareness that a consultant is available results in a "placebo" effect that strengthens consultees' abilities to confront their problems and yet maintain their psychological equilibrium (Beisser and Green, 1972). But consultants may also offer emotional support, or "nutriment" (Levine, 1972), through words of encouragement and praise. Sometimes the support most needed is simply an opportunity to ventilate feelings of hostility or anxiety. Consultants may help by conveying their acceptance of negative feelings such as anger and the wish to give up. Consultants may help consultees realize that sometimes they can increase their effectiveness by temporarily giving up—taking a few days off. Consultants can help chronically stressed consultees evaluate their situations and consider the possibility of changing to less stressful jobs. Emotional support can take many forms. Consultants should be alert to the potential usefulness of less obvious methods of support. The most needed support could be assistance in crystallizing a problem—thereby making it less ambiguous (and anxiety-producing) and more amenable to solution. The most needed support could be to provide direct advice on how to manage a particular situation or to provide information on potentially helpful resources. Sometimes consultants can offer the most support by saying nothing and allowing the consultee to put the data together (Steele, 1975).

Stress may be an agencywide phenomenon created by budget cuts or shifts in services. Administrators may be unable to provide needed support. Consultants can help staff members of agencies whose budgets are being cut talk about and mourn losses of money and people (Levinson, 1978, p. 49). Consultants can help an agency staff face and accept the reality of an impossible situation. Consultants can help members meet one another's need for support by encouraging them to share concerns and resources (Ferguson, 1969). They can function as mediators between conflicting factions (Walton, 1969).

Sometimes consultants can be most helpful by challenging consultees. They can interrupt unproductive cycles (Blake and Mouton, 1976; Goodstein, 1978; Shephard, 1969). Once-functional behaviors become dysfunctional over time. Organizational and individual behaviors often become so ritualized and mechanical as to be beyond awareness and choice. Consultants can suggest temporarily suspending action and analyzing processes—for example, decision making or the mode of communication. Consultants can ask questions that encourage consultees to examine their behaviors and assumptions. Direct confrontation can, at times, be a helpful function. Consultees may be entrenched in dysfunctional patterns. For example, they may deny problems, avoid conflict, and ignore discrepancies between their goals and their actual operations. In many cases a risky procedure, but one that can be extremely valuable, is to express the unconfronted problem or discrepancy in a vivid and memorable way. Obviously, a consultant cannot and should not insist that consultees examine the issues they are avoiding. But a consultant can suggest that consultees consider their behavior and its apparent advantages and disadvantages. Thus, consultants can say unpleasant things that need to be said but that consultees are not saying. Consultees may be so close to the issues that they cannot see them clearly. They may be unable to articulate them. Often consultees are painfully aware of certain unproductive patterns but unwilling to say what is obvious because of fear of reprisals or fear of damaging a work relationship. Consultants can afford to take risks. They are expendable. They can protect consultees' relationships by saying aloud what some consultees are thinking. They can take the role of the scapegoat, the "ritual pig" whose sacrifice restores agency peace (Steele, 1975).

   Consultants serve as models of alternative attitudes, behaviors, and problem-solving processes. Thus, they expand consultees' options. For example, consultants model their reactions to adversity, their spirit of inquiry, their coping methods, and their sensitivity to others' needs and feelings. When an administrator complains that she is unable to get feedback from subordinates, her consultant can demonstrate, through the consultation process, how to open one's self up to criticism and how to clarify, evaluate, and use feedback. When consultees feel depressed, consultants can model hopefulness by their attitude that most problems can be confronted and solved. To illustrate, a consultant team experienced continual failure in its work with a rigid, bureaucratic organization. Members of the team felt powerless and ready to quit. They decided to call on another consultant to help them examine the impasse. As they told him of their despair and recounted details, the consultant's face became animated, and he leaned toward them, saying excitedly, "I am fascinated. What a challenging situation! Tell me more." His attitude was infectious. The team members soon became energized, too. As they continued to talk about the agency, they realized they had overlooked certain leverage points. They also saw abundant opportunities for their own learning—about themselves, about agency dynamics, and about the consultative process. Three hours of this consultation changed their emotional state and attitudes. They decided to try a number of new intervention strategies. The consultant's modeling ultimately brought about some unexpected successes in the consultation.

Finally, consultants can alert consultees to external resources, such as community services, other consultants, books, journals, and training opportunities. Consultants can also help consultees identify untapped internal resources.

Annotated Bibliography

Frankenhuis, J. P. "How to Get a Good Consultant." In C. R. Bell and L. Nadler (Eds.), *The Client-Consultant Handbook*. Houston: Gulf Publishing Co., 1979. Although the author wrote this article to help managers make decisions about the hiring of consultants, the information he presents will be of interest to beginning consultants as well. Frankenhuis discusses major ways consultants can be useful and issues related to fees. He also contrasts the advantages and disadvantages of hiring individual practitioners, rather than consultants from consulting firms.

Jay, A. "Rate Yourself as a Client." In C. R. Bell and L. Nadler (Eds.), *The Client-Consultant Handbook*. Houston: Gulf Publishing Co., 1979. Jay proposes principles for clients to make optimal use of consultants. He also points out some major "sins" of clients and consultants. This essay can help new consultants anticipate common pitfalls and learn ways of avoiding them.

Lippitt, G., and Lippitt, R. *The Consulting Process in Action*. San Diego, Calif.: University Associates, 1978. New consultants will find this volume useful in orienting them to the field. Chap. 2, "Phases in Consulting," is particularly helpful in highlighting the authors' views of the tasks associated with the different stages of consultation.

Platt, J. J., and Wicks, R. J. (Eds.). *The Psychological Consultant*. New York: Grune & Stratton, 1979. This book describes opportunities for psychologists and other social and behavioral scientists to work as consultants in public- and private-sector organizations. The book provides valuable information for professionals who want to enter the consulting field.

12

Preliminary Exploration, Contracting, and Entry

The consultant's entry into an organization usually takes place in a four-step process. First comes a preliminary exploration of agency needs and of the consultant's qualifications relevant to those needs. If the "fit" appears satisfactory, the second step, discussion of a contract, begins. If this discussion leads to a mutually satisfactory agreement, the consultant physically enters the organization to begin work—the third step. If a good fit between agency needs and consultant's competencies continues and if certain other conditions are satisfied, a marked increase in consultees' trust and confidence appears. Psychological entry, the fourth step in the entry process, has been completed. Consultees now allow the consultant to enter their work family and become privy to its secrets. Until this last step is accomplished, lack of credibility and lack of vital information impede the progress of consultation. This chapter discusses issues related to these steps and recommends guidelines for moving through them successfully.

Preliminary Exploration

The contacts and conditions that might lead an agency and a consultant to schedule an exploratory interview were described in Chapter Eleven. The objective of this interview is to exchange information that will enable both parties to make tentative decisions about whether they would like to work together. To expedite the discussion, consultants often send a résumé to agency administrators ahead of time to acquaint them with the consultant's background. Most consultants also like to expand their knowledge of an agency in advance of an interview by talking to colleagues who have worked with similar agencies or by reading journals commonly read by the staff. The information needed at this preliminary stage might take more than one interview and involve a number of agency staff members as well as more than one consultant. Usually a period of one and a half or two hours is ample for amenities and for this first exchange of information.

Agency staff members use this interview to find out whether the consultant has competencies relevant to their needs, to learn his or her style and method of working (including confidentiality policies), and to obtain an estimate of the costs and benefits of consultation. The consultant will want to find out the nature and goals of the agency, its apparent needs or problems, its degree of commitment to a consultative intervention (including money and staff energy and time), and any existing expectations about how the consultant is to be used and what outcomes are to be sought. Both parties will want to find out whether their values and working styles are harmonious. They will want to identify any constraints or conflicts that might affect their relationship. Trust will be a common concern. The interview processes, as well as the content, provide important data for answering questions.

The initial interview is usually held in the agency's offices or in a neutral setting, such as a luncheon meeting in a restaurant. Holding the exploratory interview in the agency offers the advantages of underscoring the work nature of the relationship and allowing the consultant to observe the agency environment and interpersonal processes. Sometimes agency staff members, however, prefer the neutrality and casualness of a luncheon meeting. They may view this type of meeting as less binding and formal than an office interview and as giving them greater control of consequences. Should either of the parties decide to opt out of further exploration, he or she is likely to find the rejection easier if this initial interview takes place in a "nonbusiness" environment. Sometimes administrators, to reduce feelings of obligation, ask to buy the consultant's lunch—a sort of reimbursement for time. Some consultants make a practice of buying lunches for prospective consultees. However, many consultants and administrators prefer to get their relationship on an equitable basis from the start by agreeing to a nominal sum for the consultant's interview time.

The interview often begins with a clarification of the interview objectives, the topics to be covered, and the time to be allotted to the meeting. The consultant's areas of expertise and method of working might well be the next item on the agenda. Agency administrators typically check on the background of potential consultants before this interview and review their résumés. But unless they already know the consultant well, it is safe to assume that administrators would like additional information. A brief oral presentation of credentials is often desirable. Prospective consultees may want to *hear* consultants discuss their backgrounds and to use this presentation as a springboard for asking questions. Often administrators ask "what if" questions, raising issues in a hypothetical form. Consultants may choose to respond directly to the underlying questions (usually involving concerns about the consultant's confidentiality guidelines, experience in a crucial area, values, and style of work) by seeking to explicate them, by answering them candidly, and by inviting the administrators to raise any further questions. The agency problem or need is, of course, the highest priority on the agenda. When agency representatives begin to describe their concerns, consultants begin to raise where, when, why, and how questions.

Inquiries about the results of any previous attempts to solve problems, either from within or with consultant help, are also in order.

At an early point, consultants may discover that the agency staff members are not describing a problem but instead are asking for a particular intervention, making a request on the basis of implicit diagnoses and assumptions. Such requests might be related to reports of the consultant's past success in the proposed intervention. For example, an administrator learns from the head of another agency about a successful team-building intervention by consultant X. The administrator contacts consultant X and asks for the same intervention. Requests that bypass the diagnostic process present a dilemma. The consultant may have reason to doubt that the requested intervention would alleviate agency problems. Yet, the intervention would provide an entry point from which consultant and consultees might move to a more meaningful contract. Some consultants deliberately follow the consultees' prescription even though it appears to be off-target. Their rationale is that compliance with the role and task prescribed by the consultee is likely to increase the latter's acceptance. However, a prescribed task may appear so irrelevant or destructive that the consultant declines to be involved further. For instance, it may be clear that the requested intervention would involve unethical practices or fail because of lack of necessary resources to follow through.

Many consultants prefer to establish an interactive and collaborative process from the beginning. If they find consultees are unwilling to open up the decision-making process, these consultants might terminate the entry process at this point. These consultants respond to a request for a particular intervention with a suggestion for keeping options open until sufficient data are collected to make a careful diagnosis and until a number of intervention options are considered. For example, a consultant might use a request to lead mandatory in-service training as a springboard for discussion of training goals, alternative methods for reaching them, and the likely costs and benefits of each alternative. Since the diagnosis is at this point unclear, the consultant should describe a wide range of potential interventions and illustrate them with concrete examples to convey their potential to consultees. The question whether consultation is the most feasible or efficient approach to the agency's needs should be raised, and alternative resources should be considered.

During this interview, consultants will be seeking answers to certain crucial questions. They will want to know the support within the agency for change. They will be particularly interested in how the persons participating in the interview relate to the organization and to the problem, their power to intervene, and their authority in regard to hiring a consultant. Consultants will want to identify any internal conflicts that could affect the success of the consultation. Consultants might raise questions of the advisability of further exploratory interviews with other key agency staff members. Some consultants insist on contacting any persons or groups opposing consultation, in order to avoid being seen as the "hired gun" of the administration (Goodstein, 1978).

Consultees will be interested in the probable cost of consultation. If they do not ask about fees, the consultant should introduce the topic. Expenses such as travel, food, lodgings, and materials should be discussed—if relevant—and are usually separate from fees. In some situations the length of the consultation should be discussed. However, estimates at this point are highly tentative, since the nature and scope of the problem and of the intervention itself are uncertain.

From the earliest contact, consultants are responsible for expressing their own values and alerting consultees to any significant values conflicts. A certain degree of compatibility in values is essential for an effective work relationship. To demand complete agreement, however, is unrealistic and would, in fact, be counterproductive. Consultants are hired to bring about changes (such as in processes, norms, behavior, or techniques) that ordinarily involve some degree of shift in the agency's values.[1] But important discrepancies in social or political values

---

[1] Shifts in values may also occur in the opposite direction. As consultants' understanding of an agency's work increases, they may undergo a significant change in attitudes, beliefs, or values. For example, consultants working with police significantly changed their own attitudes toward police (Bard and Berkowitz, 1969).

may appear in the exploratory period and raise questions of the appropriateness of a contract. Sometimes consultants find that an organization's values so obviously contradict their own that they immediately decide not to work with it. For example, a consultant with a pro-abortion orientation would probably decline to work with a right-to-life group. Value conflicts may not be immediately visible, however, especially to inexperienced consultants and consultees. A novice consultant—a social worker —agreed to work with a law enforcement agency to help polygraph examiners improve their interviewing skills. In the first session he discovered a values conflict that more seasoned consultants would have recognized in advance. The consultant's overriding interview goal was to help interviewees. His training and values called for him to protect clients' rights and autonomy. The goal of these officers was quite different—yet it was appropriate to their jobs. They sought to "entrap" interviewees into revealing information in order to obtain data that they needed to carry out their responsibility to protect the public. In other situations, conflicts are subtle and difficult to pinpoint and explicate.

Consultants respond quite differently to values conflicts. Some consultants accept contracts without regard for value differences; Bowen (1977), for example, questions the right of consultants to refuse to work with an organization with conflicting values. He believes conflicts can be minimized by adhering to the primary tasks of helping clients generate valid information and make free choices to which they are internally committed (Argyris, 1970). Some consultants refuse to work in situations in which conflicts are likely to arise. They contend that consultants should consider both the organization's internal values and its goods or services (Goodstein, 1978); the "consultant should have some belief in the end product of the client's efforts if his or her efforts are to have any 'payoff'" (p. 94). Levine (1972) believes consultants should not work in organizations with which there are major values conflicts and should never allow themselves to be agents of agencies or consultees who are destructive to the "human spirit." For instance, "if the sole purpose of a consulting contract in a prison was to reduce

the likelihood of riots or escapes by helping to make the custodial and security arrangements more perfect, and helping them
to make the inmates more automatonlike, then we would have
no business in the setting" (Levine, 1972, p. 18).

Much of the necessary information is exchanged in the
content of the discussion. Interview *processes* are, however,
equally important sources of data for both consultees and consultant. Professional competencies are often communicated more
convincingly through behavior than through résumés. For instance, by asking questions that help agency representatives see
their situation in new or more complicated ways or by noting a
pattern in a series of events, consultants demonstrate the ability
to bring their professional expertise into the agency's specific
context. The consultant's personal characteristics—for example,
values, interpersonal style, and responsiveness to others' feelings
and ideas—are similarly manifest in the processes of an interview. Conversely, staff behaviors provide the consultant with
cues about their openness to new ideas, commitment to change,
coping style, communications patterns, and attitude toward
consultation. For example, the administrator who asks for opinions and thoughtfully listens and responds to them is likely to
be open to new ideas. The administrator who sits behind a large
desk, ten feet and a desk away from the consultant, might be
predicted to be impersonal and controlling. Sometimes, the processes emerging in a first interview accurately predict enduring
patterns—such as conflict over control—in the consultant/con-
sultee relationship (Steele, 1975).

Consultants should strive to ensure that their behavior is
consistent with their values. Those who wish to work collabora-
tively should demonstrate their respect for consultees' views.
Consultants who value open communication should themselves
demonstrate candor in this first interview. They should be direct and open in giving opinions and in asking questions. They
should make it clear that they expect consultees to ask questions, raise concerns, and express their expectations and assumptions openly. To clearly demonstrate their values, some process-
oriented consultants begin in the initial interview to discuss ongoing processes. They comment on the progress of the interview

and invite agency representatives to do the same and to share any reactions to the interview's progress.

The exploratory phase may conclude the discussions. Either party may decide against further involvement because of a values conflict. Consultants may find the conditions imposed on their role by the agency to be unacceptable. For instance, an administrator might want a consultant to interview staff members to gather information to evaluate them. The agency may decide that the consultant lacks the necessary expertise or other qualifications. Both parties may want to think further about possibilities. A pause in the discussions helps agencies and consultants alike by giving them time to consider the information produced by the interview and to weigh the potential advantages and disadvantages of entering into a contract. The outcome may be a commitment by the consultee and consultant to enter the second phase, contractual negotiations.

Contracting

In the second stage of entry, consultant and agency representatives discuss and negotiate terms for working together. The resulting contract may be a formal, legally worded document. More often, it is a letter reviewing the terms of an informal agreement. It may be an oral agreement, a "psychological" contract that defines the nature and goals of the relationship (Goodstein, 1978; Schein, 1969). The contract, whether formal or informal, should cover most of the following elements:

1. General goals of consultation.

2. Tentative time frame.

3. Consultant's responsibilities:
    a. Services to be provided.
    b. Methods to be used.
    c. Time to be committed to the agency.
    d. Evaluation of the degree to which goals are achieved —including the type of evaluation, the nature of any reports, and dates for their submission.

4. Agency responsibilities:
   a. Nature and extent of staff contributions to consultation.
   b. Fees to be paid to consultant, including expenses such as travel, per diem, and materials.

5. Consultant's boundaries:
   a. The contact person to whom the consultant is to be responsible, the gatekeeper or primary consultee (usually the agency's chief executive officer).
   b. Persons to whom the consultant is to have access and those who are out of bounds.
   c. Consultant's access in terms of departments, meetings, and documents.
   d. Conditions for bringing in other consultants or trainees.
   e. Confidentiality rules regarding all information.

6. Arrangements for periodic review and evaluation of the consultant's work and the agency's support of that work; explication of freedom of either party to terminate the contract if consultation progress is unsatisfactory.

Problems may arise in regard to any aspect of the consultation contract—including its content and the process through which it is negotiated. Sometimes contractual discussions fail to identify discrepancies between an agency's and the consultant's expectations of the consultant's role. For instance, significant differences may exist between the consultant's input—values, behaviors, or technology—and agency values, norms, and technology. To illustrate, a halfway house for adolescent offenders obtained a grant to train staff members in counseling skills. The administrator hired a distinguished psychotherapist to consult with and train the staff. After the first meeting, however, staff members avoided the consultant. Eventually, the administrator discovered that the consultant, whose orientation was psychoanalytic, was suggesting psychodynamic explanations and solutions that were contradictory to the behavioral approaches in which the staff had been trained. Caught in a bind between the consultant's concepts and their own philosophy and methods, they resolved the bind by not showing up for consultation at all.

To avoid problems of this type, consultants should provide clear information on the range and limits of their competencies in relation to problems and services being discussed. Consultants should also make explicit any professional and personal biases and values that are likely to affect their work. In the contractual negotiations (and periodically throughout a consultation) consultants should raise the following questions:

Are the consultant's resources relevant and adequate for the agency's needs?

Does the consultant have sufficient independence and objectivity to be effective?

Are the consultant's values and objectives compatible with those of the agency?

Does the consultant have the time, interest, and commitment to follow through with the consultation?

Another common problem in the contractual stage is the failure to obtain the sanction of the agency's chief executive officer, the official "gatekeeper." Consultants ordinarily should not enter an organization without this person's explicit sanction and confirmation of the consultant's goals, methods, and boundaries. Often agency administrators delegate to subordinates the authority and responsibility for contracting with consultants and subsequent management of this relationship. But it is risky to finalize a contract without at least a brief face-to-face meeting with the agency's chief. Agencies and the clients they serve are composed of multiple constituencies, and consultants' services inevitably benefit certain staff members, clients, policies, or departments more than others. The person who represents the agency in the contractual decisions becomes the consultant's gatekeeper—the person who determines how and for whose benefit the consultant is to be used, channels the entry into the organization, establishes confidentiality rules, and receives the consultant's feedback and interpretations. This person's interests and consultation goals may differ from those of the agency's chief administrator; but without a careful review, differences—even serious conflicts—may not be apparent. To illustrate, the associate director of a large child guidance clinic, who had obtained a grant to develop a comprehensive program to teach parenting skills to a particular target group of parents, contracted with a consultant, a specialist in program evaluation, for assistance. After working together for two months, the consultant and consultee discovered that the agency director was opposed to the program and unwilling to provide needed space and staff support. Furthermore, the program had become a source of controversy within the board of trustees and the entire community. The consultee, nevertheless, was determined to implement the program. The consultant was forced to decide whether to continue to work with a program that the chief administrator and other powerful persons were determined to defeat or terminate the consultation. Apparently, the two administrators had failed to communicate in the inception and early planning of the program. By requesting the approval of the chief administrator for the consultation contract, the consultant might have helped them identify and resolve their differences and thus avoid a major conflict.

But sanction granted by a director does not automatically transfer to other staff members, and another common problem in contracting is the failure to go beyond the top administrator to involve all key persons, groups, and systems in consultation decision-making processes. Unless all staff members who are to participate in consultation are involved in the negotiation process, there is likely to be difficulty in getting relationships off the ground. The administrator (or other staff member) who initiates the consultation is ordinarily far more eager for change than other staff members. This person may also be unrealistically optimistic about the staff's attitudes. Sometimes an administrator (or conditions related to funding) requires a staff to participate in consultation. Pressures may be subtle, but their subtlety may only increase consultees' uneasiness and feelings of helplessness. Consultees who are forced to consult are likely to enter the relationship with resentment and undermine the consultation's success by overt or passive resistance. Those who are relatively vulnerable are likely to play a deceptive game. A consultee in such a position may feign a collaborative attitude and "keep the consultative process moving slowly enough to be no real threat, keeping his nose clean, and making attentive noises which reduce the attempts to influence him or those above him in the hierarchy" (Steele, 1975, p. 42). What consultees learn under these conditions is, of course, not how to diagnose and solve the targeted problems but how to play power games.

Problems such as these can be prevented if, when negotiating a contract, consultants insist, as a condition for their involvement, that all staff members to be involved in a consultation participate in its planning. If this kind of participation is not possible, consultants can request that all consultation be voluntary. They can also increase consultees' trust and motivation to work by holding meetings to explain the contract, the consultant's role and boundaries, and the expected outcomes.

Beneath the verbalized contract may lie hidden agendas that jeopardize the achievement of legitimate, explicit goals. Consultants should be alert to signs that consultees have covert expectations and encourage them to bring all their hoped-for goals into contractual discussions for consideration and eventual acceptance or rejection. Agency administrators, for instance, may hire consultants with the expectancy that they will somehow be useful in bringing troublesome staff members into line (Zusman, 1972). A hiring agency may expect consultants to make recommendations that support a predetermined plan—such as a decision to shift priorities, to shut down a particular program, or to fire or hire certain individuals. Consultants may be hired to convince staff members that they will enjoy participation in a new program and that the program will benefit clients. Occasionally, an administrator hires a consultant with the hope that he or she will give legal testimony about incompetent personnel. Administrators may expect to use consultants as conduits to deliver sensitive messages to employees. Staff members may expect a consultant to tell administrators about their problems, needs, or successes. Consultees may hope the consultant will serve as a relay station from whom they can learn what other employees are doing and how the boss regards certain individuals. An agency may engage consultants for "window dressing" purposes; funding practices sometimes foster this practice by giving extra points to agencies with ongoing consultation (Rae-Grant, 1972). Outside pressures—for instance, from dissatisfied parents who demand change in school programs or from a blue ribbon commission investigating prison abuses— may lead an agency to seek an outside consultant, not to help in a true examination and reform of its policies and procedures, but because it hopes to create the appearance of flexibility and cooperation—at least until the pressure is off (Heller and Monahan, 1977). In still other situations, administrators expect consultants to help them solve marital or other personal problems.

Although unsuspecting consultants are startled to discover consultees' hidden agendas, they, too, may have covert goals. Consultants may, for instance (unwittingly or otherwise), seek to make the management more democratic or to move the agency toward providing certain services and reducing others. They may expect to use consultation contracts to promote their own products—for instance, diagnostic surveys, training packages, or books. These hidden agendas, too, should be brought into contractual discussions.

Problems such as those just discussed are common in consultation. At the time contracts are made, the parties involved often do not have adequate knowledge to anticipate all their needs, their goals, and the conditions through which they can be satisfied. Consultants can prevent serious difficulties from developing by meeting regularly with the chief administrator and other key persons to review the consultation contract and progress. Including in the contract a requirement for periodic reviews makes it much easier to identify and correct costly mistakes and avoid long-term involvement in unsatisfactory contracts. (In pointing out the need for continual reexamination of the contract, Graziano, 1972, cited a case in which undetected differences between a consultant and a board of directors persisted for years—each party blocking the other's achievement of goals.) It is also a good idea to include a proviso for a review at any time that either party feels a need and for termination of the contract if problems cannot be resolved. Many consultants, and agencies, too, prefer to limit contracts to one step at a time.

One-step, short-term contracts force progress reviews and provide a mechanism for regularly bringing into open discussion crucial issues that might otherwise remain hidden.

Entry

Physical and psychological entry may occur simultaneously. More often, consultants work with members of an agency for many weeks or months before being sufficiently trusted and accepted to be allowed into their social system. Evidence that entry has been achieved often comes through a series of "initiation" rituals, such as jokes of which the consultant bears the brunt, a gift of a coffee cup to be placed on a communal shelf, an invitation to a staff party, or shared gossip about the organization's secrets.[2] Consultants sometimes must penetrate several layers to achieve full entry. The social-psychological layers may be marked by physical boundaries. Crossing physical barriers heralded one consultant's penetration of two social strata. She made five or six visits to the agency before she was invited to join the staff in a private lounge. She then congratulated herself on her entry. A few weeks later, however, after a particularly tense meeting, a consultee—a senior staff member—invited the consultant to join him for a cup of coffee. He then led her to a tiny but cozy lounge that she had not known existed. It was the private domain of three senior staff members. The consultant had made entry at still another layer and had thus increased both her access to crucial information and her influence. She had yet, however, to earn the director's full confidence and acceptance.

[2] Consultants may find it difficult to decide whether to allow, encourage, or refuse to listen to disclosures about "company secrets." Often these disclosures concern norm-violating behaviors. For instance, Jones is going to be fired because he is dating a client, Chuck and Martha are bitter enemies and refuse to speak to each other even in staff meetings, the boss was once arrested for drunken driving. Revelations such as these may be offered to entertain the consultant and, at the same time, to draw her or him into the family circle. Occasionally, this kind of gossip is relevant to consultation goals. Often it is helpful in understanding an agency's culture and interpersonal dynamics. In many cases, however, to encourage such disclosures is unethical and diverts consultation from its proper course.

Resistance to consultants is a natural phenomenon. The integration of any new person into an ongoing social structure unbalances it, creating reactions and forcing members to make adjustments. Newcomers inevitably displace certain members by assuming some portion of their responsibilities, roles, and functions. Since newcomers' attitudes and behaviors are unknown, members are typically uneasy because they are uncertain what changes they will be required to make and whether they will gain or lose in the transactions. They will therefore feel a need to predict and control the new person's behavior so as to protect their own interests. Threat is heightened when the newcomer is a consultant, since consultants—because of their expertise—are assumed to carry some kind of special authority (Glidewell, 1959). Responses to entering consultants are also more pronounced because this role is closely associated with demands to change and disruption of the status quo. Change may be associated with feelings of dependency and awkwardness and fears that one will not be able to learn required skills or behaviors. To work with a consultant involves some degree of commitment to self-examination—a commitment that demands energy and that cannot easily be made without trust in the consultant and confidence that the outcomes will be positive. Even when consultees are working under painful circumstances, they may prefer the status quo, with its known problems, to the uncertainties associated with change.

Because of these natural reactions, all staff members—even those who were most eager to initiate consultation—are likely to feel ambivalent toward the consultant. Hopeful that the outcomes will be successful, they fear failure. Will the hoped-for benefits be achieved? Can the consultant really help? Should another consultant have been hired? Would it not be best to live with the present problems a bit longer? Can the consultant's activities and boundaries be controlled? How far can the consultant be trusted with confidential information?

A consultant might well "assume that the consultee system is a bit paranoid about his entry and it is useful if his attitude, although not his overt behavior, is a bit paranoid, too. It is comforting to note, however, that there are reasons to welcome such early problems because they indicate strength in the social system. How difficult it would be to work with an (admittedly hypothetical) psychotherapy patient who never showed any resistance and thus showed little ego strength! Similarly, how difficult it would be to work with a social system (equally hypothetical) that had so little ego strength (or such malevolent intent) that it immediately opened its arms wide and seemed ready for total embrace and thus ready for total change or disruption" (Altrocchi, 1972, p. 498).

It is useful to think of consultation entry as a developmental process. The degree to which consultees trust the consultant and perceive the consultant's expertise to be relevant to their work grows with time and experiences that confirm the consultant's competency and trustworthiness. A scale has been developed to enable consultants to assess the degree to which each consultee is ready for or resistant to consultation (Cherniss, 1978). Ratings on this scale can guide consultants in setting realistic goals, in adjusting their interactions with consultees to fit their readiness level, and in helping them move to the next highest level in the developmental sequence. At the lowest level no relationship exists. Consultees may be hostile or indifferent toward consultation. They may simply not have had contact with the consultant. At the second level a social relationship exists. The consultee does not, however, introduce work issues into discussions, and if they are introduced, the consultee obviously does not wish input from the consultant. Limited work relationships are found at level three. Cherniss identifies two types of consultees at this level. One type wants help but is not amenable to changing her or his behavior and, therefore, does not follow through. The other type discusses the problem but does not actively participate in developing solutions. Consultees operating at level four are open to the consultant's introducing discussions about problems, and they cooperate in discussions regarding solutions. However, the consultee is dependent on the consultant for initiating consultation. The consultee does not accept responsibility for identifying problems that are appropriate for consultation. Consultees at level five take initiative for contacting the consultant and bringing up work problems. In level six, consultees seek consultation whenever they need it and encourage other consultees to use the consultant.

The preceding discussion emphasized the effects of con-sultees' and consultants' roles on the entry process. But consul-tants must also understand the effects of complex agency dy-namics on entry processes. Each agency is an intricate system with uniquely patterned relationships, "themes," and norms for appropriate behavior. Reactions to consultants are intimately associated with these knotty dynamics. Moreover, a contagion effect occurs in which persons—such as consultants—who enter an agency find themselves feeling, thinking, and behaving in ac-cordance with its pervasive patterns. The stress under which most consultants work heightens this effect.

In most agencies, for instance, a "splitting" phenomenon is evident in which "good" and "bad" characteristics are polar-ized so that individuals and groups are viewed as either wholly good or bad. Splitting, a primitive response to anxiety, reduces uncertainty and simplifies relationships. Splitting is evident when perceptions are systematically biased so that objects are viewed as unrealistically positive or negative. For example, Mary is a good supervisor; moreover, she is superb in every way. Susie is a terrible supervisor and completely incompetent. An admin-istrator is highly responsible; staff members are irresponsible. Or staff members are well trained and skilled, but clients and their problems are hopeless. Unwary consultants may discover that their own observations have been distorted by such perva-sive perceptions. Moreover, consultants become the objects of splitting tendencies and may, to illustrate, be ascribed either saintly or satanic qualities.

Splitting is often related to an agency's internal conflicts. One individual or group holds perceptions that are antithetical to those of another individual or group. These factions usually compete to control an entering consultant. If one side or the other succeeds, consultants thereby lose their potential to help. Their perceptions are no longer objective. Moreover, they are re-jected by members of the losing group. A consultant working with a children's protective service illustrates this dilemma. The director of the target unit, a young man, supervised five sub-units. Three of these components were headed by young women whose idealistic ideas about ways to help clients differed dra-matically from the views held by the director and the older women heading the other subunits. The younger consultees regarded the director as cynical and stodgy. He, along with the older women, regarded the young women as naive, dreamy "kids." The consultant, drawn into the perceptual world of the younger women, soon adopted an adamantly negative attitude toward the other staff members. He had become a part of the organization's schism.

Entering consultants should carefully assess the agency's social system and its dynamics. These dynamics are, of course, the focus of some types of consultation; but because of their pervasive influence, they are a crucial area for all consultants to study. Consultants should be especially cognizant of interpersonal schisms and pressures to take sides. Otherwise, they may find themselves polarized and lacking the credibility needed to work with the entire staff.[3] Consultants can greatly increase their effectiveness if they can recognize their own feelings and reactions to agency phenomena and use them as instruments to diagnose the system's tensions and to guide their entry.

Several additional guidelines can help consultants make a successful entry. Contractual boundaries should be carefully respected. This guideline refers to time, topics, people, and spaces. Consultants, for instance, should not appear on a Tuesday if their contract calls for them to come on Wednesday. They should not make inquiries about the administrator's conflict-management style unless their contract authorizes them to work in this area. They should consult only with persons identified in the contract as consultees. Consultants should not intrude in physical areas that they have not been explicitly authorized to enter.

---

[3] Another possibility is that consultees will eventually "scapegoat" the consultant. Staff members usually have some degree of ambivalence about the substantive issues of conflicts and, in addition, are likely to feel anxious and guilty over involvements in adversarial roles and processes. These feelings act as counterforces to divisive pressures and, over time, may precipitate overtures to reach a compromise and reconciliation. The consultant may then become a handy dumping ground for displacement of negative feelings and be scapegoated out. Since the scapegoat carries away some of the anger and bitterness, agency reintegration at a more adaptive level becomes possible. Hence, in some cases, the scapegoating role performs a uniquely helpful service.

Consultants should be especially careful during the entry period to identify and respect agency norms and taboos. The degree to which a consultant's entry creates tensions depends to a large extent on the "goodness of fit" between the consultant and the agency staff (Glidewell, 1959), including the degree to which the consultant's behaviors are congruent with those expected by and consistent with the staff. For example, in early visits consultants should take care that their clothing does not create an "unclosable psychological gap" in the consultees' minds (Steele, 1975, p. 171). In subsequent interviews, since much more information becomes available, physical cues decline in importance. Consultants should use the terminology of the agency as much as possible, avoiding professional jargon that sets them uncomfortably apart and that, in addition, is likely to confuse consultees and lead to misunderstandings. Consultants should respect agency routines and, as much as possible, take them into consideration when scheduling consultation activities.

Accessibility to the staff members with whom the consultant is to work is especially important during the entry period. Frequent visits during this time and rounds of the places where consultees work can accelerate entry by increasing opportunities for consultant and consultees to get acquainted, to increase their awareness of any questions that need to be asked, and to voice any problems or reservations about working together. Consultants can sometimes facilitate entry by attending agency work and social meetings. Attendance at staff conferences, ceremonies, celebrations, and parties can speed the entry process by bringing the consultant more quickly into the work family. However, consultants should be alert to the possibility that loosening of work protocol at parties sometimes leads to problems—such as internal and external pressures to reveal confidential information.

A Place to Work

The physical setting in which consultation takes place affects both the process and content of the interaction (Steele, 1975). Physical properties—including visual stimuli, such as light, color, architectural features, and furnishings, and physiological stimuli, such as music, uncomfortable chairs, smells, temperature, moisture, and noise—influence work processes and content. Consultation in a room adjoining a cafeteria or restroom is likely to be different in content and outcomes from consultation in a quiet, private office. Physical properties elicit memories, fantasies, and feelings and suggest symbolic meanings. For example, a closed door or an executive's desk and chair that are far removed from the chairs of other parties to an interview can be used to maintain control and to send status messages. The effects of the physical environment were illustrated in the first meeting between a consultant and an administrator. The secretary led the consultant into the administrator's large, formal office and seated him in an uncomfortable chair. The administrator came in fifteen minutes later and seated himself in an easy chair behind his huge desk. He interrupted the conference several times to receive phone calls. The consultant felt intimidated and incompetent. Because he felt controlled, he failed to take appropriate initiative during the interview.

Decisions whether to conduct a consultation in the work setting or in an off-site retreat should be based on consideration of a number of factors. Work interference is reduced in off-site work. Participants are removed from the observation of other members of their organization. A retreat setting sets a mood of exploration, contemplation, and objectivity. It encourages "unfreezing." However, those back at work often speculate and fantasize about the consultation activities. Their distorted images may lead to suspicion and distrust and undermine the efforts of the staff members returning from the retreat. On-site consultation provides a rich source of information about the agency, its employees, and their use of consultants. Experimental interventions can be tried and their effects studied on the spot.

Consultants sometimes need a place of their own for a brief period in order to counteract the feelings of marginality and the fatigue that often accompany consultation. Assignment to a permanent office is contrary to the nature of the role. However, arrangements can usually be made for a temporary refuge to rest, take notes, review events, and plan future activities.

Annotated Bibliography

Beisser, A., and Green, R. *Mental Health Consultation and Education*. Palo Alto, Calif.: National Press Books, 1972. In chap. 5, "The Entry Phase: Opening with the System," the authors outline the major issues related to the entry phase. They explain why administrators often appear ambivalent about consultation and suggest ways consultants can gain administrators' trust and sanction.

Caplan, G. *The Theory and Practice of Mental Health Consultation*. New York: Basic Books, 1970. Chap. 4, "Building Relationships with a Consultee Institution," discusses institutional and consultant factors that are likely to interfere with effective entry. Caplan outlines principles and methods for successful entry and contracting.

Chandy, J. M. "The Effects of an In-Service Orientation on Teacher Perception and Use of the Mental Health Consultant." Unpublished doctoral dissertation, Department of Educational Psychology, University of Texas at Austin, 1974. Chandy shows that an in-service program that demonstrated the role of the consultant increased consultees' use of consultation services. The procedures outlined by Chandy could be used by many consultants to reduce resistance.

Gallessich, J. "Organizational Factors Influencing Consultation in Schools." *Journal of School Psychology*, 1973, *11,* 57-65. The external and internal forces affecting consultants' entry and effectiveness in educational settings are similar to those in other human services agencies. This article identifies these forces and their implications.

Glidewell, J. C. "The Entry Problem in Consultation." *Journal of Social Issues*, 1959, *15* (2), 51-59. This article comments on the general problem of introducing new persons into existing social systems. According to Glidewell, a key factor in determining the ease of entry is the degree of congruence between the perceptions of consultant and of client-organization staff in regard to needs, values, role expectations, and dependency issues. Theories presented in this article explain entry phenomena and suggest ways consultants can accelerate the entry process.

Goodstein, L. D. *Consulting with Human Service Systems.* Reading, Mass.: Addison-Wesley, 1978. Chap. 5, "Entry Issues in Organizational Consultation," discusses issues related to the initial contact and exploration period, the contracting process, and value dilemmas that often arise in these early stages.

Pipes, R. B. "Consulting in Organizations: The Entry Problem." In J. C. Conoley (Ed.), *Consultation in Schools: Theory, Research, Procedures.* New York: Academic Press, 1981. Pipes discusses advantages and disadvantages of internal and external consultants' perspectives. He also points out the differences in consultees' attitudes and expectations when they—rather than their administrator or a consultant—initiate consultation, and he discusses contractual issues.

Schein, E. H. *Process Consultation: Its Role in Organization Development.* Reading, Mass.: Addison-Wesley, 1969. In chap. 9, "Establishing Contact and Defining a Relationship," Schein provides an excellent description of the initial contact and of the content and process of contractual negotiations.

Swartz, D., and Lippitt, G. "Evaluating the Consulting Process." In C. R. Bell and L. Nadler (Eds.), *The Client-Consultant Handbook.* Houston: Gulf Publishing Co., 1979. These authors point out the importance of a written contract and include a sample contract form.

13

Building
Working
Relationships

The quality of the relationship between consultants and consultees is a critical factor in their success. This relationship is the medium through which consultants learn about consultees' unique problems and circumstances and through which new perspectives, knowledge, and skills enter the agency. Ideally, mutual respect and trust are present to facilitate the free exchange of information, questions, ideas, and feelings. But this relationship is highly susceptible to tensions that must be worked through if it is to be successful. These tensions and recommendations for managing them are the focus of this chapter.

Sources of Tension

Typically, consultation relationships begin in a climate of organizational tension. An atmosphere of crisis and feelings of ambivalence characteristically greet entering consultants. Certain inherent features of the consultant role and of the consultation relationship exacerbate these tensions.

The Consultant's Role. Marginality and transiency characterize the consultant's role. Consultants leave the comfort and security of their offices to work in unfamiliar settings. They are separated from their own professional peers. Consulting relationships are brief or intermittent in nature. Paradoxically, these features enhance consultants' capacities to help their consultees. Marginality increases objectivity and flexibility (Cotton, Browne, and Golembiewski, 1977). However, the lack of a genuine home base and the thwarting of the human need for affiliation can lower morale and thus diminish consultants' effectiveness.

Consultants' membership in the social fabric of the agency is always provisional. They did not share the agency's past. They do not share its future. During their relatively brief period of service, they are present for only a portion of the agency's workday. They miss the daily routines and rituals, the periodic crises, successes, and celebrations that bind workers together into a common culture. Thus, even when consultants are at the peak of their involvement in agency life, they remain outsiders. Poignant reminders of their marginality become routine. During a break in a consultation, consultees ignore the consultant to discuss work issues unrelated to consultation. They share in-house jokes, discuss the coming return visit of a beloved former colleague, and plan a surprise party for the boss's birthday. A consultant reads in a newspaper about an agency's success with a new program that he designed. His contract ended with the planning stage. No longer needed, he is no longer in contact with the program or its staff. Consultants are also marginal in relation to their professional peers. Consultants' goals and activities usually differ from those central to the other members of their professions (see Chapter Two). Moreover, a close identification with their professional worlds could weaken their ability to relate to consultees. "Consultants who move too far into the world of the client tend to accept the norms, values, and expectations of the client, and, as a result, lose their precious objectivity. On the other hand, if they move too far into their own professional world, they can be seen as too professional, too detached, and remote from the problems of the client system.

This overprofessionalism interferes with the communication of trust, respect, and understanding necessary for a successful client-consultant relationship. The dilemma creates a continual conflict for many consultants as they try to balance the appeals of the two worlds" (Goodstein, 1978, p. 156).

The stress associated with marginality may reduce consultants' ability to cope. They may then react in any of a number of ways. They may become so emotionally distant as to ignore consultees' feelings. They may become preoccupied with success and feel compelled to be successful—but they then lose their freedom of choice and become rigid and restrictive (Argyris, 1970). To illustrate, a consultant working with a medical group found one member of the staff highly resistant and successfully blocking the efforts of the "troublemaker" (consultant). Even her boss, after attempting to change her through placating, allowed her to overrule his plans for reorganization. The consultant became so angry and self-preoccupied that he missed the opportunity to help staff members look at the important dynamics involved. Consultants may violate their standards by trying to please consultees. They may overrespond to their consultees' demands and frustrations in order to gain support and to form alliances to reduce alienation. Consultants may overidentify with certain consultees. Young, inexperienced consultants are likely to identify with the "underdogs" of the agency. Low-ranking consultees often discover a rich vein of support in young consultants, who project positive qualities onto these consultees. Some consultants, of course, young or old, identify with the power figures; they may join with the boss and become the eyes and ears of management. Stress may also lead to "burnout," a common phenomenon in consultation (Mitchell, 1977).

Consultation is also characterized by ambiguity and lack of control over outcomes. Consultants often find themselves overwhelmed by the complex and uncertain nature of their task. They must organize and sort voluminous, complex information. Moreover, the ever-expanding and often contradictory nature of the data calls for frequent revisions in the diagnosis. Enormous flexibility is needed. Choices of directions and methods are manifold. Yet criteria for making these choices are difficult to formulate and keep in mind, especially since the consultant's formulations are often quite different from those of the consultee. The contract—including boundaries and goals—may become blurred. At the same time, consultants are usually keenly aware that—since they have little or no authority over staff members' actions—they have little control over outcomes of their work. Moreover, results may be intangible or slow in coming. Consultants must often continue to function for long periods with little feedback about their impact. In many cases, they never learn what happened after a consultation. Consequently, they often experience a sense of incompletion, alienation, and powerlessness.

Consultants' work involves them in sensitive problems and tasks. The depth and scope of consultees' problems can be disturbing. Consultants sometimes feel guilty—accusing themselves of voyeurism—as they view the organization's "innards" (Levinson, 1978). Discovery of the human flaws of authority figures produces anxiety in some consultants and leads them to exaggerated interpretations. They may overlook administrators' strengths and the situational influences on problems. In their disillusionment, consultants may fantasy that since these administrators are flawed, the whole organization is doomed to collapse. In such overreactions, consultants may fear that their diagnosis has destructive powers and therefore withhold needed feedback. Or they may, in a reaction formation, decide to "give it to them straight" and make an inappropriate attack on the consultee and the agency (Levinson, 1978, p. 40). The process of changing people may create guilty feelings (Steele, 1975).

Tensions Due to Differences in Roles and Perspectives. Certain tensions are inherent in consultation because of differences in the ways the two parties are involved. The roles are complementary—not symmetrical. One is a helper and the other is a "helpee." This condition generally leads to at least a little discomfort for both parties but particularly for consultees. Their best efforts have not solved their problems, and they are likely to feel uneasy over their inadequacies, over "looking bad," over needing help to perform their jobs. For example, the failures of a human services administrator who prides herself on her competence in working with people may threaten her self-concept. Consultees' reactions to a particular failure may be overgeneralized. They may feel not only inadequate but frightened over the implications for their future in the agency. But consultants need consultees in order to practice. In some cases, the consultant's neediness may exceed that of the consultee. For example, a particular contract may have high stakes, especially for the beginning consultant. However, the needs of most consultants are qualitatively different from the needs of the consultees. The consultant needs consultees in order to practice competencies, while the consultee needs a consultant because of some kind of deficiency or problem. The consultant's competency in a specialized area complements the consultee's deficiency. Consultees sometimes resent the parasitic nature of the consultant, who "lives off" their problems. The inequity may threaten consultees' self-esteem and aggravate infantile feelings of deference, dependency, and anger (Moore, 1970).

Furthermore, consultants are usually hired to help organizations make changes and are therefore associated with demands to give up well-established behaviors and attitudes. But while consultees are expected to change, consultants are not required to make basic changes. Changes are frequently difficult to make; and consultees, because of the importance of their jobs, are often especially uneasy over making changes. The consequences are not always predictable and may, in fact, have negative effects on work conditions. Consultees are often particularly fearful that change will reduce their power and status. They are likely to be inept in the new behaviors and feel a loss of self-esteem over their awkwardness. Consultants symbolize the threatening demands. Consultees, therefore, react to them with fear and mistrust. Consultants may, in turn, respond with a sense of self-doubt and of being on trial, asking themselves, Why am I here? Should I be a consultant? Am I truly competent? "Self-inflicted trial and mistrust could lead to a decrease in one's own confidence, a greater degree of anxiety, and a higher probability of failure" (Argyris, 1970, p. 134).

Consultees' "set" toward problems is to *do* rather than to

think. They are more likely, therefore, to be oriented to the moment than to the future (Levine, 1972). Constant daily pressures to make decisions and to act force them to focus on the concrete and practical, to narrow considerations, to focus on specifics, and to achieve closure. They live with their problems and cannot often walk away from them. The demands on consultants are not as urgent and omnipresent. Consultants can walk away from the stressful work situation. Consequently, they are more comfortable with ambiguity and with the more abstract and theoretical aspects of problems (Moore, 1970). Moreover, consultees may view certain situations as crises that consultants, who may have been involved in dozens of similar situations, consider routine (Hughes, 1958). And since consultants are likely to be more concerned with the quality of their input than the product, they are more inclined than their consultees to continue searching for breadth and depth of understanding of the consultees' situation. Similarly, consultants also are more likely to emphasize competent processes of the work, while consultees are concerned with producing satisfactory products.

Other differences in views of the problem pose difficulties. Consultees usually see other staff members or clients as the source of their problem—not their own behavior—while consultants tend to see the source of the problem as the consultee. (Consultants may, however, be blind to problems related to their own attitudes and behavior, such as implicit agendas or alignments with agency factions.) Often consultant and consultee conceptualize problems differently because they come from different professional specialties. Each may bring such a narrowly specialized body of expertise that communication and integration of their points of view are difficult. Differences in priorities stemming from value differences create another source of tension. "The consultant has one set of objectives and the consultee another. Often at the beginning of the consultation relationship, these two sets are completely different" (Zusman, 1972, pp. 35-36). For example, a consultant with strong concern for client mental health is likely to seek different outcomes than a consultee whose top priority is job stability. Conflicts occur between the consultant who prizes participative decision making and the manager-consultee who is most concerned with immediate compliance of staff members. Despite careful, explicit contracting, goals will differ because of these discrepancies in priorities. Over time, however, "as the relationship matures, the objectives on both sides change and begin to overlap" (Zusman, 1972, pp. 25-26). The two parties become more aware and accepting of each other's values and goals and more tolerant of differences. If, instead, objectives continue to diverge, the relationship will probably dissolve.

Differences in definitions and measures of success also add tensions to the relationship. Consultants may push for consultee changes because their own sense of success depends on the job they do on the consultee. Consultees' self-esteem, however, is conditional on their fulfillment of assigned tasks, on the job they do for the client or the agency. These two goals seldom coincide completely. A consultant may feel successful as a result of helping consultees increase their depth and breadth of understanding. At the same time, these consultees, though aware that the new perspectives are valuable, may feel they have failed because they are unable to use this new information immediately to perform more effectively. In fact, consultees' performance may deteriorate while they are assimilating new data and incorporating new ideas and behaviors (Birney, 1977).

Furthermore, consultants can buttress their role with a theoretical rationale and body of professional literature. In addition, some consultants belong to reference groups that reinforce the consultant role, such as outreach teams or consultant firms. Agency staff members do not have much reinforcement for the consultee role. They are generally unacquainted with consultation theory and literature, and often their reference groups are unsupportive or ambivalent about the role of consultee (Steele, 1975). In their work groups, they are likely to discuss matters related to other roles and relationships far more often than their experiences as consultees.

As a consequence of these role tensions, consultant and consultee regard the relationship and their roles in it quite differently. Consultants may be more invested in being consultants than consultees are in being consultees. The consultant role is the primary professional identity and commitment for many consultants. Agency staff members have other, more pervasive and positive identifications than the consultee role and may not often think of themselves as consultees (Steele, 1975). They may perceive themselves primarily as administrators, probation officers, nurses, educators, or ministers. They may perceive the role of "consultee" in negative terms and assign it a low priority. If they perceive the positive aspects of their professional self-concepts, such as competence and authority, as contradictory to the role of consultee, they may resolve the conflict by minimizing identification with and involvement in the consultee role.

Because of these differences, the two parties approach the relationship with different levels of enthusiasm, commitment, legitimacy, and knowledge. The consultee role is likely to activate personal and professional anxieties. Consultees' distrust of consultants may be manifest in withdrawal (both physical and psychological), denial of problems, or overt hostility. Consultants exacerbate consultees' negative feelings if they attribute them to resistance—when instead the consultees' attitudes are normal consequences of agency and role pressures. Much of what we view as resistance is resentment or anger that arises because consultees experience the relationship as demeaning and the consultant as too controlling (Steele, 1975).

Tensions Due to Similarities in Roles and Functions. When consultants enter an agency, they are likely to find some staff members whose training, competencies, or areas of responsibility are similar to their own. The consultants' input is more supplementary than complementary to the work of these persons. Because of the overlap between roles and functions, these relationships may become competitive (Moore, 1970; Znaniecki, 1965). For instance, mental health consultants working in a school find counselors, nurses, and visiting teachers who also possess specialized mental health skills and whose jobs include responsibilities for helping teachers solve problems. It is natural for these staff members to feel threatened. They may fantasize that they will be fired, lose control over decisions in their areas, or lose recognition from their peers (Caplan, 1970). Consequently, they may covertly block the consultants' entry. If they have sufficient power, they may insist on being intermediaries between the consultant and others in the organization; they may ask to be present at all meetings in which the consultant is involved in order to monitor the consultant's work. The presence of these internal staff members may prevent some members from open discussion of problems or undermine their confidence in the consultant.

However, if in the entry phase or in subsequent activities, the consultant bypasses these persons, they are likely to undermine the consultation efforts. Consultants in the entry phase should find out the agency's existing resources and avoid competing with them and thus interfering with agency use of its own resources. Frequently, consultants encounter consultees who do not utilize the talents of their internal resources but, instead, turn to the consultant for assistance, thus setting up competition with existing services and duplicating them. The consultant who complies with such requests intrudes on the internal staff's territory. Unless there is a compelling reason to the contrary, the best policy is to work with the internal specialists who possess similar skills from the beginning, thus supporting and reinforcing the existing problem-solving structure.

Individual Characteristics and Stereotypes. Personal attributes (age, gender, social and political values, and communication style, for example), occupational characteristics (such as professional values and status), and personal needs (such as to be in a superior role, to be universally liked, or to be a "rescuer") affect the nature and fruitfulness of the consultation relationship and may exacerbate tensions. Because the consultant's role is often perceived as ambiguous and threatening, the persons involved tend to overrespond to familiar characteristics such as age and professional identity. Hence, they attempt to reduce ambiguity by relating on the basis of stereotypes. Age and status stereotypes are common in consultation. A young staff member of a university counseling center, though exceptionally competent, was unable to establish credibility as a consultant to a dean; the middle-aged director of the center, however, found immediate legitimization with this administrator. A famous psychiatrist found it difficult to consult with junior public health nurses because the status differential made a peer relationship impossible. Consultees were unable to interact freely with him (Caplan, 1970). Stereotypic reactions to gender are also common. Consultees often respond quite differently to male and female consultants. They tend to regard female consultants with greater skepticism, since they do not fit the cultural stereotype of the professional. Yet, in some cases, consultees prefer female consultants because they are associated with relatively low power and are therefore perceived to be less threatening than males. Consultants, of course, are not immune to these stereotyping tendencies.

The following case study illustrates the complex interaction of personal and agency characteristics in a consultation relationship. The consultee, the director of a home for juvenile offenders, was a tall and physically imposing man fifty-eight years old. Although he preferred to consider himself democratic, he was actually authoritarian and directed the staff with a benevolent, paternalistic style, seeking both submission and affection. He hired a consultant to help him develop and implement an innovative program. The consultant, a young, petite female, was the newest member of a consultant firm. Although she valued democratic, egalitarian approaches, her work with agencies had thus far been limited to a directive or expert role, based on her considerable expertise in program evaluation. Ambivalent about the "expert" role and its power and potential for manipulation, she wanted to move into a more collaborative style. Yet, because she felt uneasy about her relative youth and inexperience, she continued to use her expert power (authoritative information) to keep control, to gain status and recognition. At the same time, because she was anxious about working with "authority figures," she felt compelled to be "nice" and compliant. Her behavior betrayed an underlying need for approval and fear of rejection by authority, especially older, paternal males.

The personal needs and styles of the consultee and consultant shaped their interaction. The relationship became personalized and subtly sexualized. The director insisted on buying her lunch and opening doors for her. He told her how pretty she was. He talked about his personal life and his interest in dancing. At the same time, he took the role of the benevolent yet authoritarian father; he was nurturing yet controlling. His friendly, supportive, "helpful" manner increased her need to comply and thus controlled her. His attitude to her was "You can do whatever you want as long as it's what I want you to do." He gently told her she didn't take enough authority. Yet when she presented an expert analysis and interpretation of an agency survey, he abruptly changed the topic and directed her to "process" a meeting, a task which was not a part of her contract and for which she was not prepared. She found herself behaving like a "sexy" daughter and reacting with extreme ambivalence to his authority.

A major theme of the agency, pervasive at all levels, was "the kids against father." The clients were the "bad" kids. The staff members were the "good" fathers who helped the "kids" by paternalistic control. This theme was independent of consultation dynamics; yet it aggravated the consultant's anxieties over the need to control and the need to bow to paternal authority. In this particular situation, a group of workers organized to oppose the director and tried to draw the consultant into their plan. By recognizing the theme and agency dynamics and her own dysfunctional reactions, the consultant was able to control her own behavior and defuse a volatile situation.

During this consultation, the consultant became engaged and showed off her new ring to the director and other staff members. Shortly afterward, the director's flirtatious behavior ceased. He became more task-oriented and less concerned with authority issues in the consultation relationship. The unambiguous implications of the engagement dispelled the consultee's sexual fantasies. A comfortable work relationship developed.

Sometimes consultants' awareness and strenuous efforts are unable to modify stereotypic patterns. A young Jewish social worker, a member of the outreach staff of a community guidance center, arranged to consult with a priest, the head of a Catholic service agency. Although she was certain she had no preconceptions that would diminish her effectiveness, she soon found that the priest's clerical attire and references to his beliefs rekindled long-forgotten stereotypes from her early childhood. The priest, who previously had worked well with professionals from different religious backgrounds, began to show signs of distrust and withdrawal. As in most troubled relationships, the sources of difficulty were multidimensional. The consultant was terminating a long-term affair. The priest, a gentle, traditional, and idealistic person, reminded her of qualities that had precipitated conflicts with her lover. Despite her acute awareness of the sources of her negative attributions and considerable emotional support from her own staff in working through her biases, the consultant was unable to change her behavior in time to prevent rapid deterioration of the relationship. In contrast, another young Jewish consultant was exceedingly successful in working with the faculty of the schools in a Catholic diocese. His acceptance was due not only to his professional competence but to his easygoing acceptance of religious differences and his interest in learning about other faiths. His enthusiastic and accepting attitude was contagious. His consultees affectionately referred to him as "our own Dr. Freud," and they annually asked him to make a presentation to their community on Hebrew traditions.

Professional characteristics are also the basis for stereotyping. Consultants' stereotypes of clergy (McWhirter, 1968), police (Brodsky, 1977), and professors (Whittington, 1968) have been noted. Consultees' conception of their mental health consultant as a "shrink" may inhibit them or lead them to ask inappropriately for help on personal problems. Consultants or consultees may behave so as to confirm and perpetuate stereotypes. For instance, consultants with clinical training may find it difficult to resist "therapizing" consultees.

Consultants and consultees often have personal dispositions or needs that interfere with the relationship. Either may relive some unresolved problem of the past in the consultation relationship. When one is confronted with ambiguity, regression may occur and prevent even the most healthy professionals from viewing the situation realistically. For example, a consultant may unrealistically perceive certain individuals as "underdogs" and inappropriately take on the role of rescuer. Consultants may identify with power and align themselves with administrators in ways that undermine their effectiveness. Consultants may need continual ego reassurance and insist on being recognized as the expert who has the answers to all problems.

Differences in cultural norms and values may also create tensions. For example, Levine (1972) describes a group of teachers who used indirect terms to discuss profanity. When the consultant responded with direct terms, the teachers were shocked and angry. The consultant learned that to be accepted, he must abide by their norms. Graziano (1972) reports a somewhat humorous example of the effects of clients' personal values on their attitudes toward a professional helper. He obtained a federal grant to establish and direct a token-economy program for prison inmates. After a period of work with the prisoners, he missed several weeks because of illness. During his absence, his prestige with the prisoners soared; but it plummeted to disgust when he returned. The prisoners, who had not been told of the reason for this absence, concluded he had absconded with the grant money. He lost status with them when he reappeared and thereby revealed himself as "straight."

Power Issues. A common source of tension in the consultation relationship is conflict over power. Ordinarily consultees have the authority to determine the work area and problem to be the focus of consultation and to determine what actions, if any, are to be taken. Consultant and consultee alike have expert power (knowledge relevant to the problems being discussed). Typically, their areas of expertise are different, and they depend on and defer to each other for certain kinds of expert opinions and information. But either party may question or intrude on the other's authority. In rare instances, a consultant may go to a consultee's supervisor to report incompetencies that threaten the welfare of a client or the agency's operations (Caplan, 1970). Consultees may reject a consultant's "expert" opinion because they have sound reasons for questioning its legitimacy. Most often, however, conflicts over authority represent defensive responses to the ego-threatening conditions described earlier. Consultants may seek to bolster their egos by abdication of the peer role and a takeover of the consultee's authority (Hughes, 1958).

Judith, for instance, a doctoral trainee in a counseling

psychology program, was particularly anxious to perform effectively in a consultation placement. However, she found that the administrator with whom she worked did not accept her ideas as readily as she had hoped. She reported to her supervisor that he appeared increasingly inattentive and indifferent to her efforts to help him. Her supervisory group role-played the consultant/consultee interaction. Judith, playing herself, immediately took on a controlling manner, quite different from her usual style. She took an interrogatory stance, implicitly expecting the administrator to accept her lead in deciding the topics to be discussed as well as her formulations of problems. Her behavior implied that her expertise was superior to his and that she was responsible for identifying and solving his problems. The "consultee," in response to Judith's intrusion on his domain, became increasingly passive and guarded. Because of her anxiety about her own competence, she was oblivious to her presumptiousness and the hostility it was generating.

The role of expert "is a quite seductive one for the consultant; all the more so in behavioral science, since the variables and their relationships are often very fuzzy and complex. It can be quite personally gratifying to have others see me as someone who really 'knows' what is going on or what should be done in a given situation" (Steele, 1975, p. 148). Professional traditions reinforce the notion of the consultant as the doctor and expert who knows what is best for the patient or consultee. Consultees' needs and their stereotypes of themselves may also pull the consultant into a dominating role (McWhirter, 1968). The question "Doc, what should I be doing?" is often a signal that the consultee wants the consultant to put on a "white coat." The expert role can temporarily meet the needs of both consultant and consultee by binding their anxieties. However, although rapport may appear excellent, beneath the surface a consultee's resentment over the deferent posture may smolder and defeat the goals of consultation. Moreover, the consultee's input is diminished. Consequently, the data for decision making are less complete. In addition, the consultee's commitment to and responsibility for decisions tend to decline.

Consultees may reject a consultant's expert power (knowledge) for good reasons. A consultee may be skeptical of the motives behind a consultant's statements or suggestions—suspecting either a lack of objectivity or a deliberate but covert shaping of input so as to move the consultee in certain directions. Consultees may perceive that a consultant has overstepped the boundaries of the role and may wish (like Judith's consultee described earlier) to even the score. Consultees may reject consultants' expertise as a defensive reaction to the ego threats described earlier.

When power issues dominate a relationship, *deskilling* often occurs. Deskilling is taking place when one person behaves in such a way as to cause another to behave in a less competent way than is consistent with his or her actual abilities. Consultees may deskill their consultants, but the reverse occurs also. The deskilling may be unintentional. Caplan (1972) described a minister who visited an elderly parishioner weekly and successfully helped her cope with her problems until a mental health consultant, a psychiatrist, pointed out that the woman was schizophrenic. Thereafter, the minister refused to visit her because he felt incompetent. Often deskilling is subtle. Sometimes it is blatant, as in the following example, taken from the log of a young community psychiatrist, Bill, who was in the early stages of consultation with Randall, the newly hired director of a volunteer service agency.

In the first interview, Bill noted Randall's defensiveness. "In general, Randall seemed guarded and uncertain as to what he wanted from me. He had some ideas about my screening volunteers and leading in-service training. He also had thoughts about some team building with his staff, which is the kind of consultation I am interested in. But he seemed to be a bit defensive about my working with his staff. This might be related to his experiences with consultants in his last position in Boston, a job which he talked about at great length. I am not sure that his previous experience with consultants was really positive. He might have been burned in some personal ways. He talks about it as if it were more of an encounter experience with a number of people not being able to take it. My feeling is that he does not want this consultation to end up being a harsh and evaluative experience. He seems to feel vulnerable. I sensed that he may be feeling challenged or threatened by me for some reason, but I will have to see what develops concerning that issue."

From Bill's report, it appears that Randall's defensiveness is coming from his own insecurity and fears that the consultant will intimidate him. Without more data, it is impossible to know the true source of the apparent defensiveness. It is possible that Bill was actually behaving in a threatening way.

A few days later, in a conference to plan a team-building workshop, Bill noted Randall's rivalrous behavior: "I think the session went okay except for my frustration in dealing and interacting with Randall. He just seems evasive and guarded. I know he pushes some of my buttons. He comes on as if he knows more about whatever it is you are talking about. He also seems ready to catch you at whatever you are up to. It is a kind of cat and mouse game. I used some term when talking about our consultation and he jumped right on it. I think I said something about needs assessment and he said that he was waiting to see how long it would be before we used some jargon. It will be a task to get his trust."

The workshop did take place, and the consultant reported some progress in the team-building goal, but he found himself upset by Randall's competitiveness. "Almost every time I stood up to lead a discussion or to direct activities, Randall would interrupt me several times. Sometimes he just would add his own comments to mine, but there were several times when he questioned my choice of activities or my interpretations or processes. I found myself more and more uneasy and angry but couldn't decide to confront him on what he was doing to me."

Soon the consultee had thoroughly deskilled the consultant, who wrote, "I found myself looking at him pretty often to see how he was taking whatever I was doing—so pretty early he began to control me and the direction of the workshop." The consultee was increasingly in charge: "We had planned to do a fishbowl with him, me, and the associate director early in the afternoon. But just before lunch, Randall suddenly announced that he did not think it would be helpful and that instead we would have small-group discussions on goals for the agency—so we did."

Coping with Relationship Tensions

How can consultants manage these tensions? Several characteristics are associated with a successful relationship.

Characteristics for Successful Coping. Successful consultants are *self-conscious* about their thoughts, feelings, actions, needs, and impact. They know how they—as the major instruments for delivering services—are calibrated. They can usually predict how they will behave in given situations, anticipate the likely consequences of their behaviors, and make adjustments for their biases. The following notes taken from the log of a beginning consultant demonstrate early steps in her self-analytic process.

> My professional values are not necessarily in line with the organizations I have served. I value a democratic approach to decision making—the sharing of control. I value open and honest communication. The rights of minority groups—such as women and blacks—are important to me. I have noticed that these values affected my interaction with the police department. Because I had a hidden agenda which was discrepant from our contract (so was theirs'), I inappropriately pushed my ideas about women and minorities. Only later was I clear about the discrepancies between their goals and mine. There are two consultee variables which at times create problems for me. One is the sex of the consultee. My reaction to some men is to acquiesce, especially when they seem self-assured and aggressive. I get particularly threatened when I perceive they are attracted to me and I start to feel quite unprofessional—that I am not taken seriously. But my response is to become more task-oriented and to lose some of my sensitivity. The other side of this issue is my attraction to consultees. I don't like to be interested in a consultee because then I become less effective. The second variable is the authority of the consultee. If the consultee is powerful and somewhat silent and reserved, I become more deferent. Then, to

counter this tendency, I became excessively independent.

I allowed myself to be deskilled in one agency
because of poor contracting, lack of self-confidence,
and attractive male consultees. In another agency, I
am not aware of being deskilled. Instead, the director
attributes more expertise to me than I actually have.
In response I feel guilty, but at the same time my ego
gets a gratifying boost.

Self-confidence is also essential to success. Consultants
need to be free to follow their own intuitions and use themselves—their feelings, fantasies, thoughts—as data to generate
hypotheses (Steele, 1975, p. 84). Belief in one's strengths is
needed for looking at all data and prolonging ambiguity when
the facts are incomplete and fuzzy. Consultants need confidence that there will be a denouement and a fair rate of success;
otherwise they will be predisposed to premature closure.

Along with self-confidence, consultants need *self-discipline* in order to curb their own impulses, to withstand manipulation without reacting emotionally, and to learn from the experience of being manipulated (Argyris, 1970, p. 175). They must
walk the very fine line between spontaneity and self-control.
When the situation is such that spontaneous expressions (for
example, of anger, affection, disappointment) might interfere
with the consultee's growth, such expressions—though self-grati-
fying—must be controlled and perhaps expressed at other times
when their effects are likely to be neutral or positive. The following case illustrates a consultant's ability to remain firm despite strong internal and external tugs to react.

The administrator and staff of a free legal clinic asked
John, a young professor and a specialist in organizational communication, to help them resolve coordination problems. Terms
were negotiated, including a provision that for a specified length
of time—before beginning actual intervention into work processes—John was to observe their usual meetings and other work
activities. The first staff meeting John attended was tense. Indirect but heated barbs flew between staff members. Obviously,
serious conflicts were being kept under wraps but were interfer-

ing with work. As the meeting came to an end, a staff member turned to John and demanded, "Give us some feedback about what you saw today." Everyone looked at John, who, startled from his intensive concentration on the complex nonverbal and verbal exchanges he had just witnessed, was nonplused. All eyes suddenly focused on him, and another staff member muttered dubiously, "Well, we must look like a pretty tough case."

John felt sorely tempted to share his impressions. He was acutely aware of his desire to accommodate the group and to impress the consultees with his competence by making sage observations. But he knew that to do so would break the contract, and there was not time left in this meeting to properly negotiate a new agreement. Furthermore, he surmised that by maintaining a stable, deliberate posture, he could be an effective counterforce to this staff's volatility. He replied, "I'm sorry to disappoint those of you who would like me to react right now, but I want to stay with our earlier agreement and get better acquainted with your agency before beginning to help you look at your staff processes. I'll be observing the remainder of this week and be ready to continue with the second part of our plan next week."

John's self-confidence and self-discipline helped him stay objective in this high-pressure situation. His resistance to their impulsive demands actually increased staff members' confidence that their consultant had both the personal strength and the professional skills to help them. Less confident consultants might have capitulated and undermined staff trust by breaking the agreement, by giving premature, ill-considered feedback, and by demonstrating that they could be manipulated into inappropriate action.

Since objectivity is a crucial ingredient of consultation, consultants need to be sufficiently *detached* to perceive and interpret data accurately. Yet they must at the same time be committed to the host agency and alert to the needs and feelings of consultees. In a sense, "loners" may be best able to function in this marginal role. Yet *sensitivity* to others is crucial.

Successful consultants satisfy their own personal and professional needs in ways that are compatible with their consultees' needs. Consultants need to be comfortable with *low needs for control* and with a *relatively low profile*. If their need for power is strong, they may encourage consultees' dependency or become embroiled in the agency's power battles. Most successful consultants learn to satisfy their needs for power in other domains of their lives.

Since client agencies differ greatly and since their norms and values are typically different from those of the consultant, this role calls for acceptance, understanding, tolerance, and adaptiveness by the consultant (Brodsky, 1977). Successful consultants accept and respect their consultees' language and dress and, more important, their values. What does a consultant do on finding he or she dislikes or disrespects certain consultees? The consultant then tries to "get into their shoes" so as to be able to understand and accept them. If acceptance is not possible, there should be no contract.

Successful consultants learn to minimize the effects of stereotyping on their relationships. They are alert to and monitor their own stereotypes. They include among their friends a wide variety of individuals who help them modify harmful stereotypes. They are also alert to consultees' stereotypes and dissipate them by refusing to reinforce them. When, for example, a male consultee flirtatiously comments on the attractiveness of a female consultant, she responds pleasantly and casually with a smiling "Thank you" and gently moves the focus back to work. Or when, during a conference, a consultee mentions a marital problem, consultants accept the information casually without probing, thus disconfirming the attribution of "shrink" and the assumption that they will analyze personal problems.

Consultants differ in their preferences for indirect or direct methods for coping with the sensitive issues that arise in their relationships with consultees. Some prefer to deal with relationship issues openly (Goodstein, 1978; Schein, 1969; Signell and Scott, 1971; Steele, 1975), assuming that the direct approach is more effective in establishing and maintaining an effective working relationship. Other consultants prefer to manage sensitive issues indirectly (Caplan, 1970). For instance, Meade and

Hamilton (1979, p. 8) advise consultants to avoid the "danger of stimulating strong transference or resistance" by "overtly" processing the personal interactions in the relationship and thus intensifying transference. Mental health professionals are probably more likely to use indirect methods because of their professional socialization (see Chapter Seven). Either direct or indirect methods can be used successfully. To illustrate, in the beginning of a consultation, a consultee introduces a personal problem subtly expressing a wish for the consultant to take a "doctor" role. The consultant wants to be acceptant and helpful and yet remain within the limits of the contract. One consultant takes an indirect approach, implicitly saying no to the inappropriate request by refocusing. This consultant might ask, "How does this problem affect your work?" Or the consultant might make a "me, too" response: "I know that can be tough, I went through that last year." The underlying message is "I do not possess superior insight or curative powers." Another indirect response is to suggest several agencies through which assistance might be obtained. Other consultants prefer a direct response that clarifies and reinforces the relationship boundaries. They might interrupt the consultee to say, "Before you go any further, I need to clarify my role and contract. I am to work with you only on concerns related to your work. If this personal problem is affecting your performance at work, maybe we can talk about how you can prevent it from interfering. Otherwise, we might discuss some professional resources that you might find helpful." The process of such a response—as well its content—confirms the expectation of an open and direct peer relationship.

Sensitivity in regard to *timing* is important in consultation (Lippitt and Lippitt, 1978). Effective consultants are able to judge the optimal time for confronting troubling situations. They are sensitive to the times when support is needed and when it is most helpful to say nothing, allowing the consultee to put the data together (Steele, 1975). The following case study illustrates how a consultant's sensitivity to a consultee's need for a good listener and for *tacit* support strengthened the relationship.

One of my early visits with Paul, the new administrator, was at a time he was providing evaluation feedback to staff. There were two supervisees about whom he was concerned because of interpersonal inadequacies which seriously affected their work. Because of his need to be gentle and likable, he was experiencing considerable discomfort in confronting them on these issues, although there was no question but that he would. His concern, apart from those individuals, was that the issue, if unconfronted, might eventually affect the overall morale and functioning of the agency.

He asked me to take a walk with him. During the time that we talked, it appeared that he was well in touch with the conflict between his personal needs and his desire to maintain high standards and morale. I contributed little to the discussion, beyond rare questions or supportive statements. Apparently, that was all that was needed of me. The "intervention" seemed to be beneficial to him. Afterward he appeared more relaxed and at ease with his decision to confront these two individuals.

Rapport building is a mutual exchange. Not only did I feel that the interchange had served to develop a higher trust of me in him, but I was also affected. During and after the conversation, I felt that we had moved onto a higher level of mutual respect and trust. To him, I believe that the incident demonstrated my willingness to listen to his concerns without passing judgment, offering a solution, or otherwise "doing something" about the situation. For me there was a feeling of warmth growing from the knowledge that I had been entrusted with a confidence about a sensitive personal and organizational issue.

Getting Help. Successful consultants know when to ask for help. In consultation "there are times when you get in over your head . . . particularly when you are on that other person's turf, or when there is a mass of things flying in the air" (Levinson, 1978, p. 39). Confronted with situational ambiguity, an emotionally charged atmosphere, and the uncertainties of practicing in a new field, consultants often need help. They need someone who speaks their language to help them review what is happening, to look at themselves, to find out what they are doing that is dysfunctional, and to understand consultees' behavior (Steele, 1975).

Consultants may turn to a "shadow" consultant, who provides personal support and opportunities for the consultant to review and critique his or her work (Schroeder, 1974). Consultants also obtain help by working in teams. Teams can reduce the feelings of isolation and marginality that often accompany consultation. Sharing of responsibility can lower anxiety. In addition, team members, especially when their competencies and styles are different, learn from observing each other. They also benefit from giving and receiving feedback. Teams can bring different specialties into consultation, and members often form a complementary unit. Teams also can accomplish more and intervene in two places simultaneously.

However, consultant teams, like other human systems, may develop interpersonal problems that affect their performance. Differences in style and goals and feelings about each other can complicate their relationships. Consultees' interactions with and differential responses to team members add to the complexity of team relations. Several types of team problems appear (Steele, 1975). Successful teamwork requires a great deal of communication and coordination. Communication failures may result in disconnected actions. "The different styles of the various consultants get acted out in this manner, with each step making sense for itself but not particularly connected with those before or after it" (p. 119). Consultants on a team may work at cross-purposes because of competitiveness or differences in perceptions, style, or values, thus pulling the agency in conflicting directions. Weaknesses may be contagious. One team member may imitate the weaknesses of another, thus amplifying dysfunctional behaviors. Consultees may split consultants into "good" and "bad" categories. One is viewed as warm and loving, the other as cold and uncaring. To conform with these attributions, consultants may alter their behavior by interacting in constricted, stereotypic patterns. Sometimes consultants separate out territories. They become less and less like each other. Each stays with her or his strongest areas and, in deference to the superior expertise of the other, pulls back from certain work. The tendency to split the territory may be reinforced by consultees' differential responses to team members. A one-upmanship spiral may develop. Instead of team gains and losses, one member gains and the other loses in each transaction. Team members may spend a disproportionate amount of time and energy in overprocessing their internal problems and have little left for consultation.

The following guidelines can help teams function effectively (Steele, 1975):

1. *Structure.* Teams should clarify their goals and methods. The roles and assignments of each team member should be agreed on and explicated.
2. *Openness.* Members of teams should be open not only to each other but to consultees. Agency members often fantasize about the relationships between team members. Face-to-face meetings with open discussions can help overcome these fantasies.
3. *Self-consciousness.* The effective team systematically studies itself and uses other consultants as process observers in order to obtain objective input. The use of video- and audiotapes for playback and discussion is helpful. Surveys of consultee reactions can provide valuable information.
4. *Heterogeneity.* Teams are most effective when their members come from different professions and have different styles and perspectives. However, the differences should not be so great as to prevent mutual understanding and shared goals.

Annotated Bibliography

Beisser, A., and Green, R. *Mental Health Consultation and Education.* Palo Alto, Calif.: National Press Books, 1972. The covert needs of consultant and consultee are discussed in chap. 4, "The Interface Between Consultant and Consultee."

The authors point out, for instance, that consultees may want the consultant to comfort them and make them feel better. The consultant may want to be a teacher and to give consultees the "right" answers. This chapter is useful in expanding consultants' understanding of and ability to manage relationship tensions.

Caplan, G. *The Theory and Practice of Mental Health Consultation*. New York: Basic Books, 1970. Following the perspective of psychoanalytic theory, Caplan describes principles and procedures for building effective relationships with consultees in chap. 5, "Building the Relationship with the Consultee." Caplan includes guidelines to prevent consultation from turning into psychotherapy.

Ford, C. H. "Developing a Successful Client-Consultant Relationship." In C. R. Bell and L. Nadler (Eds.), *The Client-Consultant Handbook*. Houston: Gulf Publishing Co., 1979. The author points out typical reasons behind breakdowns in the consulting relationship and illustrates them with brief case studies. He discusses common consultant failures, such as failure to clarify the role, and typical client failures, such as neglecting to inform the staff of the consultant's role and goals.

Levinson, H. "Organizational Diagnosis in Mental Health Consultation." In T. E. Backer and E. M. Glaser (Eds.), *Proceedings of the Advanced Workshop on Program Consultation in Mental Health Services*. Annapolis, Md.: National Institute of Mental Health, Mental Health Services Development Branch, 1978. Levinson presents a pithy description of a psychoanalytically oriented consultant's views of the consulting relationship.

Rogers, C. "The Characteristics of a Helping Relationship." In C. R. Bell and L. Nadler (Eds.), *The Client-Consultant Handbook*. Houston: Gulf Publishing Co., 1979. Written by a distinguished humanistic therapist, this article identifies and discusses generic characteristics of helping relationships, including those involving organizational consultation. The emphasis is on the helper's ability to facilitate growth.

Steele, F. *Consulting for Organizational Change*. Amherst: University of Massachusetts Press, 1975. The consultant/consultee relationship is a central theme throughout this book. Chap. 1, "The Consulting Function," and chap. 3, "Learning and the

Client's Role," by outlining consultant and consultee roles and functions, are especially valuable in illuminating relationship issues. Steele contrasts the different roles of the two parties and discusses possibilities for consultants' misinterpretations of consultees' behaviors as a consequence of these differences. This book contains one of the most thorough descriptions of consultants' feelings and reflections. Steele's recommendations are provocative and pragmatic.

14

Data Gathering, Diagnosis, and Intervention

The complex and often precarious tasks of data collection, diagnosis, and intervention are at the heart of the consultant's work. Chapters in Part Two describe specific ways of managing these challenges. This chapter discusses generic processes and suggests guidelines to increase consultants' effectiveness, regardless of the model or combination of models they are using.

Collaborative and Cyclical Processes: Assumptions and Principles

Central to the points of view presented in this chapter are two basic assumptions and principles derived from them. First, it is assumed that the most effective interventions come from the shared efforts of agency staff members (administrators and others who will be affected by changes and whose cooperation is needed to carry them out) and their consultants. Collaborative approaches have the advantage of bringing a wide range of data and expertise to bear on problems. Moreover, involvement in these processes increases consultees' ownership of and commitment to the diagnoses and interventions thus produced. Consequently, as a general principle, consultants and consultee should collaborate in the data-gathering, diagnostic, and intervention processes. Exceptions to this rule may be warranted at times, however. The clinical or medical model, in which the consultant makes diagnostic decisions and recommends solutions, may be appropriate when a consultant has more relevant knowledge than the consultee or when the consultee wants and needs only an opinion without elaboration—for instance, when the explanation would be highly technical, irrelevant to the consultee's actions, or of little value to the consultee (Schein, 1969). The purchase model, in which consultees assume complete responsibility for determining the nature of the problem and the expertise needed, may at times be appropriate—for instance, when the consultant's understanding of the agency is quite limited. This model may also be called for when, before the consultation, an agency staff has made a careful assessment of needs.

A second assumption is that data collection, diagnosis, and intervention are continuous and intricately related processes. Data collection never ceases and is an inherent part of every stage of consultation—from preliminary exploration and entry to evaluation and termination. Diagnosis is an ongoing activity, not a finished product. Even the most carefully formulated diagnosis can best be regarded as a hypothesis. Moreover, consultants, through such actions as raising issues and making observations, intervene continuously. Their greatest impact may, in fact, occur in the first contact in the form of questions or statements that challenge and expand consultees' perceptions and cognitions of their problems and of their options for solving them. In turn, consultees' changing ideas and increased awareness of organizational phenomena are continuing sources of new data. Consultants usually find it helpful, at the beginning of a consultation, to establish explicit procedures for periodically gathering and reviewing information and reevaluating earlier diagnoses and interventions. Figure 7 depicts a typical

Figure 7. The Cyclical Nature of Diagnosis and Intervention

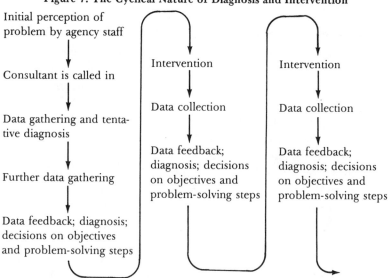

Initial perception of
problem by agency staff

↓

Consultant is called in

↓

Data gathering and tenta-
tive diagnosis

↓

Further data gathering

↓

Data feedback; diagnosis;
decisions on objectives
and problem-solving steps

Intervention

↓

Data collection

↓

Data feedback;
diagnosis; decisions
on objectives and
problem-solving steps

Intervention

↓

Data collection

↓

Data feedback;
diagnosis; decisions
on objectives and
problem-solving steps

Source: Adapted from French, W. "Organization Development: Objectives, Assumptions, and Strategies." In N. Margulies and A. P. Raia (Eds.), *Organization Development: Values, Process, and Technology.* New York: McGraw-Hill, 1972, p. 36.

pattern. These three processes are, however, separated in the following discussions to allow each one to be examined in detail.

Scanning

It is usually wise to begin a consultation by scanning the entire context rather than focusing immediately and narrowly on the presenting problem or need. Scanning can provide data to either verify or reject the initial diagnosis, to detect deeper-level problems underlying manifest ones, and to identify leverage points and resources that might be used in interventions, along with potential barriers.

Scanning procedures can prevent the costly mistakes that often result from a priori judgments of the nature and sources of problems and the means for solving them. Unfortunately, consultants often bypass the scanning process. For instance, in certain action-oriented intervention programs, data collection is minimal or nonexistent (Lorsch and Lawrence, 1972); a predetermined plan decides what data—if any—are to be collected and limits the phenomena considered to a narrow range. The ready availability of prepackaged programs and related survey instruments reinforces the tendency to overlook or minimize the unique and complex circumstances found in each agency. But consultations based on these predetermined approaches are usually "shots in the dark" that are, at best, wasteful.

Scanning can also be helpful in counteracting consultants' professional and personal biases and limitations. A consultant, for instance, in focusing on narrowly conceived technical problems and solutions, may fail to consider the relation of human processes to these problems and the organization's capacities to make technical changes. Another consultant may —either because of naivete or through a personalized reaction —erroneously conclude that an administrator's behavior is "good" or "bad." Careful scanning can help consultants more accurately assess phenomena in relation to their total context. For example, a close examination of what appears to be an administrator's irresponsible avoidance of conflict may reveal that the organization lacks the resources to work through and resolve conflicts. The administrator's past attempts to surface and work through conflicts may have been disastrous. Avoidance may, therefore, be an adaptive method of preventing disruptive and unproductive battles. Similarly, an in-group/out-group schism may appear demoralizing. It may, in fact, be demoralizing to some persons, but it may also function to unify and stabilize the core of permanent staff members, the persons who maintain and perpetuate the agency. Such a schism may also create productive tension in new staff members that accelerates indoctrination and socialization processes. Similarly, behavior that appears functional may have negative consequences. The administrator who appears to use a trust-inspiring democratic style, for example, may actually be sidestepping problems and the responsibility for protecting the agency's interests against the personal ambitions of its staff.

Conceptual Guidelines. The realm to be scanned is well nigh boundless. Practical considerations, however, force consultants to limit the range of their explorations. In selecting areas to be scanned, consultants are strongly influenced by their assumptions (which are often tacit) about the relative salience of particular domains in providing information on the sources of problems and on the leverage points through which they might be solved. By explicating these assumptions and their conceptual bases, consultants can more fully explore their relevance to a given situation and, at the same time, be alerted to their limitations. This chapter suggests a two-part conceptual framework to organize the scanning process. Based on open-systems theory and a developmental view of organizations, this framework, selected for its breadth, assumes that organizations can best be understood and their problems solved by considering (1) relations between their subsystems and to their environments and (2) their cyclical nature. Descriptions of other models that are helpful in scanning and in subsequent activities are found in Part Two and in Chapter Three.

The *open-systems approach,* following the concepts outlined in Chapter Three, calls for scanning of all agency subsystems in order to obtain an organic and dynamic perspective. The following checklist suggests the major areas to be surveyed.

An Open-Systems Checklist for Agency Diagnosis

1. History.

2. Purposes and nature:
   a. Societal mandates and underlying values.
   b. Other goals and priorities and underlying values.

3. General state of health.

4. Inputs:
   a. Clients.
   b. Staff.
   c. Funds (grants, taxes, endowments, client fees) and conditions governing funding.
   d. Materials and equipment.
   e. Community attitudes and expectancies.

5. Structure:
   a. Hierarchy of responsibility and authority.
   b. Distribution of tasks.
   c. Coordination and integration between units and activities.

     d.   Personnel: characteristics, competencies.
     e.   Recruitment and orientation procedures.
     f.   Financial structure and budgets.
     g.   Physical setting and facilities.

6. Technological processes (service delivery):
     a.   Intake and screening procedures.
     b.   Procedures, steps, phases, cycles.
     c.   Technologies involved.
     d.   Existing procedures.

7. Human processes:
     a.   Leadership: distribution of power, leadership style, forms of compliance used (such as rewards, punishments).
     b.   Decision-making patterns.
     c.   Communications patterns.
     d.   Methods for managing conflict.
     e.   Staff attitudes: commitment to agency, morale, satisfaction, attitude toward clients.

8. Output:
     a.   Clients.
     b.   Information.
     c.   Contacts with clients and community.
     d.   Contacts with other agencies.

9. Environmental interactions:
     a.   Community; consumers.
     b.   Professional.
     c.   State.
     d.   Federal.

The relations between the presenting problem and these areas should be reviewed and the environment scrutinized to detect any existing or imminent changes that have implications for the agency—for example, new technologies, shifts in funding priorities, and changing characteristics of the target population. Internal discrepancies, such as those between an agency's purposes and its actual operations and outputs, can be flagged for study.

Obviously, an open-systems analysis identifies potential points of intervention as well as sources of data with which to formulate diagnoses. The following case illustrates the application of the open-systems framework to data-gathering and diagnostic processes.

Morris, the director of an adult probation office, asked Phil, an organizational consultant with extensive experience in probation work, to carry out an intervention based on the former's assessment. Morris, poised for action, explained, "I am introducing a new program. I plan to recruit housewives and college students as volunteers to work with probationers under the supervision of my staff. Volunteers will allow us to give probationers a lot more attention, and we will be the first in the state to have a systematic volunteer program. Your job is to give the recruits a short course in working with probationers and the regular staff a workshop on supervising volunteers." The consultee had created a plan to enhance the agency's status through changes in its technical processes and in its structure and interpersonal processes. He diagnosed the immediate problem as deficiencies in the staff's knowledge and skills and assigned the consultant the role of educator-trainer.

Instead of accepting Morris's diagnosis, Phil suggested they first make sure the diagnosis was accurate before beginning training. Morris insisted that no further diagnosis was needed but finally agreed to suspend plans until diagnostic data could be gathered and interpreted. Working together at some times and separately at others, the two scanned the system. Together they reviewed agency materials that described its history, objectives, policies, jobs, and procedures. They discussed trends in the criminal justice system. Phil observed members of the agency in their staff meetings and in their work with probationers. He talked to probation officers about their goals, current operations, and problems and about the proposed program. He administered a job satisfaction survey.

These explorations revealed two previously undiagnosed problems that had crucial implications for Morris's plans. First, it became clear that staff members were fearful over what they perceived to be a significant shift in responsibilities and rewards.

Most did not want to become supervisors. They preferred to work directly with probationers. Moreover, since most came from lower-class, blue-collar backgrounds, they were uneasy about the prospect of working with and supervising volunteers, who they expected would be college-educated and middle-class. The second problem, more basic than the first, was their fear of open disagreement with their boss. They were afraid to express their feelings about the project for fear they would be punished. These unanticipated problems obviously posed serious barriers to Morris's project. Consequently, he altered his plans and his goals for consultation.

Developmental concepts of organizational life provide another heuristic framework for the consultant's work. Organizations are constantly changing. They are created and develop. They go through periods of expansion and decline. Some disappear. Others revitalize and reorganize and begin new trajectories (Kimberly, Miles, and Associates, 1980). The agency's stage of development affects the degree to which resources are available to confront problems and the staff's openness and energy level. It also has implications for the kinds of help needed from consultants. A developmental framework, therefore, can be useful in guiding consultants in collecting relevant data and in evolving cogent diagnoses and interventions.

A comparison of the developmental status of two agencies will illustrate the usefulness of this perspective. Agency A is in a period of expansion. Its budget and funding are increasing yearly; its leadership is vigorous; staff members are characteristically exuberant and productive. Agency B is in a state of crisis. It recently suffered a huge budget cut. Anxiety has—for the moment, at least—immobilized its administrators. Staff members are competing for dwindling funds and slots. Agency A is proactive; its approach to problems is preventive and long-range. Agency B's problem-solving mechanisms are in shambles. Several key staff members are preparing to leave. Valid data are difficult to obtain and even more difficult to accept, since staff members are reluctant to acknowledge their declining prospects. Consultants working with Agency A find that their ideas and skills are rapidly and effectively used. Consultants to Agency B find staff members resistant, unrealistic, and at times illogical.

A consultant's failure to realize that a serious decline in agency resources and viability (as well as a personal crisis) was impairing a consultee's abilities to cope is illustrated in the following case.

Marjorie, the director of a large daycare center, requested consultation services from the local community mental health center. Edith, whose background was in program development and evaluation, was assigned to this job. She found the organization in chaos because of impending budget cuts that would require massive cutbacks in services and staffing. It soon became apparent that although Marjorie was a ten-year veteran in her job, her management of the situation was blatantly incompetent. Moreover, Edith found Marjorie "resistant" to consultation. She tended to focus on peripheral issues. She had not begun to plan and organize responses to imminent cuts. She ignored the staff's needs for clear information and for emotional support. Moreover, in conferences Edith found Marjorie, whose sister had recently died, preoccupied with personal concerns.

Over time the relationship became polarized. Edith, intent on helping, impatiently pressed Marjorie to take certain logical steps. The administrator was less and less interested in discussing forward-looking plans and actions. After four months, Edith terminated the relationship.

In a subsequent analysis of the consultation, Edith realized she had failed to consider that Marjorie, in a state of psychological shock as a result of the organizational and personal losses, had hoped to get support from an empathic consultant. When support was not forthcoming, she had been either unwilling or unable to accept Edith's pressures to focus on problems. In this somewhat unusual situation, the consultant might have tried to help Marjorie regain her equilibrium by offering empathy for the dual loss and acceptance of her anxious feelings and desire to withdraw. Edith could also have discussed with Marjorie community resources where she could obtain counseling.

When organizations are, like Agency B, in a period of decline, consultants are likely to discover that rational problem-solving approaches and the input of technical information are of little help. A state of mourning prevails. Denial, depression, and anger interfere with agency functioning. Consultants may first become aware of an agency's state of decline in such signs as lowered energy, denial of problems, rigid and fruitless problem-solving efforts, overt negative emotions such as anxiety and fear, deepening of rifts (such as between departments or between minorities and majorities), frequent illnesses and absences, and decreases in the number of agencywide staff meetings and social activities. Consultants can determine whether these signs are related to a downswing in the agency's trajectory by checking on trends in such areas as funding, number and quality of staff members, morale and attrition, community sanctions, and numbers of services and numbers of clients served.

The following items (adapted from Beckhard, 1975; Fordyce and Weil, 1971; and Schein, 1965, 1969) make up a convenient checklist for assessing an agency's coping effectiveness.

Characteristics of Healthy Organizations

1. *Goals.* High consensus on goals and high commitment to achieve them.
2. *Attitude toward problems.* Openness to expose and work on problems; optimism toward potential for solving them.
3. *Decisions.* Decisions are data-based and made by persons who will be affected by them and who will implement them.
4. *Communication.* Communication channels are open for frequent intake and dissemination of reliable information.
5. *Rewards.* Rewards are consistently administered and are consistent with and supportive of organizational goals.
6. *Coordination.* Subsystems are coordinated and support the goals of the total system.
7. *Individuals.* Individuals are respected as valuable resources and actively supported in their continuing growth. Flexibility and creativity are encouraged.
8. *Conflict.* Conflict is open and is constructively managed so as to benefit the organization while minimizing the potential for destructive effects on individuals.
9. *Feedback.* The organization is continually involved in obtaining feedback from its environment and from internal operations. Performances receive regular and thorough feedback.

10. *Adaptiveness.* Staff members learn from new information and are flexible in adapting to changing conditions.
11. *Resources.* Optimal use of internal and external resources.
12. *Realism.* Administrators are realistic in assessing the agency's strengths and weaknesses and in assessing its relationship to the environment.

Criteria similar to those just listed have been used as the basis for surveys through which members of organizations indicate their perceptions of the organization's coping effectiveness (Schein, 1969, p. 62). Use of a checklist or survey such as this can quickly identify agencies experiencing developmental difficulties whose members are likely to need help in dealing with their emotions before they can clarify their problems, accept the realities of their situations, and begin to confront them. Consultants should be alert to the need to adapt their roles and functions accordingly or suggest to consultees that they seek help from other sources.

Data Collection

Scanning and later processes, such as diagnosis, intervention, and evaluation, call for data—information about the organization, its staff, and its environment. Consultants need to gather sufficient data to provide a reasonable basis for a valid diagnosis and to guide the process of selecting goals and intervention methods to fit the agency's particular circumstances, needs, and resources. Data may be written or oral. They may be "soft," such as impressions of internal political schisms, or "hard," such as statistical reports of clients' use of agency services or of supervisees' attitudes toward their supervisors. The following pages highlight the wide range of commonly used data-collection methods and the unique advantages and disadvantages of each. (Additional information concerning data-collection methods is found in Chapter Fifteen.) Most of these methods involve interaction between consultants and consultees (they often increase interaction between consultees, as well) and, therefore, are useful not only in diagnostic activities but as intervention strategies.

Archival Data. Agencies always have archives from which

potentially valuable data can be obtained with relative ease. For instance, consultants may examine job descriptions, agency policies and manuals of operating procedures, historical records, annual reports, budgets, audits, personnel statistics (including attrition and absenteeism statistics), orientation procedures, promotion policies, program descriptions, grant proposals, client demographic profiles, surveys of client use of services, public information brochures, logs, appointment calendars, and case records. Agencies may also have in their files reports from task forces, records left by previous consultants, and relevant legislative documents.

Probably the biggest advantage of using archival data is its unobtrusiveness. This method is more likely to yield valid information than methods such as those that require that consultees be asked sensitive questions. Permission to examine archival data is usually easy to obtain and does not require consultees' time and cooperation, as do most data-gathering methods. Archives, however, rarely contain all data vital to consultants' work. Often records are incomplete. Moreover, they may be maintained so haphazardly that information drawn from them is unreliable and misleading.

Interviews. Interviews are the most frequently used method of obtaining data and are especially valuable in the early phases of diagnosis, when the consultant is looking for leads to the underlying sources of problems, and when direct data about attitudes and perceptions are needed (Cannell and Kahn, 1972). Interviews are more flexible and fluid than surveys. Interviews can probe and shift focus when unexpected information suggests that new domains should be explored. If the consultant-interviewer is skillful in establishing rapport, individual interviews can yield much richer and more confidential material than any other method. Group interviews can also be useful in generating valuable data—including observations of members' processes as well as interview content. Obtaining information through interviews, however, depends on the subject's willingness to respond and on his or her knowledge. If the interviewee does not know the answer, observations may be the best means of gathering data. Carefully conducted interviews can sometimes obtain information unknown to the respondent, but gathering information from an individual without consent is an ethically questionable practice.

The place where data is collected affects the quality of the information obtained (Steele, 1975). This axiom has implications for all data-gathering methods but especially for interviews and observations. To illustrate his point, Steele points to the contrast in the views of the patient when seen by a psychiatrist in the hospital and when seen in the patient's home. Similarly, in seeking data on organizational morale, information obtained in a reception room will differ from that obtained in a board meeting room or in a one-to-one conference over lunch in a country club.

Surveys. Surveys are predetermined, self-administered, paper-and-pencil interviews (Nadler, 1977). Through surveys, consultants ask organizational members, clients, or community residents direct questions about their feelings, attitudes, perceptions, and evaluations. Surveys most often are used to gather information from staff members and may focus on a single issue, such as Likert's "Organizational Climate" survey, an instrument designed to identify members' perceptions of the leadership style of their organizations, ranging from authoritarian to participative (see Chapter Three). Items include such questions as "How much confidence is shown in subordinates?" and "Are subordinates' ideas sought and used if worthy?" A survey may instead be based on a broad theory or model of organizational functioning and used to obtain a comprehensive diagnosis, such as the "Organizational Diagnosis Questionnaire" developed by Preziosi (1980) and based on Weisbord's six-box model of organizational diagnosis (1976). This instrument includes five items on each of seven dimensions:

1. *Relationships.* The ways organizational members manage interpersonal conflicts and conflicts between people and technologies.
2. *Purposes.* The basic goals of the organization.
3. *Structure.* Arrangements for dividing work and responsibilities.

4. *Leadership*. The methods by which the organization is managed.
5. *Rewards*. The incentives for performing tasks.
6. *Helpful mechanisms*. The degree to which technologies are adequate to the organization's goals and the extent to which technological tasks are coordinated.
7. *Change*. The degree to which members of the organization are open to making changes.

Surveys have many advantages. They are inexpensive and quickly and easily administered, quantified, and summarized. They can be administered to large groups and in a time series. Hence, they can produce and be used to process a large volume of data. Surveys are useful in all stages of consultation—from exploration to evaluation and termination. However, since surveys consist of predetermined questions, they may miss major issues. Moreover, respondents often find it difficult to "warm up" to a paper-and-pencil interview (Nadler, 1977), and responses may be distorted by respondents' biases.

A major question in using surveys is whether to rely on standardized instruments or on specially constructed ones. Standardized instruments contain predetermined questions designed to apply to organizations in general; custom-designed surveys are constructed to fit the needs of a particular situation. The advantages of the standardized instruments are that they have been pretested and refined and their reliability and validity have been established. The "Survey of Organizations" (Taylor and Bowers, 1972) is an example of a widely used and well-developed instrument. However, specially constructed surveys may be needed to focus on issues relevant to a particular situation. They are, however, more time-consuming to prepare, and since they have not been standardized, they are less reliable. But since their relevance is usually highly apparent, respondents are more likely to answer them thoughtfully.

Consultants can capitalize on the advantages of both types by customizing standardized instruments through adding the organization's title and a suitable introduction. They can also tack onto the end of a standardized survey form specially constructed items relevant to the particular situation.

Process Observations. Through observing staff processes, consultants gather information related to interpersonal relations, administrative procedures, communications and decision-making processes, service delivery practices, and many other activities (see "Process Consultation," Chapter Nine). Observations are probably most useful in getting data that consultees would not be able to give directly because of lack of awareness. Staff members, for example, are usually unaware of their decision-making patterns. Unstructured process observations are most useful when problems are not clearly formulated. Structured observations—for example, records of the amount of time spent by a staff on various topics, the number of interruptions, and patterns such as who encourages whom—are most valuable when problems are beginning to crystallize and observation categories can be planned in advance. Stop-action strategies that encourage consultees to pause in their work to examine processes are useful when the purpose is not only to gather data but to intervene.

Case Studies of Critical Incidents. Case-study approaches in which consultants help staff members review and analyze critical incidents can reveal important patterns, such as reactions to crisis situations, planning procedures, use of resources, leadership styles, and conflict management. This approach can also help consultees identify and bring into sharp focus differences in perceptions and interpretations of the same events. This method elicits data that most methods fail to tap. It is probably most useful when followed by a forward-looking group discussion.

Mirroring Exercises. Another method for generating hard-to-get data is the use of organizational mirroring exercises. Through surveys such as organizational climate and job satisfaction questionnaires and through structured exercises, agency staff members describe their impressions of the organization. Members of the different subsystems describe their own and other units. The use of mirroring exercises is illustrated in a consultation with a counseling services center. The consultant noted subtle tensions between divisions (training, outreach, direct services, and testing) that seemed to be related to the director's expressed concern over lack of cooperation; yet interviews and surveys yielded little information about the sources and nature of these tensions. In an effort to produce information, the consultant created a mirroring exercise. She separated the staff by divisions. The director and associate director formed a separate group. Each of the five groups was then invited to depict the organization and its parts through whatever media it wished. Drawing materials and other aids were available. Each work group used different media to communicate its perceptions—including a drawing, a mime production, a still-life arrangement, and a human "sculpture." All "mirrors" revealed a common family theme. The director was portrayed to be in a close relationship with two "favorite children." Intense, rivalrous feelings were apparent. The mirrors opened up an emotional and informative discussion of phenomena of which the director was unaware and which were the underlying cause of the staff's failure to collaborate.

Confrontation Meetings. The principles of the confrontation meeting are similar to those of the more intricate and ongoing Quality Control Circles, originated by Japanese managers in 1949 (Ouchi, 1981). In this strategy, employees who work together form circles that meet weekly to study problems. Typically, a group studies one problem over a period of months. Members systematically collect and analyze data and formulate and implement problem-solving steps.

Meetings in which a staff focuses on problems can generate valuable data. First described by Beckhard (1967) as a means of assessing an organization's state of health, this strategy can quickly elicit data and can often help a staff move quickly toward the diagnosis and solution of problems. The major steps in such a meeting are these:

1. A good work climate is established, goals for the meeting are set, and any necessary background information is provided.
2. Group processes needed for a successful meeting are described—for example, openness in communication and willingness to listen to others' points of view.
3. Work groups for the meeting are identified. Groups may be

composed of members of the same department or of people
from different units.

4. Groups identify and list problems facing the organization.
5. Groups share their ideas about problems.
6. Consultant or administrator helps members categorize
   problems by clustering together those that appear related.
7. Problem-solving groups are established to work on different problems. Their task is to determine priorities, list alternative solutions, and recommend specific actions for the
   solution of the problem to which they are assigned.
8. Plans are made for a subsequent meeting to review progress.
   At that time each group reports its successes and failures to
   the total group. The problem definitions and solution strategies are critiqued, and needed revisions are made.

Establishing the Diagnosis

The scanning procedure produces data that must then be
sorted, related, and analyzed in order to formulate a diagnosis
of the problem or needs. It is often fruitful to examine the data
from several perspectives, not just the framework that guided its
collection, to find the one that best fits the available information. In addition to open-systems and developmental theories,
for example, a consultant might check the relevance of transactional analysis concepts to data drawn from the human processes
domain or the meaning and implications of the organization's
metaphors. The data analysis may suggest new hypotheses that
require further scanning and data collection to test their validity. Using the cyclical process depicted in Figure 7, consultants
should try to achieve fairly firm definitions of problems before
attempting major interventions.

Following are excerpts from a case report in which a consultant, following the open-systems and developmental framework, organized a plethora of problems into a coherent diagnosis
and set the stage for formulating and prioritizing goals. The client organization was Planned Parenthood, a local affiliate of the
Planned Parenthood Federation of America. The data for this
part of the consultant's report came from interviews with the
agency's executive director.

Founded in the 1940s to provide birth control education and information to poor families, the services of Planned Parenthood expanded significantly throughout the 1970s. Coordination and cooperation with other local social service agencies increased, as did the numbers of clients served. As federal funding grew and both state and federal legislation became less restrictive, Planned Parenthood became an accepted and welcomed member of the community services team. The medical community, howbeit reluctantly, gave the agency its support.

In 1981, however, numerous and far-reaching problems threatened the agency's continued existence. External problems included (1) significantly decreased federal funding, (2) increasingly hostile attitudes from local and state medical communities, (3) powerful and vocal anti-abortion and Moral Majority forces, and (4) the prospect of more restrictive legislation at both state and federal levels. The agency faced the prospect of substantial cuts in federal funding and a change in procedures for granting of whatever monies were available. Block grants to the states were being proposed that, if implemented, would mean this agency would find itself applying for funds to a state system that had openly opposed many of its goals. The changing economics of the city further complicated the funding situation. Inflation made it difficult to obtain financial support from the community. Moreover, a large influx of physicians into the area increased competition for patients. These physicians viewed the agency as a financial threat. Some called into question the agency's medical practices and procedures.

At both local and national levels, anti-abortion forces gained new strength and vitality from the election of the Reagan administration. The Planned Parenthood Federation was one of the groups specifically targeted for extinction. The agency in this case, although it met only limited local opposition, felt the sting of the national anti-abortion campaign. Local politicians and business leaders, because of pressures from their constituencies, were increasingly reluctant to support Planned Parenthood. In addition, the state legislature was considering a new medical practices act. Strong lobbies representing physicians and pharmacists sought to strengthen the positions of their respective professions by limiting the services that could be provided by clinics such as those operated by Planned Parenthood. The proposed act would require more extensive use of physicians and pharmacists in these clinics, thereby significantly increasing the cost of their operations.

Internal problems facing the organization were equally substantial: (1) a leadership crisis, (2) the management team's difficulties in working together, (3) lack of a mechanism for determining work roles, responsibilities, and reporting procedures, and (4) lack of responsiveness to the external threats outlined above. The executive director had been in his position only a few months. Although he had extensive experience in family planning, he had no experience in management. Furthermore, he followed in the rather "large" footsteps of a strong and charismatic leader, who led the agency from obscurity to a place of relative prominence in the community and who had commanded the respect of her staff. She had maintained tight control of the organization. Her decisions, although frequently made unilaterally, were seldom questioned. The new director's authority had not been fully accepted by the management staff. His style was more democratic than his predecessor's. To his staff he appeared indecisive. The situation had deteriorated to the extent that the management team insisted on a "management by committee" approach that, in effect, took away a large measure of the executive director's authority. The team, however, lacking the strong leadership its members had come to rely on, was in chaos. Each member, with little regard for the organization as a whole, sought to strengthen his or her own turf. Most felt threatened and distrustful of their fellow workers. Work roles became fuzzy and confused as each director sought to gain power through seizing control of any "gray" areas. More and more meetings were held for longer and longer periods of time, yet less and less was accomplished. Efforts to develop contingency plans for dealing with external pressures were blocked by internal haggling. Frustrations were extremely high.

The executive director and I agreed that massive external forces demanded that Planned Parenthood, if it were to survive, must carefully assess the changes taking place in its environment and quickly respond with appropriate steps. However, difficulties in leadership and team collaboration prevented the agency from using its resources (including a capable and dedicated staff, well-developed service operations, a large and satisfied client population, and a few powerful community leaders) to react appropriately.

Making Intervention Decisions

The usefulness of the cyclical process is again apparent as the consultant moves from diagnosis to intervention. A diagnosis suggests goals and methods for reaching them, but feasible goals and intervention methods typically cannot be chosen without a great deal of information. A new cycle of scanning and data gathering is often needed to identify options and to weigh the advantages and disadvantages of each.

In the case just described, for instance, the consultant and consultee might return to the guidelines found in "An Open-Systems Checklist for Agency Diagnosis" and "Characteristics of Healthy Organizations," earlier in this chapter, to generate an array of possible goals and methods through which diagnosed problems might be solved. They would then gather information to answer questions of feasibility relative to any strategies considered—such as costs and any constraints and facilitative resources that might be anticipated. They would also estimate positive and negative consequences of any steps considered. Following are brief examples of alternatives that might emerge at this stage.

Goal: prevent financial crisis

Possible strategies for reaching goal:
Convert to a fee-for-service basis of operations
Replace certain paid staff members with volunteers
Delete the most costly services
Seek new funding sources by exploring the possibilities of obtaining grants from private foundations

Goal: improved community relationships

Possible strategies for reaching goal:
Publicize dilemma through news media
Influence public opinion through endorsements from powerful supporters, such as prominent educators and clergy
Change attitudes of local physicians through personal contacts and liaison with the local medical association

Goal: strengthen agency's coping capacities

Possible strategies for reaching goal:
Increase executive director's leadership effectiveness through coaching and training
Increase the degree to which staff members collaborate through confrontation of distrust and territorialism
Increase management team's problem-solving skills through training in areas such as use of feedback, use of resources, decision making, and conflict management

Given even the most simple problem, solution options are likely to be extensive. (A more detailed discussion of these options is found in Chapter 4.) How does one go about choosing the goals, intervention strategies, and consultant role that will be most helpful to an agency? There is no simple answer to this question. However, the collaborative, cyclical, and scanning processes discussed earlier can greatly facilitate the selection of effective intervention plans. In addition, criteria that have been recommended to guide these decisions can be useful. Several goal-setting criteria have been proposed. One is urgency. For instance, crisis theory calls for intervention at the "sickest" point in the organization, the area experiencing the most pain. The assumptions are that it is here that the need is most acute and that the energy available for change will be greatest. A commonly used criterion is probability of success. For instance, an intervention might be directed to the healthiest department or the individuals or subsystems that are the most central, powerful, or influential. The rationale is that these interventions, by tapping the organization's strengths, are most likely to be successful. Moreover, through a ripple effect, the impact on these sturdy elements can spread to the weaker ones. Feasibility is another important consideration. Goals may be set to involve the individuals or departments that are most "ready" for an intervention or those with the most plentiful resources for carrying it out. A goal might be chosen because it could be achieved at relatively low cost in time and money. Criteria for choosing intervention methods include potential effectiveness, costs in time and money, and feasibility factors—for instance, the degree to which staff members could be expected to support a particular intervention technique. It is usually important to give particular attention to available sources of power and the types of influence most likely to bring about changes associated with chosen goals.

In the case described above, the consultant and the executive director decided that the highest priority should be given to the goal of mobilizing the agency's internal resources. The rationale was that until these resources could be tapped, attempts to cope with external problems would be futile. Since, at this point, the management team was not willing to be involved in any consultative intervention, the only feasible goal was to increase the executive director's leadership effectiveness. Methods included coaching and feedback. Eventually, changes in the executive director's style and the intensification of external threats led the management team to express interest in improving its work processes. The members of this team asked the consultant to provide training and to work with them as a process consultant. Over a period of weeks the team gradually learned, and began to use, more constructive group processes. A major change in work relations and in productivity occurred after a survey feedback meeting in which staff members discussed their need for stronger leadership; the executive director (well prepared through the consultant's coaching) began, on the spot, to assume greater decision-making responsibility. Team members eventually expressed and resolved most of their feelings of anger and evolved and implemented plans for responding to the external forces threatening to wipe out their agency.

Annotated Bibliography

Glaser, E. M., and others. "The Round Table." *Consultation*, 1981, *1* (1), 34-43. After the presentation of a case brief of a consultation failure, four consultants discuss their analyses of what went wrong and what they might have done to bring about a more successful outcome.

Levinson, H. *Organizational Diagnosis*. Cambridge, Mass.: Harvard University Press, 1972. This book presents a data-gathering guide for a case-study approach to organizational diagnosis based on both psychoanalytic and open-systems theory. A lengthy case study that demonstrates the application of this approach includes an analysis, interpretation, and feedback report.

Margulies, N., and Raia, A. P. (Eds.). *Organizational Development: Values, Process, and Technology*. New York: McGraw-Hill, 1972. Part Three, "The Process and Technology of Organizational Development," is divided into sections on data gathering, diagnosis, and intervention. Each section includes chapters by several authors. These readings provide consultants with an overview of the different approaches to these central tasks.

Nadler, D. A. *Feedback and Organization Development: Using Data-Based Methods*. Reading, Mass.: Addison-Wesley, 1977. Based on the theory that information influences and directs behavioral changes, this book takes a broad approach to the use of data as a tool for organizational diagnosis and intervention. The author discusses and illustrates the uses of a wide range of data-gathering and feedback methods.

Pfeiffer, J. W., Heslin, R., and Jones, J. E. *Instrumentation in Human Relations Training* (2nd ed.). San Diego, Calif.: University Associates, 1976. The chapters in Part I, "Instrumentation," address technical and pragmatic concerns in regard to use of instruments. Part II reviews a large number of instruments, including those assessing organizational climate, management style, and supervisor/subordinate relations. The information presented in this book will help consultants understand the use and limits of instruments and decide which ones to use in particular situations.

15

Evaluation
and Termination

Evaluation is the measurement of the positive and negative consequences of actions intended to achieve changes in individuals or groups (Riecken, 1977). Although evaluation may be informal and qualitative, today the word *evaluation* is most often used to refer to the applied science in which the investigator operationally defines and quantifies the variables of interest —such as intervention procedures and their effects—and seeks to control other variables as much as possible (Glass and Ellett, 1980). The evaluator uses the designs and methods of the researcher, but evaluation differs from research in its greater specificity. An evaluator is concerned with one program, one time, and one place (Matuzek, 1981), whereas a researcher seeks generalizable answers to basic questions. The general purpose of evaluation is to provide information for decision making.

Consultants are finding that a careful evaluation is an increasingly important aspect of their work. Administrators, faced with tight and often dwindling budgets, must demonstrate that interventions accomplish their intended effects. Consultants can find a ready supply of evaluation tools in the growing field of evaluation methodology. Methods for human services evaluation are especially well developed (Anderson and Ball, 1978; Atkisson,

1978; Meyers, 1981), as are methods for evaluation of behavioral consultation. The quality of evaluation in other models of consultation, though uneven, is steadily improving (Carter and Cazares, 1976; Medway, 1979; Porras and Berg, 1978).

Because of the complex and dynamic nature of the consultative process and its context, an adequate evaluation can be difficult to achieve. Specialized competencies are often needed to design an evaluation, to select and refine measures, and to perform statistical analyses. If, as is often the case, consultants do not possess needed competencies, they must consult with evaluation specialists. Often interventions involving extensive resources and goals include provisions for an internal or external evaluation specialist. In many cases, however, consultants are responsible for evaluation of their interventions and therefore need at least basic competencies in evaluating the kinds of interventions they are most often involved in.

One purpose of this chapter is to highlight evaluation concepts and methods as they relate to consultation. References are provided to help readers expand their competence in this field. A second purpose is to discuss issues related to termination and to suggest guidelines for successfully concluding a consultation.

Evaluation of Consultation

Consultants are usually concerned with one or more of the following types of information:

- The degree to which the desired goals were reached.
- The factors that contributed to both positive and negative outcomes.
- Interim feedback about how an intervention is progressing.
- The cost/benefit ratio of interventions.
- The consultant's overall effectiveness and effectiveness in the various stages and processes of consultation, such as contracting and diagnosis.

Consultants need evaluation models that fit the particular

characteristics and goals of their services. A complete model would recognize the cyclical nature of consultation processes, in which feedback from each intervention leads to a more precise diagnosis and a more carefully designed intervention (depicted in Figure 7, in Chapter 14). In order to focus on the evaluation process, however, a model is proposed here to represent only one segment of this cycle: one diagnosis, one intervention, one set of outcomes. Figure 8 suggests a generic framework for exploring ways to evaluate such a segment. The elements of this model are as follows:

1. *Targets of the intervention*—for example, a consultee's knowledge and/or skills in using a problem-solving model, a client's health, a community's crime rate, an agency's communications processes, or the attrition rate of staff in a rape crisis center. (Measures of the initial state of target variables are usually obtained for baseline data against which to later compare outcome measures.)

2. *Intervention inputs* such as agency funds, staff time, and consultants' services—such as teaching, advising, negotiating conflicts, or demonstrating techniques.

3. *Processes* related to or affecting the intervention: (a) the steps or procedures of the intervention, including changes or failures to follow through, schedule of the intervention, critical incidents, and interactions between inputs and individual and organizational behavior—for example, a personal crisis interfering with certain aspects of an intervention; (b) milestones such as achievement of subgoals, the short-term or intermediate effects that are needed to reach the goals of the intervention.

4. *Outcomes* expected from the intervention. Outcomes may be defined in terms of the more easily measured direct and short-term effects, such as staff skills. The assumption—explicit or implicit—is, however, that these effects will bring about changes in the chain of variables shown in Figure 8 and culminate in benefits to clients and society. For example, in an intervention in which a consultant trains and coaches the staff of a welfare department in the use of computerized record keeping, outcomes might be defined in terms of staff competencies. However, the outcomes might also be defined in terms of more

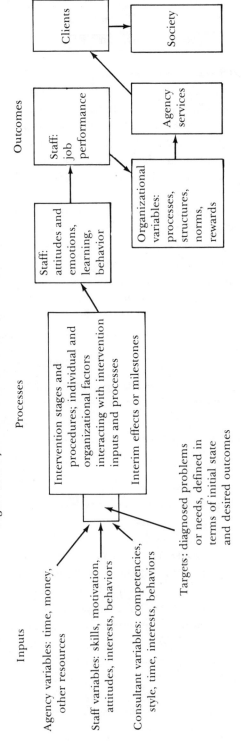

Figure 8. A Systems Model for Evaluation of Consultation

efficient agency operations, increased interdepartmental and interagency collaboration, or faster processing of clients. Benefits to society, such as reductions in the operation costs of this publicly funded agency, might be an explicit goal.

a. *Consultee outcomes.* Lockwood and Luthans (1980) identify three variables that might have relevance for a particular consultation: (1) attitudes and emotions —for example, how consultees felt about and reacted to a new administrator or a proposed program; (2) learning— the extent to which consultees acquired new skills, concepts, or information; (3) behavior—the degree to which consultees changed their behaviors; for example, the use of a new technique or increased collaboration between staff members.

These consultee variables are sometimes considered to be interim effects within the process component of the model shown in Figure 8 rather than outcomes. For example, certain changes in staff attitudes might be needed at one step in an intervention in order for the next step to be implemented (Schmuck and others, 1972).

b. *Job performance*—the degree to which actual performance changes; for example, a consultee's services to clients or an administrator's performance as a manager.

c. *Agency operations*—for example, changes in work processes or structure.

d. *Agency services*—for example, installation of a new program or improvements in the quality or quantity of services provided.

e. *Client outcomes*—for example, changes in variables such as educational achievements, mental or physical health, or employment.

f. *Societal outcomes*—for example, changes in variables such as public health, incidence of crime, and use of public transportation.

Most evaluators seek to determine the cost/benefit ratio of interventions by weighing positive outcomes against costs. If a cost/benefit ratio can be obtained for two or more interventions addressing the same need, a quantitative comparison can be made—thus providing important information to decision makers. For instance, data on the effectiveness of two alcohol counseling programs (measured by program success in keeping clients alcohol-free for six months) could be obtained along with the costs to conduct each program. But the *societal* benefits of this and other human services—perhaps the most crucial of all evaluation data—are difficult to assess, and it is virtually impossible to measure the cost of not providing services (Miringoff, 1980).

Evaluations are usually concerned with the total input into an intervention. In order to obtain feedback for professional development purposes, consultants usually want to separate out their particular performance for evaluation. Following are some of the dimensions of the consultant's task that might be evaluated:

- Were the consultant's role, purposes, responsibilities, and boundaries clear to both consultant and consultee?
- Did the consultant stay within the boundaries of the contract?
- Did the consultant inform consultees of his or her limits, values, and competencies?
- Was the consultant effective in establishing trust?
- Did the consultant respect the consultee's autonomy and responsibility?
- Did the consultant focus discussions appropriately and use time effectively?
- How effective was the consultant's overall performance?
- How effective was the consultant in each stage of the consultation process—in the preliminary exploration and in entry, for instance?

Technical Considerations

Measurement. An evaluation requires accurate measurements of important variables. Issues in obtaining useful measures are briefly described below, along with sources from which measures might be drawn. More detailed discussions of practical measurement issues are found in articles by Flaherty (1979) and Lockwood and Luthans (1980). The text by Cronbach (1970) is helpful in understanding the more technical aspects of measurement.

To be useful for evaluation purposes, information must be countable. The observation that consultees appear to be better satisfied and more productive as a result of their director's change in leadership style is not acceptable for evaluation purposes. Instead, a consultant might obtain attitudinal measures of consultees' degree of satisfaction through a questionnaire and measures of their productivity through ratings of their effectiveness by supervisors or clients or through agency records—for example, the number of clients served or percentage of days absent.

Pre- and post-intervention measures of target variables—in terms of their initial and outcome levels—are the primary bases for most evaluations. Outcomes at the earlier points in the chain shown in Figure 8 (such as consultees' learnings or job performance) are more easily defined for measurement purposes than are outcomes further removed from the intervention (such as client or societal benefits). Moreover, the further an outcome is removed from the intervention, the more difficult it becomes to separate out other influences. Most evaluations measure only one or two links in this chain. Measures of inputs and of intervention processes are usually in terms of costs, such as money and time, for the agency. Information related to other important inputs—such as consultees' attitudes and interests—can often, however, be obtained through surveys. Information on the nature of the consultant's inputs—for example, educational or diagnostic methods and directive or facilitative style—is usually not quantifiable. However, qualitative descriptions of these and other elements shown in Figure 8 are useful in interpreting other data and can add greatly to the effectiveness of the total evaluation.

Many of the methods for assessing outcomes of consultants' interventions, such as questionnaires or observations, are obtrusive. Consultees being evaluated are then conscious of, and often inconvenienced by, the measurement procedures. Consultees are likely to react negatively to these intrusions. Data gathered, therefore, may measure such variables as resentment or social desirability rather than the criterion variable. Reactivity can be reduced if the consultant carefully explains the purposes of the evaluation and allows consultees to ask questions. Some kinds of measures, such as measures of consultee/client processes, may change as a result of consultees' understanding the purposes of the measurement. However, the loss in accuracy is ordinarily less serious than the loss of trust. Consultants should be careful to avoid deception and should follow the principles of informed consent—both for ethical reasons and to increase the probability of obtaining usable data. (When consultants are working in the role of researcher, the cost/benefit contingencies related to disclosure of purposes are different from those in consultation.)

Each measure is only an approximation of the total impact of an intervention. By obtaining multiple measures of outcomes, consultants can assure a more complete and accurate evaluation. Multiple measures help correct for weaknesses and biases of any one measure. They are useful for cross-validation—to ascertain whether scores on one measure are consistent with scores taken on others. If possible, consultants should measure different *aspects* of outcomes and different *perspectives*. For instance, to obtain a more complete evaluation of an in-service training program, a consultant might measure three aspects: consultees' attitudes toward the tasks for which they were trained, their knowledge, and their behaviors in applying that knowledge. Different perspectives of outcomes could be obtained by surveying consultee-trainees, their coworkers, supervisors, and clients to obtain their opinions of the effectiveness of training.

Instruments selected for evaluation purposes should be reasonably valid and reliable. This type of information can be obtained from test publishers and from directories of tests (Lake, Miles, and Earle, 1973; Pfeiffer, Heslin, and Jones, 1976). The validity index gives information on whether the instrument is measuring what it is supposed to measure. There are several types of validity, but the most important is construct validity, the degree to which scores on an instrument are correlated with scores on a related measure that is known to measure the same construct. All measures have some degree of error. The reliability index indicates the degree of error or inconsistency in an instrument—to what extent scores are consistent when the instrument is repeatedly administered under the same conditions. Reliability is usually determined through standardization procedures in which the subjects are tested and retested either on the same instrument or on a parallel one. A large number of standardized instruments are available that have well-established validity and reliability properties. Specially constructed instruments are often more useful for evaluation purposes but require considerable work in pilot testing to establish satisfactory levels of validity and reliability.

Measures come from four major sources: agency records or archives, interviews, questionnaires, and observations of behavior (see Chapter Fourteen for further discussion). *Archival* data can usually be useful for evaluation purposes. Archival data can be obtained easily and inexpensively and, in most cases, are amenable to long-term evaluation. For example, an agency's records of staff absenteeism, attrition rates, and client no-shows for appointments can provide valuable information. A major advantage in the use of archival data is its unobtrusiveness. The reactivity of more direct methods is avoided. However, there are several disadvantages to the use of archival data (Lockwood and Luthans, 1980). The figures may be, either intentionally or unwittingly, distorted by the record keeper. The record-keeping units and methods may change over time and limit comparisons. Information related to a particular intervention may not be found in archives.

Interviews are often valuable sources of data for evaluation purposes. Generally, however, they are most useful in generating information to formulate hypotheses in the diagnostic stage. Interviews are useful in assessing such areas as feelings, attitudes, information about the job and the organization, and ideas on how problems can be solved. Unlike surveys, interviews are flexible. The interviewer can follow up unexpected leads and can clarify ambiguities. Moreover, interviews can be used to cross-validate survey data. Substantial agreement has been reported between survey and interview measures (Lockwood and Luthans, 1980). One major disadvantage in interview data is their costliness in time and money. Unless interviews are highly structured, quantifying data obtained from them is very difficult and time-consuming. In addition, the information gathered through interviews may be reactive, and interviewees may distort responses.

Questionnaires are most frequently used to gather data for evaluation (Porras and Berg, 1978). Questionnaires or surveys are useful in measuring such variables as attitudes, opinions, feelings, perceptions, preferences, motives, knowledge, and demographic data. Their major advantages are their ready availability, low cost, and ease in administering and scoring. Reliability and validity indexes of most popular surveys are satisfactory. Because of their ease of administration, questionnaires are valuable for long-term evaluations. Because anonymity can be ensured, respondents are more likely to respond candidly. Responses to questionnaire items may lack depth or clarity in some cases. But open-ended questions can reduce ambiguity and increase depth of understanding. One of the disadvantages of questionnaires is their obtrusiveness. Because respondents are being scrutinized, they may react to the scrutiny rather than to the questions. Consequently, response sets—such as social desirability—may invalidate the results. Moreover, respondents may not fully understand the meaning of survey questions. Another disadvantage is that the questionnaire may become an intervention itself and change behavior, thus confusing the evaluation of the intervention proper.

Observations of actual behaviors can be used to measure group and individual behaviors and job performance (Perkins, Nadler, and Hanlon, 1981). Numerous variables of relevance to an intervention are amenable to observational measurement—for example, the degree to which staff members use their lounge, the degree of contact between conflicted individuals or groups, the number of staff meetings, the degree to which individuals are assertive, the physical distance between conferees in staff meetings, the use of problem-solving models, and the use of the consultant. Content analyses of observations of staff interaction yield useful information—for instance, the topics of interviews between supervisors and supervisees and items discussed in staff meetings (Lockwood and Luthans, 1980). Unstructured observations can be valuable in suggesting phenomena related to productivity and morale, but to be useful for evaluation purposes, observations must be structured and systematized by categories constructed to allow phenomena to be counted.

Structured observations by neutral parties are likely to be more objective than survey or interview methods and to minimize the probability of reactivity. However, most observational methods require high levels of expertise to ensure that they are systematic and reliable. The cost, therefore, is often relatively high. Another problem is that phenomena being observed may, by their nature, differ at different times of the day, different days of the week, and across different seasons, thus interfering with the interpretation of measures. Furthermore, some reactivity is always possible, since ethically the consultant must make sure that the persons being observed are aware that they are being observed and are aware of the purposes of the observations. The consultees may then alter their behavior, so that the measures record atypical behaviors.

Several other types of measures might be useful. When it is impossible to obtain behavioral observations, simulated behaviors might be measured. For instance, consultees might role-play a relevant work situation before and after a consultative intervention. This method, however, presents many problems in management and in measurement (Flaherty, 1979). The use of self-generated measures—self-reports of performance, for instance —has been recommended (Lockwood and Luthans, 1980). Management-by-objectives consultation relies on self-generated data. These measures can be tailored to fit a particular situation and are based on consultees' criteria. They can be useful for consultees' cyclical self-feedback processes. In most cases, however, self-reports are susceptible to respondent bias. Measures may be inaccurate because the consultee unwittingly or knowingly distorts performance records.

Supervisor and peer ratings can sometimes be helpful in an evaluation. The biggest problem with this type of measure is that the ratings are likely to be influenced by the raters' feelings and attitudes. The following guidelines can be used to reduce the subjectivity of supervisor and peer ratings (Flaherty, 1979):

1. The characteristics to be rated should be carefully linked to the objectives of the consultation and should have been agreed on by both the consultant and the consultee.
2. The attributes to be rated should be specified and defined as concretely as possible.
3. Behaviors should be rated on a scale of frequency. The range of the scale should be determined by the extent to which both consultant and consultee think the rater can reliably discriminate the specific target behavior.
4. Wherever possible, ratings should be obtained from several persons in order to reduce the effects of rater bias.

Evaluating the Consultant's Performance. Often the most informative method for evaluating the consultant's performance is through open-ended interviews. If consultees are assured that the consultant wants and needs their candid opinions for the purpose of professional growth, individual interviews usually yield valuable data. Conferences with groups of consultees can also generate useful information about the consultant's impact. However, most consultants find that, in addition, questionnaires —because of their anonymity—help them obtain a more complete evaluation. A questionnaire for this purpose, "Consultation Evaluation Survey" (Table 9, Chapter Eighteen), can be used. Additional forms for evaluation of the consultant's performance are available from numerous other sources (Human Resources Research Organization of Alexandria, Virginia; Survey Research Center of the University of Michigan; Larsen, Norris, and Kroll, 1976).

Design. Following is a brief discussion of the basic issues in evaluation design.* The major problem in the design of an

---

*Readers are referred to Schmuck and others (1972) and Weiss (1972) for introductions to design and to Campbell and Stanley (1966) for a more sophisticated discussion.

evaluation is to separate out intervention effects from other influences. One of the simplest approaches to this problem is the use of preintervention measures as baseline data. For example, the goal of an intervention is to improve communication of a work group. The amount of time spent by the group each week in work-focused discussions is selected as the criterion. The consultant obtains a baseline measure on this criterion before the intervention and another measure afterward. The evaluation design is illustrated below:

$$O_1 \quad X \quad O_2$$

O_1 is the baseline measure, X represents the intervention, and O_2 is the postintervention measure. If O_2 is superior to O_1, it can be inferred that the intervention achieved the desired results. This design is useful for relatively uncomplicated consultation goals and also as a preliminary check before deciding whether to perform a more extensive evaluation.

But how can the consultant be sure that the intervention was responsible for the change? Other influences might have produced the rise in O_2. For example, staff members might be communicating more because, at the same time as the intervention, their morale was boosted by an across-the-board increase in pay or by the resignation of an incompetent agency director. Quasi-experimental designs can help control such factors that are extraneous to the intervention (Weiss, 1972). One approach calls for adding to the design described above a comparison group. The consultant looks for a similar work group that is not to be involved in the intervention but that is otherwise operating under the same conditions (the new agency director and the pay raise) as the experimental group (the group receiving the intervention). Since the two groups may have started out with different communications patterns, it could be argued that differences in postintervention measures are due to original differences. Baseline measures control for differences in beginning levels. The design is then:

| Experimental group | O_1 | X | O_2 |
| Comparison group | O_3 | X | O_4 |

If the difference between O_1 and O_2 is greater than the difference between O_3 and O_4, the intervention can be considered successful. In using this design, however, it is important to ensure that the comparison group is as similar as possible to the experimental group in every way except for the intervention. In consultation work, however, it is frequently impossible to find a suitable comparison group. Usually, the group asking for consultation differs in significant ways (such as motivation and resources) from those not asking for consultation (Ahmed and Tims, 1977). Moreover, the problem is compounded by the fact that the characteristics that are salient and that therefore need to be matched are often unknown. In many cases, the problems involved in obtaining a comparison group may cost more in time and money than is justified.

Another quasi-experimental design calls for a time series of measures taken before and after the intervention (Weiss, 1972). No comparison group is required. The pattern is illustrated in Figure 9. If the postintervention measures, O_3 and O_4, show a

Figure 9. A Time Series Design

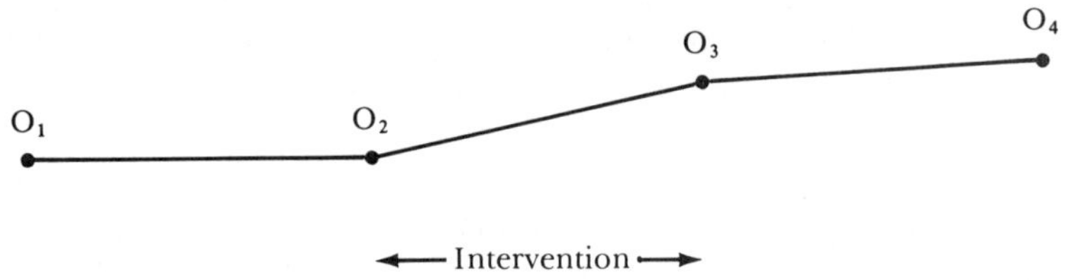

sustained rise in the desired direction, as shown here, the implication is that the intervention achieved the wanted outcome. Although a time series design does not require a comparison group, it is enhanced by the addition of one or more comparison groups and sets of time series measures to serve as an additional check on the influence of the intervention.

Still another problem exists, however. Changes that appear to be associated with the intervention may actually be due to random variation. By chance, either the experimental group or the comparison group may have characteristics that predispose it to change in certain directions. For example, in the illustration described earlier, a member of one work group may have been in the process of resigning. The circumstances surrounding the resignation might have affected the attitudes and behaviors of that group and thus influenced the criterion measure. Or one member may have had previous training in communications processes and, consequently, grasped and used the information presented in the intervention. These random effects could be controlled by an experimental design, in which the units to be evaluated (individuals, work groups, clients, departments, organizations) are drawn from a large pool and randomly assigned to experimental and control conditions. The experimental design is usually out of the question in consultation, however. A pool of potential units is usually unavailable. Furthermore, random assignments are not possible, because the request for consultation usually specifies the units to receive the intervention. None of the evaluations of OD interventions examined in a recent survey used a true control group, although about half used comparison groups (Porras and Berg, 1978).

Data Analysis. Through taking measurements, consultants obtain countable data that can then be tallied and compared in a design such as one of those described above. For instance, pre- and postscores of staff members' job satisfaction are obtained and compared. The postintervention score is found to differ from the earlier score in the desired direction. But is the difference large enough to make the intervention worthwhile? A test of significance can help the agency staff and consultant answer this question. Resources to help consultants with this question and others related to statistical analyses include Cohen and Cohen (1975), Guilford and Fruchter (1973), and Weiss (1968).

Processes

The agency context is basically inhospitable to evaluation procedures, and consultants' interventions are particularly difficult to evaluate. Administrators are often unable to follow through with the necessary time and money for evaluation.

Political conflicts may force changes midway through a consultation project. Staff members are often resistant to participation because of uneasiness over being scrutinized and because of the disruption of their work. Moreover, in the consultation process, new problems are often uncovered that lead to shifts in goals. Consequently, the original design and baseline measures are no longer relevant.

Because of these problems, consultants and consultees should carefully weigh the advantages and disadvantages of evaluation before investing in an evaluation design. These are some of the questions that should be raised:

- Are the problems sufficiently crystallized and the goals and interventions sufficiently defined so as to be quantifiable?
- Will persons in positions of authority use evaluation findings?
- Are resources such as budget, time, and energies adequate to carry out an evaluation?

If, after weighing the answers to these questions, the decision is to perform an evaluation, plans should be laid in the earliest stages of consultation. Building in evaluation planning from the beginning of consultation enhances the evaluation in the following ways (Nicholas, 1979):

- It provides the opportunity to get baseline measures, to pilot test instruments, and to refine the design before the consultation begins.
- Evaluation procedures that are integrated into consultation from the beginning become a natural part of the intervention and are then much less disruptive.
- The persons who are to use the evaluation information can be identified early. Consequently, evaluation criteria and methods can be selected to fit their informational interests and needs. Moreover, the sanction of these persons is ascertained. If their approval is not forthcoming, decisions about consultation need to be reconsidered.
- Constraints and resources can be identified ahead of time—for example, a scheduled conference that will prohibit staff

participation during a two-week period—and can be considered in the design.

Evaluation planning also helps clarify the goals and methods of consultation. However, a good evaluation design allows for feedback during the intervention and flexibility in accommodating changing needs. The following case illustrates the need to keep evaluation plans (and intervention goals) flexible. A social work consultant and a prison chaplain agreed to a goal of increasing the latter's understanding of the dynamics of a long-term counseling group. The consultant obtained preintervention measures of the chaplain's understanding of group processes and skills in group leadership. During the consultation, however, it became obvious that the focus and goals of consultation had shifted. The chaplain's "long-term" group disbanded. At the same time, he needed a diagnosis of a despondent prisoner and guidance in working with him. The chaplain also needed to learn methods for teaching social skills to new, short-term groups of prisoners being prepared for release. The predetermined criterion and baseline measures were no longer relevant. A second, more global criterion—such as increased understanding of prisoners' psychosocial needs—might have been set as a second criterion. But, because of its lack of specificity, this criterion would be more difficult to measure.

Consultants should explore with consultees all evaluation possibilities and problems to help the latter decide on evaluation goals and methods. Evaluation is less threatening to staff members when they participate in all of its phases (Miringoff, 1980). Ideally, from the beginning, evaluation is a collaborative process in which agency staff members, client representatives, and any other constituencies join with the consultant in considering alternative evaluation plans. Consultees are particularly helpful in identifying criteria for measuring outcomes and, later, in making post hoc analyses of process variables affecting the intervention. Moreover, through participation in evaluation plans, they will be more likely to help implement them and to understand, accept, and use the information that comes out of them.

The contract evolving out of these discussions should identify the evaluation goals, methods, and schedule. Particularly important is identification of the persons responsible for various tasks, including data collection, analysis, and interpretation and the writing of a report. (If the consultant is to be responsible for these tasks, the costs—such as consultant time, clerical assistance, and computer time—should be estimated and included in the contract.) Who should take major responsibility for the evaluation? Consultant? Agency staff? An outsider? If the consultant or an agency employee conducts the evaluation, some objectivity is lost. However, external evaluators, though more objective, are less familiar with agency procedures and often are less able to obtain cooperation for evaluation procedures. The ideal solution to this dilemma is to use an outside specialist as a consultant to the persons more closely involved in the consultation and the evaluation.

Feedback of the findings of the evaluation should go to all agency staff members. Ideally, all consultees receive both a written report and opportunities to discuss findings with one another and with the consultant. Feedback can be a powerful tool in helping agency employees perceive their work problems more clearly, in motivating them to make needed changes, and in helping them decide what kinds of changes are needed. The feedback design is an important factor in the ways the information fed back is regarded and used. An article by Nadler (1979) is helpful in identifying a wide range of feedback designs (for example, family group, intergroup, peer group) and criteria for making design decisions.

Termination

For some reason, consultants are reticent about discussing termination of their interventions and working relationships. The consultation literature contains little information regarding the issues associated with this process or guidelines for managing it. Several aspects of termination—criteria for termination, the emotional reactions that often accompany termination, and principles for effective management of this process—are discussed in the following pages.

When should termination occur? Often consultants and consultees give this question little thought. The possibility of terminating may rarely be considered, for instance, when a consultant has a contract of indefinite duration. More often the contract calls for planned phases; the concluding point is predetermined and regarded as non-negotiable. But termination should always be considered a viable option—even if the contract is of indefinite length or the consultant has not yet concluded tasks specified in the contract (see Chapter Eleven). Political or budgetary concerns may arise that indicate a consultation should be dropped. Evolving diagnoses may reveal unexpected problems outside the consultant's competencies. Either the consultant or consultees may discover that the relationship itself is unsatisfactory and/or unproductive. For example, a consultant may choose to terminate when "clients refuse or are unable to be open, to accept responsibility for their behavior, to experiment and to learn" (Argyris, 1970, p. 346). Either party may distrust the other, thus interfering with work; significant discrepancies between consultant and consultee values may appear. In such cases, termination is appropriate and may serve as a stimulus for both parties to define more carefully their values and professional goals.

In some consultations, such as those involving short-term contracts or impersonal services, termination is a relatively simple and matter-of-fact process. But when a consultant has worked with an agency over a long period, become deeply involved in its culture and functions, or participated in its crises and other significant events, the termination process is likely to be complicated by emotional reactions in both consultants and consultees. For all concerned, the consultant's departure in these situations may mark the ending of an era of excitement, growth, and deeply satisfying work and a return to more routine patterns. Termination is often the end of a meaningful relationship and shared events—confrontations, failures, discoveries, crises, and successes. Termination may escalate minor or submerged dynamics such as feelings of dependency and closeness, resentment and anxiety—thus creating conflicting, confusing feelings (Levinson, 1972).

As a consequence of these reactions, consultees often feel

more dependent on consultants when the time of departure approaches. Consultants may encourage this dependency, reflecting their own ambivalence about leaving. Emotional reactions may be expressed in a variety of ways. Consultants may discover the agency has new problems, new needs that require their continuation. Consultees may attempt to prolong consultation by presenting a surge of requests for assistance. They may, through phone calls and lingering in interviews, seek to continue the relationship. They may introduce important information and feelings related to consultation and its goals that they previously held back. Hence, reworking of some aspects of consultation is necessary.

Several guidelines can help prevent termination problems:

1. *Explication.* From the beginning of consultation and in reminders through unequivocal statements expressed throughout the consultation, the consultant can explicate the timing of the termination. Emphasizing the developmental nature of consultation and the changing relationship and tasks at each stage can be helpful.

2. *Gradual transfer of responsibility.* Wherever appropriate, the consultant's responsibilities should be gradually transferred to internal staff.

3. *A period of disengagement.* A disengagement period can prevent abruptness in the termination (Bell and Nadler, 1979). Disengagement could include (a) a period of testing to find out whether the intervention is completed sufficiently for consultees to maintain changes, (b) reduced consultant involvement—perhaps to half time or less of the previous activity level, and (c) use of telephone conferences when contact is needed.

4. *Rituals.* Rituals help clarify the reality of transitions. They can help bring to the surface and resolve emotional reactions to termination. Rituals could include a meeting, perhaps a month or more before the termination date, between consultant and staff to identify any unfinished tasks and to establish priorities for the remaining time. During the last few weeks, consultants can hold individual conferences with major consultees to review work, to give and receive feedback, to complete unfinished business, and to say good-bye. The termination could be

concluded with a formal staff meeting and a social activity such as a luncheon or party.

Annotated Bibliography

Argyris, C. *Intervention Theory and Method: A Behavioral Science View*. Reading, Mass.: Addison-Wesley, 1970. Both consultees and consultants have the authority and responsibility to terminate their relationship if it is unproductive. Argyris outlines criteria for terminating a consulting relationship in chap. 16, "Terminating Ineffective Client Relationships." He points out that termination, by stimulating inquiry, can be a positive intervention for both consultant and consultees, and he illustrates his hypothesis with several case studies.

Bell, C. R., and Nadler, L. (Eds.). *The Client-Consultant Handbook*. Houston: Gulf Publishing Co., 1979. In Part VI, "Disengagement and Closure," are chapters on evaluation and termination that outline procedures for successful management of these two phases of consultation.

Flaherty, E. W. "Evaluation of Consultation." In J. J. Platt and R. J. Wicks (Eds.), *The Psychological Consultant*. New York: Grune & Stratton, 1979. This article is concerned mainly with evaluation of program consultation. The author describes steps, processes, and methods of needs assessment and of the evaluation of outcomes.

Lippitt, G. L. "Evaluating Consultation Services." *Consultation*, 1981, *1* (1), 17-26. Lippitt presents a model for evaluation of organizational consultation. He highlights key issues concerning purposes and methods. Beginning consultants will find this article useful in helping them decide whether to perform a formal evaluation.

Meyers, J. "Specific Strategies for Research in Consultation." Paper presented at 82nd annual meeting of the American Psychological Association, New Orleans, September 1974. Meyers outlines the formidable problems that must be overcome in evaluating mental health consultation and suggests a systems model as a guide in developing effective evaluation strategies.

Meyers, W. R. *The Evaluation Enterprise.* San Francisco: Jossey-Bass, 1981. The major focus of this book is program evaluation, but the principles it discusses are relevant to all models of consultation. Of particular interest to most consultants will be the discussions in chap. 6 through 9 of conceptual issues related to evaluation decisions.

Nicholas, J. M. "Evaluation Research in Organizational Change Interventions: Considerations and Some Suggestions." *Journal of Applied Behavioral Science,* 1979, *15* (1), 23-39. The author of this article stresses the use of a carefully constructed preevaluation design. He discusses methodological problems and suggests ways of overcoming them.

Schmuck, R. A., and others. *Handbook of Organization Development in Schools.* Palo Alto, Calif.: National Press Books, 1972. In chap. 10, "Evaluation at Beginning, Middle, and End," are well-organized and comprehensive guidelines for evaluation of organizational consultation from a systems model. Consultants who lack evaluation skills will find this reference especially valuable in explaining evaluation issues and how to plan and conduct an evaluation.

 *Part IV*

Developing
the Potential of
Consultation

What lies ahead for the new profession of consultation? Part Four resumes the sociological analysis begun in Part One by examining some of the forces shaping consultation, identifying developmental problems, and delineating proposals to enhance the future of consultation.

How will consultation fare in the face of drastically changing social conditions? In particular, how will these shifts affect human services consultation? Chapter Sixteen reviews environmental forces that are affecting the future of consultation. And because peer groups also influence the evolution of professions, this chapter examines several leading consulting associations and their effects on the profession's development and on its ability to respond to changing societal needs. Developmental problems are identified and solutions are suggested to enable the profession to grow in status and in its potential to serve society.

Members of professions traditionally commit themselves to serve society and establish standards to uphold this commitment. Consultant associations have been slow to evolve codes to cover the unique activities and circumstances of consulting. To enhance their service to society and to protect the future of the profession, peer associations must establish and enforce ethical codes that address the specific problems of consultation. Chapter Seventeen proposes principles for a consultant's code of ethics.

Training patterns also help shape professions. Chapter Eighteen traces the evolution of two consultation training patterns: (1) intraprofessional training, offered in traditional institutions to prepare people to practice consultation as a subspecialty of a primary field and (2) interdisciplinary training, offered in nontraditional settings, which tends to separate consulting activities out from established professions and thus fosters the growth of consultation as an independent profession. The chapter proposes two training models. The first, based on an existing program, provides members of established professions with the minimal background needed to practice consultation as a subspecialty. The second model proposes a curriculum for advanced study leading to a Ph.D. in consultation and careers as consultant practitioners, scholars, and researchers.

16

The Shaping of
a New Profession:
Problems
and Prospects

Over the past two decades, social needs and the explosion in technology have created and institutionalized the role of human services consultant. Consultants have organized a number of associations and begun the process of professionalization. But the conditions that fostered the growth of consultation have changed. The organizations that deliver human services are in flux. What lies ahead? What are the prospects for the profession and practice of consultation? In an effort to answer these questions, the following pages examine two major influences on evolving professions—environmental forces and peer associations—and the challenges that appear on the horizon.

Environmental Forces

Environmental forces are powerful factors in creating occupations and shaping their trajectories. What does the current milieu suggest for the future of the human services consultant? The two conditions essential to the growth of a new role are still present. Needs are immense. For instance, crime is at an all-time high. The institutions of family and community continue to deteriorate. Environmental health hazards are increasing. Technological resources for alleviating social problems and improving the quality of life are available and in many areas, such as health care, offer truly remarkable possibilities.

Changes in the nation's economy and dominant ideology are, however, creating sweeping changes in human services. Marked by diminishing resources and financial austerity, the 1980s are witnessing drastic reductions in federal funds for health, education, and welfare. A conservative philosophy replaces the liberal spirit of the 1960s and early 1970s that attributed many human problems to the social environment and held society responsible for their amelioration. Today, the dominant view—reminiscent in some ways of the social Darwinism of the 1880s—attributes problems to the individual and holds that publicly financed services inhibit the growth of desirable characteristics such as independence and resourcefulness as well as charitable actions by neighbors, friends, and philanthropic organizations. Citizens are now less willing that government funds be spent for such purposes as support for the chronically unemployed or for services that could be paid for through consumer fees. Decentralization and deregulation of government control, also characteristic of the 1980s, embody economic and ideological trends. Control over a large proportion of remaining federal funds has been decentralized. The Federal Omnibus Budget Reconciliation Act of 1981 (P. O. 97.45) redirects more than ninety federal categorical funding programs into a series of block grants to the states. (Most federally funded health care programs, for example, are now incorporated in block grants. An Alcohol, Drug Abuse, and Mental Health Services Block Grant replaces federal alcohol and drug abuse formula grant authorities and grant programs under the Community Mental Health Centers and Mental Health Systems Acts. A block grant for Preventive Health and Health Services replaces about ten health prevention and health service programs, including rape crisis programs. A Primary Care Block Grant replaces the Community Health Centers program and enables states to take over this program in 1983.) Some services are being deregulated. Sunset laws passed in most states require careful reviews of the social need for regulatory agencies and more austere budgets for most of those that are renewed. The rationale is that regulatory laws often serve not to protect the public but to protect special-interest groups, restrain trade, and keep the costs of services high.

These shifts are bringing about profound changes in human services. Many programs and entire agencies have disappeared. In surviving public agencies, finding funds to maintain services is often the most engrossing concern. With the loss of federal grants, their mainstay for years, these agencies are now seeking funds from state and local governments and from private foundations. Some agencies are increasing the proportion of services offered for fees. These funding changes are altering agency priorities. Services for disadvantaged groups and preventive services, priorities the federal government once enforced through funding contingencies, have been greatly cut. Since priorities are more often determined by local values, they are more diverse. In general, however, they are becoming more conservative, because the needs of the status quo tend to prevail when competition for grant money is intense and when competition takes place within the relatively narrow and personalized local political arena. Moreover, agencies shifting to fees must, of necessity, serve needs of the middle-class citizens who are able to pay.

Employees of these agencies are in turmoil. Administrators, once accustomed to expanding budgets and programs, are cutting out and reducing services, competing for shrinking resources, lobbying in new arenas, learning new funding rules, and adapting their services to fit changing criteria. They are searching for ways to bring in revenues from consumers. They are struggling to manage remaining resources more economically, to find the most efficient technologies, to cut services with minimal damage to primary functions, and to evaluate services and employees more carefully. Some are collaborating with other agencies to share resources, but a "lifeboat ethic" is working against cooperation (Barnet, 1980). Staff cuts are, in most public agencies, extensive. Competition for remaining jobs is intense. Ideological changes often exacerbate the problems created by budget cuts. For example, employees of agencies that provide abortions and of those that provide aid to indigent populations are strongly criticized by members of conservative groups who question the necessity and the social desirability of these services.

The scene in some human services organizations is brighter. Cutbacks in certain public agencies—especially those that provide traditional mainstream services, such as education and public transportation—are often minor. Some institutions are growing through such means as absorbing services being cut out of other agencies, finding new funding sources, and converting to a fee-for-service basis of operation. Interagency linkages in some fields, such as health care, are helping maintain needed services and, at the same time, seeking to improve quality and reduce costs (Marks and Broskowski, 1981; Pincus, 1980). Private-sector human services—such as daycare, education, and physical fitness facilities—are expanding. In addition, business and industrial organizations are offering employees increased services in such areas as health care, childcare, and recreational programs. Developments in health care are especially noteworthy as corporations recognize the effects of the work environment on stress-related and degenerative disorders and the consequences of these problems for organizational productivity (Manuso, 1981). Freed of constraints of traditional health care systems and of governmental red tape, corporate programs for prevention and amelioration of health problems may revolutionize the health care field.

Changes in human services consultation parallel those in the organizations they serve. Money shortages have—for the time being, at least—diminished the calls for human services consultants, despite continuing needs for their specialized expertise. Many publicly funded agencies no longer use consultants or use them sparingly; others, however, are using consultants to generate revenue—for instance, by hiring them to lead workshops for paying groups such as professional, business, and industrial organizations. Increased demands from privately funded organizations are, to some extent, offsetting reductions by publicly funded agencies. But efficiency, a favorable input/output ratio, is a primary concern in all human services organizations. Negotiations for consultation now involve more discriminating selection of services and more careful consideration of costs. Consultants must therefore be more accountable. They must be more careful to tailor their services to meet particular needs, more cost-conscious, and more expert in documenting outcomes.

The needs for which consultants are called are changing. Consultation regarding direct services is, for example, more widely sought by mental health agencies than consultation regarding preventive services (Rogawski, 1979). Administrators of declining agencies—when funds are available—call on consultants for help in appraising environments, using resources more efficiently, and helping staffs cope with technological and emotional problems associated with reductions. At the same time, staffs of many organizations, especially those in the private sector, need assistance in expanding services. The expertise most wanted today includes the following:

- Concepts and methods for diagnosing and solving problems at all levels, including those associated with changes in technology and in the political and social environment.
- Change skills to help staff members effect needed changes, including adaptations to declining resources.
- Methods for evaluation of performances at all levels, including individual, program, departmental, agency, and consultation.
- Management of information systems.
- Skills in human relations, including recruiting, motivating, and retaining competent employees, conflict management, and team building.
- Instructional theories and techniques to help staff members learn new skills and retool outdated ones.
- Stress-management techniques for individuals and organizations.
- Skills in interorganizational linkages.
- Knowledge of resources, such as specialized bodies of information, materials, equipment, and human resources.

Understanding of the nature and problems of increasingly specialized organizations—for instance, the unique characteristics of women's centers, hospices, and physical fitness centers.

The pivotal change is the new emphasis on accountability. Human services consultation was for many years supported by federal funds that often required little or no evidence of effectiveness and fostered the growth of carelessly contracted and often useless services.[1] The scarcity of public funds and the entrepreneurial traditions of expanding private-sector human services organizations demand more responsible practices. This demand has the potential for forcing consultants to improve the quality of their services and their tarnished image.

Influence of Peer Associations

Societal forces create and shape occupations, but peer groups also influence their development. Through explicit and implicit socialization processes, these organizations shape their members' role, values, and norms. They influence the purposes for which the profession's knowledge is used, its responsiveness to social change, its character and reputation, and its very survival. The following pages examine the functions and activities of some of these peer groups and their implications for the profession's future.

The professionalization scale described in Chapter Two, an instrument constructed of criteria typically used by sociologists to measure the development of professions, will be the gauge for this assessment. The assumptions underlying this scale, briefly reviewed below, are (1) that professionalization enhances a profession's potential to serve society and its members as well and (2) that a profession cannot move to higher levels of the

---

[1]Twenty years of wasteful practices in hiring consultants are described in a report to Congress by the comptroller general of the United States, "Government Earns Low Marks on Proper Use of Consultants" (Washington, D.C.: U.S. General Accounting Office, Report # FPCD-80-48). Detailed comments on this report are found in Backer (1981).

scale until lower-level tasks have been accomplished (Moore, 1970).

1. *Full-time.* The first criterion separates professionals from amateurs and from ancillary members of a field. Professions are full-time occupations and the principal source of their members' incomes. Professions are neither subordinate to other professions nor stepping stones to them. Like several other criteria on this scale, this one has two dimensions: (1) full-time practice and (2) practice in the profession as an independent discipline.

2. *A calling.* The profession represents a primary and enduring identification. Morever, its members are bonded by "shared mysteries, exemplified in technical language and common styles of work and often even in common attire" (Moore, 1970, p. 9). This criterion has two dimensions: (1) commitment to the activities, values, and principles of the profession and (2) bonding.

3. *Organization.* Members of professions organize associations to serve two purposes: to protect and enhance their own interests and to establish and uphold standards to protect the public.

4. *Education.* Professions possess "esoteric but useful knowledge and skills, based on specialized training or education of exceptional duration and perhaps of exceptional difficulty" (Moore, 1970, p. 6).

5. *Service orientation.* This criterion, representing a high level of professionalization, clearly establishes service to society as the profession's primary purpose and requires this commitment to be demonstrated through rules of competency and ethical and conscientious performance that protect clients and the general public.

6. *Autonomy.* The ultimate achievement is autonomy, freedom from lay evaluation and control. Autonomous professions are entrusted to receive and protect privileged information. They determine their standards of education and training. They help shape the legislation that regulates their practices. Furthermore, members of autonomous professions are typically self-employed and work for fees. Autonomy becomes possible

when, because its expertise is salient to important social needs, a profession is in a position of relative power and when its body of knowledge is so highly specialized as to be esoteric—hence, laypersons cannot challenge the professional's judgments. But according to the assumptions underlying the professionalization scale, society does not confer autonomy on a profession until it has demonstrated its primary commitment to the public welfare.

Although a relatively new field, consultation is a major concern of numerous professional associations. An appendix at the end of this book lists names and addresses of leading peer organizations. These groups fall into two major categories, intraprofessional and interprofessional, reflecting the two forms through which consultation is being professionalized. A brief review of the stages in the evolution of consultation (discussed in Chapter Two) will help differentiate these two categories. In the first stage of development, consultation is practiced only as an occasional and peripheral activity by members of established professions; no consulting associations are needed. In the second stage, however, a clearly defined consultant role with distinctive concepts and methods emerges and is practiced as a subspecialty of established professions. Although these consultants identify primarily with their profession's major organizations, they also begin to form smaller groups within their professions in order to discuss consulting concerns. In the third stage, subspecialties begin to separate out from their parent bases and merge to create a new field. Because practices and concerns of individuals at this stage differ, often radically, from those of their original fields, they form new associations, composed of individuals from various fields, to address these changing interests.

Because intraprofessional and interprofessional organizations professionalize consultation in different ways, they differ in their import for the future of this field and will therefore be examined separately. Five peer groups will be reviewed. Two belong to the intraprofessional category: the Division of Consulting Psychology of the American Psychological Association and the Managerial Consultation Division of the Academy of Management. Three are interprofessional: NTL (National Training Laboratories Institute for Applied Behavioral Science), the OD

(Organization Development) Network, and CCI (Certified Consultants International, formerly International Association of Applied Social Scientists, or IAASS). These organizations were chosen because of their diverse functions and the degree to which they influence the practice of consultation.

The review consisted of an examination of official documents, including publications and, in some cases, personal communication with officers. Specific questions concerned membership criteria and characteristics, purposes, activities (especially those related to education and training), and the existence and nature of standards for ethical and competent performance. Obviously, the ultimate impact of these associations is difficult to assess through the information available for this review. Moreover, since some consultants belong to two or more associations, it is impossible to separate out their influence. Yet, official policies and functions and published statements regarding goals, achievements, and problems should give at least a reasonable estimate of their influence on the future of consultation.

The Division of Consulting Psychology, one of the special-interest groups within the American Psychological Association (APA), was created in the 1930s. It was originally a division of the American Association of Applied Psychology, an organization that merged with APA in 1945. As a part of the bylaws of the merger, the consulting division was chartered into APA. Currently, this group has about 750 members. To be eligible for membership, a person must meet APA's minimal requirements and have a major professional interest in psychological consultation. Members of this group are seasoned professionals; more than half hold diplomates from the American Board of Professional Psychology, and nearly half are fellows of APA. They practice a wide range of consulting models in human services, business, industrial, and research organizations.

The objectives of this organization are:

a. the encouragement of high standards of psychological consultation
b. the promotion of scientific research on psychological problems, especially in the area of consulting psychology

    c.   the facilitation of exchange of information and experience among the members

    d.   the support of the APA in the advancement of psychology

    e.   the fostering of cooperative relations with allied groups on consulting problems (quoted from the division's brochure, "Consulting Psychology," The Division of Consulting Psychology, 1980).

To reach these goals, the division offers educational, training, and social activities during the annual APA convention. It publishes a newsletter and has a dozen standing committees. The division does not have its own code of ethics; its members rely on guidelines of the parent body, APA.

The Managerial Consultation Division, a professional division of the Academy of Management, has about 1,050 members, most of whom are academicians who work part-time as consultants (personal communication from Robert L. Mathis, past chairperson of the Managerial Consultation Division). Only members of the parent body may join this division. Its purposes are to encourage professionalism in management consultation, scholarship, and research and to promote the exchange of professional information among its members. To reach these goals, the organization publishes a newsletter four times a year; and at the annual meeting of the academy, the division presents panels and papers. Occasionally, this organization also sponsors preconference workshops. In 1978 the association approved a document designed to aid members in self-regulation, the "Standards of Professional Conduct for Academic/Management Consultants." This code, rare in that its sole concern is the practice of consultation, reflects this group's awareness of the special ethical problems of consulting and commitment to protect clients. It explicitly states that service to clients is the members' primary goal and provides numerous guidelines for protecting clients. For example, members are to decline to serve under conditions that would impair their objectivity or if an assignment is so narrowly defined that a consultant would be unable to advise consultees of the impact of any recommended changes.

Guidelines also establish principles for confidentiality and avoiding conflicts of interests, for practicing within the members' areas of competence, and for encouraging research and dissemination of findings.

These two associations illustrate the effects of the subspecialty form of consultation on professionalization. Members, firmly linked to their primary professions, do not satisfy even the first criterion on the professionalization scale—practice in consultation as an independent discipline. Yet, members of both organizations are strongly identified with consultation (for instance, nearly half the members of the Division of Consulting Psychology are full-time consultants), and they have brought the practice of consultation as a subspecialty to a high level. But bonding is, for the most part, within the major profession, as are the members' education and training. Both associations, either through their own standards or through those of their parent group, express a commitment to serve the public, but the two groups differ in the degree to which they have identified unique principles and standards for consultation services. Members of the Division of Consulting Psychology rely on the APA code, which does not fully cover certain consultation problems—for example, those related to intraorganizational controversies and confidentiality issues. The Managerial Consultation Division, through its standards of practice, more clearly differentiates the consultant role from the broader field of management and more clearly explicates a commitment to serve society through this role. Through their primary identifications, members of these associations—particularly those in the psychologists' group—have achieved some of the criteria on the highest rung in the professionalization scale, autonomy.

Although all three interprofessional associations to be reviewed foster the development of consultation as an independent field, they vary in purpose and in their impact on the profession and will therefore be examined separately. The National Training Laboratories Institute for Applied Behavioral Science (NTL) was founded in 1947 as a nonprofit, independent organization. The founding place was Bethel, Maine, the site of early human relations training and research. Its purpose is broad, "helping people learn how to use available, but relatively un-used, knowledge and gain the skills of working effectively with others" (NTL Institute Program Calendar, Spring-Fall 1981-82). The original focus was the development of the human relations laboratory, the T-group (training group), in which individuals work in small groups to learn more about themselves, about others, and about group processes. In 1967 the institute expanded its interests to include community development, organization development, and development of individual potential through personal growth programs. In its early years, NTL staff members had a small, informal network. Members met face-to-face to discuss problems, including "generic problems of rationale and value orientation" (Lippitt and others, 1975, p. 485). The institute, however, grew into an elaborate organization with about 700 members and expanded its functions by establishing competency standards and accrediting mechanisms. Conflicts over purposes and use of resources led to disbanding of the network and elimination of the accrediting function in 1970. (A newer organization, the International Association of Applied Social Scientists, took over accreditation activities.) NTL reorganized in 1975 and is now a professional member organization into which new members enter through a peer selection process.

The institute sponsors extensive training programs, including workshops and institutes held across the country and throughout the year, and the *Journal of Applied Behavioral Science,* a publication concerned with theory, research, intervention practices, and related social issues. Recently, NTL established an ethics code, "NTL Values and Ethics Statement." This code is concerned with the particular problems that confront laboratory trainers and, in particular, those who work in NTL programs. It does not address the complex problems associated with consultation within agencies. Within its framework, however, the code covers many ethical problems encountered by all consultants. For example, it establishes guidelines for providing consumers with pertinent information, evaluating outcomes, and protecting clients, especially minorities. It stresses the importance of self-awareness, the need to practice within one's area of competency, and the desirability of helping clients clarify and uphold their own values.

NTL's domain, applied behavioral science, is broad. Consultation is only one of its interests, and professionalization is not its purpose. Yet, this organization's impact on consultation is extensive. In particular, through its training programs and publications, NTL has contributed more than any other organization to the education and training of consultants. It disseminates new concepts and practices that help consultants adapt to environmental changes. Articles in the *Journal of Applied Behavioral Science* strengthen the scientific foundations of consultation practice; they call attention to controversial areas and attempt to crystallize different views. NTL activities promote interdisciplinary communication and colleagueship. NTL has not, however, addressed the professionalization tasks facing consultants—such as the establishment of standards of competency and guidelines for unique ethical problems. The code, for example, refers to the people "qualified" to apply behavioral science but does not indicate the criteria for qualification.

The OD Network is an independent, nonprofit organization that began in 1964 as the Industrial Network, an affiliate of NTL. The original purpose was to bring together the few persons who were at that time applying laboratory training methods to work organizations. Today, the Network is independently chartered and has a membership of 2,500. Any interested person may join.

The objectives of this organization are to provide opportunities for personal and professional colleagueship, professional development, and to extend the peripheries of OD through intersecting with other groups, disciplines, and practices. The rationales for these objectives are given in the Network's official statement (quoted from an undated brochure):

1. The success of the Organization Development practitioner depends heavily on the use of self as an "instrument of change" and on one's familiarity with the wide range of techniques many of which are unrecorded but used by others in the field. It is an

objective of the Network to facilitate personal and professional development among its members regarding this kind of learning.

2. There are common organization development problems for which the current body of technology is inadequate. The Network is in a unique position to focus attention on these problems and to stimulate new ideas and approaches and to share this information.

3. The success of the Organization Development field can be materially aided by a strong, synergistic relationship among its principal contributors. These include the internal organization practitioners, external consultants, members of the academic community, and organizations such as NTL. Providing an opportunity for these groups of people to come together is a significant purpose of the OD Network.

4. Providing affiliation and linkage among people who have common interests, motives, and values and who like one another is an explicit objective of the Network.

The principal methods through which this organization reaches its goals are twice-yearly national meetings and the *OD Practitioner,* a publication that disseminates information about OD theory, techniques, case studies, book reviews, and news items. Recently, the Network has also begun to sponsor special-interest conferences on innovative topics, illustrated by three conferences planned for 1982: a conference on ecology of work and one on wellness in the workplace, to be cosponsored with NTL, and a conference on OD in health care settings, offered in collaboration with the American Society of Health, Manpower, Education and Training, a division of the American Hospital Association.

This association has satisfied, at least in part, the first four criteria on the professionalization scale. For example, many of its members work full-time as consultants and identify themselves professionally as OD consultants. The OD Network emphasizes the commonalities of consultants from different professional backgrounds and promotes interdisciplinary bonding. Its work in rapid dissemination of information on environmental changes and their implications for consultants and in offering opportunities for training in new techniques is especially outstanding. However, the association does not include a service commitment in its purposes. It has not evolved standards for ethical performance and for competent practice; consequently a state of ambiguity appears to jeopardize this group's professional growth, capacity for service, and credibility. OD consultants' commitments to their stated values are often weak (Bowen, 1977; Friedlander, 1977; Friedlander and Brown, 1974; Fullan, Miles, and Taylor, 1980; Tichy, 1978). Without a definitive guide and a commitment, practitioners may be "pulled apart by external forces" (Alderfer, 1981). They may, for instance, allow themselves to be used by administrators to exploit employees, or they may take an adversarial role against management. (It is possible that management's uncertainty and fear lie behind the growing demand for internal consultants who, because they are employees, are more clearly under administrative control and in seminars on "maintaining control of development consultants" offered by the American Management Association [Krell, 1981, p. 317].) They may also succumb to internal temptations to use the role to meet personal needs (Argyris, 1970).

Certified Consultants International (CCI, formerly the International Association of Applied Social Scientists, or IAASS) is also a spin-off of NTL. IAASS was incorporated in 1971 for the purpose of accrediting and became CCI in 1980. CCI has nine regions, including Canada and Europe, and has about 270 members, professionals from a wide variety of occupational backgrounds.

The purposes of this group are "to establish clear criteria of competence, to develop and publicize standards for applied behavioral and social science practitioners, and to foster the sound development of the profession," and its primary focus is "the responsible delivery of professional services to client groups and organizations" ("Applicant's Guide: Certified Consultants International," undated brochure). CCI certifies members in five areas: personal-professional development consultation, group development consultation, internal organization development practice, organization development consultation, and social change. CCI has defined the purposes and functions of each of these areas of certification and identified major competencies needed to practice in each area. For instance, the purpose of the OD consultant is to introduce long-term planned and system-wide changes into organizations by helping staff members define problems, develop solutions, and set and implement goals. Needed competencies include skills in data gathering, diagnosing organizations, identifying and developing resources, and long-term intervening and planning. The certification process is highly individualized. It involves the examination of extensive materials presented by applicants, including evaluations from clients with whom the candidate has worked, and face-to-face examination of candidates by a review panel. The review emphasizes the demonstration of competence rather than training credentials. Candidates are required to demonstrate an ethical commitment and concern for "dehumanization." Members are reviewed every two to five years.

CCI does not have an ethics code, but it does have an ethics committee and a discipline committee. It also has committees on special constituencies (such as women and minorities), standards and admission, education of the public, and institutional network. The organization offers no training.

Among the achievements of this organization are its rigorous peer review process and the differentiation of the purposes, functions, and needed competencies of five consulting specialties. CCI's major deficiency in professionalization is its failure to construct an ethics code. Given this association's primary function of accrediting and its ten years of existence, this failure is surprising. In 1975 the ethics committee of this organization reported a study of the ethics of "laboratory practice" that revealed extensive disagreements among members over whether a code should be established and what principles such a code should contain (Luke and Benne, 1975). It seems likely that continuing internal conflicts regarding the consultant's responsibilities and boundaries lie behind the failure to establish an ethics code. Moreover, although CCI is dedicated to the sound development of consultation and to the protection of clients and the public, its impact in these areas appears minimal. It influences the practices of a relatively small number of practitioners, and its services to the public appear to be limited to providing information to potential client organizations of these 270 certified members.

Many peer associations—with varying purposes and functions—are shaping the consulting field. As a profession, however, consultation remains at an early stage of development. Certain developmental deficits appear to be impeding its growth and its ability to serve a society that is demanding higher standards of accountability.

The subspecialty form of consultation is highly developed and stabilized. In many ways, it is responsive to the needs of human services and other types of organizations. It is especially suited to consultants from well-established professions, enabling them to keep updated in their specialty areas and, at the same time, providing them with many professional privileges. The disadvantage of this form is that since the consultant role and practices are secondary in importance, it is unlikely to foster high standards of excellence in consultation. Competence in the specialized content of consultation, rather than its process and its organizational context, is the major concern. The consultant role and its unique problems may not be well differentiated from the parent field, whether it is psychology, management, or some other occupation, such as communications, education, or public health. To illustrate, the Division of Consulting Psychology, though almost fifty years old, does not yet have ethical standards for consultation. Lack of a clearly defined role and standards leaves consultants without guidelines for certain important decisions. For instance, the major sources of confusion (and controversy) among psychologists who attended the National Conference on Consultation Training (Alpert and Meyers, in press) were role-boundary issues—the place of the consultant's social and political values in his or her work and the propriety of consultants' use of behavioral techniques to control consultees. At the same time, the potential for traditional professions to adapt their knowledge, principles, and practices to the consultant role and to the changing environment is demonstrated in the standards of the Managerial Consultation Division and in articles such as "Areas of Consulting in the 80s," published in the *Academic Consultants' Communique* (Lippitt, 1981a).

The emphasis of these groups on substantive specialties also tends to fragment consultants and thus prevent them from discovering their similarities and from having exchanges that might lead to improved practices and to clearer role definitions and standards. Fragmentation of consultants into specialized areas is apparent even within professions. The Division of Consulting Psychology, for example, represents only a small proportion of psychologists involved in consultation. Other APA divisions (such as the Divisions of Industrial and Organizational Psychology, Health Psychology, School Psychology, and Community Psychology) are also concerned with the practice of consultation. An estimated two thirds of the 5,000 members of the Academy of Management practice consultation; yet only a fifth of these persons belong to the Managerial Consultation Division (Arnold, 1981).

Interdisciplinary associations are growing in number and influence and pulling consultants in the direction of an independent field. They are highly successful in bringing together people, ideas, and experiences from diverse professions. They have contributed to consultants' knowledge and ability to adapt to changing needs. However, these associations are not establishing performance and ethics standards and service commitments. These failures reveal basic uncertainties regarding the consultant's social role and purposes.

This review indicates that professional associations are not fully preparing their members to provide the high-quality and responsible services needed by society. The groups reviewed here have, in general, failed to accomplish certain tasks that would move consultants to higher levels of accountability. The profession badly needs service commitments, ethical codes, standards of excellence, and educational standards or competency-based criteria for practice. Other important tasks facing the profession are systematization of the body of knowledge and practice principles and exploration of issues related to professional autonomy—such as legal barriers that might prevent consultants from practicing. Already some state laws, such as those regulating the practice of psychologists, restrict certain kinds of consultation to licensed members of various professions. Specialists in evaluation or management, for example, are not allowed to consult in regard to certain problems defined by state laws as psychological in nature.

Both intraprofessional and interprofessional associations have the potential for leadership in accomplishing these developmental tasks. But an underlying problem, failure to clarify the consultant's social role, purposes, and boundaries, is impeding their progress.

Underlying Role-Related Problems

The role of the consultant is to help. But what are the parameters of the role? How and for what purposes is the consultant's technology to be used? What knowledge and skills are needed for competent service? What biases are likely to interfere with consultants' effectiveness? The following pages examine some of the major role-related dilemmas facing the profession and suggest resolutions for them.

Boundary Clarification. A crucial problem is lack of clarity about the consultant's boundaries. The major questions in this area are these: Whose agent is the consultant? To what extent are consultants responsible for consultees' decisions and actions? What is the place of the consultant's political and social values?

Whose agent is the consultant? Who is the primary client, the person or group to whom consultants are responsible and whose interests they are obliged to serve? The complex issues related to this question are salient in all consultation because of inherent conflicts between and within groups—staff members, administrators, boards of trustees, and consumers—on the exact nature of organizational goals, the best means for reaching them, and expectations of their consultants (Kouzes and Mico, 1979). These conflicts are especially intense in those public agencies in which competition for resources is great (such as community hospitals and public schools) and in management/worker relationships. Some consultants argue that the primary client is the public or the individuals and groups served by the agency and use the consultant role as a means of protecting the special interests of these clients. Other consultants contend that they are responsible for protecting workers against exploitation by management.

The position taken here is that consultants are the agents of the hiring agency and must, therefore, support and protect agency goals and interests. Consultants are neither advocates nor adversaries of individuals or groups within or outside the agency. When their work brings them into conflicts, consultants should seek to help staff members find compromises consistent with agency goals. But the chief executive officer, as the organization's official representative, is the final authority in resolving conflicts, and in all their actions, consultants should support this person's interpretation of agency interests.

What are the consultant's responsibilities to other constituencies? In regard to staff, consultants' major responsibility is to provide competent professional services within the boundaries of their contract. Consultants working in human services agencies are also responsible to the agencies' clients—the ultimate beneficiaries of their services. But within the consultant role, this responsibility is fulfilled through delivery of high-quality services to the agency staff. Consultants can, in addition, serve the public by using knowledge gained through the consultant role (being careful, however, to protect the confidentiality of their sources of information) to provide feedback to professional groups, to training institutions, and to the general public concerning social conditions and needs and concerning ways of responding to them (Feldman, 1979; Levine, 1972; Rogawski, 1979). Consultants also may serve society through contributing to the theoretical and empirical bases of their profession. These contributions, however, are not delivered through the consultant role but through other professional or private roles.

To what extent are consultants responsible for consultees' decisions and actions? This question concerns the limits of the consultant's professional authority. Some consultants assume that, because of their scientific and technical expertise, they—in the tradition of the doctor—know what is best and should therefore formulate consultees' problems and decide the actions to be taken. Others argue that the consultant's authority is limited to the role of adviser or facilitator.

The proper role of the consultant is that of professional resource. Agency staff members have the responsibility and authority for making decisions. Agency officials consider the technical advice of other sources—such as their own staff and other consultants—and other bodies of information, such as agency goals and values and political and fiscal constraints. Consultants, who have no official legitimization for making decisions and who can (and do) walk away from the consequences of decisions, are not responsible for agency decisions and actions. Consultants are, however, responsible for providing competent services through information, recommendations, points of view, and principles. They may raise questions about the parameters of problems and the kinds of information relevant to them. They may facilitate the processes through which diverse views are brought into decision making.

What is the place of the consultant's political and social values? This question is the subject of the most heated controversy within the profession. Consultants, like other specialists, occupy positions of relative power, as they are often the sole authorities on certain technical problems and their implications. Their power is increased when, as often happens, consultees are in a crisis state and, consequently, highly susceptible to influence. Moreover, consultants sometimes assume, like the ancient sage described in Chapter Two, that their particular social and political values and views are superior and, therefore, feel justified in using the power of their role to impose these values on consultees.

This phenomenon is best illustrated in consultants' attitudes toward change. Many consultants assume that certain changes are needed and, moreover, that it is their responsibility to help organizations make these changes. This view is closely linked to the atmosphere of social reform in which consultation flowered. Humanistic values, such as concern for all members of society to have access to needed services and for the prevention of exploitation of employees, are part of the professional and personal ideologies of the majority of consultants from mental health professions and from the field of organization development. OD consultants, for instance, often enter a contract with an implicit, predetermined diagnosis based on their values (Bowen, 1977) and seek to make such changes as decentralizing decision making and establishing more open communication and more organic cultures (Beckhard, 1969; Burke, 1980; French and Bell, 1973; Golembiewski, 1972). Frequently, however, consultants' diagnoses and recommendations appear to owe more to their commitment to change technologies than to humanistic ideals (Krell, 1981).

Another point of view holds that agency staff members should be fully responsible for choosing the social and political values governing their work and that it is the consultant's responsibility to support consultees' values. This position—and the values it represents—appears to be the only tenable one for consultants to take. Consultants who specialize in change processes, then, should help agencies change only in directions explicitly chosen by their staff. Consultants who promote their values through persuasion or through any other efforts to control consultees are exploiting their role. It would be naive, of course, to think that consultants' social and political values do not influence their professional practice. Consultants are responsible for clarifying their values—both to themselves and to their consultees—and the effects of these values on their work. The most appropriate and effective way for consultants to express their values is in choosing which agencies to serve. But agency values and conflicts related to them are often unclear—to employees as well as to their consultants. Consultants can help consultees identify value-related dilemmas, clarify their own values, and make decisions and take actions consistent with them (Argyris, 1970; Bowen, 1977; Gallessich, 1974). This process may uncover unsuspected differences between consultants' and consultees' values and lead them to terminate their contract.

Consultants should not allow their expertise or their role

to be used in ways they believe are harmful to clients, staff members, or the public. They should confront consultees whom they perceive to be involved in unethical practices—of either a professional or a moral nature—and attempt to help them understand the issues involved and make needed changes. If consultants decide they can no longer support an agency's policies or actions, they should formally terminate their contracts. For instance, a consultant might choose to leave an agency because of an administrator's rigidly autocratic or deceptive management style or because an agency's services are discriminatory and do not reach the minority groups specified in its funding guidelines.

After terminating, a consultant may choose to take an advocate role for a group or individual whose interests appear to be jeopardized and in so doing take a role as adversary of the agency or the element within it that is associated with unethical or immoral actions. (It should be clear that advocates are not necessarily proponents of social reform. The advocate's goal may, for instance, simply be to obtain adequate services for a single client or eliminate discriminatory treatment of an employee and involve no policy or institutional change.) The advocate's actions include power strategies outside the consultant role. The advocate may confront a consultee, administrator, or board of trustees and insist that that person or body make changes. The advocate may also mobilize external forces. An advocate, for instance, might exert pressures on the agency by organizing, educating, and training community action groups, through news media, or through exerting political pressures on influential individuals, such as members of city councils, legislatures, and licensure boards. An advocate might offer to help a union whose members are being unfairly treated by an agency administrator.

Consultants usually turn to the advocate role only after a series of frustrating experiences and painful weighing of the costs and benefits of different actions. Chesler, Bryant, and Crowfoot (1975, p. 15) described the poignant dilemmas of the sociologist-consultant working in a school system. "You are in a meeting with school system administrators. They are discussing the problems of a high school which draws exclusively from a lower class neighborhood. One administrator says, 'There are students in this school who could go to college if they were not too lazy to apply and go to school a few more years.' As you look around, most of the rest of the administrators nod. What would you do?" And in another situation, a consultant observes physical violence that he is sure is psychologically as well as physically abusive. "In a black high school you are walking down the hallway with the black assistant principal. Approaching you is a black teacher with a board paddle on his shoulder. As he meets students in the hallway who are late for class, he asks them to bend over and vigorously applies the paddle to the butts. How do you respond? What do you say to the principal and the teacher? Do you attempt to stop the behavior?"

Before turning to advocacy, consultants should generally exhaust all strategies within the consultant role. For example, the consultant in the schools described above might seek to use informational and facilitative strategies to increase the consultees' understanding of their clients' behaviors. He or she might, through seminars, films, discussion groups, recommended readings, and conferences, seek to help teachers and administrators identify a variety of reasons that certain students appear "lazy," clarify their goals for these students, and explore alternative methods for reaching them. If these approaches failed, the consultant might directly confront the staff members on the destructive consequences of their behavior. Finally, the consultant might terminate the contract and mobilize external forces to bring pressures on the school or join the staff of an agency devoted to eliminating institutional racism.

Role Specialization: Problems and Opportunities. Like other open systems, professions tend to become more differentiated and specialized over time. Moreover, consultation is inherently specialized. Demands for highly specialized consultants will continue and even increase as a result of the complex nature of modern work organizations and human services and the availability of sophisticated technology. But with specialization come certain problems. Specialization narrows the perceptual field and the range of conceptualization. It therefore increases the probability of consultant "myopia" and the tendency to deliberately or unwittingly formulate problems in narrow terms.[2] Specialization increases consultants' difficulties in understanding the work of other professionals. It increases the barriers to communication while, at the same time, increasing the need to communicate.

Most problems confronting human services providers cannot be solved without careful consideration of a wide range of specialized information and communication among many specialists. Successful consultation depends not just on expertise in a substantive area but on other competencies, such as skills in the process of communicating with and helping professional peers and knowledge of organizational structures and processes. Similar competencies are needed by all consultants, regardless of their particular specialty areas.

These generic competencies—the concepts, principles, and skills needed for practice in the consultant role—must be identified and integrated in the standards of consultant associations and in their educational and training activities. Moreover, organizations sometimes need consultant generalists—persons who are highly skilled in broad areas, such as organizational problem solving and resource utilization—and guidelines for their preparation should be established. The particular strengths and limitations of both the specialist and the generalist must be identified in order to help consumers choose the consultants who will best fit their needs.

Scientist and Practitioner: Role Integration Difficulties. Consultants often think of themselves primarily as practitioners, change agents, or simply helpers; but they are also applied scientists. Sometimes their role is limited to technical advising or services. More often, consultants have opportunities to go beyond the technician's role—to bring various bodies of knowledge to bear in helping consultees apply scientific methods in diagnosing and solving problems. Consultants use scientific tech-

[2]Mechanic (1974) demonstrated the marked effects of specialization on diagnosis. In the United States, where specialization of physicians is especially common and the most numerous specialty is surgery, the per capita rate of surgery is double that in England and Wales, where specialization is far less frequent.

niques to gather evidence and to evaluate their services. A few, through research and theory building, contribute to the profession's body of knowledge.

The practitioner role, however, is always paramount in consultation, and the roles of practitioner and scientist are often difficult to integrate. The setting and the task often prohibit the use of refined scientific methods. Consultants work with complex, difficult-to-quantify data such as political conflicts and actions, emotions, and crisis events. Intervention inputs and processes are, at best, difficult to isolate and measure. Experimental designs are usually out of the question because of the lack of appropriate control groups. Moreover, consultants often lack theoretical grounding (Fullan, Miles, and Taylor, 1980) or cannot relate theories to the practical problems they find (King, Sherwood, and Manning, 1978) and, consequently, must turn to their case experiences—or to intuition—for guidance (Steele, 1975).

Consultation, like other professional practices, will never be an exact science; but most practitioners could greatly enhance their services by more fully integrating the scientist's perspectives and methods. Unfortunately, the body of knowledge on which consultants base their practices is relatively unsupported by empirical evidence. Little is known, for instance, about the relations among consultants' inputs, processes, and outcomes. Research contributions by senior professionals—which to date are quite modest—are badly needed to establish a more scientific basis for consultation practice (Mannino and Shore, 1980). Professional associations, through their activities and through reward systems, could strengthen their members' identification with the role of scientist.

Pathologies. Each profession creates unique, systematic biases in its members' attitudes and behaviors. Members of professions, for instance, tend to adopt stereotypic and narrow attitudes toward the world in general and toward their work in particular, to overprize their areas of expertise, to reduce the numbers of persons with whom they are able to relate, and to diminish their involvement in the broader social and intellectual domains of life. Familiar instances of these professional "pathologies" are the absent-minded professor, the lawyer who is more concerned about property than about personal rights, and the civil servant who makes a fetish out of the principles of seniority (MacIver, 1966). Professional pathologies affect the quality of their members' services and harm their reputations.

What are the pathologies of the consultant role? Consultants' tendencies to impose their values on consultees and to recommend change for change's sake were noted earlier in this chapter. All professionals tend to create unnecessary dependency in their clients; and mental health consultants, in particular, tend to see their expertise as a magic cure-all and to draw consultees into dependent or "sick" roles. Some consultant groups appear to be anti-intellectual (Alderfer, 1981), to reject the reality of expert, authoritative knowledge and its responsibilities (Lippitt and others, 1975), and to insist on individualistic and situational interpretations of ethics (Luke and Benne, 1975). Entrepreneurialism is characteristic of some consultation, and when it leads to exploitation, may be regarded as a pathology. Probably most consultants are careful to treat their clients fairly, but exploitative practices such as exorbitant fees, fraudulent advertising, careless contracting, and disregard of conflicts of interest have been noted (Backer, 1981; Luke and Benne, 1975).

Sexism is clearly one of consultation's pathologies. Women are more seriously underrepresented in consultation than in most other professional fields. This bias is illustrated in authorship credits in consultation publications. For instance, all twenty-three chapters in a book on organizational consultation edited by Bell and Nadler (1979) were written by males. All twenty-eight authors of papers presented in an OD conference and later published in a book were male, although women attended the program and some, in traditional supportive roles, helped produce the book (Burke, 1978). All primary authors of the articles published by the *Journal of Applied Behavioral Science* in 1979 were male; five of the forty-three authors were female, but they were listed in secondary positions. Women are somewhat more visible in publications related to mental health consultation. Typical is a 1979 book edited by Platt and Wicks (both males) in which two of the thirteen contributors (15 percent) were female. Moreover, several books concerned with mental health approaches to consultation have been authored, edited, or coedited by women (Alpert in Alpert and Meyers, in press; Conoley, 1981a; Green in Beisser and Green, 1972; and Newman, 1967). Ethnic minorities are probably as underrepresented in consultation as women. A more intensive investigation would be required to obtain ethnicity information to verify this assumption; however, it is clear that both Spanish and Asian surnames are rare in the consultation literature.

Some of these pathologies may be key factors in the profession's identity and developmental problems. Professional associations need to determine the biases to which their members are susceptible and find ways of counteracting them.

The Need for Leadership

Consultants are not fulfilling their potential for delivering the high-quality services badly needed by our troubled society. If they are to serve society more responsibly, consultants must, through their professional associations, accomplish certain developmental tasks. Fragmentation into numerous specialized groups poses a barrier to progress. But cross-disciplinary collaboration (achieved by several associations reviewed in this chapter) has failed to accomplish some crucial tasks. A fundamental impasse is apparent: lack of clarity about the consultant's social role and purpose. Incipient pathologies may be contributing to this impasse.

Many consultants—as individuals—are well equipped to diagnose these systemic professional problems and recommend interventions for solving them. However, only visionary, socially responsible, and vigorous *group* actions can move the profession forward. Both intraprofessional and interprofessional associations have the resources for offering the needed leadership and could exert influence in numerous ways. For example, associations could reward activities designed to stimulate and raise members' consciousness of developmental problems and to elicit ideas for solving them. Illustrative of the possibilities is the joint sponsorship of a competition for papers on "Ethics and

Communications Consulting" by the Applied Communication Section of the Speech Communication Association and the *Journal of Applied Communications Research.* Winning papers will be presented at the 1982 convention of the association and later published in the journal. Associations could lead by organizing intergroup councils to focus on common professional problems. (Several of the organizations reviewed here, including the Division of Consulting Psychology of APA and the OD Network, state as one of their major purposes the promotion of such activities.) An example of such an intervention was the National Conference on Consultation Training, which brought together a group of psychologists (Alpert and Meyers, in press). Although this was an intraprofessional rather than an interdisciplinary conference, it made a giant step forward by bringing together different specialists within psychology to discuss common training problems (and, somewhat incidentally, to discover their conflicting assumptions regarding the consultant's role and boundaries). Interprofessional councils—by bringing together representatives of all major consultant groups to focus on current dilemmas—might speed the work of professionalization.

Annotated Bibliography

Backer, T. E. "Organizational Consultation: Where We Stand in 1981." *Consultation,* 1981, *1* (1), 5-11. Backer discusses trends in consulting and critical issues faced by organizational consultants—such as defining the word *consultation,* control of unethical practices, and expansion of research.

Hughes, E. C. *Men and Their Work.* New York: Free Press, 1958. This book is an outstanding resource for understanding the ways professional organizations influence the contract between professionals and society.

Lippitt, G. L. "Areas of Consulting in the 80s." *Academic Consultants' Communique,* 1981, *9* (2), 1-2. The author reports the result of a survey of twenty-two organizational executives to determine their major concerns for the coming decade.

Lippitt, R. O., and others. "The Professionalization of Laboratory Practice." In K. D. Benne and others (Eds.), *The*

Laboratory Method of Changing and Learning: Theory and Application. Palo Alto, Calif.: Science and Behavior Books, 1975. This chapter provides an overview of the practice of laboratory training and discusses the professionalization of this occupational field. The authors identify crucial issues in professionalization that are relevant to all consultation specialties.

Meyer, M. W., and Associates. *Environments and Organizations: Theoretical and Empirical Perspectives.* San Francisco: Jossey-Bass, 1978. The theories and research discussed in this book are helpful in identifying and interpreting the political, economic, social, and technical forces that control organizations' growth and decline.

Moore, W. E. *The Professions: Roles and Rules.* New York: Russell Sage Foundation, 1970. Moore's review of the development and expansion of professions is helpful in understanding the effect of collective action on the evolution of professions and their role in society.

Rogawski, A. S. (Ed.). *New Directions for Mental Health Services: Mental Health Consultations in Community Settings,* no. 3. San Francisco: Jossey-Bass, 1979. Several chapters in this book examine changing social and economic conditions and their implications for the practice of mental health consultation.

17

Establishing
a Professional
Code of Ethics

The professional/client relationship is inherently one of unequal power. Clients, as laypersons in the professional's specialty, lack sufficient information to judge whether a performance is competent and ethical. They must depend on the integrity of the professional for the choice of technology and its skilled application. The gap between the knowledge of the professional and the layperson increases with specialization.

The power of the professional poses a social problem. Power and privilege can be used in harmful ways. Professionals, for example, may offer poor-quality services, charge unreasonably high fees, restrict entry into the profession so as to create scarcity and deny competent practitioners the right to offer services, betray confidences, and use the client relationship for their own benefit (Greenwood, 1966). The universal and centuries-old approach to this problem is the social contract through which professional organizations institutionalize a service orientation by committing their members to put social welfare above their own and to use their knowledge for the benefit of the pub-

391

lic. A major expression of this orientation is a code of ethics, and the degree to which a profession explicates its social contract in a code is a crucial index of its maturity. The ethics codes of the more highly developed professions are distinguished by their altruism, their service orientation, and their "explicit, systematic, and binding nature" (Greenwood, 1966, p. 15). The primary concern of these codes is to regulate practitioners' behaviors in relationships with clients. However, ethical codes often include standards for relationships to the larger society, to colleagues, and to members of other professions. Codes embody not only professional principles but the moral values of professions' members, which typically reflect social mores. Codes avoid controversial social and political issues. Professions attempt to separate out particular values, interests, likes, and dislikes from professional standards and practices in order to relate to clients on a neutral basis (Parsons, 1939).

Professions enforce their ethical codes through three basic processes. Self-discipline is the primary means of enforcement. Members of professions are expected to be alert to ethical dilemmas and voluntarily adhere to their professions' codes. They are taught the code during their training and are periodically reminded of it through various activities and publications. Informal disciplinary methods—such as peer consultation and review—also enforce ethical codes. A formal review by an ethics committee is used to investigate reported cases of malpractice. Disciplinary actions might include debarment from the professional organization, license suspension, a requirement of extended supervision, or submission to some form of rehabilitative treatment.

The Ethical Dilemma

The Need. Like other professionals, consultants need an ethical code to ensure that their services are competent and ethical. Consultees are often unqualified to "appraise the quality of service being offered or the risks involved and, therefore, may have to rely for support and protection on the helper's standards of conduct and on the network of professional peers"

(Lippitt and Lippitt, 1978, p. 57). But because the field is new and complex and because clear definitions and standards are lacking, many otherwise qualified persons are not aware when an ethical dilemma is present or, if aware, do not know what response would be most appropriate. The most skilled and principled consultants sometimes find themselves in ethical dilemmas, unsure what to do. For instance, responding to the needs of one group of employees, a consultant discovered he was jeopardizing the interests of another group and perhaps the agency's stability as well. Another consultant found that a report in which she discussed a survey of staff morale was subtly reworded and distorted by an administrator in order to support a grant proposal.

Ethical dilemmas are especially serious in consultation because of the numbers of people affected by a consultant's ethical principles. For instance, in working with the directors of several large agencies, a consultant influences decisions that affect the morale and productivity of hundreds of employees and the services to thousands of clients. Consequently, consultants' ethics have become a social issue. A 1980 report to Congress by the Comptroller General of the United States illustrates one type of criticism: the charging of exorbitant fees by consultants (cited in Backer, 1981, p. 7).

> GAO has issued six reports since 1961 which have questioned the reasonableness of fees paid for consulting services. In addition, the Department of Energy's Inspector General and the Subcommittee on Civil Service and General Services, Senate Committee on Governmental Affairs, have questioned the reasonableness of these fees. For example, the Department of Energy paid a consulting service contractor $500 a day for 15 days to critique the first issue of a new journal. The same contractor had worked within the past year as a Department of Energy subcontractor at $250 a day.

Consultants, too, have expressed concern about the malpractices of their colleagues (Benne, 1969; Pfeiffer and Jones, 1977; Lippitt and Lippitt, 1978; Walton and Warrick, 1973).

Members of one consultant association noted the "shoddy and unprofessional offerings of services that are now being foisted on an unknowing public," especially through consultants' incompetence, fraudulent advertising, and failure to take responsibility for clients' welfare (Luke and Benne, 1975, p. 493). However, judging from the literature, the profession is surprisingly unconcerned about ethical issues. For instance, two recent, comprehensive books on mental health consultation in the schools do not include chapters on ethics and make scant reference to ethical problems (Conoley, 1981; Meyers, Parsons, and Martin, 1979). And a bibliography of 884 publications in the mental health consultation field between 1973 and 1978 lists only six references on ethics, in contrast to twenty-one on consultant/consultee relationships and twenty-eight on evaluation (Grady, Gibson, and Trickett, 1981).

The Missing Codes: Caveat Emptor. Consumers get little help from professional associations in distinguishing the able and ethical consultant from the charlatan. Few organizations have established codes for consultants' specialized practice. Divisions of consultants within larger organizations—such as APA's Division of Consulting Psychology—tend to rely on the codes of the broader profession, rather than developing unique consulting codes. Yet the codes written for other professions either do not address the problems specific to consultation or are so general that they offer little guidance (Walton and Warrick, 1973). Among the exceptional organizations are NTL Institute and the American Society for Training and Development; their codes, however, are directed toward the ethical issues arising in only one consultation model (laboratory training) and are concerned with individual rather than organizational dilemmas.

Why the shortage of ethics codes for consultants? One barrier to the development of consultants' codes was identified by Benne (1969) more than a decade ago. "Part of the difficulty of developing general ethical codes for group and organizational consultation is that the present practitioners of the art are drawn from numerous rather than single primary professional identifications. It is unwise and impossible for psychologist-consultants to legislate norms of appropriate behavior for psychiatrist-consultants, however attractive the prospect might be for psychologists. And the reverse is true. And so it runs for sociologists and social workers, anthropologists and educators, or any combination of these" (p. 603).

But this explanation does not help us understand why within-profession groups do not evolve unique ethics codes to govern their consultation practice. Nor does it tell us why emergent professional groups—such as OD practitioners—who have been practicing under a common theoretical and methodological framework for many years have not yet developed codes. The complexity of the consulting process and its context is undoubtedly a factor in the missing codes. But a more important source of difficulty is the conflict within the profession over the boundaries of the consultant role and, hence, differences in regard to what is and is not ethical (see discussion in Chapter Sixteen on role identity problems). Moreover, some consultants question the need for an ethical code. Respondents to a survey regarding ethical concerns of laboratory training consultation administered by the Ethics Committee of the International Association of Applied Social Scientists contended that consultant situations are often so complex that a code cannot possibly cover all contingencies (Luke and Benne, 1975). Ethical decisions, therefore, must be based on the unique features of each situation. This view overlooks the possible effects of personal factors—motives, needs, interests—in creating perceptual distortions that might prevent an accurate appraisal of situations. Moreover, the situational view of ethics "calls for more self-discipline in commitment to values than most people are able to mobilize" (Lippitt and Lippitt, 1978, p. 61). Respondents to this survey also questioned whether an external code would have the desired effect of internalizing standards. "In fact, codes may work in the opposite direction. Laboratory practitioners who comply with a *legal* code of ethics prescribed by their professional organization may feel that they have solved their 'ethical' problems and fail to confront the ethical issues internal to their work and to continue growing, ethically as well as technically" (Luke and Benne, 1975, pp. 494-495). The respondents offered still another reason that an ethical code is unnecessary.

They reported that when they work in the consultant role as laboratory trainer, moral and legal judgments may, at times, be suspended in the interest of learning! Yet, their professional expertise in no way qualifies or entitles consultants to overrule the laws and norms created by society to protect its members.

The questions raised here point to the need for ethical codes. At the same time, they reveal some of the reasons that few organizations have established them. Obtaining agreement, even within a small group, is sometimes impossible. Yet viable ethical codes can come into existence only when members of professional groups are able to agree on their principles—and when these principles are sanctioned by the larger society.

Public Education, a Poor Alternative. Public education offers another means for protecting the public against unethical and incompetent practitioners. Consultants can offer information to help consumers choose, negotiate with, use, and evaluate a consultant (Bell and Nadler, 1979; Fuchs, 1975). Consumers can be advised of consultants' limits and potential areas of malpractice. Training of consultees is another way consultants can offer protection (Bardon, 1977; Chandy, 1974; Steele, 1975). However, when carried out by individuals, these efforts have much less impact than would programs conducted by professional organizations. Several organizations—for example, the American Society for Training and Development (ASTD) and Certified Consultants International—have established committees to provide the public with information. These public information services are likely to carry much more weight when, like ASTD, they have a statement of ethical principles endorsed by the association.

A Position Statement. The position taken here is that consultants' codes of ethics are urgently needed. Reliance on individual standards is insufficient for public protection. Individuals' experiences, knowledge, and judgments are limited by idiosyncratic biases. The wisdom of the larger group (including input from consumers and from other professions) is needed to create a sound code. The profession has sufficient knowledge accumulated through decades of practice to identify common ethical dilemmas and to establish working principles.

This task must be accomplished by peer groups. Without the support and enforcement of professional organizations, no code will have extensive influence. The code serves as a symbol through which the public and the members of the profession can measure the profession's commitment to the social contract. To leave members without guidance and consumers without protection is irresponsible.

An intergroup discussion of ethical problems and exploration of possibilities for a generic code would also serve the public's interests by broadening the perspectives for viewing ethical issues. The initiative might be taken by associations, such as APA's Division of Consulting Psychology or the OD Network, that include among their purposes the promotion of cooperative work by allied groups on common problems.

A Consultant's Code of Ethics

The following pages describe a comprehensive code of ethics for consultants. This code builds on recommendations of several individuals (Benne, 1969; Pfeiffer and Jones, 1977; Lippitt and Lippitt, 1978). It also draws on principles of several organizational codes (American Psychological Association, 1972; Managerial Consultation Division of the Academy of Management, 1978; NTL Institute, 1980). This code is suggested (1) as an interim guideline for individual practitioners, (2) for use in educational and training settings, as a stimulus for alerting trainees to potential problems and providing them with guidance, (3) as a basis for discussion of ethics within and between consultant organizations, and (4) to help consumers protect themselves from unethical practices.

Principle 1. Consultants' clients are the agencies that hire them. Consultants place their clients' interests above their own. They do not allow their own motives, needs, and interests to interfere with their clients' welfare and goals. When their work brings them into conflicts, consultants seek to help agency staff members find compromises consistent with agency goals. Consultants recognize the agency director, its chief executive officer, as the organization's official representative and final authority in making decisions. In all actions, consultants support this person's interpretation of agency interests.

Principle 2. Consultants are responsible for safeguarding the welfare of their consultees and client organizations. Consultants inform consultees of any potential risks in consultation activities and help consultees make informed decisions on whether or not to use any service.

Although consultants are usually hired to help organizations increase their coping capacities, in some cases the task is not to increase effectiveness but rather to maintain organizational integrity and prevent severe deterioration. Interventions by consultants who are oversold on the value of change can be destructive. Consultants are alert to the condition of agencies and individuals they work with. In collaboration with agency administrators, they seek to help agencies under stress maintain their equilibrium. Consultants avoid, for example, focusing on intra-agency conflicts when it is clear that they are severe and that the agency lacks the resources to alleviate them. Consultants are especially careful to provide administrators with any needed guidance in relation to an intervention, since these individuals carry heavy responsibility for the welfare of the entire agency and its functions.

Consultants protect the confidentiality of all information related to their consultees and client agencies. Consultants, in general, do not reveal the names of their client organizations and do not discuss agencies with outside persons. Several exceptions to this general rule might be made, however. A consultant may, with an administrator's permission, use the latter as a reference. With permission, a consultant may report a case study or research in a professional journal, at a conference, or in a training context. For the purpose of obtaining assistance, a consultant may discuss a problem situation in a confidential interview with a colleague. But in these cases, the consultant is careful to preserve the anonymity of the agency and of its staff or to obtain the staff's informed consent for disclosure.

Principle 3. Consultants present their professional qualifications and limitations accurately in order to avoid misinterpretation. They immediately correct any misunderstandings about their credentials and experience. They also inform consultees of any professional or personal relationships, biases, or values that are likely to affect their work.

Principle 4. Consultants are careful to present their knowledge accurately. They avoid magnifying agency problems and needs. They do not make unrealistic promises about the benefits of their services. Consultants will not knowingly distort any information. They strive to correct any distortions made by others.

Principle 5. When consultants perceive a consultee to behave in an unethical manner, they express their observations and the reasons for their concern to the person involved. Consultants are not responsible for consultees' behavior, but they are responsible for clear communication with them in regard to any ethical concerns and for providing an opportunity for a collegial discussion of issues involved.

Principle 6. Consultants avoid involvement in multiple roles and relationships that might create conflicts of interest and thus jeopardize their effectiveness in the consultant role. When there is doubt about the existence of a conflict of interest, the consultant brings the relevant information to consultees' attention so that an informed decision can be made. Consultants do not enter into contracts with competing agencies. Consultants decline to work with agencies when an ongoing personal relationship with an agency member would reduce their objectivity and freedom of expression, alter their commitment to the agency, or otherwise create a conflict of interest. Consultants do not allow themselves to be drawn into any roles that are incompatible with their stated purposes and contract. Sexualizing of a consultant/consultee relationship is one clear type of violation of ethical conduct (Jones and Pfeiffer, 1979). However, improprieties occur in many other areas—for example, by allowing one's interests in gathering research data to interfere with one's services as a consultant or by agreeing to an administrator's request for confidential information about another consultee or to a request for personal counseling.

Principle 7. Consultants avoid manipulating consultees. Instead, they seek to increase consultees' independence and freedom of choice.

This principle involves thorny issues related to consultants' use of their influence to control consultees' behavior. Sometimes a consultant may deliberately control a consultee's behavior to ensure that it is in accordance with the consultant's recommendations. In other cases, a consultant may be unaware that he or she is manipulating. There are three ways consultants can reduce the probability of their manipulating consultees (Kelman, 1969):

- Increasing consultants' and consultees' active awareness of the manipulative potential of consultation and explicating the values and assumptions of any interventions. Consultants label their own biases and encourage consultees to label their values and to challenge the consultant's values.
- Deliberately building protection against manipulation or resistance to it into the consultation process by minimizing the consultant's values and maximizing the consultee's values as the dominant criteria for change.
- Setting the enhancement of freedom of choice as a central goal and use of the consultant's knowledge and skills and of the consulting relationship to increase both the consultee's range of choices and her or his freedom to choose.

Principle 8. Consultants accept contracts only if they are reasonably sure that the client agency will benefit from their services. They do not agree to provide services without ascertaining whether these services are relevant to and consistent with the organization's needs and goals. Consultants are careful not to "sell" a point of view. They help consultees examine and clarify the needs or problems underlying requests for consultation. They help consultees explore all potential sources of problems and varied solutions to these problems and the potential cost/benefit ratios of any consultative services, materials, and instruments.

Principle 9. Consultants establish clear contracts with well-defined parameters. They ascertain that they are sanctioned to enter an agency through the express permission of its executive officer. Consultants make sure not only that they are in agreement with the administrator on the terms and purposes of the contract but also that this information is communicated to all staff members who participate in consultation activities and that the implications of their participation are understood. Consultants are then careful to behave in ways that are congruent with this contract.

Principle 10. Consultants fulfill their contracts and remain within contractual boundaries. Consultants provide all the services agreed on. Changes are made only through explicit recontracting with the administration and any staff members involved in the consultation. Consultants are careful not to extend their activities beyond contractual boundaries. If, at any time, evidence indicates that consultation is ineffective or harmful, the consultant brings this evidence to the attention of the consultee and either changes the consultation to make it beneficial to the consultee or terminates the relationship.

Principle 11. Consultants strive to evaluate the outcomes of their services. They determine, insofar as they are able, whether the goals established for consultation were achieved. They help consultees interpret and make use of evaluation findings.

Principle 12. Consultants assume responsibility for assisting administrators in establishing confidentiality policies to govern consultation and communicating these policies to the staff members involved in consultation activities. Generally, consultants need complete freedom to protect individual confidences, but consultants may be unnecessarily handicapped if they promise to keep all information strictly confidential. Certain information given confidentially may be useful when presented anonymously to an administrator. But unless evaluation of persons is specifically defined as a consultation objective, no information about the performance of individuals or work groups should be provided to supervisors. Consultants must keep all staff members advised of any limitations or qualifications of this policy.

Principle 13. Consultants acquire the basic body of knowledge and skills of their profession. They keep abreast of new theoretical, empirical, and technical developments related to consultation. They seek to maintain the highest possible standards of competence in their practice by giving their best services to their consultees.

Principle 14. Consultants know their professional strengths, weaknesses, and biases. They monitor themselves to ensure that constraints resulting from their particular professional "sets" do not distort their perceptions, attitudes, and behaviors so as to interfere with the needs of their client organizations. The unique features of the organization and the presenting problem—not consultants' particular technological or theoretical biases—determine their diagnoses and recommendations. It is unethical for consultants to define situations to fit their particular professional specialties—as illustrated by the consultant who automatically recommends a confrontation meeting or a packaged training program or by one consultant who persuaded an agency and staff to channel their consultation funds into a series of human relations weekend retreats rather than meeting their expressed need for training in interviewing skills.

Principle 15. Consultants are aware of personal characteristics that predispose them to systematic biases. They are alert to the possibility that such factors as ethnicity, age, sex, and social status may distort their perceptions, interpretations, and recommendations. They are also aware of the more subtle effects of personal needs and motives—such as the need for recognition or difficulties accepting authority—on their attitudes and behavior. Consultants monitor themselves to prevent these personal biases from distorting diagnoses and from interfering with the provision of competent, appropriate, and ethical services. In some cases, consultants terminate a consultation or disqualify themselves from certain consultative activities to be sure that their biases do not interfere with their responsibilities to their clients.

Principle 16. Consultants are alert to differences between their own social and political values and interests and those of client organizations. They inform consultees of any significant ideological conflicts. Consultants do not enter into contracts with an agency whose values are antithetical to theirs.* When

*Whereas most professions' codes of ethics require that they provide services to any client asking for them regardless of such characteristics

consultants become aware of conflicts between their own values and those of a client agency, they share this information with the appropriate administrator or consultee so that together they can decide whether to continue their relationship. Consultants do not have the right to change an organization's goals or operations or to align them with their own convictions. However, they are responsible for expressing their values.

Society traditionally expects professionals to keep personal beliefs separated from their social roles, perpetuating a "myth" of value-free services that allays societal concerns and the professional's own anxieties about conflicts (Gouldner, 1969). But most professional services, and certainly those of consultants, involve value-laden choices. Some conflicts are immediately apparent—for example, when a liberal is asked to consult with a reactionary organization, when an agnostic is asked to consult with a religious organization, and when a conservationist is asked to consult with a nuclear energy plant. More often, conflicts emerge only after a consultative relationship is underway. For instance, liberal consultants sometimes find they are unable to function effectively with certain law enforcement institutions. Conservative consultants may feel incompatible with the values of the staff and clients of shelters for drug abusers. Some values conflicts come from differences in social roles and responsibilities. Ministers' "righteousness" may be appropriate for their role but inappropriate for other professionals (Caplan, 1972).

Values conflicts also arise when consultants discover that agencies are involved in questionable practices, such as funding irregularities, exploitative behavior by administrators, and distortion of data—such as data contained in reports to the press or to boards of trustees.

Principle 17. Consultants regularly assess their strengths and weaknesses in relation to current and future work. They solicit feedback from consultees. They develop and implement

---

of the client's as values and political beliefs (Greenwood, 1966), consultants may properly refuse to work with client organizations whose values are antithetical to theirs because of the value-laden nature of organizational policies and actions—and their social consequences.

individualized continuing education programs—self-directed readings and participation in workshops, university courses, and seminars—to update their professional knowledge and skills. They periodically ask peers to coconsult or to review cases. They take advantages of opportunities to work with teams and with colleagues to maximize their learning.

Principle 18. When advertising or otherwise promoting their services, consultants are careful to describe them accurately and to avoid fraudulent information or claims.

Principle 19. Consultants serve public interests through offering a proportion of their time to agencies that are financially unable to pay for consultation services. They also contribute through voluntary service on boards or committees of organizations that are concerned with the public welfare.

Principle 20. Consultants contribute to the growth of knowledge through their own research and experimentation. They conduct research on their activities and report findings through professional media so that they can be used for the benefit of the public. They experiment with new techniques, but they take care to inform consultees of the innovative nature of any services and obtain their informed consent before experimentation.

Principle 21. Consultants are alert to the public's welfare. They are careful that their own behavior does not endanger the public. When aware that actions or policies of consultees or agencies are detrimental to the public welfare, consultants discuss their concerns with the persons whose behavior they question. If the consultant still perceives that consultees' behaviors are harmful, he or she encourages them to change. If the consultees refuse to change, the consultant should step out of the consultant role. In certain cases, it may be necessary for the consultant to take further actions to protect the public (see Chapter Sixteen).

Principle 22. Consultants contribute to the training of less experienced consultants.

Principle 23. Consultants behave so as to protect the reputation of their profession.

Principle 24. Consultants cooperate with other consultants and with members of other professions:

- By sharing scientific and technological knowledge.
- By refraining from competitive activities that would interfere with collegial relationships.
- By a supportive demeanor with clients. The consultant does
  not jeopardize colleagues' authority with their clients or
  with the general public.

Principle 25. Consultants acquaint themselves with the current fee standards in their area of expertise and in the agency's geographic location. They stay within the normative range for fees. They do not undercut other consultants by inappropriate fee reductions.

Principle 26. When a consultant observes another professional to behave in an apparently unethical way, the consultant goes to that person to discuss these perceptions. If the perceived impropriety continues, the consultant calls on another professional or professional group for a review.

Principle 27. Consultants contribute to their profession by participating in the activities of peer associations and supporting their standards.

Principle 28. Consultants take active steps to maintain and increase their effectiveness. They take care of their physical and mental health. They are aware when illness, stress, crisis, or emotional reactions interfere with their normal functioning, and they do not practice when their condition would prevent them from delivering effective services. When aware that their behavior is dysfunctional, consultants suspend or terminate the work relationships that are affected, and if they are unable to resolve personal problems, they seek professional help. Also, when signs indicate that professional problems are occurring, consultants seek the counsel of peers. Consultants meet their personal needs outside the consulting relationship in order to prevent exploiting consultees by using them to meet social or emotional needs.

Annotated Bibliography

Bowen, D. D. "Value Dilemmas in Organization Development." *Journal of Applied Behavioral Science,* 1977, *13,* 545-558. In this thoughtful article, Bowen describes five basic ethical dilemmas that commonly arise in consultation. He points out that the definition of the consultant role is related to these dilemmas. He contends that the OD assumption regarding the necessity and desirability of change is a defect in this model of consultation and recommends that the goal of change be reconsidered.

Fanibanda, D. K. "Ethical Issues of Mental Health Consultation." *Professional Psychology,* 1976, *7,* 547-552. In this article, Fanibanda discusses seven areas of ethical concern for mental health consultants and proposes principles to guide consultants' behavior.

Glaser, E. M. "Ethical Issues in Consultation Practice with Organizations." *Consultation,* 1981, *1* (1), 12-16. This article reports a survey of organizational consultants that included questions about ethical concerns and principles. The author points out the need for more attention to ethical issues in the training of consultants and for the development of principles to guide consultants' practice.

Lippitt, G., and Lippitt, R. *The Consulting Process in Action.* San Diego, Calif.: University Associates, 1978. Chap. 5, "Ethical Dilemmas and Guidelines for Consultants," describes a number of ethical problems in consultation and reviews the ethics codes of several professional organizations. The authors then draw on these existing codes as the foundation for a set of ethical principles they propose for consultants.

Luke, J. R., and Benne, K. D. "Ethical Issues and Dilemmas in Laboratory Practice." In K. D. Benne and others (Eds.), *The Laboratory Method of Changing and Learning: Theory and Application.* Palo Alto, Calif.: Science and Behavior Books, 1975. This chapter is concerned with the need for an ethics code for consultant trainers. The authors describe a project designed to lead to such a code of ethics for the International Association of Applied Social Scientists (now Certified Consultants International). They report some of the reactions of members of this organization to a preliminary survey of ethics concerns.

18

Training Patterns: Present and Future

Most consultants practicing today learned how to consult not through formal training but through on-the-job experiences. However, this situation is changing rapidly as more and more trained consultants enter the field. There are two major patterns of training for the practice of consultation. One is intraprofessional; many professions offer consultation training at preservice and continuing education levels. But a second pattern is playing a dynamic role in the training of consultants. People who want to learn how to consult are finding they cannot always obtain the knowledge and skills they need from their own professions. To meet their demands, consulting practitioners are offering training through nontraditional organizations that are not constrained by professional boundaries or by the turfdom issues found in most colleges and universities. This pattern is now at the leading edge of consultation training.

What patterns will appear in the future? And how can training best serve social needs? This chapter examines consultation training from the perspective of a profession in transition.

The goals are (1) to understand the direction in which the profession is moving, (2) to identify the competencies needed in order for the profession to respond to the demands being placed on it, and (3) to propose training designs to produce the competencies that will enable consultation to fulfill its potential.

Training Patterns and the Evolution of Professions

A high educational level is the fourth criterion on the professionalization scale discussed in Chapter Two and Sixteen. To reach this level of professionalization, training must be specialized and acquired in a formal program, usually as a final part of a general education (Moore, 1970). Formal training emerges slowly and usually lags far behind actual practices.

When a new specialty begins to break out of disciplinary boundaries and form a new field, the establishment of training programs is delayed by certain barriers. The emergence of a new field inevitably encroaches on existing territories. Professions are naturally not interested in offering training for practices that do not fit into their boundaries. Established departments and programs within universities oppose new structures that might offer content overlapping theirs. Besides these turf issues, the conservative nature of established institutions slows down the training for new specialties. New skills—although society demands them and even though they may be technologically advanced—are often ignored by professions and universities for years.

But when society urgently needs new services, it provides inducements, such as money and prestige, to obtain them. Market demands and rewards associated with them act as magnets to pull people out of other fields into the new occupation, and these individuals seek training to acquire the necessary skills. The first generations of practitioners are usually unable to obtain needed training from established professions and university programs. The first generation must often learn through on-the-job experiences. These pioneering practitioners then fill the gap by offering informal training and supervision to newcomers, thus creating the profession's first pattern of training. (This pat-

tern was followed in medieval Europe by craftspersons who provided informal training, often under guild auspices, to members
and apprentices.) When training progresses from this stage to a
more formal one, it usually moves first to vocational schools or
other organizations that are not connected to colleges or universities (Hughes, 1958). Eventually, however, most evolving professions seek to move their training—or some part of it—into
universities, because affiliation with these institutions hastens
the process of authentication and legitimization. Training also
shifts to universities because trainers and students find these settings better equipped to offer systematized and broad-based
preparation.

Consultation Training Patterns

Because of issues related to territorialism and identity,
locus is a pivotal factor in the evolution of consultation training. Consultation practices first evolved in traditional professions, where consulting is practiced not as an independent new
field but as a subspecialty of the profession. The first locus for
consultation training, therefore, and one that is well established,
is within older professions. These institutions—especially the
fields of mental health and management—nurture the new practice, but at the same time, they control its development by
keeping its content and methods within their own disciplinary
boundaries. Thus, they delay the emergence of an independent
profession. With the rapid growth of an interdisciplinary body
of knowledge and as market demands for practitioners with
highly developed and comprehensive consulting skills intensify,
traditional settings have been unable to contain training activities. A new pattern, led by practitioners and innovative organizations, is dominating the preparation of consultants. Just beginning to appear is a third pattern—university-based preparation
for the practice of consultation as an independent discipline.

The Intraprofession Pattern. In its earliest stage of development, the practice of consultation does not require any specialized preparation. Established professions tend to regard consultation as a tangential activity. However, they may value

consultation but regard extensive experience in their basic practices as the proper preparation for this role. From this perspective, preparation for consultation comes with years of experience in one's primary field, not from a different area of specialized knowledge. Consultation is a crowning experience reserved for senior professionals (Hughes, 1958).

Mental health professions, beginning with psychiatry, led in the introduction of formal preparation for consultation into their training programs almost thirty years ago. In the early 1950s, as a result of a 1952 conference held by the American Psychiatric Association, psychiatric residency programs began to include formal preparation for consultation.* Communication was stressed as the key to effective consultation (Barnes, Busse, and Bressler, 1957; Brosin, 1968). Formal training to prepare psychiatric residents for the clinical and educational models of consultation became common (Abrahamson, 1968; Aldrich, 1968; Schwab, 1968). Training for the newly developed mental health model of consultation was first offered at the postdoctoral level in the Harvard School of Public Health in 1955 to professionals from several fields of mental health (Caplan, 1970). With the passage of the Mental Health Centers Act of 1963 and with training grants from the National Institute of Mental Health, training for mental health professions rapidly expanded. As early as 1969, Kern estimated that NIMH was supporting at least twenty residency training programs in community psychiatry, all of which included consultation training. The focus of some of these programs included organizations as well as clients. Preservice training for doctoral students in professional psychology programs was begun in 1962 at the University of Texas. Beginning as an informal seminar and field experience to train students for mental health consultation, the course has expanded its scope along with developments in the field and

*A report that came out of the Cornell Conference on Training, sponsored by the American Psychiatric Association, criticized residency programs for their failure to prepare residents for preventive psychiatry (Whitehorn, 1953). The trainers were urged to include in their curricula preparation for working with other professions and with all kinds of community groups and organizations in order to promote mental health.

now includes preparation for organizational consultation and for the education and training model of consultation (Gallessich, 1974, 1980b; Iscoe and others, 1967). Many other professional psychology programs now include training for various consultation models (Alpert, 1977; Colligan, 1973; Conoley, 1981b; Dorr, 1978; Hartsough, 1972; Hyman and Meyers, 1973; Keys, 1980; Kratochwill and Bergan, 1978; Lambert, Yandell, and Sandoval, 1975). The professions of social work and psychiatric nursing also offer training for consultation (Kaslow, 1977; Smith, 1975).

Training for consultation in the mental health professions is still more fully developed than in other professions, perhaps because of the strength of demands for clinical, mental health, and behavioral consultation, leadership from mental health professionals, and the theoretical elegance of the mental health model and its potential for ameliorating social problems. But other professions are moving rapidly to prepare their students to practice consultation as a subspecialty (Campbell, 1978). Many professional management training programs and schools of business include courses in consultation. Courses in organizational consultation and in other models of consultation appear in other settings—for example, in departments of rehabilitation counseling, labor and industrial relations, communications, human development, and education. The following examples illustrate the varied sources and scope of preservice consultation training.

The Communication Analyst Program of the Department of Communication of Ohio State University offers a master's degree with a specialty in organization development and organizational behavior, with a strong emphasis on consultation. The Speech Communication and Human Relations Division of the University of Kansas offers a similar program at both the master's and doctoral levels. The Department of Psychology of the State University of New York at Buffalo offers a Ph.D. in social psychology that emphasizes organizational psychology and consultation skills. The Department of Organizational Behavior and Intervention of the Harvard Graduate School of Education offers M.Ed. and Ed.D. degrees in organization development and organizational behavior. This program emphasizes process consultation, consultation skills training, and personal development. The Graduate Center for Human Development of Fairleigh Dickinson University offers a master's degree in human development that includes consultation training, along with teacher education, group leadership, and human relations training.

In university-based training programs, consultation is usually regarded as a subspecialty, but a few new academic programs now feature consultation as a major. For example, a master's degree program in organizational development and analysis at the Department of Organizational Behavior of Case Western Reserve University offers courses in several consultation models and a wide array of supportive courses, such as community development, administration, health care management, general systems theory, and personal development (Campbell, 1978). Programs such as this one appear to be moving toward recognition of consultation as an independent profession.

In addition to offering preservice preparation for consultation, professions offer training in the form of convention seminars and workshops, in institutes, and through in-service training. To illustrate, the 1981 annual meeting of the Speech Communication Association included a number of workshops and short courses concerned with technological competencies relevant to consultation, such as "Negotiation in the Organization: The Role of Argumentativeness," "A Teachers/Consultants/Trainers Guide for Developing Workshops on Male-Female Dynamics in the Organization," "Setting Up Your Own Consulting Business for Profit and Research," "A Short Course on Communications Consulting," and "Workshop Consulting: How to Design and Administer Effective Workshops." In-service consultation training is found in clinics, counseling centers, school districts, welfare departments, and state schools and hospitals (Aiken, 1974; Broskowski, Khajavi, and Mehryar, 1973; Gallessich and Ladogana, 1978; Leonard, 1979; Signell and Scott, 1972; Walsh, 1973).

The Leading Edge: Training Outside Professional Boundaries. As a result of responses by professional consultants to the needs of people who want to increase their consultation skills, the leading edge of training has moved outside traditional institutions. This movement is not a consolidated effort but the work of varied individuals and groups. Training in this new pattern is available through innovative, interdisciplinary organizations that offer workshops, seminars, and publications and through informal arrangements for supervision from experienced consultants.

An interdisciplinary educational organization, the National Training Laboratories Institute of Applied Behavioral Science, leads the training in this second pattern. For thirty-five years NTL has trained professionals from a variety of disciplines in new specialty areas. Beginning with training in group dynamics and human relations, it expanded its offerings to include other specialty areas. For the past fifteen years it has offered training in organization development and consultation. NTL's scope and interdisciplinary nature are illustrated in its 1982 training calendar (NTL Institute Program Calendar, Fall-Spring 1981-1982). Extended workshops—ten days in length—on consultation skills are available in four major cities, along with briefer workshops on OD skills. Also on the calendar are numerous workshops and seminars on technology needed by consultants. The topics include career development, managing human resources, facilitating and managing complex systems change, ecology of work, stress, principles of Japanese management, and management of declining organizations. The subject of one seminar is "how to manage a consultant practice: personal, financial, and value considerations." The NTL Institute also contributes to the preservice training of professionals from a variety of disciplines through the Graduate Students Professional Development Program (GSPDP). This program offers training in personal and professional development, in workshop design and leadership, and in consultation. In addition, the institute publishes, through the *Journal of Applied Behavioral Science,* numerous articles that contribute to the education of consultants.

Another nontraditional organization is offering vigorous leadership in consultation training. University Associates offers an extensive array of workshops, clinics, and seminars, as well as a year-long internship program. For example, the 1981 offering included numerous workshops (offered in cities in the United States and Canada) on such topics as OD, concepts and instruments for assessment of organizations, team building, and consultation skills. This organization is a prolific publisher of materials for self-directed learning. Its extensive catalogue includes an annual handbook for group facilitators, a series of books on human relations training, volumes concerned with survey instruments, and numerous publications concerned with specialized technologies.

Many other organizations—for example, the American Society for Training and Development and the OD Network—are contributing to training in the nontraditional sector.

Many people acquire consultant skills through informal arrangements. They organize their own programs through readings, workshops, and seminars. The area in which it is most difficult to obtain training is supervision of actual experiences in consulting. However, it is sometimes possible to find an experienced consultant with whom a beginner can work as an apprentice or a cotrainer or coconsultant. Some organizations, such as University Associates, offer internship opportunities. Consultation skills can also be acquired through membership in peer support groups composed of consultants who meet regularly to discuss practical and theoretical issues. Some midcareer professionals work in agencies that are willing to provide in-service consultant training. Private consulting firms sometimes offer on-the-job training to new staff members (Lippitt and others, 1975).

Today training for consultation is in a state of ferment. Training opportunities are widely available both within and outside established professions and universities and at all points in the career span. Led by mental health and management professionals, consultation training has been institutionalized as a subspecialty in traditional settings. Outside traditional institutions, new, interdisciplinary organizations offer wide-ranging programs that attract large numbers of trainees. The intraprofessional pattern provides a stable base for training in new practices and helps traditional professionals fit their specialized skills to agency needs. The interdisciplinary pattern serves as a catalyst at the periphery of the new field. It brings to consultants new practices that reflect new technology and changing needs.

The next development in consultation training will be the establishment of university-based programs and departments in which consultation is an independent discipline. Already, some universities have interdisciplinary doctoral programs that offer preparation in applied behavioral science—with an emphasis on consultation—with courses from departments of education, social work, business administration, public administration, and public health (Lippitt and others, 1975).

Proposals: A Training Model for Today and One for Tomorrow

The training activities described in the preceding pages prepare consultants for one of two basic roles: (1) practice of consultation as a subspecialty or (2) practice as a professional consultant. Human services agencies need both types of consultants. They need people who are specialists in a traditional field (such as nursing, law, or educational administration) and who, in addition, are competent consultants—experts in transmitting their specialized knowledge to staff members. Agencies also need people whose specialty is human services consultation, professionals who are experts in human services and in helping agency staff members solve problems.

To respond to these needs, two training proposals are outlined here as models for training two types of consultants. One is a basic consultation course that provides a minimal background for practice of consultation as a subspecialty. The second is a program for advanced study in consultation. It prepares people for careers as professional consultants.

The Minimal Core: A Basic Course. The minimal core is provided through a two-semester course and related field experiences. The course content, which follows the material in this book, can be used by trainers in a number of ways. Here it is designed to fit a nine-month academic calendar. The design, however, could be the nucleus for an expanded program extending over a two-year period. It could, in addition, be adapted to fit into nontraditional training programs—for example, in an institute or in a series of workshops and seminars or in-service training.

The course is titled "Consultation Theory and Process." Various versions of this model have been used to train students since 1970 (Gallessich, 1974; Gallessich and MacDonald, 1981). It was described in a paper, "Training Psychologists for Consultation with Organizations," presented at the National Conference on Consultation Training in 1980 (Gallessich, 1980b) and published in the proceedings of this conference (Alpert and Meyers, in press). In its present setting it is, in many ways, traditional. It is offered in the department of educational psychology within a college of education. It is taught by a psychologist, and the majority of the students come from professional psychology programs (school, counseling, clinical, and community). The graduates' primary identification is with psychology, and they view consultation as a subspecialty. The course is innovative, however, in its interdisciplinary content and in its inclusion of students from numerous fields—such as communications, management, special education, and educational administration.

Most students are in the third or fourth year of Ph.D. programs when they enroll in this course. They have received basic preparation in their primary disciplines and have had related practicum experiences. Thus, before entering consultation training, all these students have developed competencies in a primary field. They have expertise to offer client organizations at several levels. Most can consult with staff members about agency clients. For example, a trainee might help a probation officer work more effectively with a rebellious adolescent. Some students are qualified to consult with agencies in regard to in-service training and to lead workshops and laboratories. To illustrate, a trainee might lead a workshop on interviewing skills for the staff of a Planned Parenthood center, on counseling skills for the staff of a hospice, on assessment skills for first-grade teachers, and on theories of aging for the staff of a senior citizens' center. Some trainees are also qualified to consult with administrators of these agencies in regard to program development. A school psychology student might help a school administrator plan a program for gifted children or design the evaluation of such a program. A counseling student might assist the staff of an abortion center design and implement a counseling component to expand its services. A community psychology student might work with the staff of a low-cost housing agency to assess resident needs and to mobilize community resources to respond to those needs. Some students have achieved considerable knowledge of administration or management through course work and experiences. They might, for example, be familiar with management theory and practice or with the processes of work groups and, therefore, be qualified to consult in these areas.

The objectives of the course are listed in Table 4, "Consultation Training: Generic Objectives." The primary topics and

Table 4. Consultation Training: Generic Objectives

---

1. Competency in specialized models: understanding of the theoretical and methodological bases of one or more specialized models of consultation, such as behavioral or organizational consultation. Competency in applying one or more models to agencies, to help individuals, groups, and organizations diagnose problems and make changes.

2. Understanding of the generic role and functions of consultation: awareness of the consultant's social purpose and role boundaries and their implications for practice.

3. Competency in generic consultation processes: entry, contracting, diagnosis, establishing effective and ethical working relationships with consultees and with other consultants, and evaluation.

4. Understanding of one or more theories for understanding organizations and their environments and competency in applying a theoretical framework (such as open-systems, developmental, or management theories) to organizations.

5. Self-understanding: awareness of the effects of one's characteristics—such as style, values, competencies, gender, and age—on consultation processes and outcomes. Ability to monitor and change one's behavior as needed to ensure delivery of ethical, competent services that are consistent with agency needs and congruent with one's own personal and professional values.

---

methods for reaching the objectives are shown in Table 5, "Topics and Methods of a Year-Long Consultation Course." A typical outline for the two semesters is shown in Table 6, "Consultation Theory and Process: Course Outline."

A didactic method takes precedence over all others in the first six weeks. A conceptual framework is presented through lectures, readings, and class discussions. Table 7, "Consultation:

Table 5. Topics and Methods of a Year-Long Consultation Course

Topics	Primary Methods[a]
I. Conceptual framework	
A. Understanding agencies	
1. Agencies as open sociotechnical systems	Didactic
2. Management theories/practices	Didactic/field
3. Group processes	Didactic/field/laboratory/supervision
4. Adaptive and planned-change processes	Didactic/field
5. Culture/characteristics of particular types of agencies	Didactic/field/supervision
B. Understanding consultation	
1. Origins	Didactic
2. Generic functions/roles	Didactic/supervision/field/laboratory
3. Specialized models	Didactic/field/supervision/laboratory
II. Skills	
A. Preliminary exploration and contracting	Didactic/field/laboratory/supervision
B. Entry	Didactic/field/laboratory/supervision
C. Building working relationships	Didactic/field/laboratory/supervision
D. Data gathering, diagnosis, and intervention	Field/laboratory/supervision
E. Self-understanding	Field/laboratory/supervision
F. Evaluation and termination	Didactic/field/supervision
G. Ethics	Didactic/field/supervision

[a]*Didactic* methods include lectures, readings, and written assignments. *Laboratory* methods include simulations, structured exercises, role play, and video playback. *Field* refers to placement in an agency, working 8–10 hours/week as a consultant. *Supervision* refers to small-group supervision in which field placements, consultation issues, group processes, and individual styles are discussed and video playback is used.

Table 6. Consultation Theory and Processes: Course Outline

First Semester		
September 3		Distribution and discussion of syllabus and outline
September 10	9:30-12	Agencies as open systems (history and functions; openness to environment; cycles of events)
September 17	9:30-12	Subsystems: clients, management, human resources
September 24	9:30-12	Sociotechnical processes

Table 6 (Continued)

October 1	9:30-12	Adaptive mechanisms and processes
		Consultation: generic functions and roles
October 8	8:00-12	Laboratory (process observation)
October 15	8:00-12	Organizational consultation
		Laboratory: entry and contracting
October 22	9:30-12	Organizational consultation (continued)
		Mental health consultation

Small-group supervision begins.

November 5	11:00-12	Ethics
November 12	11:00-12	Evaluation
November 19	11:00-12	Practice issues
December 3	11:00-12	Practice issues
		Second Semester
January 15	9:00-12	Discussion of syllabus; process laboratory
January 22	11:00-12	Process consultation: practice issues
January 29	11:00-12	Guest speaker from a consulting firm: consultation careers
February 5	11:00-12	Workshop leadership
February 12	11:00-12	Guest speaker: consultation outreach from a university counseling center
February 19	11:00-12	Structural assessment of organizations: consultant implications
February 26	11:00-12	Panel of practicing consultants
March 4	11:00-12	Panel of consultees
March 18	11:00-12	Open systems: implications
March 25	11:00-12	Developmental perspectives of organizations: implications
April 1	11:00-12	Guest speaker, NTL training opportunities, graduate student program
April 8	11:00-12	Class reports
April 15	11:00-12	Class reports
April 22	11:00-12	Class reports
April 29	11:00-12	Wrap-up; evaluation

Table 7. Consultation: Curriculum Guide[a]

I.   Conceptual framework

         A.   Understanding agencies

                1.   *Agencies as open sociotechnical systems*
                         Demone and Harshbarger (1974)
                         Galbraith (1973)
                         Gallessich (1982), Chapter 3[b]
                         Hasenfeld and English (1975)
                         Katz and Kahn (1978)
                         Kimberly, Miles, and Associates (1980)
                         Meyer and Associates (1978)
                         Miller and Rice (1967)
                         Perrow (1970)

                2.   *Management theories/practices*
                         Blake and Mouton (1964)
                         Drucker (1980)
                         Likert (1961, 1967)
                         McGregor (1960)
                         Miringoff (1980)
                         Ouchi (1981)

                3.   *Group processes*
                         Bion (1961)
                         Hare (1976)
                         Schein (1969)
                         Zander (1977)

                4.   *Adaptive and planned-change processes*
                         Clark (1969)
                         Drucker (1980)
                         Kotter (1978)
                         Roeber (1973)

                5.   *Culture/characteristics of particular types of agencies*[c]

         B.   Understanding consultation

                1.   *Origins*
                         Gallessich (1982), Chapter 2

                2.   *Generic functions/roles; specialties*
                         Altrocchi (1972)
                         Argyris (1970)
                         Gallessich (1982), Chapters 1, 4, and
                           16

Table 7 (Continued)

---

3. *Specialized models*

    a.   *Education and training*
        Benne and others (1975)
        Cooper and Heenan (1980)
        Gallessich (1982), Chapter 5
        Pfeiffer and Jones (10 volumes of *Annual Handbooks for Group Facilitators* and 8 volumes of *A Handbook of Structured Experiences for Human Relations Training*)
        Training and Development Journal
        Training: The Magazine of Human Resources Development

    b.   *Clinical*
        Caplan (1970), Chapters 6 and 10
        Gallessich (1982), Chapter 6
        Levinson (1972)
        Mendel and Solomon (1968)

    c.   *Mental health consultation*
        Alpert (1976)
        Altrocchi (1972)
        Beisser and Green (1972)
        Caplan (1970), Chapters 7 and 11
        Gallessich (1982), Chapter 7
        Grady, Gibson, and Trickett (1981)
        Rogawski (1979)

    d.   *Behavioral consultation*
        Bergan (1977)
        Gallessich (1982), Chapter 8
        Glenwick and Jason (1980)
        Keller (1981)
        O'Brien, Dickinson, and Rosow (1982)
        Reppucci and Saunders (1974)
        Russell (1978)
        Tharp and Wetzel (1969)

    e.   *Organizational consultation*
        Argyris (1970)
        Blake and Mouton (1976)
        Consultation (a journal concerned mainly with organizational consultation)
        Gallessich (1982), Chapter 9

(continued on next page)

Table 7 (Continued)

Goodstein (1978)
Journal of Applied Behavioral Science
(issues of this journal often include articles on organizational consultation)
Lippitt and Lippitt (1978)
Merry and Allerhand (1977)
Schein (1969)

f. *Program consultation*
Anderson and Ball (1978)
Backer and Glaser (1978)
Gallessich (1982), Chapter 10
Matuzek (1981)
Rogawski (1979)

II. Skills

A. Preliminary exploration and contracting
Gallessich (1982), Chapters 11 and 12
Goodstein (1978), Chapter 5
Schein (1969), Chapter 9

B. Entry
Beisser and Green (1972), Chapter 5
Caplan (1970), Chapter 4
Gallessich (1982), Chapter 12
Glidewell (1959)
Goodstein (1978), Chapter 5

C. Building working relationships
Beisser and Green (1972), Chapter 4
Caplan (1970), Chapter 5
Ford (1979)
Gallessich (1982), Chapter 13
Levinson (1978)
Rogers (1979)
Signell and Scott (1971)
Steele (1975), Chapters 1 and 3

D. Data gathering, diagnosis, and intervention
Gallessich (1982), Chapter 14
Glaser and others (1981)
Levinson (1972)
Margulies and Raia (1972), Part Three
Merry and Allerhand (1977)
Nadler (1977)
Pfeiffer, Heslin, and Jones (1976)

Table 7 (Continued)

E. Self-understanding
    Gallessich (1982), Chapter 13
    Lippitt and Lippitt (1978), Chapter 7
    Sinha (1979)
    Steele (1975)

F. Evaluation
    Flaherty (1979)
    Gallessich (1982), Chapter 15
    Lippitt (1981b)
    Lockwood and Luthans (1980)
    Meyers (1974)
    Nicholas (1979)
    Schmuck and others (1972), Chapter 10
    Swartz and Lippitt (1979)

G. Termination
    Argyris (1970), Chapter 16
    Bell and Nadler (1979), Part Six
    Gallessich (1982), Chapter 15

H. Ethics
    Bermant, Kelman, and Warwick (1978)
    Bowen (1977)
    Fanibanda (1976)
    Gallessich (1982), Chapters 16 and 17
    Glaser (1981)
    Kelman (1969)
    Lippitt and Lippitt (1978), Chapter 5

---

[a]Complete bibliographic information is provided in the references at the end of this book.

[b]Gallessich (1982) entries refer to chapters in this book.

[c]Readers may contact the author for a list of references on various types of human services organizations.

Curriculum Guide," lists references for each major topic. Following the outline of this book, the topics include agencies as open sociotechnical systems, management theory and practice, group processes, planned change, and the culture of particular types of agencies, such as schools, police organizations, and volunteer organizations. The second major topic is consultation theory. The origins and generic functions of consultation are explored, and six specialized models (clinical, mental health, behavioral, education and training, program-centered, and organization-centered) are examined and compared.

Midway through the fall semester, laboratory work begins, and the concepts presented earlier (such as group processes and consultant roles and processes) are related to and integrated with the experiences that evolve through the structured laboratory format, which includes use of videotape playback facilities. In addition, new topics related to skills building are introduced both through didactic means and through laboratory experiences (see Table 6). Some students—usually those from counseling and clinical programs—enter this course well prepared with interpersonal skills because of previous practicum experiences that stress feedback on personal style and interpersonal skills training. Students from programs that do not emphasize interpersonal skills and the effect of individual style on professional behavior need additional laboratory training and feedback. (Another way of managing the wide range of interpersonal competencies is to use this variable as the basis for determining composition of the small supervisory groups so that experiences in these groups can be better tailored to fit student needs.)

By the eighth week, small-group supervision begins, and students prepare to enter field settings. The fieldwork provides opportunities to practice skills and apply concepts. Small-group supervision helps students organize their experiences and develop skills in analyzing consultation processes, in pinpointing choice points, and in weighing the consequences of alternative actions. Increasingly they learn to make decisions based both on a theoretical framework and on a realistic assessment of the actual field situation. Papers are assigned to help students conceptualize their experiences. An early assignment requires students to write a systematic description of their agencies and of their emergent contract. They are given the following guidelines:

1. *Organization.* Name, type, primary purpose, services, or products.
2. *Clients.* Characteristics.
3. *Environment.* Identify the important environmental forces

influencing the organization and the nature of their impact (for example, federal laws and/or funding contingencies, political events).

4. *Location.* Characteristics of immediate neighborhood and any implications for organization.

5. *Physical plant.* Salient characteristics and their impact on productivity and morale.

6. *Services technology.* Describe the major features of the service delivery processes.

7. *Administrative structure.* Describe and draw a simplified organizational chart.

8. *Chief administrator.* Professional training and experience, dominant values, concerns, subgroups, norms.

9. *Staff.* Background of professional training and experience, dominant values, concerns, subgroups, norms.

10. *Entry process.* Describe the processes. How were you received and how are you perceived? What can you say about the openness of the agency to you? What are your personal reactions?

11. *Contract.* Exactly what is your contract at this point? Objectives? Your functions and role? Time set for renegotiation?

12. *Growth opportunities.* How do you think you can best use this contract for your own professional development?

At the end of the first semester, students also write an integrative paper in which they relate their field observations and experiences to theory through discussing such topics as the effects of their behaviors on the development of a relationship with a consultee or their difficulties or successes in following a particular model of consultation.

In the second semester, except for a few didactic presentations by guest speakers (experienced consultants), conceptual input is informal and closely connected to students' field experiences and concerns in the small supervisory group. The small group is the major vehicle for accomplishment of course goals in the second semester. It serves a variety of functions. The supervisory responsibility is, of course, paramount in fostering the development of competent, ethical practices and the integration of theory and practice. The intensive small group is a substitute for the apprenticeship model; it allows supervisors to monitor and guide student progress. The major drawback is that the student does not have an opportunity to observe the supervisor in continuous real-life practice and therefore misses the vivid modeling that facilitates learning. However, supervisors describe their own work and provide modeling through role-play demonstrations.

In addition, the small group provides the following benefits: (1) Peer feedback, an important catalyst for increasing awareness of impact and for stimulating professional development (Gallessich and MacDonald, 1981). Usually this feedback is sensitive and perceptive, and it is often easier to accept than criticism from supervisors. To generate more abundant data for peer feedback, trainees often form two- or three-person teams, and team members accompany each other to field placements once each semester for the purpose of observation and feedback. (2) Opportunities to sharpen skills in critiquing consultation practices through analyses of the experiences of the different group members, often easier through focus on others than when the focus is on self. (3) Exposure to different styles of consultation. (4) Experience in working with members of different specialty areas, thus building a basis for future collaboration. (5) An opportunity to learn about the operations of a number of organizations through the reports of other members of the group.

Another advantage of the small-group supervision is that the group provides an analogue to the field placement but with conditions that are more amenable to trainee insight and change. Any systemic interpersonal difficulties or "themes" arising in the trainees' field setting often arise also in the group context in a more clear form than is possible in the context of one-to-one supervision. For example, there may be authority problems or subgroup conflicts, or a student's particular style may be counterproductive. The group then becomes an analogue for identifying and interpreting behaviors and provides support for trying out new insights and behaviors.

The instructor of this course sometimes makes arrangements for the field placement. However, students often initiate contacts with agencies to explore consultation possibilities. Each arrangement has costs and benefits. In the supervisor-initiated contact, for example, the agency administrator is often more likely to accept a trainee, but the trainee may have to work harder to be recognized and legitimized. In student-initiated contacts, the "student" status is minimized. One drawback, however, is that the supervisor in these situations may have less knowledge of the field placement. Most students work in only one field setting. However, some work in two or more, either sequentially or simultaneously. Sometimes the extra setting involves team consultation, in which two trainees share consultation responsibilities. Team consultation and an additional site increase the data for feedback and for learning about systems and are a valuable supplement to the primary placement.

Several types of evaluation are used with this course. The "Consultant Self-Assessment Form," Table 8, is administered at

Table 8. Consultant Self-Assessment Form

1 = little knowledge and skill
5 = great knowledge and skill

1. Self-awareness: Awareness of personal needs that might be served in the consultative relationship (and perhaps limit effectiveness).	1 2 3 4 5
2. Skill in organizational assessment: Ability to identify salient organizational characteristics through various kinds of data gathering.	1 2 3 4 5
3. Knowledge of alternative methods of consultative intervention: Understanding of a number of consultative models, their assumptions, values, strategies, strengths, and weaknesses.	1 2 3 4 5
4. Awareness of training and experience biases that affect your perceptions and decisions (thus affecting your consultation).	1 2 3 4 5
5. Entry: Knowledge of entry processes—awareness of the organizational variables and the consultant variables affecting the entry into an organization.	1 2 3 4 5

(continued on next page)

Table 8 (Continued)

6. Contractual skills: Knowledge of the basic elements of a consultative contract and ability to negotiate contracts, including renegotiation and termination. Clarity about boundaries.	1 2 3 4 5
7. Ethics and values: Understanding of ethical issues related to consultation and ability to establish and maintain explicit values. Clarity and ethical behavior in relation to value conflicts.	1 2 3 4 5
8. Relationship-building skills: Ability to develop and to maintain constructive working relationships with consultees.	1 2 3 4 5
9. Team-building skills: Ability to build a team that provides both mutual support and challenge to consultants.	1 2 3 4 5
10. Evaluation skills: Ability to use formal and informal feedback mechanisms to monitor the consultative performance.	1 2 3 4 5
11. Termination of consultative relationship: Knowledge of the termination process and skill in termination with consultees.	1 2 3 4 5
12. Skill in mental health consultation.	1 2 3 4 5
13. Skill in workshop leadership.	1 2 3 4 5
14. Skill in process consultation.	1 2 3 4 5

the beginning of the year, midway, and at the end of the year to obtain a self-reported assessment of initial competencies and changes during the year. This form evaluates growth of students and the effectiveness of the training also. A questionnaire is administered at the end of the year to evaluate the effectiveness of the various training methods. In addition, students usually administer the "Consultation Evaluation Survey" (Table 9) to obtain feedback from consultees.

Table 9. Consultation Evaluation Survey

Confidential

The following information is being collected to assess services provided by consultation training interns from the Educational Psychology Department of the University of Texas. *Please answer as candidly as pos-*

Table 9 (Continued)

sible. Your responses are completely confidential. Your name or other identification is not needed. Your responses will *not* influence the grade received by your consultant intern, and they will not be seen by her/him. Grades in this course are on a credit/noncredit basis. Your responses will be pooled with others and the results will be reported to your consultant. Your responses will provide valuable feedback to your consultant and help the faculty responsible for training to evaluate the training program.

Your organization _____ Date _____

Consultant's name _____

Number of years you have worked in this type of organization _____

Sex (circle one):   Male   Female

Have you had previous experience with consultants?   Yes   No

To what extent have you made use of the consultant this year?

_____ Not at all
_____ Very little, 1 or 2 times
_____ To a moderate extent, about 3 to 6 times
_____ To a considerable extent, about 6 to 10 times
_____ To a great extent, more than 10 times

In general, how helpful has the consultant been to you? (Circle the number that is most descriptive)

Not at all   1 2 3 4 5 6 7   Very helpful

Did you work with the consultant in a group situation?   Yes   No

Did you work with the consultant on an individual basis?   Yes   No

Please respond to the following items by circling the number that best describes your perception of your consultant. Response options range from 1 (not at all descriptive) to 7 (very descriptive). If an item does not seem applicable to your consultation, circle N.A.

The consultant:

1. Offers useful information.   1 2 3 4 5 6 7 N.A.

2. Understands my working environment.   1 2 3 4 5 6 7 N.A.

3. Presses his/her ideas and solutions.   1 2 3 4 5 6 7 N.A.

(continued on next page)

Table 9 (Continued)

---

4. Is skilled in forming good working relationships.   1 2 3 4 5 6 7 N.A.

5. Is a good listener.   1 2 3 4 5 6 7 N.A.

6. Helps me find alternative solutions to problems.   1 2 3 4 5 6 7 N.A.

7. Increases my self-confidence.   1 2 3 4 5 6 7 N.A.

8. Helps me identify resources to use in problem solving.   1 2 3 4 5 6 7 N.A.

9. Is not concerned with my point of view.   1 2 3 4 5 6 7 N.A.

10. Encourages me to make my own decisions.   1 2 3 4 5 6 7 N.A.

11. Helps me find ways to apply content of our discussions to specific situations.   1 2 3 4 5 6 7 N.A.

12. Respects values that are different from his/hers.   1 2 3 4 5 6 7 N.A.

13. Fits easily into our work setting.   1 2 3 4 5 6 7 N.A.

14. Stimulates me to see situations in more complex ways.   1 2 3 4 5 6 7 N.A.

15. Relies on one approach to solving problems.   1 2 3 4 5 6 7 N.A.

16. Explains his/her ideas clearly.   1 2 3 4 5 6 7 N.A.

17. Has difficulty understanding my concerns.   1 2 3 4 5 6 7 N.A.

18. Encourages me to try a variety of interventions.   1 2 3 4 5 6 7 N.A.

19. Helps me in ways consistent with my own needs.   1 2 3 4 5 6 7 N.A.

20. Encourages communication between me and others with whom I work.   1 2 3 4 5 6 7 N.A.

21. Increases my understanding of basic psychological principles.   1 2 3 4 5 6 7 N.A.

22. Makes helpful suggestions.   1 2 3 4 5 6 7 N.A.

23. Does not appreciate the pressures of my job.   1 2 3 4 5 6 7 N.A.

24. Makes me feel comfortable in discussing sensitive problems.   1 2 3 4 5 6 7 N.A.

25. Encourages our work group to cooperate.   1 2 3 4 5 6 7 N.A.

Table 9 (Continued)

26. Supports my efforts to solve problems.	1 2 3 4 5 6 7 N.A.
27. Has knowledge relevant to my work.	1 2 3 4 5 6 7 N.A.
28. Helps me understand myself better.	1 2 3 4 5 6 7 N.A.
29. Helps me develop a wider range of problem-solving skills.	1 2 3 4 5 6 7 N.A.
30. Rushes into premature solutions.	1 2 3 4 5 6 7 N.A.
31. Is sensitive to my feelings.	1 2 3 4 5 6 7 N.A.
32. Helps me see my situation more objectively.	1 2 3 4 5 6 7 N.A.
33. Knows how and when to ask good questions.	1 2 3 4 5 6 7 N.A.
34. Is reliable about appointments.	1 2 3 4 5 6 7 N.A.

Methods of consultation vary with each consultant, and sometimes a consultant uses a combination of methods to offer services. Indicate which of the following methods your consultant uses (1) most frequently, (2) second most frequently, (3) third in order of frequency, and (4) least frequently. Place a 1, 2, 3, or 4 before each category to indicate your perceptions of your consultant's methods:

_____ Category A Gives information, supplements knowledge, offers advice.

_____ Category B Helps me understand problems and find various ways to solve problems; encourages me to make decisions as to which solutions to use.

_____ Category C Works out a plan for me to follow in solving a problem; coordinates my activities.

_____ Category D Evaluates my performance.

Please indicate by rank order (1, 2, 3, or 4) your preference as to consultation method:

_____ Category A Gives information, supplements knowledge, offers advice.

_____ Category B Helps me understand problems and find various ways to solve problems; encourages me to make decisions as to which solutions to use.

_____ Category C Works out a plan for me to follow in solving a problem; coordinates my activities.

_____ Category D Evaluates my performance.

(continued on next page)

Table 9 (Continued)

This consultant will be consulting in the future. What suggestions do you have to help him/her improve in consultation skills? Remember, this information will NOT be used for grading; it will be extremely helpful to your consultant as feedback.

What did you like most about his/her work?

What did you like least about his/her work?

If you did not use this consultant, why not?

Training for Tomorrow: A Doctoral Program in Consultation. For the profession of consultation to continue to develop, it must eventually be recognized as an independent discipline. The two patterns described earlier—traditional intraprofessional training and innovative, interdisciplinary training—have helped consultation evolve. They have given it stability, expanded its peripheries, and helped it respond to societal needs. Contributions from both these patterns will be needed in the future. But a third pattern—university based training for consultation as an independent field—will be needed to legitimize the profession, to strengthen its scientific foundations, and to integrate and systematize the bodies of knowledge that are now scattered across different fields.

A proposal that anticipates this next development is presented in Table 10. This four-year program would lead to a Ph.D. in Consultation in Human Services Agencies. The coursework provides a comprehensive background in consultation and includes generic theory and process and the concepts and practices of several specialized models.

Students learn about organizations through a two-semester core in social systems and electives in specialized organizations, such as federal agencies or religious organizations. A basic course

Table 10. Proposed Program of Work Leading to a Ph.D. in
Consultation to Human Services Agencies

Courses	Semester hours
Consultation theory and process	
Required The social role of the consultant; generic theory and process	3
Laboratory: consultation processes	3
Electives 3 electives to be taken from such courses as the following: behavioral, mental health, or organizational consultation; human resource development; laboratory training (each course to be 4 semester hours and to include a theoretical component, a review of research, and a field placement or practicum)	12
Organizational theory	
Required 2 courses in social systems, including open-systems, sociological, and psychological theories of organizations	6
Electives 2 electives to be taken from such courses as the following: public health agencies, educational agencies, private-sector human services, law enforcement agencies	6
Management	
Required Management theory	3
Conflict management	3
Electives 2 courses in special areas of management, such as management of health services or management of decline	6
Government	
Required Social policy	3
Elective A second government course, such as political science or community organizing	3
Interviewing	
Required Interviewing theory and research	3
Interviewing skills laboratory	3
Group process	
Required Theory and research	3
Group experience course	3

(continued on next page)

Table 10 (Continued)

Courses	Semester hours
Quantitative methods	
Required 2 courses in basic research theory and methods	6
a consultation research project	3
2 courses in evaluation models and methods	6
a consultation intervention evaluation project	3
Minor To be selected from such fields as management, social work, nursing, psychology, religion, sociology, communications, business administration, special education	18
Dissertation	12
Internship (one year full-time or two years half-time in a supervised field placement)	12
Total semester hours	120

in management theory and one in conflict management are required, as well as electives in particular management topics—such as management in law enforcement agencies or management of decline. A required course and an elective in government add an important social perspective. Required courses in group processes and interviewing equip students with both theoretical and interpersonal competencies in these areas. Four basic courses in research and evaluation (including design, measurement, and statistical methods) and projects requiring the application of research and evaluation skills prepare students to be effective practitioners and scientists who can contribute to the body of consultation knowledge. These courses are also essential in preparing students for the dissertation.

Students elect a minor in an appropriate field, such as social work or communications, to give them expertise in a second discipline. The minor is chosen to fit students' internship and career plans. Students apply newly acquired concepts and skills in an internship. This internship, a full-time twelve-month placement or a half-time placement for two years, is supervised by consultation faculty members. The dissertation requirement includes a strong recommendation that the research topic be related to some aspect of consultation.

This program could be most easily implemented as an interdisciplinary program in which several academic departments participate. Some of the courses could be offered through a cooperative arrangement with nontraditional organizations or with human services agencies. For persons who already have doctorates in some fields (for instance, management or sociology) the course of work listed in Table 10 could be modified to create a one- or two-year postdoctoral program.

Annotated Bibliography

Alpert, J. L., and Meyers, J. (Eds.). *Training in Consultation.* Springfield, Ill.: Charles C Thomas, in press. This volume includes the papers presented at the National Conference on Consultation held in Montreal in 1980 and the editors' commentaries on the training issues discussed in this landmark event.

Campbell, S. "Graduate Programs in Applied Behavioral Science: A Directory." In J. W. Pfeiffer and J. E. Jones (Eds.), *The 1978 Annual Handbook for Group Facilitators.* San Diego, Calif.: University Associates, 1978. Campbell surveyed members of the International Association of Applied Social Scientists to obtain information about graduate programs in such areas as organization development, human relations training, and laboratory education. She then sent questionnaires to the directors of the programs thus identified. The responses of these directors are reported in this article, including the degree offered in each program, its content areas, value orientations, accreditation, approximate enrollment, and residency requirements. This article is of interest to persons seeking training in fields related to consultation and is useful in assessing the recent growth of programs in these fields.

Conoley, J. C. "Emergent Training Issues in Consultation." In J. C. Conoley (Ed.), *Consultation in Schools: Theory, Research, Procedures.* New York: Academic Press, 1981. Conoley outlines and discusses some of the major issues in consultation training. Of particular value is a table that identifies needed competencies, relevant learning experiences, and methods for assessment of trainees' acquisition of competencies.

Gallessich, J. "Training the School Psychologist for Consultation." *Journal of School Psychology*, 1974, *12* (2), 138-149. This article reviews currently popular consultation models and their implications for training and describes a training model that provides theoretical and experiential preparation for a broadly conceived approach to consultation.

Gallessich, J., and Ladogana, A. "Consultation Training Program for School Counselors." *Counselor Education and Supervision*, 1978, *18*, 100-108. This article describes outcomes of two consultation training models: a 65-hour pilot program and a 35-hour revised form of the earlier model. The authors draw on the experiences and outcomes of this project to recommend sequential models for consultation training.

Gallessich, J., and MacDonald, J. "Facilitating Professional Development Through Group Analogic Methods." *Professional Psychology*, 1981, *12* (2), 209-215. The authors describe the use of a group analogic method in helping consultant trainees with such developmental tasks as appropriate assumption of responsibility.

Lippitt, G., and Lippitt, R. *The Consulting Process in Action*. San Diego, Calif.: University Associates, 1978. In chap. 7, "The Consultant's Skills, Competencies, and Development," the authors present criteria for assessing consultants' capabilities and list a number of skills and qualities that they consider related to effectiveness in the consultant role.

Appendix

Organizations Concerned with Consultation

American Society for Training and Development
    600 Maryland Avenue, S.W., Suite 305
    Washington, D.C. 20024
    (202) 484-2390

Certified Consultants International
    Box 1625, Station B
    Nashville, Tennessee 37235
    (615) 322-4978

Development Publications
    5605 Lamar Road
    Bethesda, Maryland 20816
    (301) 320-4409

Division of Consulting Psychology
    American Psychological Association
    631 A Street, S.E.
    Washington, D.C. 20003
    (202) 547-8808

Managerial Consultation Division
    Academy of Management
    Dr. R. A. Fosgren, Director of Membership
    College of Business Administration
    University of Maine
    Orono, Maine 04473
    (207) 581-7958

NTL Institute
    P.O. Box 9155
    Rosslyn Station
    Arlington, Virginia 22209
    (703) 527-1500

OD Network
    1011 Park Avenue
    Plainfield, New Jersey 07060
    (201) 561-8677

University Associates: Publishers and Consultants
    8517 Production Avenue
    P.O. Box 26240
    San Diego, California 92126
    (800) 854-2143

References

Abrahamson, S. "Methods of Teaching." In W. M. Mendel and P. Solomon (Eds.), *The Psychiatric Consultation.* New York: Grune & Stratton, 1968.

Ahmed, P., and Tims, F. "Some Considerations in Evaluating School Consultation Programs." In S. Plog and P. Ahmed (Eds.), *Principles and Techniques of Mental Health Consultation.* New York: Plenum Medical Book Co., 1977.

Aiken, J. "Community Outreach via a University-Based Counseling Center." Paper presented at 82nd annual meeting of American Psychological Association, New Orleans, August 1974.

Alderfer, C. "Organization Development." *Annual Review of Psychology,* 1977, *28,* 197-223.

Alderfer, C. "Comments on the Preceding Article: The Marketing Orientation of OD." *Journal of Applied Behavioral Science,* 1981, *17* (3), 324-325.

Aldrich, C. K. "A Specialized Teaching Program for Residents in Psychiatry." In W. M. Mendel and P. Solomon (Eds.), *The Psychiatric Consultation.* New York: Grune & Stratton, 1968.

439

Alpert, J. L. "Conceptual Bases of Mental Health Consultation in the Schools." *Professional Psychology,* 1976, 7 (4), 619-626.

Alpert, J. L. "Training and Conducting Research in Consultation: Can They Be Done Simultaneously?" Paper presented at 85th annual meeting of American Psychological Association, San Francisco, September 1977.

Alpert, J. L., and Meyers, J. (Eds.). *Training in Consultation.* Springfield, Ill.: Thomas, in press.

Altrocchi, J. "Mental Health Consultation." In S. E. Golann and C. Eisdorfer (Eds.), *Handbook of Community Mental Health.* New York: Appleton-Century-Crofts, 1972.

Altrocchi, J., Spielberger, C. D., and Eisdorfer, C. "Mental Health Consultation with Groups." *Community Mental Health Journal,* 1965, *1,* 127-134.

Anderson, S. B., and Ball, S. *The Profession and Practice of Program Evaluation.* San Francisco: Jossey-Bass, 1978.

Argyris, C. *Intervention Theory and Method: A Behavioral Science View.* Reading, Mass.: Addison-Wesley, 1970.

Arnold, W. J. "From the Outside, Looking In." *Academic Consultants' Communique,* 1981, *9* (2), 2.

Atkisson, C. C. *Evaluation of Human Service Programs.* New York: Academic Press, 1978.

Bacharach, S. B., and Lawler, E. J. *Power and Politics in Organizations: The Social Psychology of Conflict, Coalitions, and Bargaining.* San Francisco: Jossey-Bass, 1980.

Backer, T. E. "Organizational Consultation: Where We Stand in 1981." *Consultation,* 1981, *1* (1), 5-11.

Backer, T. E., and Glaser, E. M. (Eds.). *Proceedings of the Advanced Workshop on Program Consultation in Mental Health Services.* Los Angeles: Publication sponsored by National Institute of Mental Health, Mental Health Services Development Branch, and Human Interaction Research Institute, 1978.

Bales, R. F. *Interaction Process Analysis.* Reading, Mass.: Addison-Wesley, 1950.

Bandura, A. *Social Learning Theory.* Englewood Cliffs, N.J.: Prentice-Hall, 1977.

Bard, M., and Berkowitz, B. "A Community Psychology Consultation Program in Police Family Crisis Intervention: Preliminary Impressions." *International Journal of Social Psychiatry*, 1969, *15*, 209-215.

Bardon, J. I. "The Consultee in Consultation: Preparation and Training." Paper presented at 85th annual meeting of American Psychological Association, San Francisco, September 1977.

Barnes, R. H., Busse, E. W., and Bressler, B. "The Training of Psychiatric Residents in Consultative Skills." *Journal of Medical Education*, 1957, *32* (2), 124-130.

Barnet, R. J. *The Lean Years.* New York: Simon & Schuster, 1980.

Bass, B. M. "A Systems Survey Research Feedback for Management and Organization Development." *Journal of Applied Behavioral Science*, 1976, *12*, 215-229.

Bass, B. M., and Barrett, G. V. *Man, Work, and Organization: An Introduction to Industrial and Organizational Psychology.* Boston: Allyn & Bacon, 1972.

Bass, B. M., and Valenzi, E. R. "Contingency Aspects of Effective Management Styles." In J. G. Hunt and L. Larson (Eds.), *Contingency Approaches to Leadership.* Carbondale: Southern Illinois University Press, 1974.

Beckhard, R. "The Confrontation Meeting." *Harvard Business Review*, 1967, *45*, 149-155.

Beckhard, R. *Organization Development: Strategies and Models.* Reading, Mass.: Addison-Wesley, 1969.

Beckhard, R. "Organization Development in Large Systems." In K. D. Benne and others (Eds.), *The Laboratory Method of Changing and Learning: Theory and Application.* Palo Alto, Calif.: Science and Behavior Books, 1975.

Beer, M. "The Technology of Organizational Development." In M. D. Dunnette (Ed.), *Handbook of Industrial and Organizational Psychology.* Chicago: Rand McNally, 1976.

Beisser, A., and Green, R. *Mental Health Consultation and Education.* Palo Alto, Calif.: National Press Books, 1972.

Bell, C. R., and Nadler, L. (Eds.). *The Client-Consultant Handbook.* Houston: Gulf Publishing Co., 1979.

Benne, K. D. "Some Ethical Problems in Group and Organizational Consultation." In W. G. Bennis, K. D. Benne, and R. Chin (Eds.), *The Planning of Change.* New York: Holt, Rinehart and Winston, 1969.

Benne, K. D., and others (Eds.). *The Laboratory Method of Changing and Learning.* Palo Alto, Calif.: Science and Behavior Books, 1975.

Bennis, W. G. *Organizational Development: Its Nature, Origins, and Prospects.* Reading, Mass.: Addison-Wesley, 1969a.

Bennis, W. G. "Unsolved Problems in Organizational Development." *The Business Quarterly,* Winter 1969b, 80-84.

Bennis, W. G., Benne, K. D., and Chin, R. (Eds.). *The Planning of Change.* (2nd ed.) New York: Holt, Rinehart and Winston, 1969.

Bergan, J. R. *Behavioral Consultation.* Columbus, Ohio: Merrill, 1977.

Bergan, J. R., and Tombari, M. "Consultant Skill and Efficiency and the Implementation and Outcomes of Consultation." *Journal of School Psychology,* 1976, *14* (1), 3-13.

Berlin, I. N. "An Effort to Update Mental Health Consultation Methods." Unpublished paper, 1973.

Bermant, G., Kelman, H. C., and Warwick, D. P. (Eds.). *The Ethics of Social Intervention.* Washington, D.C.: Hemisphere, 1978.

Berne, E. *Games People Play.* New York: Grove Press, 1964.

Bernstein, S. B., and MacLennan, B. "Community Psychiatry with the Communications Media." *American Journal of Psychiatry,* 1971, *128* (6), 722-727.

Bidwell, C. "The School as a Formal Organization." In J. G. March (Ed.), *Handbook of Organizations.* Chicago: Rand McNally, 1965.

Bion, W. R. *Experiences in Groups.* New York: Basic Books, 1961.

Birney, D. H. "The Effects of Consultee-Centered Administrative Consultation on the Supervisory Effectiveness of the Directors of Child Development Centers." Unpublished doctoral dissertation, Department of Educational Psychology, University of Texas at Austin, 1977.

Blake, R. R., and Mouton, J. S. *The Managerial Grid.* Houston: Gulf Publishing Co., 1964.

Blake, R. R., and Mouton, J. S. *Consultation.* Reading, Mass.: Addison-Wesley, 1976.

Bockoven, J. S. *Moral Treatment in Community Mental Health.* New York: Springer, 1972.

Boss, R. W. "It Doesn't Matter if You Win or Lose, Unless You're Losing: Organizational Change in a Law Enforcement Agency." *Journal of Applied Behavioral Science,* 1979, *15* (2), 198-220.

Bowen, D. D. "Value Dilemmas in Organization Development." *Journal of Applied Behavioral Science,* 1977, *13,* 545-558.

Bowers, D. G. "O.D. Techniques and Their Results in 23 Organizations: The Michigan ICL Study." *Journal of Applied Behavioral Science,* 1973, *9* (1), 21-43.

Bradford, L. P., Gibb, J. R., and Benne, K. D. (Eds.). *T-Group Theory and Laboratory Method.* New York: Wiley, 1964.

Brodsky, S. L. "The Ambivalent Consultee: The Special Problems of Consultation to Criminal Justice Agencies." In S. C. Plog and P. I. Ahmed (Eds.), *Principles and Techniques of Mental Health Consultation.* New York: Plenum Medical Book Co., 1977.

Brookover, W. B., and Erickson, E. L. *Sociology of Education.* Homewood, Ill.: Dorsey Press, 1975.

Brosin, H. W. "Communication Systems of the Consultation Process." In W. M. Mendel and P. Solomon (Eds.), *The Psychiatric Consultation.* New York: Grune & Stratton, 1968.

Broskowski, A., Khajavi, F., and Mehryar, A. "An Evaluation of an In-Service Training Seminar on Community Consultation and Education." *Journal of Community Psychology,* 1973, *1* (2), 174-176.

Budson, R. D. "Consultation to Halfway Houses." In A. S. Rogawski (Ed.), *New Directions for Mental Health Services: Mental Health Consultations in Community Settings,* no. 3. San Francisco: Jossey-Bass, 1979.

Burke, W. W. (Ed.). *The Cutting Edge: Current Theory and Practice in Organization Development.* San Diego, Calif.: University Associates, 1978.

Burke, W. W. "Organization Development and Bureaucracy in the 1980s." *Journal of Applied Behavioral Science,* 1980, *16* (3), 423-437.

Burns, T., and Stalker, G. M. *The Management of Innovation.* London: Tavistock, 1961.

Campbell, D. T., and Stanley, J. C. *Experimental and Quasi-Experimental Designs for Research.* Chicago: Rand McNally, 1966.

Campbell, S. "Graduate Programs in Applied Behavioral Science: A Directory." In J. W. Pfeiffer and J. E. Jones (Eds.), *The 1978 Annual Handbook for Group Facilitators.* San Diego, Calif.: University Associates, 1978.

Cannell, C. F., and Kahn, R. L. "The Collection of Data by Interviewing." In N. Margulies and A. P. Raia (Eds.), *Organizational Development: Values, Process, and Technology.* New York: McGraw-Hill, 1972.

Caplan, G. *Principles of Preventive Psychiatry.* New York: Basic Books, 1964.

Caplan, G. *The Theory and Practice of Mental Health Consultation.* New York: Basic Books, 1970.

Caplan, G. "Mental Health Consultation: Retrospect and Prospect." In S. C. Plog and P. I. Ahmed (Eds.), *Principles and Techniques of Mental Health Consultation.* New York: Plenum Medical Book Co., 1977.

Caplan, R. B. *Psychiatry and the Community in Nineteenth Century America: The Recurring Concern with the Environment in the Prevention and Treatment of Mental Illness.* New York: Basic Books, 1969.

Caplan, R. B. *Helping Helpers to Help.* New York: Seabury Press, 1972.

Carter, B. D., and Cazares, P. R. "Consultation in Community Mental Health." *Community Mental Health Review,* 1976, *1* (5), 4-13.

Case, J., and Taylor, R. C. R. (Eds.). *Co-ops, Communes, and Collectives.* New York: Pantheon Books, 1979.

Chandy, J. M. "The Effects of an In-Service Orientation on Teacher Perception and Use of the Mental Health Consultant." Unpublished doctoral dissertation, Department of Educational Psychology, University of Texas at Austin, 1974.

Cherniss, C. "The Consultation Readiness Scale: An Attempt to Improve Consultation Practice." *American Journal of Community Psychology,* 1978, *6* (1), 15-21.

Chesler, M. A., and Arnstein, F. "The School Consultant: Change Agent or Defender of the Status Quo?" *Integrated Education,* 1970, *8* (4), 19-25.

Chesler, M. A., Bryant, B. I., and Crowfoot, J. E. "Consultation in Schools: Inevitable Conflict, Partisanship, and Advocacy." Paper presented at 83rd annual meeting of American Psychological Association, Chicago, August 1975.

Chin, R., and Benne, K. D. "General Strategies for Effecting Change in Human Systems." In W. G. Bennis, K. D. Benne, and R. Chin (Eds.), *The Planning of Change.* (2nd ed.) New York: Holt, Rinehart and Winston, 1969.

Clark, C. C. "Reframing." *Ameican Journal of Nursing,* 1977, 77 (5), 840-841.

Clark, J. V. "A Healthy Organization." In W. G. Bennis, K. D. Benne, and R. Chin (Eds.), *The Planning of Change.* (2nd ed.) New York: Holt, Rinehart and Winston, 1969.

Cohen, J., and Cohen, P. *Applied Multiple Regression/Correlation Analysis for the Behavioral Sciences.* Hillsdale, N.J.: Erlbaum, 1975.

Colligan, R. "Training School Psychologists for Consultation." Paper presented at 81st annual meeting of American Psychological Association, Montreal, Ont., August 1973.

Comptroller General of the United States. *Government Earns Low Marks on Proper Use of Consultants.* Washington, D.C.: U.S. General Accounting Office (GAO Report No. FPCD-80-48), 1980.

Conoley, J. C. (Ed.). *Consultation in Schools: Theory, Research, Procedures.* New York: Academic Press, 1981a.

Conoley, J. C. "Emergent Training Issues in Consultation." In J. C. Conoley (Ed.), *Consultation in Schools: Theory, Research, Procedures.* New York: Academic Press, 1981b.

Cooper, C. L., and Marshall, J. (Eds.). *White Collar and Professional Stress.* New York: Wiley, 1980.

Cooper, S., and Heenan, C. *Preparing, Designing, Leading Workshops.* Boston: CBI Publishing, 1980.

Cotton, C. C., Browne, P. J., and Golembiewski, R. T. "Marginality and the OD Practitioner." *Journal of Applied Behavioral Science,* 1977, *13* (4), 493-506.

Cremin, L. A. *The Transformation of the School.* New York: Random House, 1961.

Cronbach, L. J. *Essentials of Psychological Testing.* (3rd ed.) New York: Harper & Row, 1970.

Cronbach, L. J., and Snow, S. E. *Aptitudes and Instructional Methods.* New York: Irvington, 1977.

Crowfoot, J. E., and Chesler, M. A. "Contemporary Perspectives on Planned Social Change: A Comparison." *Journal of Applied Behavioral Science,* 1974, *10* (3), 278-303.

Curtis, M. J., and Zins, J. E. (Eds.). *The Theory and Practice of School Consultation.* Springfield, Ill.: Thomas, 1981.

Davidson, G. O., and Kreul, R. W. "Pastoral Care and Community Mental Health." *AMHC Forum,* 1976, *23* (3), 89-92.

Davis, J. M., and Sandoval, J. "Metaphor in Group Mental Health Consultation." *Journal of Community Psychology,* 1978, *6,* 374-382.

Davison, G. C., and Stuart, R. B. "Behavior Therapy and Civil Liberties." *American Psychologist,* 1975, *30,* 755-763.

Demone, H. W., and Harshbarger, D. "Issues in the Management and Planning of Human Service Organizations." In H. W. Demone and D. Harshbarger (Eds.), *A Handbook of Human Service Organizations.* New York: Behavioral Publications, 1974.

Dorr, D. "Training for Rapid Behavioral Consultation." *Professional Psychology,* 1978, *9* (2), 198-202.

Douglas, M. E. "Stress and Personal Performance." *Personal Administrator,* 1977, *22,* 60-63.

Drucker, P. F. *The Practice of Management.* New York: Harper & Row, 1954.

Drucker, P. F. *Managing in Turbulent Times.* New York: Harper & Row, 1980.

Dworkin, A. L., and Dworkin, E. P. "A Conceptual Overview of Selected Consultation Models." *American Journal of Community Psychology,* 1975, *3* (2), 151-159.

Eldridge, J. E., and Crombie, A. D. *A Sociology of Organisations.* London: Allen & Unwin, 1974.

Emery, R. E., and Marholin, D. "An Applied Behavior Analysis of Delinquency." *American Psychologist,* 1977, *32* (10), 860-873.

English, J. "Mental Health Consultation with a Government Agency." In W. M. Mendel and P. Solomon (Eds.), *The Psychiatric Consultation.* New York: Grune & Stratton, 1968.

"Ethical Standards of Psychologists." Washington, D.C.: American Psychological Association, 1972.

Etzioni, A. *A Comparative Analysis of Complex Organizations.* New York: Free Press, 1961.

Everett, P. B., Hayward, S. C., and Meyers, A. W. "The Effects of a Token Reinforcement Procedure on Bus Ridership." *Journal of Applied Behavioral Analysis,* 1974, *7,* 1-9.

Eysenck, H. J. "The Effects of Psychotherapy: An Evaluation." *Journal of Consulting Psychology,* 1952, *16,* 319-324.

Eysenck, H. J. "The Effects of Psychotherapy." In H. J. Eysenck (Ed.), *Handbook of Abnormal Psychology.* New York: Basic Books, 1961.

Fanibanda, D. K. "Ethical Issues of Mental Health Consultation." *Professional Psychology,* 1976, *7,* 547-552.

Faust, V. *The Counselor-Consultant in the Elementary School.* Boston: Houghton Mifflin, 1968.

Feiner, J. S., and Tarnow, J. D. "Expanding the Base for Child Mental Health Service and Training." *Journal of Special Education,* 1977, *11* (1), 49-58.

Feldman, R. E. "Collaborative Consultation: A Process for Joint Professional-Consumer Development of Primary Prevention Programs." *Journal of Community Psychology,* 1979, *7,* 118-128.

Fenster, C. A., and Schlossberg, H. "The Psychologist as Police Department Consultant." In J. J. Platt and R. J. Wicks (Eds.), *The Psychological Consultant.* New York: Grune & Stratton, 1979.

Ferguson, C. K. "Concerning the Nature of Human Systems and the Consultant's Role." In W. G. Bennis, K. D. Benne, and R. Chin (Eds.), *The Planning of Change.* (2nd ed.) New York: Holt, Rinehart and Winston, 1969.

Fiedler, F. E. *A Theory of Leadership Effectiveness.* New York: McGraw-Hill, 1967.

Fine, M. J. "Some Qualifying Notes on the Development and

Implementation of Behavior Modification Programs." *Journal of School Psychology,* 1970, *8,* 301-305.

Flaherty, E. W. "Evaluation of Consultation." In J. J. Platt and R. J. Wicks (Eds.), *The Psychological Consultant.* New York: Grune & Stratton, 1979.

Ford, C. H. "Developing a Successful Client-Consultant Relationship." In C. R. Bell and L. Nadler (Eds.), *The Client-Consultant Handbook.* Houston: Gulf Publishing Co., 1979.

Ford, R. N. *Motivation Through Work Itself.* New York: American Management Association, 1969.

Fordyce, J. K., and Weil, R. *Managing with People.* Reading, Mass.: Addison-Wesley, 1971.

Frank, J. D. "Foreword." In A. Kiev (Ed.), *Magic, Faith, and Healing.* London: Free Press of Glencoe, Collier-Macmillan, 1973.

Frankenhuis, J. P. "How to Get a Good Consultant." In C. R. Bell and L. Nadler (Eds.), *The Client-Consultant Handbook.* Houston: Gulf Publishing Co., 1979.

French, J. R., and Raven, B. H. "The Bases of Social Power." In D. Cartwright and A. Zander (Eds.), *Group Dynamics: Research and Theory.* (2nd ed.) New York: Harper & Row, 1960.

French, W. "Organization Development: Objectives, Assumptions, and Strategies." In N. Margulies and A. P. Raia (Eds.), *Organization Development: Values, Process, and Technology.* New York: McGraw-Hill, 1972.

French, W. L., and Bell, C. H. *Organization Development: Behavioral Science Interventions for Organization Improvement.* Englewood Cliffs, N.J.: Prentice-Hall, 1973.

French, W. L., and Bell, C. H. *Organization Development.* (2nd ed.) Englewood Cliffs, N.J.: Prentice-Hall, 1978.

Friedlander, F. "OD Reaches Adolescence: An Exploration of Its Underlying Values." *Journal of Applied Behavioral Science,* 1977, *12* (1), 7-51.

Friedlander, F., and Brown, L. D. "Organization Development." *Annual Review of Psychology,* 1974, *25,* 313-341.

Fuchs, J. H. *Making the Most of Management of Consulting Services.* New York: Amacom, 1975.

Fullan, M., Miles, M. B., and Taylor, G. "Organization Development in Schools: The State of the Art." *Review of Educational Research,* 1980, *50* (1), 121-183.

Gagné, R. M., and Briggs, L. J. *Principles of Instructional Design.* New York: Holt, Rinehart and Winston, 1974.

Galbraith, J. *Designing Complex Organizations.* Reading, Mass.: Addison-Wesley, 1973.

Gallessich, J. "A Systems Model of Mental Health Consultation." *Psychology in the Schools,* 1972, *9* (1), 13-15.

Gallessich, J. "Organizational Factors Influencing Consultation in Schools." *Journal of School Psychology,* 1973, *11,* 57-65.

Gallessich, J. "Training the School Psychologist for Consultation." *Journal of School Psychology,* 1974, *12* (2), 138-149.

Gallessich, J. "Consultation." In U. Delworth, G. R. Hanson, and Associates, *Student Services: A Handbook for the Profession.* San Francisco: Jossey-Bass, 1980a.

Gallessich, J. "Training Psychologists for Consultation with Organizations." Paper presented at National Conference on Consultation Training, Montreal, Ont., August 31, 1980b.

Gallessich, J., and Ladogana, A. "Consultation Training Program for School Counselors." *Counselor Education and Supervision,* 1978, *18,* 100-108.

Gallessich, J., and MacDonald, J. "Facilitating Professional Development Through Group Analogic Methods." *Professional Psychology,* 1981, *12* (2), 209-215.

Gartner, A., and Riessman, F. *The Service Society and the Consumer Vanguard.* New York: Harper & Row, 1974.

Geller, E. S. "Applications of Behavior Analysis to Litter Control." In D. Glenwick and L. Jason (Eds.), *Behavioral Community Psychology.* New York: Praeger, 1980.

Gendreau, P., and Andrews, D. A. "Psychological Consultation in Correctional Agencies: Case Studies and General Issues." In J. J. Platt and R. J. Wicks (Eds.), *The Psychological Consultant.* New York: Grune & Stratton, 1979.

Glaser, E. M. "Definition of Program Consultation." In T. E. Backer and E. M. Glaser (Eds.), *Proceedings of the Advanced Workshop on Program Consultation in Mental Health Services.* Annapolis, Md., 1978.

Glaser, E. M. "Ethical Issues in Consultation Practice with Organizations." *Consultation,* 1981, *1* (1), 12-16.

Glaser, E. M., and others. "The Round Table." *Consultation,* 1981, *1* (1), 37-43.

Glass, G. V., and Ellett, F. S. "Evaluation Research." *Annual Review of Psychology,* 1980, *31,* 211-228.

Glenwick, D., and Jason, L. (Eds.). *Behavioral Community Psychology.* New York: Praeger, 1980.

Glidewell, J. C. "The Entry Problem in Consultation." *Journal of Social Issues,* 1959, *15* (2), 51-59.

Goldstein, A. P., and Sorcher, M. *Changing Supervisor Behavior.* Elmsford, N.Y.: Pergamon Press, 1974.

Goldstein, I. L. "Training in Work Organizations." *Annual Review of Psychology,* 1980, *31,* 229-272.

Golembiewski, R. T. "Organization Development in Public Agencies: Perspectives in Theory and Practice." *Public Administration Review,* 1969, *29,* 367-377.

Golembiewski, R. T., Hilles, R., and Kagno, S. "A Longitudinal Study of Flexi-Time Effects: Some Consequences of an OD Structural Intervention." *Journal of Applied Behavioral Science,* 1974, *10* (4), 503-532.

Goodstein, L. D. *Consulting with Human Service Systems.* Reading, Mass.: Addison-Wesley, 1978.

Gordon, J. S. "Consultation with Youth Programs." In A. S. Rogawski (Ed.), *New Directions for Mental Health Services: Mental Health Consultations in Community Settings,* no. 3. San Francisco: Jossey-Bass, 1979.

Gouldner, A. W. "Engineering and Clinical Approaches to Consulting." In W. G. Bennis, K. D. Benne, and R. Chin (Eds.), *The Planning of Change.* New York: Holt, Rinehart and Winston, 1964.

Gouldner, A. W. "Anti-Minotaur: the Myth of a Value-Free Sociology." In W. G. Bennis, K. D. Benne, and R. Chin (Eds.), *The Planning of Change.* (2nd ed.) New York: Holt, Rinehart and Winston, 1969.

Grady, M. A., Gibson, M. J. S., and Trickett, E. J. (Eds.). *Mental Health Consultation Theory, Practice, and Research, 1973-1978: An Annotated Reference Guide.* Adelphi, Md.: Mental

Health Study Center, National Institute of Mental Health, 1981.

Graziano, A. M. "The Consultant, the Client, and Hidden Assumptions." In J. Zusman and D. L. Davidson (Eds.), *Practical Aspects of Mental Health Consultation.* Springfield, Ill.: Thomas, 1972.

Greenwood, E. "The Elements of Professionalization." In H. M. Vollmer and D. L. Mills (Eds.), *Professionalization.* Englewood Cliffs, N.J.: Prentice-Hall, 1966.

Greiner, L. E. "Patterns of Organizational Change." *Harvard Business Review,* 1967, *45,* 119-130.

Grotjahn, M. "The Aim and Technique of Psychiatric Family Consultations." In W. M. Mendel and P. Solomon (Eds.), *The Psychiatric Consultation.* New York: Grune & Stratton, 1968.

Guilford, J. P., and Fruchter, B. *Fundamental Statistics in Psychology and Education.* New York: McGraw-Hill, 1973.

Guskin, A., and Guskin, S. *A Social Psychology of Education.* Reading, Mass.: Addison-Wesley, 1970.

Haber, S. "The Professions and Higher Education in America: A Historical View." In M. S. Gordon (Ed.), *Higher Education and the Labor Market.* New York: McGraw-Hill, 1974.

Hall, E. *The Hidden Dimension.* Garden City, N.Y.: Doubleday, 1966.

Halliday, J. L. *Psychosocial Medicine.* New York: Norton, 1948.

Halpin, A., and Croft, D. *The Organizational Climate of Schools.* Chicago: Midwest Administration Center, University of Chicago, 1963.

Hamilton, M. K. "Survey of Consultation Activities in College Counseling Centers." Fort Collins: University Counseling Center, Colorado State University, 1978.

Hamilton, M. K., and Meade, C. J. (Eds.). *New Directions for Student Services: Consulting on Campus,* no. 5. San Francisco: Jossey-Bass, 1979.

Hare, A. P. *Handbook of Small Group Research.* (2nd ed.) New York: Free Press, 1976.

Harrison, R. "Understanding Your Organization's Character." *Harvard Business Review,* 1972, *50,* 119-128.

Hartsough, D. M. "Pre-Internship Training in Consultation

Skills." Paper presented at 80th annual meeting of American Psychological Association, Honolulu, September 1972.

Hasenfeld, Y., and English, R. A. "Introduction." In Y. Hasenfeld and R. A. English (Eds.), *Human Service Organizations.* Ann Arbor: University of Michigan Press, 1975.

Hasenfeld, Y., and English, R. A. (Eds.). *Human Service Organizations.* Ann Arbor: University of Michigan Press, 1975.

Heller, K., and Monahan, J. *Psychology and Community Change.* Homewood, Ill.: Dorsey Press, 1977.

Herbert, T. T., and Yost, E. B. *Management Education and Development.* Westport, Conn.: Greenwood Press, 1978.

Hirschhorn, L. "Alternative Services and the Crisis of the Professions." In J. Case and R. C. Taylor (Eds.), *Co-ops, Communes, and Collectives.* New York: Pantheon Books, 1979.

Hirschowitz, R. G. "Consultation to Complex Organizations in Transition: The Dynamics of Change and the Principles of Applied Consultation." In S. C. Plog and P. I. Ahmed (Eds.), *Principles and Techniques of Mental Health Consultation.* New York: Plenum Medical Book Co., 1977.

Holahan, C. J. "Consultation in Environmental Psychology: A Case Study of a New Counseling Role." *Journal of Counseling Psychology,* 1977, *24* (3), 251-254.

Holahan, C. J. *Environment and Behavior.* New York: Plenum, 1978.

Homans, G. C. *The Human Group.* New York: Harcourt Brace Jovanovich, 1950.

Hopper, R., and Whitehead, J. *Communications Concepts and Skills.* New York: Harper & Row, 1979.

Howard, L. R. "Forensic Psychology and Road Accidents." *Journal of Forensic Psychology,* 1971, *3,* 4-11.

Hughes, E. C. *Men and Their Work.* New York: Free Press, 1958.

Hughes, E. C. "The Social Significance of Professionalization." In H. M. Vollmer and D. L. Mills (Eds.), *Professionalization.* Englewood Cliffs, N.J.: Prentice-Hall, 1966.

Hunt, J. G., and Larson, L. (Eds.). *Contingency Approaches to Leadership.* Carbondale: Southern Illinois University Press, 1974.

Huse, E. F. *Organization Development and Change.* St. Paul, Minn.: West, 1975.

Hyman, I., and Meyers, J. "Training for Change: A University Supervised Internship in a Single Setting." *Journal of School Psychology,* 1973, *11* (2), 161-167.

Illich, I. *Deschooling Society.* New York: Harper & Row, 1972.

Iscoe, I., and others. "Some Strategies in Mental Health Consultation: A Brief Description of a Project and Some Preliminary Results." In E. L. Cowen, E. A. Gardner, and M. Zax (Eds.), *Emergent Approaches to Mental Health Problems.* New York: Appleton-Century-Crofts, 1967.

Jacques, E. *The Changing Culture of a Factory.* London: Tavistock, 1951.

Janis, I. L., and Mann, L. *Decision Making.* New York: Free Press, 1977.

Jay, A. "Rate Yourself as a Client." In C. R. Bell and L. Nadler (Eds.), *The Client-Consultant Handbook.* Houston: Gulf Publishing Co., 1979.

Joint Commission on Mental Illness and Health. *Action for Mental Health.* New York: Basic Books, 1961.

Jones, J. E., and Pfeiffer, J. W. "Ethical Considerations in Consulting." In C. R. Bell and L. Nadler (Eds.), *The Client-Consultant Handbook.* Houston: Gulf Publishing Company, 1979.

Jongeward, D. *Everybody Wins: TA Applied to Organizations.* Reading, Mass.: Addison-Wesley, 1973.

Kadushin, A. *Consultation in Social Work.* New York: Columbia University Press, 1977.

Kahn, R. L. "Conflict, Ambiguity, and Overload: Three Elements in Job Stress." In A. McLean (Ed.), *Occupational Stress.* Springfield, Ill.: Thomas, 1974.

Kamerschen, K. "The Development of a Campus Community Mental Health Center." Paper presented at 82nd annual meeting of American Psychological Association, New Orleans, September 1974.

Kanner, L. *History of the Care and Study of the Mentally Retarded.* Springfield, Ill.: Thomas, 1964.

Kanter, R. M. *Men and Women of the Corporation.* New York: Basic Books, 1977.

Kaslow, F. W. "Community Mental Health Centers." In F. W. Kaslow and Associates, *Supervision, Consultation, and Staff*

Training in the Helping Professions. San Francisco: Jossey-Bass, 1977.

Kaslow, F. W. "The Psychologist as Consultant to the Court." In J. J. Platt and R. J. Wicks (Eds.), *The Psychological Consultant.* New York: Grune & Stratton, 1979.

Katz, D., and Kahn, R. L. *The Social Psychology of Organizations.* New York: Wiley, 1978.

Keller, H. R. "Behavioral Consultation." In J. C. Conoley (Ed.), *Consultation in Schools: Theory, Research, Procedures.* New York: Academic Press, 1981.

Kelman, H. C. "Manipulation of Human Behavior: An Ethical Dilemma for the Social Scientist." In W. G. Bennis, K. D. Benne, and R. Chin (Eds.), *The Planning of Change.* (2nd ed.) New York: Holt, Rinehart and Winston, 1969.

Kern, H. M. "The New Emphasis on Mental Health Consultation." In L. Bellak and H. H. Barten (Eds.), *Progress in Community Mental Health.* New York: Grune & Stratton, 1969.

Keys, C. B. "Graduate Training in Organizational Consultation: Three Dilemmas." Paper presented at National Conference on Consultation Training, Montreal, Ont., August 1980.

Khajavi, F., Broskowski, A., and Mermis, W. "Team Consultation to Complex Organizations: Some Emerging Issues for Mental Health Workers." *Hospital and Community Psychiatry,* 1972, *23,* 235-239.

Kimberly, J. R., Miles, R. H., and Associates. *The Organizational Life Cycle: Issues in the Creation, Transformation, and Decline of Organizations.* San Francisco: Jossey-Bass, 1980.

King, D. C., Sherwood, J. J., and Manning, M. R. "OD's Research Base: How to Expand and Utilize It." In W. W. Burke (Ed.), *The Cutting Edge: Current Theory and Practice in Organization Development.* San Diego, Calif.: University Associates, 1978.

King, L. S. *The Medical World of the Eighteenth Century.* Chicago: University of Chicago Press, 1958.

Klein, D. "Some Notes on the Dynamics of Resistance to Change: The Defender's Role." In W. G. Bennis, K. D. Benne, and R. Chin (Eds.), *The Planning of Change.* (2nd ed.) New York: Holt, Rinehart and Winston, 1969.

Klein, D., and Lindemann, E. "Preventive Intervention in Individual and Family Crisis Situations." In G. Caplan (Ed.), *Prevention of Mental Disorders in Children.* New York: Basic Books, 1961.

Knight, K. E., and McDaniel, R. R. *Organizations: An Information Perspective.* Belmont, Calif.: Wadsworth, 1979.

Koile, E. A., and Gallessich, J. "Report to the Hogg Foundation for Mental Health on the Dallas County Junior College District Group Dynamics-Communications Workshops." Unpublished report, Department of Educational Psychology, University of Texas at Austin, 1970.

Koile, E. A., and Gallessich, J. "The Dallas Human Relations Labs." *Junior College Journal,* 1971, *41* (6), 31-37.

Kotter, J. P. *Organizational Dynamics: Diagnosis and Intervention.* Reading, Mass.: Addison-Wesley, 1978.

Kouzes, J. M., and Mico, P. R. "Domain Theory: An Introduction to Organizational Behavior in Human Service Organizations." *Journal of Applied Behavioral Science,* 1979, *15* (4), 449-469.

Kratochwill, T., and Bergan, J. "Training School Psychologists: Some Perspectives on a Competency-Based Behavioral Consultation Model." *Professional Psychology,* 1978, *9* (1), 71-82.

Krell, T. C. "The Marketing of Organization Development: Past, Present, and Future." *Journal of Applied Behavioral Science,* 1981, *17* (3), 309-323.

Kurpius, D., and Brubaker, J. *Psychoeducational Consultation: Definitions, Functions, Preparation.* Bloomington: Indiana University Press, 1976.

Kutzik, A. J. "The Medical Field." In F. W. Kaslow and Associates, *Supervision, Consultation, and Staff Training in the Helping Professions.* San Francisco: Jossey-Bass, 1977a.

Kutzik, A. J. "The Social Work Field." In F. W. Kaslow and Associates, *Supervision, Consultation, and Staff Training in the Helping Professions.* San Francisco: Jossey-Bass, 1977b.

Lake, D. G., Miles, M. B., and Earle, R. B. (Eds.). *Measuring Human Behavior.* New York: Teachers College, Columbia University, 1973.

Lambert, N. M., Yandell, W., and Sandoval, J. H. "Preparation of School Psychologists for School-Based Consultation: A Training Activity and a Service to Community Schools." *Journal of School Psychology,* 1975, *13* (1), 68-75.

Larsen, J. K., Norris, E. L., and Kroll, J. *Consultation and Its Outcome: Community Mental Health Centers.* Washington, D.C.: Publication sponsored by Department of Health, Education, and Welfare, National Institute of Mental Health, Mental Health Services Branch (Grant No. R 12 MH25121), 1976.

Lasch, C. *Haven in a Heartless World.* New York: Basic Books, 1977.

Lawrence, M. M. *The Mental Health Team in the Schools.* New York: Behavioral Publications, 1971.

Lawrence, P. R., and Lorsch, J. W. *Organization and Environment.* Homewood, Ill.: Irwin, 1967.

Leavitt, H. J. "Applied Organizational Change in Industry: Structural, Technological and Humanistic Approaches." In J. G. March (Ed.), *Handbook of Organizations.* Chicago: Rand McNally, 1965.

Leonard, M. "Training Consultants." In M. K. Hamilton and C. J. Meade (Eds.), *New Directions for Student Services: Consulting on Campus,* no. 5. San Francisco: Jossey-Bass, 1979.

Levine, M. "The Practice of Mental Health Consultation: Some Definitions from Social Theory." In J. Zusman and D. L. Davidson (Eds.), *Practical Aspects of Mental Health Consultation.* Springfield, Ill.: Thomas, 1972.

Levine, M., and Levine, A. *A Social History of Helping Services.* New York: Appleton-Century-Crofts, 1970.

Levinson, H. "Psychiatric Consultation in Industry." In W. M. Mendel and P. Solomon (Eds.), *The Psychiatric Consultation.* New York: Grune & Stratton, 1968.

Levinson, H. *Organizational Diagnosis.* Cambridge, Mass.: Harvard University Press, 1972.

Levinson, H. "Organizational Diagnosis in Mental Health Consultation." In T. E. Backer and E. M. Glaser (Eds.), *Proceedings of the Advanced Workshop on Program Consultation in Mental Health Services.* Los Angeles: Publication sponsored by National Institute of Mental Health, Mental Health Services Branch, and Human Interaction Research Institute, 1978.

Lewin, K. *Field Theory in Social Science.* New York: Harper & Row, 1951.

Likert, R. *New Patterns of Management.* New York: McGraw-Hill, 1961.

Likert, R. *The Human Organization: Its Management and Value.* New York: McGraw-Hill, 1967.

Likert, R., and Likert, J. G. *New Ways of Managing Conflict.* New York: McGraw-Hill, 1976.

Lindemann, E. "Symptomatology and Management of Acute Grief." *American Journal of Psychiatry,* 1944, *101,* 141-149.

Lippitt, G. L. "Areas of Consulting in the 80s." *Academic Consultants' Communique,* 1981a, *9* (2), 1-2.

Lippitt, G. L. "Evaluating Consultation Services." *Consultation,* 1981b, *1* (1), 17-26.

Lippitt, G., and Lippitt, R. *The Consulting Process in Action.* San Diego, Calif.: University Associates, 1978.

Lippitt, R. O., and others. "The Professionalization of Laboratory Practice." In K. D. Benne and others (Eds.), *The Laboratory Method of Changing and Learning: Theory and Application.* Palo Alto, Calif.: Science and Behavior Books, 1975.

Lockwood, D. L., and Luthans, F. "Multiple Measures to Assess the Impact of Organization Development Interventions." In J. W. Pfeiffer and J. E. Jones (Eds.), *The 1980 Annual Handbook for Group Facilitators.* San Diego, Calif.: University Associates, 1980.

Lorsch, J. W., and Lawrence, P. "The Diagnosis of Organizational Problems." In N. Margulies and A. P. Raia (Eds.), *Organization Development: Values, Process, and Technology.* New York: McGraw-Hill, 1972.

Lubove, R. *The Professional Altruist.* Cambridge, Mass.: Harvard University Press, 1965.

Luke, J. R., and Benne, K. D. "Ethical Issues and Dilemmas in Laboratory Practice." In K. D. Benne and others (Eds.), *The Laboratory Method of Changing and Learning: Theory and Application.* Palo Alto, Calif.: Science and Behavior Books, 1975.

McAlister, A., and others. "Mass Communication and Community Organization for Public Health Education." *American Psychologist,* 1980, *35* (4), 375-379.

McClung, F. B., and Stunden, A. A. *Mental Health Consultation to Programs for Children.* Rockville, Md.: National Institute of Mental Health, 1972.

McElvaney, C. T., and Miles, M. B. "Using Survey Feedback and Consultation." In R. A. Schmuck and M. B. Miles (Eds.), *Organization Development in Schools.* Palo Alto, Calif.: National Press Books, 1971.

McGehee, W., and Thayer, P. W. *Training in Business and Industry.* New York: Wiley, 1961.

McGrath, J. E. "Stress and Behavior in Organizations." In M. D. Dunnette (Ed.), *Handbook of Industrial and Organizational Psychology.* Chicago: Rand McNally, 1976.

McGreeny, C. P. "Training Consultants: Issues and Approaches." *Personnel and Guidance Journal,* 1978, *56* (6), 432-435.

McGregor, D. *The Human Side of Enterprise.* New York: McGraw-Hill, 1960.

MacIver, R. "Professional Groups and Cultural Norms." In H. M. Vollmer and D. L. Mills (Eds.), *Professionalization.* Englewood Cliffs, N.J.: Prentice-Hall, 1966.

MacLennan, B. W. "Mental Health Programs: Priority Setting and Funding." In A. S. Rogawski (Ed.), *New Directions for Mental Health Services: Mental Health Consultations in Community Settings,* no. 3. San Francisco: Jossey-Bass, 1979.

McWhirter, D. P. "Consultation with the Clergy." In W. M. Mendel and P. Solomon (Eds.), *The Psychiatric Consultation.* New York: Grune & Stratton, 1968.

Mahoney, M. J., and Thoresen, C. E. *Self Control: Power to the Person.* Monterey, Calif.: Brooks/Cole, 1974.

Mann, F. C. "Changing Superior-Subordinate Relationships." *Journal of Social Issues,* 1951, *7* (3), 56-63.

Mann, F. C. "Studying and Creating Change: A Means to Understanding Social Organization." *Research in Industrial Human Relations,* 1957, *17,* 146-167.

Mann, P. A. *Psychological Consultation with a Police Depart-*

ment: A Demonstration of Cooperative Training in Mental Health. Springfield, Ill.: Thomas, 1973.

Manning, P. K. "Metaphors of the Field: Varieties of Organizational Discourse." *Administrative Science Quarterly,* 1979, *24* (4), 660-671.

Mannino, F. V., and Shore, M. F. "Research in Consultation Training." Paper presented at National Conference on Consultation Training, Montreal, Ont., August 1980.

Manuso, J. S. "Psychological Services and Health Enhancement: A Corporate Model." In A. Broskowski, E. Marks, and S. H. Budman (Eds.), *Annual Review of Community Mental Health.* Vol. 2: *Linking Health and Mental Health.* Beverly Hills, Calif.: Sage, 1981.

Marcus, J. "Nursing Consultation: A Clinical Specialty." *Journal of Psychiatric Nursing and Mental Health Services,* 1976, *14* (11), 29-31.

Margulies, N., and Raia, A. P. (Eds.). *Organizational Development: Values, Process, and Technology.* New York: McGraw-Hill, 1972.

Marks, E., and Broskowski, A. "Community Mental Health and Organized Health Care Linkages." In A. Broskowski, E. Marks, and S. H. Budman (Eds.), *Annual Review of Community Mental Health.* Vol. 2: *Linking Health and Mental Health.* Beverly Hills, Calif.: Sage, 1981.

Martin, R. "Expert and Referent Power: A Framework for Understanding and Maximizing Consultation Effectiveness." *Journal of School Psychology,* 1978, *16,* 49-55.

Martin, R., and Meyers, J. *School Psychologists and the Practice of Consultation: A National Survey.* Washington, D.C.: Division 16 Corresponding Committee on Consultation, American Psychological Association, 1979.

Maslow, A. H. *Motivation and Personality.* New York: Harper & Row, 1954.

Matuzek, P. "Program Evaluation as Consultation." In J. C. Conoley (Ed.), *Consultation in Schools: Theory, Research, Procedures.* New York: Academic Press, 1981.

Meade, C. J., and Hamilton, M. K. "Campus Consultation:

Toward a Coherent Conceptualization." In M. K. Hamilton and C. J. Meade (Eds.), *New Directions for Student Services: Consulting on Campus,* no. 5. San Francisco: Jossey-Bass, 1979.

Mechanic, D. *Politics, Medicine, and Social Science.* New York: Wiley, 1974.

Medway, F. J. "How Effective Is School Consultation? A Review of Recent Research." *Journal of School Psychology,* 1979, *17* (3), 275-282.

Meichenbaum, D. H. "Self-Instructional Methods." In F. H. Kanfer and A. P. Goldstein (Eds.), *Helping People Change.* Elmsford, N.Y.: Pergamon Press, 1975.

Mendel, W. M., and Solomon, P. (Eds.). *The Psychiatric Consultation.* New York: Grune & Stratton, 1968.

Merry, U., and Allerhand, M. E. *Developing Teams and Organizations.* Reading, Mass.: Addison-Wesley, 1977.

Meyer, J. W., and Rowan, B. "The Structure of Educational Organizations." In M. W. Meyer and Associates, *Environments and Organizations: Theoretical and Empirical Perspectives.* San Francisco: Jossey-Bass, 1978.

Meyer, M. W., and Associates. *Environments and Organizations: Theoretical and Empirical Perspectives.* San Francisco: Jossey-Bass, 1978.

Meyers, J. "Specific Strategies for Research in Consultation." Paper presented at 82nd annual meeting of American Psychological Association, New Orleans, September 1974.

Meyers, J. "Consultee-Centered Consultation with a Teacher as a Technique in Behavior Management." *American Journal of Community Psychology,* 1975, *3* (2), 111-121.

Meyers, J., Parsons, R. D., and Martin, R. *Mental Health Consultation in the Schools.* San Francisco: Jossey-Bass, 1979.

Meyers, W. R. *The Evaluation Enterprise.* San Francisco: Jossey-Bass, 1981.

Miles, M. B., and Schmuck, R. A. "Improving Schools Through Organization Development: An Overview." In R. A. Schmuck and M. B. Miles (Eds.), *Organization Development in Schools.* Palo Alto, Calif.: National Press Books, 1971.

Miller, E. C. "The Parallel Organization Structure at General

Motors: An Interview with Howard C. Carlson." *Personnel,* 1978, *55* (4), 64-69.

Miller, E. J., and Rice, A. K. *Systems of Organization.* London: Tavistock, 1967.

Miringoff, M. L. *Management in Human Service Organizations.* New York: Macmillan, 1980.

Mitchell, M. D. "Consultant Burnout." In J. E. Jones and J. W. Pfeiffer (Eds.), *The 1977 Annual Handbook for Group Facilitators.* San Diego, Calif.: University Associates, 1977.

Moore, W. E. *The Professions: Roles and Rules.* New York: Russell Sage Foundation, 1970.

Moos, R. H. "Changing the Social Milieus of Psychiatric Treatment Settings." *Journal of Applied Behavioral Science,* 1973, *9* (5), 575-594.

Murray, H. A. *Explorations in Personality.* New York: Oxford University Press, 1938.

Nadler, D. A. *Feedback and Organization Development: Using Data-Based Methods.* Reading, Mass.: Addison-Wesley, 1977.

Nadler, D. A. "Alternative Data-Feedback Designs for Organizational Intervention." In J. Jones and J. W. Pfeiffer (Eds.), *The 1979 Annual Handbook for Group Facilitators.* San Diego, Calif.: University Associates, 1979.

Newman, R. *Psychological Consultation in the Schools.* New York: Basic Books, 1967.

Nicholas, J. M. "Evaluation Research in Organizational Change Interventions: Considerations and Some Suggestions." *Journal of Applied Behavioral Science,* 1979, *15* (1), 23-39.

Nisbet, R. A. *The Degradation of the Academic Dogma.* New York: Basic Books, 1970.

"NTL Values and Ethics Statement." Arlington, Va.: NTL Institute, 1980.

O'Brien, R. M., Dickinson, A. M., and Rosow, M. (Eds.). *Industrial Behavior Modification: A Learning Based Approach to Industrial-Organizational Problems.* New York: Pergamon Press, 1982.

Odiorne, G. S. *Management by Objectives.* New York: Piman, 1965.

O'Leary, K. D., and Drabman, R. "Token Reinforcement Programs in the Classroom: A Review." *Psychological Bulletin,* 1971, *75,* 379-398.

Oshry, B. "Power and the Control of Structure." *Social Change,* 1976, *6* (3), 1-2.

Osterweil, Z. O., and Marom, M. "Training Teachers as Facilitators of Mental Health: 'Psychotherapy of the Role.' " Unpublished paper, Hebrew University of Jerusalem, Israel, n.d.

Ouchi, W. *Theory Z.* Reading, Mass.: Addison-Wesley, 1981.

Parad, H. J. (Ed.). *Crisis Intervention: Selected Readings.* New York: Family Service Association of America, 1965.

Parker, B. "The Value of Supervision in Training Psychiatrists for Mental Health Consultation." *Mental Hygiene,* 1961, *45,* 94-100.

Parker, B. "Some Observations on Psychiatric Consultation with Nursery School Teachers." *Mental Hygiene,* 1962, *46* (4), 559-566.

Parsons, T. "The Professions and Social Structure." *Social Forces,* 1939, *17* (4), 457-467.

Pascale, R. T., and Athos, A. G. *The Art of Japanese Management.* New York: Simon & Schuster, 1981.

Pearl, A. "The Psychological Consultant as a Change Agent." *Professional Psychology,* 1974, *5,* 292-298.

Pedalino, E., and Gamboa, V. U. "Behavior Modification and Absenteeism: Intervention in One Industrial Setting." *Journal of Applied Psychology,* 1974, *59* (6), 694-698.

Perkins, D. N., Nadler, D. A., and Hanlon, M. D. "A Method for Structured Naturalistic Observation of Organizational Behavior." In J. E. Jones and J. W. Pfeiffer (Eds.), *The 1981 Annual Handbook for Group Facilitators.* San Diego, Calif.: University Associates, 1981.

Perloff, R., Perloff, E., and Sussna, E. "Program Evaluation." *Annual Review of Psychology,* 1976, *27,* 569-594.

Perrow, C. B. *Organizational Analysis: A Sociological View.* Monterey, Calif.: Brooks/Cole, 1970.

Pfeiffer, J. W., Heslin, R., and Jones, J. E. *Instrumentation in Human Relations Training.* (2nd ed.) San Diego, Calif.: University Associates, 1976.

Pfeiffer, J. W., and Jones, J. E. "Ethical Considerations in Consulting." In J. E. Jones and J. W. Pfeiffer (Eds.), *The 1977 Annual Handbook for Group Facilitators.* San Diego, Calif.: University Associates, 1977.

Pincus, H. "Linking General Health and Mental Health Systems of Care: Conceptual Models of Implementation." *American Journal of Psychiatry,* 1980, *137,* 315-320.

Pines, A., and Maslach, C. "Characteristics of Staff Burnout in Mental Health Settings." *Hospital and Community Psychiatry,* 1978, *29,* 233-237.

Pipes, R. B. "Consulting in Organizations: The Entry Problem." In J. C. Conoley (Ed.), *Consultation in Schools: Theory, Research, Procedures.* New York: Academic Press, 1981.

Platt, J. J., and Wicks, R. J. (Eds.). *The Psychological Consultant.* New York: Grune & Stratton, 1979.

Pollack, S. "Consultation with the Courts." In W. M. Mendel and P. Solomon (Eds.), *The Psychiatric Consultation.* New York: Grune & Stratton, 1968.

Pondy, L. R., and Mitroff, I. I. "Beyond Open System Models of Organizations." *Research in Organizational Behavior,* 1979, *1,* 3-39.

Porras, J. I., and Berg, P. O. "Evaluation Methodology in Organization Development: An Analysis and Critique." *Journal of Applied Behavioral Science,* 1978, *14* (2), 151-174.

Preziosi, R. C. "Organizational Diagnosis Questionnaire (ODQ)." In J. W. Pfeiffer and J. E. Jones (Eds.), *The 1980 Annual Handbook for Group Facilitators.* San Diego, Calif.: University Associates, 1980.

Proshansky, H. M., Ittelson, W. H., and Rivlin, L. G. *Environmental Psychology: Man and His Physical Setting.* New York: Holt, Rinehart and Winston, 1970.

Rae-Grant, Q. "The Art of Being a Failure as a Consultant." In J. Zusman and D. L. Davidson (Eds.), *Practical Aspects of Mental Health Consultation.* Springfield, Ill.: Thomas, 1972.

Rappaport, H., and Rappaport, M. "The Integration of Scientific and Traditional Healing." *American Psychologist,* 1981, *36* (7), 774-781.

Reiff, R. "The Power of the Helping Professions." *Journal of Applied Behavioral Science,* 1974, *10* (3), 451-461.

Reiff, R. *The Invisible Victim.* New York: Basic Books, 1979.

Reiser, M. *The Police Department Psychologist.* Springfield, Ill.: Thomas, 1972.

Reppucci, N. D., and Saunders, J. T. "Social Psychology of Behavior Modification: Problems of Implementation in Natural Settings." *American Psychologist,* 1974, *29,* 649-660.

Riecken, H. W. "Principal Components of the Evaluation Process." *Professional Psychology,* 1977, *8* (4), 392-410.

Robinowitz, C. B. "Consultation in Mental Retardation and Developmental Disabilities." In A. S. Rogawski (Ed.), *New Directions for Mental Health Services: Mental Health Consultations in Community Settings,* no. 3. San Francisco: Jossey-Bass, 1979.

Rodin, J., and Janis, I. L. "The Social Power of Health-Care Practitioners as Agents of Change." *Journal of Social Issues,* 1979, *35* (1), 60-81.

Roeber, R. J. *The Organization in a Changing Environment.* Reading, Mass.: Addison-Wesley, 1973.

Roethlisberger, F., and Dickson, W. *Management and the Worker.* Cambridge, Mass.: Harvard University Press, 1939.

Rogawski, A. S. "Mental Health Consultation to Welfare Agencies." In S. C. Plog and P. I. Ahmed (Eds.), *Principles and Techniques of Mental Health Consultation.* New York: Plenum Medical Book Co., 1977.

Rogawski, A. S. (Ed.). *New Directions for Mental Health Services: Mental Health Consultations in Community Settings,* no. 3. San Francisco: Jossey-Bass, 1979.

Rogers, C. "The Characteristics of a Helping Relationship." In C. R. Bell and L. Nadler (Eds.), *The Client-Consultant Handbook.* Houston: Gulf Publishing Co., 1979.

Rothstein, W. G. *American Physicians in the Nineteenth Century.* Baltimore: Johns Hopkins University Press, 1972.

Rubin, L., Plovnik, M., and Fry, R. "Initiating Planned Change in Health Care Systems." *Journal of Applied Behavioral Science,* 1974, *10,* 107-124.

Russell, M. L. "Behavioral Consultation." *Personnel and Guidance Journal,* 1978, *56* (6), 346-350.

Sarason, S. *The Culture of the School and the Problem of Change.* Boston: Allyn & Bacon, 1971.

Scandura, J. M. "Structural Approach to Instructional Problems." *American Psychologist,* 1977, *32* (1), 33-53.

Schein, E. H. *Organizational Psychology.* Englewood Cliffs, N.J.: Prentice-Hall, 1965.

Schein, E. H. *Process Consultation: Its Role in Organization Development.* Reading, Mass.: Addison-Wesley, 1969.

Schein, E. H. "Disengagement: Reducing Involvement with the Client System." In C. R. Bell and L. Nadler (Eds.), *The Client-Consultant Handbook.* Houston: Gulf Publishing Co., 1979.

Schein, V. E., and Greiner, L. E. "Can Organization Development Be Fine Tuned to Bureaucracies?" *Organizational Dynamics,* 1977, *5* (3), 48-61.

Schindler-Rainman, E., and Lippitt, R. O. "Awareness Learning and Skill Development." In K. D. Benne and others (Eds.), *The Laboratory Method of Changing and Learning.* Palo Alto, Calif.: Science and Behavior Books, 1975.

Schmuck, R. A., and Miles, M. B. (Eds.). *Organization Development in Schools.* Palo Alto, Calif.: National Press Books, 1971.

Schmuck, R. A., and others. *Handbook of Organization Development in Schools.* Palo Alto, Calif.: National Press Books, 1972.

Schroeder, M. "The Shadow Consultant." *Journal of Applied Behavioral Science,* 1974, *10,* 570-594.

Schwab, J. "Consultation-Liaison Training Program." In W. M. Mendel and P. Solomon (Eds.), *The Psychiatric Consultation.* New York: Grune & Stratton, 1968.

Scriven, M. "The Methodology of Evaluation." In R. Tyler, R. Gagné, and M. Scriven (Eds.), *Perspectives of Curriculum Evaluation.* AERA Monograph Series on Curriculum Evaluation. Chicago: Rand McNally, 1967.

Sennett, R. *The Fall of the Public Man.* New York: Vintage Books, 1978.

Shephard, H. A. "Innovation-Resisting and Innovation-Producing Organizations." In W. G. Bennis, K. D. Benne, and R. Chin (Eds.), *The Planning of Change.* (2nd ed.) New York: Holt, Rinehart and Winston, 1969.

Sigerist, H. E. "A Look at the Past." In A. H. Katz and J. S.

Felton (Eds.), *Health and the Community*. New York: Free Press, 1965.

Signell, K. A., and Scott, P. A. "Mental Health Consultation: An Interaction Model." *Community Mental Health Journal,* 1971, 7 (4), 288-302.

Signell, K. A., and Scott, P. A. "Training in Consultation: A Crisis of Role Transition." *Community Mental Health Journal,* 1972, *8* (2), 149-160.

Sills, G. M. "Nursing, Medicine, and Hospital Administration." *American Journal of Nursing,* 1976, pp. 1432-1434.

Simon, H. A. *Administrative Behavior: A Study of Decision-Making Processes in Administrative Organizations.* New York: Macmillan, 1947.

Sinha, D. P. (Ed.). *Consultants and Consulting Styles.* New Delhi, India: Vision Books, 1979.

Smith, H. L. "The Minister as Consultant to the Medical Team." *Journal of Religion and Health,* 1975, *14* (1), 7-13.

Sommer, R. *Personal Space: The Behavioral Basis of Design.* Englewood Cliffs, N.J.: Prentice-Hall, 1969.

Spielberger, C. "A Mental Health Consultation Program in a Small Community with Limited Professional Mental Health Resources." In E. L. Cowen, E. A. Gardner, and M. Zax (Eds.), *Emergent Approaches to Mental Health Problems.* New York: Appleton-Century-Crofts, 1967.

"Standards of Professional Conduct for Academic/Management Consultants." New York: Division of Managerial Consultation, Academy of Management, 1978.

Steele, F. *Physical Settings and Organization Development.* Reading, Mass.: Addison-Wesley, 1973.

Steele, F. *Consulting for Organizational Change.* Amherst: University of Massachusetts Press, 1975.

Stein, B. A., and Kanter, R. M. "Building the Parallel Organization: Creating Mechanisms for Permanent Quality of Work Life." *Journal of Applied Behavioral Science,* 1980, *16* (3), 371-388.

Stevens, B. J. "The Use of Consultants in Nursing Science." *Journal of Nursing Administration,* August 1978, pp. 7-15.

Stolz, S., Wienckowski, L. A., and Bracon, B. S. "Behavior Modification: A Perspective on Critical Issues." *American Psychologist,* 1975, *30,* 1027-1048.

Super, D. E., and Hall, D. T. "Career Development: Exploration and Planning." *Annual Review of Psychology,* 1978, *29,* 333-372.

Szasz, T. S., and Hollender, M. H. "A Contribution to the Philosophy of Medicine: The Basic Models of the Doctor-Patient Relationship." *Archives of Internal Medicine,* 1956, *97,* 585-592.

Tannenbaum, A. S. *Control in Organizations.* New York: McGraw-Hill, 1968.

Taylor, F. W. *The Principles of Scientific Management.* New York: Harper & Row, 1911.

Taylor, J., and Bowers, D. G. *The Survey of Organizations: A Machine Scored Standardized Questionnaire Instrument.* Ann Arbor, Mich.: Institute for Social Research, 1972.

Tharp, R. G., and Wetzel, R. J. *Behavior Modification in the Natural Environment.* New York: Academic Press, 1969.

Thompson, J. D. *Organizations in Action.* New York: McGraw-Hill, 1967.

Thoresen, C. E., and Mahoney, M. J. *Behavioral Self-Control.* New York: Holt, Rinehart and Winston, 1974.

Thorndike, F. *Animal Intelligence.* New York: Macmillan, 1911.

Tichy, N. M. "Demise, Absorption, or Renewal for the Future of Organization Development." In W. W. Burke (Ed.), *The Cutting Edge: Current Theory and Practice in Organization Development.* San Diego, Calif.: University Associates, 1978.

Tocqueville, A. de. *Democracy in America.* (P. Bradley, Ed.) New York: Vintage Books, 1945. (Originally published 1835-1840.)

Trist, E. L., and Bamforth, K. W. "Some Social and Psychological Consequences of the Long-Wall Method of Coal-Getting." *Human Relations,* 1951, *4,* 3-38.

von Bertalanffy, L. "The Theory of Open Systems in Physics and Biology." *Science,* 1950, *111,* 23-28.

Vroom, V. H., and Yetton, P. *Leadership and Decision Making.* Pittsburgh, University of Pittsburgh Press, 1973.

Wallin, J. E., and Ferguson, G. "The Development of School Psychological Services." In J. F. Magary (Ed.), *School Psychological Services in Theory and Practice: A Handbook.* Englewood Cliffs, N.J.: Prentice-Hall, 1967.

Walsh, J. A. "Converting Clinicians to Consultants in an In-Service Training Seminar." *Journal of Community Psychology,* 1973, *1* (3), 292-294.

Walton, R. E. "Two Strategies of Social Change and Their Dilemmas." *Journal of Applied Behavioral Science,* 1965, *1* (2), 167-179.

Walton, R. E. *Interpersonal Peacemaking: Confrontations and Third Party Consultation.* Reading, Mass.: Addison-Wesley, 1969.

Walton, R. E., and Warrick, D. P. "The Ethics of Organization Development." *Journal of Applied Behavioral Science,* 1973, *9* (6), 681-698.

Weber, M. *The Theory of Social and Economic Organization.* (A. M. Henderson and T. Parsons, Trans.; T. Parsons, Ed.) New York: Free Press, 1947.

Weick, K. *The Social Psychology of Organizing.* Reading, Mass.: Addison-Wesley, 1969.

Weick, K. E. "Educational Organizations as Loosely Coupled Systems." *Administrative Science Quarterly,* 1976, *21,* 1-19.

Weisbord, M. R. "Organizational Diagnosis: Six Places to Look for Trouble With or Without a Theory." *Organization and Group Studies,* 1976, *1,* 430-447.

Weiss, C. H. *Evaluation Research: Methods of Assessing Program Effectiveness.* Englewood Cliffs, N.J.: Prentice-Hall, 1972.

Weiss, R. S. *Statistics in Social Research: An Introduction.* New York: Wiley, 1968.

Whetten, D. "Sources, Responses, and Effects of Organizational Decline." In J. R. Kimberly, R. H. Miles, and Associates, *The Organizational Life Cycle: Issues in the Creation, Transformation, and Decline of Organizations.* San Francisco: Jossey-Bass, 1980.

White, R. K., and Lippitt, R. O. *Autocracy and Democracy: Experiments in Group Leadership.* New York: Harper & Row, 1960.

Whitehorn, J. C. (Ed.). *The Psychiatrist, His Training and Development*. Report of the 1952 Cornell Conference. Washington, D.C.: American Psychiatric Association, 1953.

Whittington, H. G. "Consultation Practice in Colleges and Universities." In W. M. Mendel and P. Solomon (Eds.), *The Psychiatric Consultation*. New York: Grune & Stratton, 1968.

Wiener, N. *The Human Use of Human Beings*. Garden City, N.Y.: Doubleday, 1954.

Winett, R. A. "An Emerging Approach to Energy Conservation." In D. Glenwick and L. Jason (Eds.), *Behavioral Community Psychology*. New York: Praeger, 1980.

Winett, R. A., and Winkler, R. C. "Current Behavior Modification in the Classroom: Be Still, Be Quiet, Be Docile." *Journal of Applied Behavior Analysis,* 1972, *5,* 499-504.

Woodman, R. W., and Sherwood, J. J. "Effects of Team Development Intervention: A Field Experiment." *Journal of Applied Behavioral Science,* 1980, *16* (2), 211-227.

Woodward, J. *Industrial Organization: Theory and Practice*. London: Oxford University Press, 1965.

"The Work of RHR: Section I: A Brief Overview." *RHR Journal,* 1976, *5* (2), 7-14.

Zander, A. *Groups at Work: Unresolved Issues in the Study of Organizations*. San Francisco: Jossey-Bass, 1977.

Znaniecki, F. *The Social Role of the Man of Knowledge*. New York: Octagon Books, 1965.

Zusman, J. "Mental Health Consultation: Some Theory and Practice." In J. Zusman and D. L. Davidson (Eds.), *Practical Aspects of Mental Health Consultation*. Springfield, Ill.: Thomas, 1972.

Name Index

Subject Index